SPREADING THE WORD

SPREADING THE WORD

Groundings in the
Philosophy of Language

by

SIMON BLACKBURN

CLARENDON PRESS · OXFORD
1984

Oxford University Press, Walton Street, Oxford OX2 6DP
London Glasgow New York Toronto
Delhi Bombay Calcutta Madras Karachi
Kuala Lumpur Singapore Hong Kong Tokyo
Nairobi Dar es Salaam Cape Town
Melbourne Auckland

and associated companies in
Beirut Berlin Ibadan Mexico City Nicosia

Oxford is a trade mark of Oxford University Press

Published in the United States
by Oxford University Press, New York

British Library Cataloguing in Publication Data

Blackburn, Simon
Spreading the word.
1. Languages — Philosophy
I. Title
401   P106

ISBN 0-19-824650-1
ISBN 0-19-824651-X   Pbk

Library of Congress Cataloging in Publication Data

Blackburn, Simon.
Spreading the word.

Bibliography: p.
Includes index.
1. Languages — Philosophy.   I. Title
P106.B47 1984   401   83-17253
ISBN 0-19-824650-1
ISBN 0-19-824651-X (pbk).

Typeset by Oxford Verbatim Limited
Printed in Great Britain
at the University Press, Oxford

Preface

Modern philosophy has been dominated by a concern with language. But modern philosophy of language is highly inaccessible. It is very hard for the ordinary student, let alone the layman, to appreciate the problems it explores, or the methods it uses. The interest of the results and their relations to other philosophical or intellectual concerns is thus largely hidden. Everyone who has any interest in modern philosophy knows the great names of the subject – Frege, Russell, Tarski, Quine – but too often even conscientious students know little more. Every philosophy teacher or examiner will know how fragile is the ordinary student's grasp of the issues they tackled, the methods they used, or the interest of their results. This book is an attempt to introduce the problems, and methods, and some of the results.

When I formed the intention of writing such a book, it seemed a modest enough aim. I felt I had at least two qualifications. One is that I like my philosophy to be clear. I tend to believe that too many of the complexities of the subject are really covers for confusions, so that when these are removed the real beauties can be revealed in clear and striking colours. I believe that too few philosophers frame the golden words of Quintilian above their desks: 'do not write so that you can be understood, but so that you cannot be misunderstood.' The other qualification I felt was that I believe in the importance of the subject. I believe that the philosophy of language ought to be widely studied, and that its results and methods are of more than merely specialist interest. I think that confusions about language underlie many other philosophical problems, and that any serious study of, for instance, the metaphysics of morals or of persons, of groups and of psychology demands at least an initial baptism into the issues I want to introduce. In sum, I believe that the great perennial problems of philosophy can be felt by any reflective persons. If we practitioners believe that we have new and better approaches to them, and that philosophical reflection upon language is a part of those approaches, then it is up to us to address that interest. We ought to be able to show why our discussions are worth hearing.

This motivation, however, soon made me realize how difficult the aim really was. Naturally, it would not do merely to survey various positions on various issues. For the point of the book was not to enable a student to go through the hoops, but to enable him to understand why the hoops are placed where they are. The keynote was to be *appreciation* of issues, not mere acquaintance with them. On the other hand, nearly all the issues have been studied in immense depth. There is no topic here on which more cannot be said, or has not already been said in the immense literature. So I began to feel that I was walking naked through a landscape where every bush concealed an army of snipers. Proper academic caution would demand digging fortified trenches after every step; but the audience I wanted to reach does not need a trench-eye view, any more than it just wants a bird's-eye view. I began to understand why the book I had in mind had not yet been written.

The solution, I felt, was to take the reader into issues by myself arguing them through: I found I could make no real distinction between introducing problems and wrestling with them, but in a way which took the intended audience with me. And this is what I have tried to do. So this is not so much an introductory 'text', or something like a survey of its domain. It is an attempt to show the student what is done by philosophizing about language. It is my own reaction to philosophical problems about language which interest me. But it is written with an audience of beginners in mind. In a sense, it is an indication of the place of the philosophy of language in many other intellectual endeavours – in particular, in the philosophy of understanding, of knowledge, and of truth. It is therefore an attempt to place some of the investigations that go under the philosophy of language, and to indicate not only their implications, but sometimes their limitations as well. Naturally, I hope that the material serves as the basis for courses on the philosophy of language. If it does, it will need supplementing, and I have indicated what I take to be the right supplements in notes to each chapter.

Because I believe that there is no deep study of language which is not also concerned with philosophy of mind, and with the nature of truth and reality, this book contains more general philosophy than its title might indicate. The philosophical aspects of language I have selected include the whole inter-action between thinkers, their language, and the world they inhabit. It is these large themes, rather than detailed technical problems, which I have tried to explore. So, for example, in connection with truth I include quite detailed treatment of particular domains of truth, such as moral truth, and of some aspects of the theory of knowledge. My main regret is that space prevented inclusion of more such examples, for instance on the theory of conditionals, or of possibilities, or of mathematics.

One of the casualties of the trench-eye view is that not only students, but thinkers from other countries and traditions, find much of the philosophy of language incomprehensible. They can then come to dismiss it as irrelevant to their concerns – the product of a "linguistic" or "analytical" school within philosophy, which can be regarded as optional or misguided. But in so far as these labels suggest some particular body of doctrines or of techniques, then I could not accept them. Indeed, in the course of the work I suggest reasons for avoiding some doctrines associated with these titles (chapters 5 and 6). The only sense in which they are appropriate is that we are concerned to think about issues raised by reflecting upon language, and to do it carefully. But doing that is something which no self-respecting philosopher, from any school at all, can hope to avoid.

I have tried to keep footnotes to a minimum, and they mention only works specifically quoted or discussed in the text. Notes giving fuller sets of references, suggestions for further reading, and sometimes subsidiary comments, are included at the end of each chapter. In order not to break the flow I have not generally included indicators to these notes in the text. I have included a small glossary of philosophical terms at the end of the book.

Conversation with many friends and students has helped to shape the book. I should like to thank especially David Bostock, Alberto Coffa, Elizabeth Fricker, Martin Davies, John Kenyon, and Ralph Walker. Edward Craig read the penultimate manu-script with enormous care and his comments helped me in many ways. I should also like to thank the Open University for permission to use parts of material which I originally prepared for them, in the chapter on reference. I owe especial gratitude to the Radcliffe Trust, for a Fellowship which freed me from my teaching duties and enabled me to contemplate the work. I owe thanks as well to the Master and Fellows of Pembroke College for allowing me to benefit from this release. Finally the text has been endlessly improved by my wife's editorial and literary skills; I owe a debt to her greatly over and above that which all writers must owe to those around them.

Pembroke College   S.W.B.
May 1983

ACKNOWLEDGEMENT

I wish to record my thanks to Lady Ethel Wodehouse and Hutchinsons Ltd. for their kind permission to use the quotation which appears as the epigraph to chapter 1; and also the permission of the author's estate and their agents, Scott Meredith Literary Agency Inc., 845, 3rd Avenue, New York 10022, USA.

Contents

PART II: LANGUAGE AND THE WORLD

PART I

OUR LANGUAGE
AND OURSELVES

CHAPTER 1

The Shape of the Problems

"When you come tomorrow, bring my football boots. Also, if humanly possible, Irish water spaniel. Urgent. Regards. Tuppy."

"What do you make of that, Jeeves?"

"As I interpret the document, sir, Mr. Glossop wishes you, when you come tomorrow, to bring his football boots. Also, if humanly possible, an Irish water spaniel. He hints that the matter is urgent, and sends his regards."

"Yes, that's how I read it, too . . ."

P. G. Wodehouse, 'The Ordeal of Young Tuppy'.

1. *A Preliminary Map*

A philosophy of language attempts to achieve some understanding of a triangle of elements:

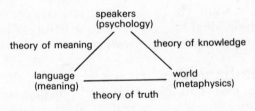

Fig. 1

The speaker uses the language. With it he can put himself into various relations with the world. He can describe it, or ask questions about it, issue commands to change it, put himself under obligations to act in it in various ways, offer metaphors, images, jokes, about what it is like. The task of the philosopher is to obtain some stable conception of this triangle of speaker, language, and world. This aim will appear somewhat different to different generations and times. The things which seem reliable and unpuzzling to one thinker come to seem crucially problematic to another. One of the difficulties of appreciating the area is just that of seeing which questions should be framed first, and which concepts are reliable and legitimate aids to answering them. Even at this point the choices are contentious. There is no one proper selection of questions and aids which philosophers of language unite in respecting. But there are more or less intelligent guides to choosing, and one good guide will also enable one to come to respect the virtues of other good guides.

At a given time, in a given philosophical tradition, one or another of the points of this triangle will appear prominent. That point will represent the primary source of understanding, so that the natural direction of enquiry is to use that knowledge to aim at conclusions about the other elements. Thus in the European tradition from Descartes until this century the moving conception has been that of the individual, with his particular capacities for experience and reasoning. The aim of metaphysics has been to attain a conception of the world which would enable this individual to know something about it (or enable him to put up with scepticism about it). The nature of his mind determines what kind of language this individual can intelligibly speak: which ideas the language can express for him. In Locke, or Kant, the prime investigation is into the kind of mind the individual has; given this, the nature of language, so far as it is important, or of the world, in so far as it is intelligible, follows on.

In a different tradition, for instance that of the Greeks, it would seem more natural to establish by metaphysical enquiry some feature of the world, of reality. Thus metaphysical argument might show that values are real, or that numbers are real, that they are unchangeable, and so on. It would then appear that we must have capacities large enough to enable us to comprehend these established objects, and from this fact would follow conclusions about our rationality, our minds, and our epistemic (knowledge-gaining) natures. More familiarly, a culture may reasonably accord such respect to the science of the day that the world as depicted by that science becomes the sole and immediate metaphysical reality. Both the nineteenth century and our own have seen philosophy dominated by scientific naturalism, in which the results and (alleged) method of the natural scientist are regarded as the real philosophical data. In the nineteenth century this attitude found expression in the views of Mill in England and the anti-Hegelian, anti-speculative empiricism of Germany: it led to a vague belief that a science of psychology would produce the only real advance in our understanding of logic, language, and thought. The same attitude has persisted throughout much empiricist philosophy of language this century, although the science which is to provide the eventual source of understanding tends to shift: psychology, formal logic, formal semantics, or structural linguistics.

But the noteworthy change is towards concentration upon language itself, rather than the mind of its user or the world he inhabits. Now it may seem odd to roll the triangle so that the investigation of language assumes primacy. A language has to be capable of describing whatever world the metaphysician allows. It has to be intelligible to whatever creature the psychologist paints. But, it might seem, its interesting properties would first be discovered by settling the nature of that world or that creature. For example, if we ask whether our numeral expressions like '6' or '7'[1] refer to things, and think of that as a question in the philosophy of language, it might seem that we have to wait until the metaphysician tells us about the reality of numbers, and until the psychologist or epistemologist tells us how we can know about them. If numbers are real and we can know about them, then presumably we can regard our numerals as referring to them. Otherwise, we must regard them in some other light. It is not clear how there could be a self-governing investigation into language with enough authority to issue commands to the other philosophical areas. But ideologies change, and it has become natural to give the nature of language considerable autonomy, and even sovereignty over the other elements of the triangle. An individual's psychology becomes whatever is needed to enable him to understand the language which stands revealed, and the world becomes whatever is necessary to make true the true statements made with

---

[1] In this work I put single quotes around a word or sentence which is being talked about. Sometimes, where it helps clarity, or a lot of words are being mentioned, I also use italics. Double quotes are used for direct quotation from other writers, and to register a deliberate distance from a particular phrasing.

that language. This is the "linguistic turn", for better or worse, of most of the important philosophy this century: this book will assemble some of the materials necessary for evaluating it.

Not only can the triangle be rotated, but whole aspects of it can wither away. It can diminish to a straight line, or even a point. This will seem a good or bad thing according to whether we want to do away with one kind of subject-matter. One concern can dominate philosophy so entirely that questions in other corners of the triangle become dismissed. One of the few things everyone has heard about logical positivism is that it claimed that metaphysics – the study of the "world" element in the triangle – was dead; at present many writers believe that epistemology has just died, and the investigations traditionally thought of as part of the theory of truth are given regular obituaries. All this arises because people find it hard to see how there can be any enquiry except into the relations of speakers and their language. We see what we are committed to by surveying the language we speak and the beliefs we express by it. There is no other philosophical study of our "world" or our relations to it – although, of course, there are scientific studies of the nature of the things it contains. It is characteristic of any dominant philosophy to be hostile to some one of the corners of the triangle and to shunt all interesting questions into the line between the other two.

Even if we believe that some one element of the triangle dominates the rest, we should beware of forgetting other possible orientations. Amongst other things, this would make it impossible to appreciate the concerns of people who have a different perspective, and it thereby causes distorted history of philosophy. To take a plain example: if we are convinced that all worthwhile philosophy is ultimately the analysis of the meanings of terms which we use, and if we are sure that Hume, or Kant, or whoever, was doing worthwhile philosophy, then we must regard them as analysing the meanings of terms. Unfortunately this corresponds to very little that they appear to have been doing. So if we persist in this diagnosis, we run the risk of judging their work by quite inappropriate standards (in the case of Hume, I show why in chapter 6). But there is in any case a more general reason for tolerating different attitudes towards elements of the triangle. This is that the flow of implications around it is subtle and hard to perceive, and it is something to which any thinker needs great sensitivity. A theory of language is likely to affect any metaphysics and epistemology, but they in turn affect most of our ideas about language. Or so I shall try to show.

2. *Kinds of Question*

What is to be done to approach this stable conception of the triangle of terms and their relations? Or to put the question another way, how is there scope for a philosopher to improve some untutored, common-sense appreciation of how we stand in relation to our language, and to the world we depict with it?

Suppose we start with the individual. The person who has mastered a language *understands* its sentences and the terms used to make them up. He gives them a meaning, and members of his linguistic community do the same. What kind of fact is this? Understanding the sentences of a language is knowing what they are used to say – which thoughts or questions or commands or wishes they express, in the mouths of speakers of that language. But what is the difference between having such knowledge and lacking it? Or is it wrong to think of some one kind of knowledge; is there only the criss-crossing of ways in which we do understand each other's sayings, and ways in which we do not – a continuous ebb and flow of tides of incomprehension? My experiences, beliefs, ideas, and attitudes are different from yours, and different again from those of people in other places and times. How can we give our words the same significance? But if we do not, how is communication possible at all – how do I pass you information, or tell you what to do, or learn anything about what is believed by other people? There is a tension between the rooted, organic, place of language in particular persons and people, at particular places and times, and the common stock of thoughts which we seem to express, enabling me to understand you, or understand and translate what was written five hundred years ago, or even timeless truths and certainties which do not change. Different temperaments feel this tension differently. Some, like the later Wittgenstein, stress the first aspect, the place of any language in the activities and relations of people at times: "Language has grown like any big city: room by room . . . house by house, street by street . . . and all this is boxed together, tied together, smeared together", wrote Fritz Mauthner.[2] How can I know my way around *your* town – how can I rely upon any points of reference (it's no good relying upon anything you *say*, since it is the significance of that which I am looking for)? We need a philosophy of mutual understanding, protecting shared understanding in the face of divergent ways and experiences.

Perhaps the mazes and labyrinths of old towns makes them unfit places for real seekers after truth, who need accurate and precise ways of describing things and understanding each other's descriptions. So there exists a vision of a genuinely scientific language: a purified, precise instrument of the discovery of truth. If our words resist accurate analysis, they should be replaced by ones which permit it; if our own inferences and modes of argument are messy and unsystematic, they should be replaced by ones which are precise and computable. The goal of a logically adequate or even perfect symbolism, pursued through the progressive refinement of artificially simple languages, has always been a preoccupation of philosophers, and indeed of scientists (it was a leading aim of the original Royal Society. See 2.2, footnote 5). When we think about almost anything hard, we are apt to fear that it is our words that are letting us down. We need to "remove the mist or veil of words" (Berkeley), or to avoid being "caught in the nets of language" (Nietzsche); the remedy is to ensure that our words relate to reality in the proper way, that our inferences are solid and our distinctions accurate. Many rationalists have shared Leibniz's dream of a *universal characteristic*, a language suitable for science and logic; the great logical work of Frege made it possible to see more clearly what such a language might be like, and the vision dominated the subsequent work of Russell, of the early Wittgenstein, of Carnap and the Vienna Circle positivists. It still suffuses much research into the semantics of various parts of language. Of course, the vision has different components, and I come to distinguish them in time. The pure vision of a rationally planned new town for scientists and philosophers, with straight roads leading from one solid unornamented block of truth to another, a Bauhaus of

[2] I owe the quotation to Hans Sluga, *Frege*.

the mind, is not now widely shared. Such places prove uninhabitable. But we learn more about the philosophy of language by examining them than by dismissing them out of hand in favour of the old, human jumble in which we feel at home.

Fairly clearly, we will not assess the issues raised by this ideal without further thinking not only about what it is to understand a language, and to understand other people's use of their language, but also about what it is to describe the world by using it. If the virtues of a good language are mainly in the direction of increased comprehension, of each other and of the world, then progress towards seeing those virtues rightly needs a philosophy of mutual understanding, and also a *theory of truth*, taking us onto the other side of the triangle. The understanding speaker uses his sentences to make judgements, which are true or false. So we need a solid conception of what it is to do this. The issues here also root deeply in the history of philosophy. There are classical theories of truth, and various newcomers. Truth is something we all respect, and want for our beliefs. But framing and answering general questions about truth is not easy. Probably the best way to feel these problems is to start locally. Particular kinds of judgement, perhaps moral and aesthetic judgements, are easily felt not to be capable of truth in the same way as more homely beliefs: they are not "objective", mark no features of "reality". The same can be felt for other things we say, such as mathematical remarks. What makes true the judgement that $7 + 5 = 12$? Even the theses of scientific theories can be seen as instruments of prediction rather than descriptions of hidden aspects of reality. Perhaps many of our commitments should not be regarded as beliefs that something is true or false (corresponds to reality), but rather should be seen in some other light. This is the way into the issues of truth, realism, and the nature of judgement. It has links with the theory of knowledge, fairly obviously, and back with the theory of understanding. But finally it connects with a much more thorough enquiry into the structural workings of our language.

At many points in discussions such as these, use has to be made of fairly obvious features of words of our languages. Some are names, some predicates; some are connectives linking different parts of discourse, some turn assertions into questions, and so on. The goal of systematic, *compositional semantics*, is to form a view about how best to describe the functioning of individual terms in sentences, and how to describe how, given this functioning of their parts, sentences come to have the meanings they do. Without this kind of knowledge our understanding of the nature of our language is exceedingly rudimentary. And the pursuit of such a theory has in one way or another attracted most major philosophers of language this century (the notable exception being the later Wittgenstein). In this book I introduce some issues making semantic description of languages interesting and difficult. But they do not dominate the philosophy from the outset. This requires some explanation: the reader may well wonder quite what place issues in compositional semantics have, in the overall attempt to understand ourselves and our languages. In some developments there might seem to be nothing for the philosopher of language to do but attempt yet more accurate descriptions of the way terms function in the generation of meaningful sentences and utterances: if this were understood, it might be thought, then there would be nothing else for the philosophy of language to worry about. In another common metaphor, a compositional semantics would form the "core" of a philosophy of language, with other issues built entirely around it. In the rest of this chapter I illustrate why I am not presenting matters quite like this, and introduce more of the compositional aspect of language.

3. *Semantic Descriptions*

All theorists of language are impressed by its compositional nature. Competent users of language are not restricted to a repertoire of previously understood sentences. We possess the skill to generate new sentences meaning new things and to know what these new sentences mean. I shall call this the *elasticity* of our understanding. It exists because new sentences contain old words in old patterns. And just as in chess old pieces making old moves yield new positions, so our familiar devices are capable of limitless recombination. Our understanding of the words and the syntax enables us to identify the meaning of new sentences. There ought to be some way of describing what the words (or other features) *do*, so that we can represent the way speakers and hearers respond to their presence when arriving at interpretations. So we would understand a language semantically if we knew exactly how the presence of words, or any other meaning-giving features of sentences, work in generating meanings. Finding this out means distinguishing various categories of expression, such as names or predicates. It will involve a description of what expressions in those categories do – e.g. that names refer to things, or predicates are true sets of things. And it will involve clauses saying how combinations of items from these various categories make up sentences meaning what they do – e.g. that a sentence consisting of a name followed by a predicate says that the item referred to by the name has the property expressed by the predicate, or belongs to the set of things associated with the predicate. Such a theory faces choices at each stage. There is difficulty over finding the right categories, over selecting quite the right description of what items in the categories do, and over formulating the right clauses stating how items combine.

This is a relatively *internal* inquiry into the way meanings are generated in a particular language – English, say, or impoverished, artificial fragments of it. But there are *external*, surrounding questions, which success in compositional semantics would evidently leave untouched. For instance, if a group spoke an extremely simple language, with only names and a fixed vocabulary of predicates, the compositional problem would be easy. It would require little more than the clause already indicated. But there would be questions about names, predicates, and sentences which this success would not answer. We would still want to know what it is in the behaviour, or mental life, or whatever, of the community which *makes it true* that a particular word is the name of a particular thing. We would want to know what makes it true that a particular word is a predicate with a particular assigned meaning, and what kind of truth it is that sentences in the mouths of the group have the overall meaning the theory calculates for them. Then there would be questions about the nature of the judgements made with this vocabulary: whether they admit of truth and falsehood, whether they are objective, correspond with the world, and how they know them.

Questions raised by compositional understanding can be illustrated by a simple example. Consider our ordinary numeral notation. This contains the familiar arabic symbols '0', '1', . . ., '9', and sequences of them, such as '437' or '501'. Any sequence of the original ten digits counts as a numeral, except those beginning with '0'. An internal enquiry into how this notation works would notice that there is a system in the way sequences of numerals refer to numbers. If there were no such system then it would be a miracle if we all took some previously unfamiliar numeral, such as '675,896,341', to refer to the same number. But we understand it readily, because, somehow, we are sensitive to the placing of the individual digits, and understand which number the expression refers to because of that placing. The rule we respond to is that which dictates counting to base ten. We can state it like this. First of all, we know what each primitive digit does:

> '0' refers to the number 0
> '1' refers to the number 1 . . .
> '9' refers to the number 9.

The form of these axioms or base clauses is just that first we mention the symbol talked about. The single quotes show that we are talking about the enclosed symbol. We then say what the symbol does, in this case by saying which number it refers to. We do that by *using* the symbol. This means that someone understands these clauses only if they can already use the notation. So the clauses would be useless for a certain purpose: they couldn't teach someone to understand the digits. But this does not unfit them for their role in the compositional theory, as we shall now see. We could just go on indefinitely:

> '10' refers to the number 10
> '11' refers to the number 11 . . .

But this would defeat the compositional aim. The aim was to represent how we use the presence of digits in their places to identify the reference of new numerals. But if each numeral got its own independent description, as if we continued this list, that would be no help. It would make it seem as if each piece of understanding was quite independent of the others, so that a child would have to be taught each numeral *separately*, and then have a skill which wouldn't *transfer* to unfamiliar numerals. In other words, we want to explain how it is no accident that, say,

'219' refers to 219. We therefore want a rule telling us how the presence of those digits, in that order, determines this fact. A rule which does it is:

> Suppose $A, \ldots, A_n$ is a sequence of digits referring to a number k. Suppose B is an individual digit referring to a number j. Then the sequence $A, \ldots, A_n B$ refers to the number $(10 \times k) + j$.

Thus '219' is the sequence '21' with '9' on the end. It therefore, by the rule, refers to $(10 \times$ whatever '21' refers to$) +$ what '9' refers to – i.e. 9, by the base clause governing that digit. What does '21' refer to? Using the rule again: $(10 \times 2) + 1$. Putting the two calculations together, the original refers to $(10 \times 21) + 9$, i.e. 219. That's a way of saying how counting to base ten with the arabic notation works.

The example is trivial, but some of the points it illustrates are not. Notice that it is not the final result that is news – we already knew that '219' referred to 219. Everyone who could use our numerals would know that. The value of the description lies entirely in showing us *why* this fact is so. We wouldn't understand how this arithmetical notation works unless we had in some sense cottoned on to the rule of composition. There are some examples, such as the Inca use of systems of knots in ropes as counting devices, which remain uninterpreted precisely because nobody is sure how complications in the knotting determined the number being referred to. Some notations would need quite complex systems of rules – the Roman system of letters, for instance.

Let us call the notation described by the base clauses and the rule, the arabic numeral notation: ANN. Then the structure of ANN has been completely revealed. So in one sense we know how we refer to numbers. We do so by using that notation. But we have not provided much of a Christmas present to any philosopher of mathematics. *His* question, 'How do we refer to numbers?', is asking what it is to refer to a number, what numbers *are* that they can be objects of reference and what the ability to refer to one has to do with other skills, such as the ability to count and add. None of these questions is advanced at all by the compositional knowledge. This is, of course, particularly blatant since the base clauses simply help themselves to the fact that the digits refer to the numbers they do. If this kind of fact is problematic to a philosopher, then they are merely examples of the problem.[3]

There is one particularly important reason why a philosopher of mathematics might pay scant attention to the structure of ANN. We believe that counting to base ten is just one amongst an indefinite number of possible ways of counting. We could have used all sorts of systems, with different numbers of primitives, different ways of combining them, and different rules for recovering the number referred to. But these would be merely alternative ways of doing the same thing – referring to numbers. The fact that someone uses a differently structured system does not prevent him from talking of the number 125, and coming to know the same things as we do: that it does not divide by 2, has a cube root, and so on. So there seems to be a clear distinction between *what* we do – talking about numbers – and the particular *way* we do it – using ANN, for instance. But understanding this distinction in general can be very difficult. What do different notations have to share if they are to be ways of talking about the same things, or expressing the same knowledge? Are there limits to the extent to which diverse ways of expressing things can coincide with sameness of thoughts expressed?

The compositional nature of language is impressive. A non-systematic numeral notation, for instance, would only enable us to count up to some fixed limit. For each new numeral would have to be learned individually, as the basic ten digits have to be learned, and we would only have time to master a small number of them. Similarly, a non-systematic language would enable its users to say only a fixed, limited, number of things. The meaning of each sentence would have to be learned individually, and this learning would provide no resources for rearranging words or other devices to make new messages. Still, counting up to a limited number is still counting. And saying only a limited number of things is not the same as saying nothing. It is thus premature to take the compositional nature of language as *the* criterion determining language, so that if a group has no ability

---

[3] For this reason, beware of shorthand titles, 'theory of reference', 'theory of sense', etc. These titles do not show what has been explained nor what has been used to do it. See also notes to 1.4.

to separate and recombine elements of messages, it is not using those elements to communicate. If this ability is to be the litmus test distinguishing linguistic from non-linguistic skills, we need an argument that communicating only a fixed, limited, number of things, and having no ability to do more, either is not communicating at all, or is at best communicating non-linguistically. The undoubted essence of ability to use a language is the ability to express and communicate information, desires, wishes, etc. by its means. Any proposed indicator of whether this is happening needs to earn its keep. We need argument that the indicator distinguishes only cases where this is happening from those where it is not.

Someone might object to the compositional description of ANN, on the quite reasonable grounds that numbers are not objects of reference at all. One might, for instance, suppose that for us to refer to a thing it has to impinge on us in some way. Since numbers are abstract objects, if they are objects at all, they do not enter into causal relationships, and therefore do not impinge on us. Hence, we do not refer to them, and the relationship between a numeral and its interpretation would have to be described differently. We would need a different kind of clause stating what numerals do, in terms of what digits do. But the insight we have into the compositional nature of ANN remains. It simply needs expressing in the preferred style. For example, noticing that numerals are introduced in counting, when they describe how numerous are sets of objects, we might try a semantics couched in terms of their adjectival role. This would say that '0' is the digit used to count sets of 0 things, . . ., '9' is the digit used to count sets of 9 things, and the rule would similarly just substitute 'used to count sets of . . . things' for 'refers to the number . . .'. The compositional insight remains the same. Ever since the pioneering work of Frege, emphasizing this aspect of numerical terminology, it has been a matter of some importance to weigh the merits of each style of description, and this introduces one way in which semantics is of more interest to philosophy than might have so far appeared. Can the adjectival style be used to compute an interpretation for sentences in which numerals do *not* appear to be functioning as adjectives describing sets, such as '7 is the sum of 5 and 2'; can it be used to develop interpretations of other sentences which appear to talk about numbers as general objects of theory, such as 'there is an infinite number of prime numbers'?

This introduces one kind of way in which semantic theory influences surrounding philosophical problems. If there are occurrences of numerals which the adjectival style cannot cover, they will provide a reason for seeking something more, and may provide a reason for reverting to thinking of numerals as genuinely referring to things, such as numbers. A different example of the same phenomenon might help. Suppose a theorist notices that 'good' functions somewhat like an adjective. He might nevertheless have doubts about whether it is used to describe things or attribute a property to them. He might be drawn to an expressive theory, which claims that a sentence 'X is good' serves some other function than describing X; its role is to convey the speaker's approval of X, perhaps. There then arises the question of whether this conception of the role of that sentence (and hence of the adjective inside it) is adequate to accounting for all its occurrences. For instance, we say such things as 'If *this is good* we should encourage it in the young', or 'I think that *this is good* but I may be wrong.' Here it seems that the embedded sentence is used to do something other than merely convey the speaker's approval of the topic, because in the first case it seems to identify some hypothesis, and in the second case to identify something about which the speaker has doubts. The question which is internal to the workings of our language is whether the expressive theory about the use of the sentence can explain and interpret these occurrences of the sentence. But understanding whether it can is no mere internal, technical issue in semantics. Until we have a clear view of it we cannot assess the expressive theory, and until we can do that we cannot form any reliable view about the metaphysics or the epistemology of ethics. I give the theory of this issue in 6.2.

These examples show how it is that, to understand the role of a term in our language, we need some understanding of its compositional possibilities. A description of its role which leaves some occurrences unintelligible, by failing to show how a word with *that* role can feature in *that* context to generate *that* meaning, is semantically inadequate. But there remain questions of what it is about a group of people which makes it true that they are speaking and understanding a language which fits a particular semantic description, of what counts as change in language, sameness of language, understanding of language in a certain way. Other questions relate more to the 'world' corner of the triangle, and can be appreciated if we draw a distinction between *needing* some semantic description and *imposing* it. If it can be shown that we need some semantic description to complete a compositional account, then one aspect of a philosophy of language is completed. In speaking the language we would be *referring* to numbers, or *describing* things as good, or whatever. But against philosophical unquiet, yielding epistemological or metaphysical argument that we *cannot* be doing these things, a purely structural argument for saying that we *must* be doing so will seem weak. Opposition will continue to look for some other way of conceiving the interpretation of the contentious terms, without implying the false conception of how they relate to the world. We have already seen a small example of how this might happen, in the different styles of describing ANN, which yet serve the same compositional aim.

This point can be put another way. A description of the compositional working of our language is, like anything else, a description which we offer in the light of our own conception of ourselves and of the world we inhabit. The compositional aim controls one aspect of the adequacy of such descriptions. An adequate compositional theory may describe us as doing all kinds of things in using the language it talks about: referring to numbers or possibilities or events or chances or properties of things; using operators with certain properties, predicates in certain ways, and so on. But our wider understanding of the triangle may make us uncomfortable with these descriptions. There are then a number of courses open. We can seek an alternative style of description, avoiding saying that numerals refer, or that evaluative sentences describe things, and so on. We can criticize the language, saying that it is rightly described by the given semantics, but that since we do not really refer, describe, etc., in the way it shows us doing, the language itself incorporates mistaken philosophical ideas – about numbers or ethics. In the last ditch we can argue that words like 'refer', 'describe', 'truth', etc., bear different senses in the contested cases from those which they normally have, so that although it is correct to allow that numerals refer, or that we refer to possibilities, chances, or whatever, this is in a rather "different sense" from that in which we refer to tables and chairs. Discovering how habitable this ditch is, or indeed whether any of these responses is permissible, involves the wider perspective of the triangle, and takes us beyond purely compositional concerns.

4. *Further Points about Words and Language*

A final cluster of points illustrated by ANN is partly terminological, but partly more substantive. There could clearly be numerical codes, or alternative numerical systems, in which the written arabic digits,. or their audible counterparts in spoken English, have different interpretations. The connection between those signs and their meanings is arbitrary, and, as we shall see, conventional. The conventions could change. The digit '5' could come to refer to the number of hands we (presently) have; the digit '2' could come to refer to the number of fingers we (presently) have on each hand. (I am told that in modern Arabic the sign shaped like '0' refers to the number 5.) The connection between the actual signs and their interpretations is mutable, conventional, and contingent – something which could have been otherwise, had human beings operated differently.

This contingency poses terminological problems and it is important to be clear about the way we solve them. Do we identify the notation ANN simply through its *lexicon* and *syntax* (the rule stating that any sequence of digits except those commencing with '0' counts as a numeral)? If this were so, after the change described, whereby '5' and '2' change functions, we would still be using ANN, because we are using exactly the same terminology. Or should we say that after such a change we no longer use ANN, but only a related cousin, ANN*: in other words, should we say that the identity of a language is created not only by the vocabulary of signs it has, and the way those signs make up sentences, but also by the meanings attached to each element? In short, do we define a language syntactically or through syntax *and* semantics? It is up to us which decision we take. But there is no chance at all of clear philosophy of language unless we remember which decision it was. I regard it as clearer to adopt the latter convention: ANN is therefore defined as that numerical notation which uses *those* signs in *those* combinations *to refer to* those numbers. A change in this last function would mean that ANN had been superseded by some related system, such as ANN*.

The change described results in the sign '2' referring to the number 5, and the sign '5' referring to the number 2. It is easy to imagine coming across a population who use this different system. They would write the numerals in this sequence: 0, 1, 5, 3, 4, 2, 6, . . ., and teach children to associate those terms with the relevantly numbered sets of things ('5: number of hands you have, . . .') Such a group would have ANN* as their actual numerical notation, in the way that we have ANN. So far as I know, no group does this: ANN and ANN* are equally good possible numerical notations, but only one is used. In fact there is an infinity of possible numerical notations. In some the digits retain the use we give them, but the significance of putting them into sequences is different (e.g. chains might need reading backwards, so that '71' refers to 17); some generate the same interpretations for numerals up to some point that ANN gives them, then go on to diverge, and so on. Transferring these ideas to language, we say that there are infinitely many possible languages, only a few of which are in actual use among human populations. A *misinterpretation* of a population happens when they are assigned the wrong actual language; that is, when they are interpreted so that sentences and utterances are given one meaning, when they in fact have another.

It is of course up to us which language we have as our actual language. It is a matter of our habits, behaviour, ways of taking the written shapes and spoken sounds which we make. Language may change as the thoughts, concepts, habits of belief and attitude, of the population change; in the idiom I am introducing, this means that one actual language is succeeded by another. This highlights the problem of *individuation*: when are we to say that a term or cluster of terms has a different sense from that which it used to have; when can we say that different terms, for instance from different languages, have the same sense? The purpose of such questions, in philosophy in general, is not to try to impose more precision than the shifting phenomena admit of. The purpose is to find the *principles* governing the verdict that terms are being taken in the same or different ways. It doesn't matter if the principles do not always yield a clear verdict. But it does matter if we have no grip of what the principles are. For in that case we do not know what counts as an argument that groups are or are not speaking the same actual language.

Because the same words could in principle be used to say different things in different languages, there is an important difference between merely telling which words someone used and telling what he said or commanded or thought. To know the second involves knowing how his words are to be taken – that is, which interpretation they may bear; or which is his actual language. To know merely what his words were does not of itself answer this. For example, Henry may affirm this sentence: 'There are 12 apples on the table', but if he uses ANN* he would thereby say that there are 15 apples on the table. Conversely he could have said that there are 12 apples on the table in any number of ways, since there is no limit to the number of languages capable of expressing that information. The distinction is usually known as that between *direct* reportage, which tells the words, and *indirect*, which tells what was said. But this way of expressing it is slightly unreliable. In normal conversation when we tell the words someone used we presuppose or assume that they bear their normal meanings, identified by whichever language we speak. It is only exceptionally that we contemplate the possibility that someone is using normal words in an idiosyncratic way. Indeed, in chapter 4 we meet reasons why we will not allow that this is happening even when on the face of it the speaker is indeed using words in a non-standard way. So normally direct reportage conveys to a hearer not only which words were used, but also what was said. Nevertheless the essential point is that these are two different things, regardless of how often we convey both together.

It should be noticed that in expressing this clear distinction in the way that I have, I implicitly treat words in one particular way. I am treating such things as a sentence, a word, a sign, or a symbol, as items which can in principle occur in different notations or languages. Thus I say that the symbol '2' could occur in ANN* as well as in ANN; that the sentence 'there are 2 apples on the table' could be common to each language, although meaning something different in each. This is a definite choice, for another way of identifying words and sentences would tie a word to its meaning. In that sense, ANN* would contain a different word, '2', from the word looking the same, which occurs in ANN. In this sense English would contain, say, *four* words looking like this: 'ruff'. Whereas in the usage which I prefer, there is *one* word, which is capable of four different meanings (a frill or folds of linen; a male bird of the sandpiper family; a small freshwater fish; a situation or move in a bridge game). There are other principles as well for counting words. An etymologist would distinguish them by history, so that if the word-in-one-meaning and the word-in-another-meaning evolved from one common source they would count, for his purposes, as the same word. And this principle too could be refined and distinguished.

For the purpose of understanding the original triangle, or in other words of doing some philosophy of language, there are advantages, and no disadvantages, in counting or "individuating" words in the way I favour. This way gives us an easy description of the difference between identifying the marks or sounds someone makes and the understanding he has of them, or the meaning his group gives to them. On the one hand, words, notation, symbols; on the other hand, their use, interpretation, or meaning, and the connection contingent and mutable, and laid bare for investigation. An alternative decision would muddy the way we identify this problem area. If different languages could not share the same words, or if we decided that difference of meaning entailed difference of word, then we would need to understand a man, before we could even know which words he was using. We would, however, need *some* description of what we can identify; the shapes he writes or the sounds he makes, where these are things which could in principle be produced with different meanings. When discussing such things as the change brought about by revisions of beliefs, or the relation between ANN and ANN*, it is convenient to have a simple way of saying what changes and what does not. I prefer to express things by saying that the words (signs, symbols, sentences) may remain the same, but that the interpretation or meaning or understanding of them changes; equally, since a language is identified by which sentences are used with which meanings, the language changes.

I labour this point, because it is a frequent cause of passion. I mentioned above the tendency to make features of our language into the key to understanding conceptual issues about, say, our minds, the world, necessity, reason, truth. One way in which this tendency is embodied is by claiming that many issues are "about words", "matters of definition", "matters of semantics", "metalinguistic". Issues about these abstract things are brought nicely down to earth, given a nice concrete subject-matter, if they are represented as issues about words. But the change of focus is merely a blurring unless the sense of 'word' which is intended is made clear. If words are regarded as identified (individuated, as it is usually put) without regard to their meanings, then it is not usually true that they are the subject of these issues, any more than the pieces of paper and metal actually in circulation are the subject-matter of economics.

Thus, consider a metaphysical thesis, that mind cannot be matter, or an arithmetical one, that $2 + 2 = 4$. These puzzle thinkers of an empirical bent, since their status and relation to ordinary experience is unclear. If they are true, they are true not only of the world that experience reveals to us, but of any possible world. They *have* to be true, if they are true. This inexorable quality is mysterious, and a nice way of removing the mystery would be to put *us* in charge of what we take to be inexorable. Perhaps as pure convention we arrange our mathematical and psychological language so as to give these remarks their protected status. Necessities emerge as products of our language, not as impositions to which we have to conform. Unfortunately, however, this conventionalism looks markedly less attractive once the necessary distinctions are made. Certainly, by changing our actual language we could come to assent to the sentence 'mind can be matter' or '$2 + 2 = 10$'. We would get the latter if we adopted ANN* and we would get the former if we came to use 'mind' to refer to stone or lead. It is within our power to do this. But this is irrelevant, for it does not show that by speaking a certain kind of language we might come to believe that $2 + 2$ is other than 4, or that mind can be matter. It simply shows that we have the authority to choose different ways of expressing things. But this is irrelevant to discovering whether there are possible or adequate ways of thinking which deny our cherished doctrines. Certainly a conventionalist can go on to urge that there are, and that it is a matter of our own decision that we do not adopt them. But the difficulty of showing this is quite hidden unless we are clear about the individuation of words and languages.

So to make it even a half-truth that such issues are "about words" there is needed a sense in which words are individuated at least in part by their meanings. In this sense there could not be a language in which the word 'mind' meant anything other than mind, or in which the word '2' meant any other number. Suppose someone then says that the word 'mind' cannot refer to matter. Does this give the metaphysical thesis some kind of linguistic or conventional explanation? Not at all. Since, by this definition, the word 'mind' must refer to mind, it cannot refer to matter if mind cannot be matter. But there is here no explanation of why this cannot be so. It simply rides on the back of the definition of the word, and the still untouched metaphysical thesis. Similarly, we might announce that the word 'claret' cannot refer to the stuff that comes from the tap, and this is just because the word must, in this usage, refer to claret, and claret cannot be the stuff that comes from the tap. And this does absolutely nothing to suggest that this last truth is a *verbal* one![4]

Are these distinctions mere nuts-and-bolts, or are more controversial issues in the air? Two points which might prove worrying should be noticed. One is a matter of common observation: when we learn another language, there is often no sharp division between learning which words we are hearing, and learning which sentences, in which meanings, we are hearing. In other words, it is only when we have a fair degree of skill at understanding speech that we can report it *directly*. The usual difficulty for the foreigner is not only being unable to interpret the sentences, but also not knowing what they are – being unable to repeat what was said. This is disguised by thinking only of written language. We expect languages from familiar cultures to be written more or less in our way: we can tell which German, Spanish, or French words are on the page, even if we do not know what they mean. A word is something which comes

---

[4] This explains why in this work I give no detailed exploration of the problem of necessary truth, although that is frequently presented as a problem in the philosophy of language. For the reasons given it seems to me that there is no theory in the philosophy of language which would start to explain why no adequate way of thinking could deny that $7 + 5 = 12$, that there are asymmetries between the past and the future, and so on for other necessary truths.

just after one gap and just before another gap in print. But we here rely upon a shared convention of writing. The theoretical point remains, that if we are working our way into a language from scratch, in principle there will be no sharp division between learning to isolate words, and learning the meanings of sentences. The second worry underpins this one. A word, as we see in chapter 4, is best regarded as a feature of a sentence; or rather, the presence of a word is a feature which matters because it is one of the features to which we are sensitive when we construct the meaning of the sentence. This makes it unsurprising that in foreign speech we cannot isolate words reliably. To do so involves becoming sensitive to the features of overall utterances which determine their meanings, and only a reasonable acquaintance with many utterances and many meanings will enable us reliably to abstract out features whose presence helps to determine meaning. When we can make reliable guesses about *what* they are saying, we will also see *how* they are saying it. But until we know this we can have no perception of which *words* – which meaning-giving features – to identify in their utterances.

These points deserve respect. But they cast no doubt on the theoretical possibility marked by allowing that the same word could have different meanings in different languages. Thinking of the presence of a word as the presence of a meaning-determining feature may be right; noticing that we are bad at identifying such features as long as we are bad at understanding the meanings of most utterances in a language is also right; it does not follow that words can only be regarded as intrinsically connected with their roles. It might take considerable acquaintance with a community to realize that some aspect of a sentence – say, writing it in red ink – affects its meaning in some determinate way. Before this is realized the feature may simply pass notice, regarded as part of the " background noise" which we blot out. We become sensitive to it only upon realizing the significance of its presence or absence. But this does nothing to diminish the possibility that two different communities should use the *very same* feature to effect *different* modifications of the meaning of a communication. Nor does it cast doubt on the possibility that at a particular stage a hearer may know quite well that the meaning of a sentence is determined by the presence of some feature, but not know what the effect is, and hence what the overall utterance of the sentence is saying. The reflections of the previous paragraph only suggest that we take care not to idealize the stages of language learning. In particular a complete lexicon and syntax of a language cannot be given before we have any grip on the interpretation its sentences bear. Common observation shows that this is not a practical division of our procedures, and the argument I have hinted at, and develop in chapter 4, shows why not. In this sense semantics precedes syntax. (There is however the curious phenomenon of brain injured patients who remain good at determining ungrammaticality, but are bad at understanding sentences. Presumably they retain in a different location of the brain kinds of sensitivity which, on this account, had a partly semantic origin and significance.)

I earlier mentioned some philosophical questions left untouched by the semantic description of ANN. One of them deserves particular respect. This is the question of what kind of skill the ability to refer to a number is. We can put the question in terms of *competence*. Let us say that a user of the notation is competent if we can recognize which sequences of symbols count as numerals, and what their references are if they do. Similarly, a user of a language is competent if he can recognize which sequences of words (or sounds) are to count as well-formed and what is meant by any sequence which is so. A semantic theory of a language, like this one for ANN, would ideally contain rules enabling anyone following them to derive a statement of what any particular sentence of the language means. A fully competent user would know that the sentence means this. But, again profiting from the example of ANN, it is obvious that a philosopher will want to probe what this knowledge *amounts to*. What is it to know what a sentence means? Is it to be able to tell when it is true? Is it to be able to make sensible inferences either to its truth, given other facts, or from it supposed truth to other consequences? The *bland* answer to this question is that the competent user knows that '219' refers to 219, and so on for any sequence of numerals, or, in the case of a full language, the competent user knows what any particular sentence means. What I shall call an *external* approach to competence probes further into what this knowledge demands of someone. The word 'external' merely reminds us that the internal description of the actual workings of the language does not itself solve such a question.

To sum up the notions introduced so far. A language is given a semantics when we can say what each sentence means. We can do this compositionally by locating which features of a sentence are responsible for its meaning, and the rules whereby those features (notably words in various positions) yield the meaning. A language is thought of as an abstract thing, identified by its containing given sentences in given meanings. A population will use some particular abstract language as their actual language by indeed using those sentences in those meanings. It is contingent (something which could have been otherwise) that words and sentences bear some meaning and not others in the mouths of any given population. This contingency is equivalent to the fact that the population speaks some language L_1 and not another one L_2 in which the words and sentences have other meanings. Finally an external theory of competence hopes to describe further what has to be true of someone who knows the meanings of the sentences of his language. This is a distinctively philosophical query, not settled simply by telling what the semantic structure of his language is.

5. *Rules and Psychology*

To end this chapter I shall introduce one difficult question in the external theory of competence. This is the question of how the ordinary user of a language stands in relation to its syntactic and semantic rules. The central question is whether the user can be said to 'know' the rules; whether they have a 'psychological reality'. The question is pressing because it is fairly clear that any adequate set of such rules (what linguists now tend to call a *grammar* for a language) will be horribly complex. So it is not as if the ordinary user can either himself say what they are, or even recognize them as reliable once they have been pointed out. (Consider that someone may be perfectly good at using ANN but fail to recognize that the rule I wrote for it characterizes the way it works.) So what is the relation between the user and the rule?

We can distinguish four basic positions. The first two allow some "psychological reality" to the rules. They suppose that if a correct grammar says that a sentence is to be certified to mean what it does in some way, then the user who understands it must have a psychology which somehow reflects this grammar. The other two deny this: one of them simply denies that anything whatsoever about a user is indicated by the fact that his language permits some grammatical description, and the other claims that all that is suggested is neurophysiological, not psychological.

(1) *Chomsky's realism*. Chomsky insists that any inference from grammar to the psychology of the user is empirical in nature. It will not follow from the fact that a language *can* be described by certain rules that the user implicitly or in some other sense follows these rules. Nevertheless, the user's competence needs to be explained somehow, and if mention of these rules is to *explain* the competence that a user has, then he must in some sense have mastered them or at least implicitly he must know them: they must characterize his cognitive system. The natural analogy is with our perceptual skills. It is a matter of empirical psychology to discover what are the cues to which we respond in making utterly straightforward, non-inferential perceptual judgements. Thus it might be that the cue enabling me to judge the direction of a sound is the time-lag between arrival of a signal at one ear and at the other. This is not something I can discover by introspection: it is my brain, rather than I, that "computes" the direction from this fact. Similarly, the nature of the mental rules and representations which underlie a perception of grammaticalness or the awareness of what a particular sequence of English sounds means, is the subject of empirical enquiry.

Two other aspects of Chomsky's realism may be mentioned here. One is the idea that the ordinary sentence which we have on the surface is the terminus of a transformational history. It may be seen as the outcome of processes of change which can include the deletion of phrases, the insertion of others, the movement of parts relative to one another. If these processes are also real then the rules governing our language faculty include knowledge that they preserve meaning and preserve grammaticality – otherwise we would lightheartedly transform sentences into others which mean something different, or mean nothing. These rules will be immensely complex. To give a simple example, you might think that prepositional phrases can be moved fairly liberally: 'I get bored in France' means the same as 'In France I get bored.' But 'I didn't have a good time in France or England' does not mean the same as 'In France or England, I didn't have a good time.'[5] The rules governing transformations have to determine why this is so, and which transformations are permissible to avoid the undesirable consequences. This complexity leads to the second, notorious aspect of Chomsky's ideas: the large part played by innateness. The central idea is that of the "poverty of stimulus". This means that after a relatively small "exposure" to examples, to the vocabulary of its native tongue, and to ways of combining the vocabulary, the child masters an enormous and precise set of rules, adequate to all the baffling complexity of the syntax and semantics of that language. According to Chomsky the best explanation of this is an innate "universal grammar", or biological inheritance of syntactic and semantic categories and of rules concerning such things as the movement of phrases, permissible substitutions of pronouns, and so on. This inheritance encodes the fundamental features of any possible human language. In learning it is primed, as it were, with knowledge of the actual exemplars of such things as nouns, phrases, pronouns, verbs etc. in an actual language such as English, and the user is then equipped with an indefinitely elastic range of syntactic and semantic competence. The innate cognitive structure fills the gap between the impoverished, fragmentary input and the rich and extended output.

The argument from the poverty of stimulus is queried by philosophers including Putnam, Ryle and Goodman.[6] Ryle for example urges that we could only talk in Chomsky's way of exposure to a stimulus if we had forgotten what happens in a normal childhood. An infant is helped, encouraged, guided, taught, trained; he models sayings on those of others, practises, impersonates, invents, and so on: "As Aristotle said, what we have to do when we have learned to do it, we learn to do by

---

[5] *Rules and Representations*, p. 156.

[6] Putnam, Goodman, 'Symposium on Innate Ideas', in *The Philosophy of Language*, ed. Searle.

doing it . . ."[7] Ryle castigates Chomsky for representing the infant as a solitary thinker, unfostered and alone ('Mowgli in Babel') trying out solitary hypotheses about which noises count as sentences amongst the strangers around him. If that were his predicament, unless a kind nature had restricted the number of possible grammars he could try out, he would have far too many to choose from. But this is not his task. His task is not to think and select, but to imitate, to enter wholeheartedly into the ways of his parents and friends.

Ryle's point is to expand our understanding of what happens during language learning, to close the gap between what you might expect the learning to achieve and what it does achieve (the gap which innatists fill with an endowed structure of possible grammars – "clouds of biological glory" in Ryle's view). The gap is also closed if we can see how the apparently idiosyncratic, shapeless, and arbitrary rules which users appear to follow may actually have a *point*. If we can make the rules involved intelligible, there is so much the less miracle about the speed with which the learner absorbs them. Making them intelligible means in particular seeing how the *semantic* role of terms explains their *syntactic* oddities. Consider a simple example. If we classify phrases such as 'any fish' and 'no fish' as noun phrases, we might expect them to fill the same grammatical positions. 'You may eat any fish that you catch' and 'you may eat no fish that you catch' are thus equally well-formed. Unfortunately, 'if you catch any fish you may eat them' is well-formed, whereas 'if you catch no fish you may eat them' is not. How do we master such syntactic quirks? Obviously not by an innate sense of grammar, but by realizing (roughly) that given the supposition that I catch no fish, there is no reference for the pronoun 'them' to pick up, hence no permission to be given by the sentence. Whereas in the former case there is. (Precise rules for sentences involving pronouns are still intensely hard to find.) If there is a point to a rule, the learner's achievement is easier to understand. By analogy, consider a theorist trying to find principles of permissible classical composition by analysing musical scores, paying attention only to written shapes. A horrendous task. Yet some musicians mastered them in early childhood! This is not however because

[7] Gilbert Ryle, 'Mowgli in Babel', in *On Thinking*, pp. 101–2.

they had an innate grammatical endowment: it is because they mastered a very simple notational device, and had *ears* to tell which of the indefinite kinds of combination were acceptable. They had no innate propensity to select shapes at all.

(2) This takes us in one direction away from Chomsky's kind of psychological realism. This is towards insisting that the rules of semantics and syntax of our language should be conceived not as hidden and largely innate mechanisms guiding our competence, but as intelligible, open, means for serving our ends. They should be discoverable, not by experiment, in the way that our use of visual and auditory cues in detecting distances are discovered, but by reflection upon the purposes for which we use language and the means we have naturally developed to serve those purposes. The *way* we use our language is open before us; reflection on it should enable is to tell how we control our sayings, and to see the point of the rules which guide us in doing so.

Chomsky is adamant that his position is the only empirically respectable stance in this matter. But the second position is empirical enough, although it may still await development. It marks a "research programme" of diminishing Chomsky's gap: of showing how a child's needs and training render it unsurprising that it conforms to the rules of its native language, since those rules mark not meaningless and arbitrary restrictions on patterns of combination of terms, but natural consequences of the need to communicate. Before coming back to this, I shall contrast it with the final two positions.

(3) Quine emphasized the important distinction between behaviour which *fits* a rule and behaviour which is *guided* by it. "Behaviour *fits* a rule whenever it conforms to it; whenever the rule truly describes the behaviour. But the behaviour is not *guided* by the rule unless the behaver knows the rule and can state it. This behaver observes the rule."[8] Thus one can imagine immensely complicated mathematical rules for giving a denotation to the sequences of digits in ANN: rules involving exponentiation, rules which take, say, the first hundred numer-

---

[8] W. V. Quine, 'Methodological Reflections on Current Linguistic Theory', in Davidson and Harman (1972), p. 442.

als as primitive, instead of only the first ten, and so on. These rules could end up giving the same numerals the same references. But there is no sense in which we observe them. Our behaviour fits them, but is not guided by them. Or consider a computer chess programme. Perhaps it ends up playing the same way as a tournament player, in that the kind of move it would make in any position is the same as his. The output is the same. But the rules may be very different. The computer may get there by brute force: it scans millions of possible outcomes, and selects according to predetermined features. Whereas the evidence is that even Grand Masters consider only some thirty or so positions on their "lookahead tree" (compare the answer of Richard Reti, asked how many moves ahead he looked in tournaments: "One . . . the right one"). The computer's rules fit the competence of the player, but the player does not follow those rules.

Quine uses this distinction to cast doubt on any notion of guidance by implicit rules. Even if we had an adequate set of syntactic and semantic rules for English, they could stand to the ordinary user as the computer's programme stands to the ordinary player. There is no reason to believe that the user embodies those rules, even implicitly. If we imagine two different sets of rules issuing in a pairing of the same meanings with the same sentences, Quine would deny that it makes any empirical sense to ask which of them guides us. Chomsky is well aware that there is an issue here.[9] He does not simply confuse the idea of an adequate grammar with the idea that its rules are realized in the users of the language. But he thinks that empirical evidence can favour the view that we are implicitly guided in one way rather than another (after all, it is empirical evidence, for example from skill at lightning chess, which suggests that players do not go through millions of computations). Quine's position is that this is not so. Questions of the psychological reality of semantic and syntactic rules guiding a user in his recognition of meaning and well-formedness are not to be raised. The most that we can do is generate a set of rules such

---

[9] He is especially scornful of philosophers who (a) fail to see that the issue is an empirical one, and (b) therefore take him to be giving the wrong answer to the question whether it follows from the fact that a grammar is adequate that it is also guiding us; e.g. *Rules and Representations*, pp. 129 ff.

that *if* someone follows them, they are competent with the language as we are; you can never use this and other observations as evidence that these are rules which do actually guide us. It will be seen that on this third position semantic and syntactic rules play no part in explaining our competence. It is sometimes said that they would merely 'model' our competence, or give a 'theoretical representation' of it. But this is just an unclear way of saying that *if* we knew the rules and followed them, we *would* end up knowing what we do know about what it is that sentences mean.

(4) The fourth position finds the missing link between us and the rules in neurophysiology. The idea is that our brains have a causal structure. Some "bits" are responsible for some aspects of our competence, and other "bits" are not. This causal structure could be found to be the same shape as the structure of some system of rules, in the following sense. Let us say that a set of semantic and syntactic rules for English would be *crippled* if some particular rule or rules or axioms saying what particular words or other features do, were removed. The removal will mean a definite impoverishment: sentences which needed just those rules for their interpretation will be lost. For instance, if there is a rule permitting just a certain movement of noun phrases within sentences, and it is removed, sentences depending on that operation will no longer be permitted. But others, not dependent on that rule, will remain. So a particular crippling would have a pattern of effects. Now we might find that some particular damage to a person's brain produced just the same pattern of effects: after removal of some bit he cannot understand the very sentences which a particular crippling also deletes. This would be empirical evidence that the rule or axiom is actually embodied in the user's neural processes. The evidence could of course be extended: for example, it might be that in some semantic set-up a quick computation of what a sentence means could proceed using some rules, but a circuitous one could arrive at the result without it; equally a particular injury might lead to a much slower comprehension of the sentence. Ultimately a structure underlying the user's competence might be found which is, as it were, causally the same shape as a

semantic system.[10] This makes the semantic system a correct description of the speaker.

The fourth suggestion need not be incompatible with Chomsky's psychological realism. It may be that we should allow a "psychological reality" corresponding to the neural operations, so that talk of implicit knowledge, inherited grammar, representations of grammatical categories, etc. would be only a way of saying that our brains have the suggested causal structure. But if so, it is a bad, mysterious, and potentially misleading way of saying it. For whilst it sounds exciting and strange to say that an infant inherits a universal grammar, it is not nearly so strange if this translates into saying that the infant has a brain which under normal conditions of development will come to have a causal structure of the kind described.

An analogy due to Quine helps to locate the issues.[11] We can compare our competence in telling the meanings of sentences with the visible foliage of a tree. The 'grammar we use' would be the supporting branches and twigs. Quine's position is that the shape of the foliage does nothing to indicate the underlying structure of branches and twigs. Chomsky's position is that it does: evidence, for example from the pattern of growth of the foliage can confirm particular structures. The fourth position is that if we shot bits out we could watch which patterns of foliage fall, and that this would be evidence that our language is structured as described by some grammar, although not evidence that we "implicitly follow" the rules of that grammar. The second position is that we are like squirrels constantly scampering around the structure. We know what it is because we know our way around it.

Although the fourth position sounds initially attractive, I think it is not adequate. The idea is that it is the causal structure of our brains which creates or constitutes the fact that our language has some particular semantic structure. But it *might* be that our brains are like holographs, which do not encode information bit by bit. It is simply not true of them that if you

---

[10] Gareth Evans, 'Semantic Theory and Tacit Knowledge' in Holtzman and Leich (1981), p. 127. The position is described and developed well in Martin Davies, *Meaning, Quantification and Modality*, ch. 4. See also L. Fricker, 'Semantic Structure and Speaker's Understanding', *Proceedings of the Aristotelian Society* (1982).

[11] Also used by Davies, op. cit., p. 82.

destroy a particular area you lose one particular piece of information. You only get a somewhat less good overall picture. If we were like this – and it is not of course a matter of armchair theorizing to tell whether we are or not – then nothing would correspond to destroying bits of foliage by knocking out particular twigs or branches. And then on this account it would not be true that our language has a particular semantic structure. For example, suppose it turned out that there is simply no neurophysiological way of destroying someone's competence with the numeral '7' (his awareness that it refers to 7) by itself. No pattern of damage is isomorphic with the 7-crippled numeral system which would be left if that numeral were deleted from ANN. On this account it would follow that the given rule was not the correct one, the one which describes the actual structure of the numeral system. And that seems incredible. It seems right to say that we know that '719' refers to what it does *because* of the presence of '7' in its actual place, although we do not know that any 7-crippling, localized brain damage could be brought about. Whether it can be brought about is pure speculation, but it is not one on which our knowledge of how the numeral system works depends. We know that because we can control the reference – we can substitute digits at will to refer to what we like – and we can see how we accomplish that control. If this generalizes to natural languages, it establishes the second position, that the way we use our language is open to view and ought to be capable of being known by reflecting on our control of our devices. This damages the analogy which is sometimes made between recognizing meaning in a remark, and interpreting a visual presentation. In perception we may be quite ignorant of the cues which we use (or, more accurately, which our perceptual mechanisms and brains use) in order to recognize what we are seeing. But just for that reason we are not good either at controlling those cues. In advance of theory, most of us cannot produce perceptual illusions; we do not know how to arrange the significant features in order to make it look to someone as though he is, for instance, in a tapering room when in fact he is not. We would need expert help. Whereas in communication we are extremely skilled at selecting and organizing exactly the meaning-determining features which result in our messages communicating what we want.

The following argument is also relevant. Consider a simple language containing only twelve names and twelve simple predicates, any of which can be applied, truly or falsely, to any of the named things.[12] There can only be 144 sentences. A compositional semantics could proceed like this: it could say what each name refers to ('Fred' refers to Fred . . .) and which feature each predicate ascribes to a thing ('bald' applies to bald things . . .) Finally a rule would say that the result of placing a name next to a predicate is a sentence saying of the thing named that it has the feature expressed by the predicate. There are twenty-four axioms, and one rule. But we could have given a wooden list correlating each of the 144 sentences with a meaning. From Quine's standpoint each is an adequate semantics for the language; there is no real question of which one is embodied by speakers. From the first standpoint, learning theory can tell us that one is better: in particular we can see whether a child knowing what 'Fred is bald' means, and knowing what 'John is fat' means, may see without further training what 'John is bald' means. This confirms the compositional account. It is not true that each sentence requires a separate, independent, description. The fourth position relies on an underlying neurophysiology. It urges that damage would knock out, say, twelve sentences (the 'Fred' sentences) at a time, or, if it knocked out one sentence at a time, this would make the wooden view true.

But these views are all lacking any connection between the structure and the very fact that the sentences mean what they do. They allow that in principle, if the learning or the neurophysiology were different, the wooden account might be true of one part of the population, and the compositional account of the other, yet they would communicate and understand each other perfectly. Yet what reason could there be for allowing that a person means that Fred is asleep by some noise, unless the noise is structured in a way which permits us to see it as made of a name for Fred, and a predicate for being asleep? To use a sentence to mean that Fred sleeps is to have a certain understanding of it: that it refers to Fred, and says that he is asleep. Now indeed in a code a sign might be dictated to perform these two functions without itself containing elements

[12] Evans, op. cit., pp. 122–3.

which correlate with either. 'Zzz' means that at three minutes past ten the contact will come out of the second alley . . . But the code is parasitic upon another language where different elements have the different functions. If a community had no such language, it is plausible to say that they could not take sentences in the alleged way (see also 4.5, 4.6). In that case the wooden list for each of the 144 sentences misinterprets any population which does indeed use them woodenly. It pretends they are saying complex things when the absence of any elements corresponding to the complexities proves that they are not.

The result is that you cannot speak a natural language (a first language) and mean by a sentence that Fred sleeps unless you can take an element of it and use it to say other things about Fred, and take another element and use it to say that other things than Fred are asleep. This is not a natural fact about us, but a philosophical truth about the conditions to be satisfied if we are to mean something by an utterance.[13] But now, how could you have the right kinds of skill with the elements of such a sentence without being in a position to know that you have them (by being made aware of the different powers and capacities for redeployment the terms have)? You may not have thought quite which semantic categories are needed to describe your language. But it could not be wholly surprising to the competent user, possessing the skill to redeploy 'Fred' and *thereby* certified as understanding 'Fred sleeps' to mean that Fred sleeps, that the terms has something particular to do with Fred.

If this argument is generalized, it again favours the doctrine that our control over our language, the way we can deploy words to generate understood effects, is the fact making it true that our language is semantically structured in a given way. Even if we cannot ourselves describe what we do, an adequate description must answer to our own knowledge of our own skills: it ought to be recognizable as a description of what we do. We know that the description of ANN is right, because we can see it in the way we create and respond to any numeral we wish.

---

[13] Strawson, *Individuals*, p. 99. Evans, *The Varieties of Reference*, 4.3, emphasizes the same point about thoughts. But the principle which Evans calls the generality constraint is stronger than anything I am relying upon.

Even if this argument is accepted, it certainly does not prove that the second position is right. The second position, like Chomsky's, represents an empirical belief: in this case the belief that we can find pointful rules underlying our grammatical and semantic competence, and narrow the gap between what happens during learning, and the competence we end up with. This is a more optimistic belief than its three competitors. But that does not ensure that it is true.

This chapter has been a bare introduction to many issues which are subsequently considered again, and has toured a large territory. Problems of truth, of speakers and their understandings, of semantics, and of psychology all jostle their way around the triangular path. Crowds have a bad way of shutting out the light. So I now turn to a more detailed view of what a language might be, and how we are to think of ourselves as understanding one.

Notes to Chapter 1

1.3 'not provided much of a Christmas present . . .'
The numerical example is intended to be quite important, in enabling the reader to avoid confusions of the 'theory of . . .' kind. Nothing is more discouraging than reading about the theory of force, the theory of sense, the theory of meaning, the theory of reference, etc. without having much grasp of the problems these theories set out to explain, and the devices used to do the explaining. Of course, much philosophical energy goes into discovering good questions to concentrate upon, but the student can hardly appreciate that unless he knows accurately which questions are the ones being tackled at any given time. This section is intended to arm the student against automatic and parochial assumptions that it is just known, and beyond controversy, that a theory of meaning ought to be doing just this or that. This is as sensible as supposing that there is just one thing which a theory of beer or a theory of boots ought to be doing. It all depends on what we want to explain, about beer or boots or about meaning.

1.4 'to make features of our language into the key . . .'
The logical positivists developed a conventionalist approach to necessary truth, and the belief that linguistic arrangements somehow organize our world-view, and therefore determine what we count as unalterable and inexorable, is also implicit in Wittgenstein. Students might try:

A. J. Ayer, *Language, Truth and Logic*, ch. 4.

W. C. Kneale, 'Are Necessary Truths True by Convention?', *Proceedings of the Aristotelian Society*, Supplementary Volume (1947).

E. J. Craig, 'The Problems of Necessary Truth', in Blackburn (1975).

B. Stroud, 'Wittgenstein and Logical Necessity', *Philosophical Review* (1965).

C. Wright, *Wittgenstein on the Foundations of Mathematics*, esp. chs. 22–5.

C. Lewy, *Meaning and Modality*, chs. 1–5, for a general attack on conventionalism.

The work of Quine and Wittgenstein (especially the *Remarks on the Foundations of Mathematics*) is also important in this connection, but better read in the light of later chapters.

1.5   Although the topic of this section is central to our conception of ourselves as language users, the literature is not encouraging. Many discussions proceed in the light of particular compositional theories, and particular views about the indeterminacy of grammar, and may be better read after chapter 8. Apart from the works mentioned in the text footnotes, the following might be consulted:

N. Chomsky, 'Knowledge and Language', in Gunderson (1975).

C. Graves *et al.*, 'Tacit Knowledge', *Journal of Philosophy* (1973).

S. P. Stitch, 'What Every Speaker Knows', *Philosophical Review* (1971).

——— 'Grammar, Psychology and Indeterminacy', *Journal of Philosophy* (1972).

CHAPTER 2

How is Meaning Possible? (1)

> Still, thou are blest, compar'd wi' me
> The present only toucheth thee
> But och! I backward cast me e'e
> On prospects drear!
> An' forward, tho' I canna see,
> I guess an' fear!
>
> Robert Burns, 'To a Mouse'.

1. *Representation and the Dog-leg*

The best philosophical problems arise in the following way. We get a sense of what the world is like, what it must be like. We see it as made up from some kinds of thing, permitting some kinds of arrangement, capable of making up some kinds of fact or states of affairs. Then, we find that there are judgements we make, commitments we enter into, which seem not to fit at all into this picture of the world. We are at a loss to "give an account" of them, or in other words to imagine a kind of fact which could make them true, or whose absence might make them false. Thus a scientific world view might picture the world in terms of an evolving spatial distribution of particles or forces: how can this dance of atoms make room for consciousness, agency, causation, or value? How can it even allow my particular perspective on the world, from one place and one time?

In this chapter and the next I try to introduce the problem of gaining some conception of what meaning *is*: how is it even possible for a world – a natural world of things in space and time, and made of flesh and blood – to contain some things which *mean* other things? As Burns notes, in our thoughts we represent to ourselves the way the world is, or was, or will be. We think of absent things, events, and states of affairs, and perhaps believe in them or desire or fear them, or hope they do not exist or will exist. This is the 'intentionality' or directedness of thought. With our language we can express judgements, desires, or hopes about what we thus conceive, communicating with another. But our words bear no natural connections with whatever it is that they signify. It is our use of them, our habit of taking them in one way and not in another, which confers their powers on them, just as our arrangements confer their powers on pieces of chess, or tokens which serve as currency. So we need to say something about the relation between language and thought, on the one hand, and language and things on the other: to complete the original triangle, in other words.

The central and obvious truth about words is that we understand them: we confer their powers, know how to use them, make them work for us. The difficulty, then, is to gain some appreciation of the kind of fact this might be. What kind of truth is it that I can use a word to mean something, or express a thought about something? How can any world make room for a fact of this sort? I come at this by describing the pressures which tempt philosophers – and not only outdated, classical philosophers, but also the most up-to-date investigators – into what we call a *dog-legged* theory. In this, words are thought of as reinterpreted into another medium, such as that of Ideas, whose own powers explain the significance words take on. This idea, I shall argue, is destroyed by considerations which are by now quite familiar in modern philosophy of language. But I shall go on to suggest some essential similarities between this discredited approach, and others, due to Quine and Dummett, in which meaning is explored through thinking about interpretation, or the manifestation of meaning to each other. Classically, we would understand meaning by mapping words back onto ideas; in this approach we do so by interpreting them back into a home medium or language which an interpreter brings with him. And the obstacles and limitations may prove to be similar in each case. Having explored this, I turn in chapter 3 to a more direct approach to meaning, which seeks to understand what it is to use a word in a principle-governed way, without relying upon any illicit comfort in the way of reinterpretation of words back into some other currency.

Aristotle[1] supposed that men confronted by things external to their minds form mental likenesses of them. Spoken words

---

[1] *De Interpretatione*, 16ᵃ3.

are signs of those mental likenesses, and thence derivatively, of things in the world. On this view words, as Hobbes put it, "signify the cogitations and motion of our minds". The classic statement of this view in modern philosophy is Book III of Locke's *Essay Concerning Human Understanding*. It is treacherous to suppose that throughout the *Essay* Locke meant one definite kind of mental representation of things by his term 'Idea', but at this point he clearly follows Aristotle and Hobbes. He begins chapter II of this book:

Man, though he have a great variety of Thoughts, and such, from which others, as well as himself, might receive Profit and Delight; yet they are all within his own Breast, invisible, and hidden from others, nor can of themselves be made appear . . . Thus we may conceive how *Words* which were by nature so well adapted to that purpose, come to be made use of by Men, as the *Signs* of their *Ideas*; not by any natural connexion that there is between particular articulate Sounds and certain Ideas, for then there would be but one Language amongst all Men; but by a voluntary imposition . . . The use men have of these Marks, being either to record their own Thoughts for the Assistance of their own Memory; or as it were to bring out their Ideas, and lay then before the view of others: *Words in their primary or immediate Signification, stand for nothing, but the Ideas in the Mind of him that uses them* . . . [Locke's italics.]

Locke had an argument for giving Ideas this prime position in the theory of understanding. A man cannot make a word into a sign, but not a "sign of his Ideas at the same time", for "Words being voluntary signs, they cannot be voluntary signs imposed by him on things he knows not. That would make them Signs of nothing, Sounds without Signification." The premise of this argument, that we cannot make signs signify something unless we in some sense know about that thing, surfaces in many forms, and we shall encounter it again. But Locke's use of it in this argument depends upon a suppressed premise: that it is only our ideas which we "know". This comes as a surprise. We might accept that we cannot make words into signs of things about which we do not know, but claim that we know a good deal about chairs and tables, numbers and electrons, rights and duties: the whole world of common sense, or of scientific, mathematical, or ethical theory. Why the restriction to our own Ideas, conceived of as private, hidden, and invisible to others?

Clearly, Locke is arguing within a generally representative theory of knowledge. We do know about external objects, other people, their thoughts, and perhaps some more exotic entities as well. But we know them only derivatively, through the immediate acquaintance we have with our own Ideas of them. So perhaps his argument is best restated in terms of what we in some sense immediately or primarily know – words must immediately or primarily signify objects of immediate or primary knowledge; but these are Ideas, secret, within our own breasts, hidden and invisible. Notoriously, this theory of knowledge makes it difficult (most philosophers would say, impossible) to have any reason to suppose that we know anything at all about the world: we cannot tell whether an Idea adequately represents the world if we only have the Idea to go on, any more than we can tell whether a painting is a good likeness if we are denied any chance of comparing it with the sitter. Hence the Idealist response, made in this instance by Berkeley, that the knowable world must be shrunk to within the immediate objects of knowledge – the private, hidden, personal ideas. This is an argument within the theory of knowledge. But it is essential to see that the parallel move applies with just as much force in the theory of understanding. For how can I so much as get the thought that my words can signify not *only* a hidden, private, personal item within my own breast, but *also* some external object or feature of the world, such as a chair? Certainly I have the idea of the chair. But that is just an *idea*. My words can, let us suppose, stand as marks of such a private thing – there is still no way of understanding how they *point through* such things to a different range of items for which they derivatively stand. Thus the second stage of this dog-leg turns out to be impassable. Whenever we try to understand our words as referring beyond the circle of our ideas, we can do no more than present further ideas to ourselves. It is as if we tried to get someone to understand that a portrait might represent a sitter, but just by showing more and more portraits; or as if we tried to get someone confined to a cinema for all his experience to understand that the films represent objects other than themselves, but could only attempt this task by showing more and more films.

At this point it might be suggested that the highly visible

model, according to which Ideas are something like private reproductions of reality, is letting us down. The presence of the reproduction is, it turns out, no explanation of how words can be understood to refer *through* it, to the world which it itself reproduces. The reproduction must need itself to be taken as representative of the external world, and we so far lack any account of what it is to so take it – how we can understand it to point beyond itself. But there is a more general moral to be drawn, which will apply to theories which do not postulate a particularly visual intermediary, or one which in any very natural way reproduces features of the thing signified. The general moral is that any dog-legged theory needs to avoid what we might call the "regress-or-elephant" problem. The form of a dog-legged theory is that we understand the way in which words have significance in two stages: they are associated with elements of an interpreting medium (in this case, Ideas), and the elements of this medium have their own representative powers. They have "lines of projection" onto the world whereby they signify aspects of it. The argument we have just gone through highlights the problem on this second part of the leg. We face a *regress* of interpretations if we need to introduce another medium whose powers explain the powers of any given medium. And we are in danger of not advancing at all if the powers of elements of the medium to signify things are left unexplained. This would be like the theory which explains why the world stays where it is in space by its being carried on an elephant, and changes the subject when asked what carries the elephant. Of course, any explanation must start somewhere. But it is pointless, a mere shuffle, to introduce an element which can be seen to require just the *same kind* of explanation of the original. So a dog-legged theory must always show how it avoids the regress-or-elephant dilemma. Notice that this is not an impossible demand. The intermediary may be of such a kind that it is in some way easier to see how it can have significance, and by its presence help to explain how words do.

The line of thought leading to a dog-legged theory is this. The words of a natural language like English have no intrinsic connections with what they signify. We could use them to mean different things, were we to come to speak different languages, or we could use them like parrots with no understanding at all.

We need to know what they signify, if we are to understand them. But the argument goes, *knowing what* they signify demands that we have some *way of representing* to ourselves what they signify. So consider what we must demand of this representation. Suppose it were merely the substitution of some different words for the originals. Then the problem arises again about the substituted words (the regress). If they are not understood, their presence is irrelevant. If they are, then there must be some further way of representing what they stand for. So the conditions on anything which is to serve as the intermediary tighten. If it is not merely to be a shuffle, introducing just another demand for a way of representing to oneself what *it* represents, it must be *essentially representative* – that is, its mere presence to the mind must itself guarantee that we know which item or feature in the external world is thereby represented. Its connection with a feature of the world needs to be, as it were, transparent, so that there is no further act of interpreting it one way or another. If its own connection with whatever it represents were mutable and contingent, in the way that the connection of words with things is, then there would exist the possibility of taking it one way or another; there would then be a need to show what determines how it is being taken. But that would introduce *another* way of representing the candidates, so that one could ask whether one took the original to mean this one or that one. This would lead to the regress of interpretations. At every stage, therefore, if the connection is variable or needs to be established, it introduces the demand for a manner of representation which is guaranteed, whose *mere presence* ensures that it also represents the right thing. There must be a *medium which carries its own interpretation with it*, so there is no possibility of misunderstanding what is thought of, once it is present.

Furthermore, the possibilities and guarantees talked of here need to be extremely strong. For suppose it is a merely natural or contingent matter that once a human being has one of these essentially representative items in mind, he is thinking of, say, a chair. There is then the bare logical possibility that thinkers of a different, rather inhuman, nature should have the same items in mind but be thinking of, say, a bed. But what difference can this be, on the theory? The inhuman character is to take the item one way, whereas humans take it the other. But the essentially representative nature of the item is there precisely to plug this gap: there is to be no further fact that it is taken in one way or another. Its presence *supplies the way it is taken*, for otherwise we never get an interpretation of the word which we understand by its means, but only a regress of substitutes, each posing the same problem.

2. *Images*

Images were once popular candidates for the intermediaries now sketched. For the presence of an image in the mind might well seem to guarantee intrinsically that a particular object, or feature of the world, is represented by its presence. Images have another nice property, in that our ability to create them, as faint copies or reproductions of experiences we have had, just as photographs are copies of scenes which the camera points at, seems to be a nice, relatively unmysterious kind of ability. It promises an easy theory of how we come to understand words, as well as a simple story about what that understanding consists in. Unfortunately it is inadequate. For the presence of an image far from guarantees understanding, even in any weak sense, and its absence far from guarantees lack of understanding.

We can sense that something must be wrong. For how is a world in which some things mirror others, or possess mirror images of others, also a world in which anything *means* anything? If we imagine a landscape with only unthinking, unmeaning things in it (including perhaps creatures which move and interact with things), it is impossible to see why adding mirrors and pictures, even placing them in the internal parts of the things that move, introduces significance. The landscape and its pictures may reflect each other perfectly well, but this in itself gives us no ground for saying that the pictures or their possessors are thinking of features of the landscape, any more than that the features of the landscape signify the features of the picture. This general inadequacy is usually held to be the problem with the very static picture or diagram theory of meaning which Wittgenstein espoused in his early work and later rejected. We can understand the general inadequacy by working through some arguments.

Firstly, there is bound to be a gap between having an image

on the one hand, and taking it to represent one or another feature of the world on the other. Wittgenstein makes the point with a pithy example: imagine an old man climbing up a hill. Concentrate upon your image carefully. Now, might it not be an image of an old man sliding backwards down a hill? That it was an image of one and not the other is not a matter of anything intrinsic to it, guaranteed by the image, but is a matter of the way it is taken. So its presence as the final explanation of what it is to take words (say, the words 'an old man climbing up a hill') one way or another is redundant. It itself requires interpretation as much as the words do. The point is that however naturally it comes to regard a picture in one way or another, as a picture of this, or a sample of that, or as representing one kind of thing and not another, this is in effect adopting one "method of projection" rather than another. But then the presence of the image is not by itself an explanation of what it is to do that, and the dog-legged theory using images collapses.

This kind of argument was anticipated by Berkeley in his famous attack on Locke's account of "abstract ideas". The problem concerned the general significance of words. Consider my understanding of what it is for a shape to be triangular. If this is a matter of associating the term with an image standing as an intermediary through which I understand the term, what properties must the image have? Since it is in some sense to represent any triangle, perhaps it had better not be too specific, having some particular geometry. If it were, for instance, right-angled, then I might take it to represent only *that* kind of triangle, in which case I would misunderstand the general term 'triangle' by using it. Perhaps then I should in some sense blur it, making its particular geometry indistinct, so that it is neither definitely one kind of triangle nor another. But now its representative capacity is threatened in another way. Perhaps it represents only blurred triangles. Or, suppose it is like a photograph sufficiently indistinct to be plausibly taken to be a picture of any triangle. Then it would also plausibly be taken to be a picture of something which isn't a triangle at all, such as the segment of a circle, or a trapezoid. Berkeley saw the problem. He also saw the right thing to say, which is that in so far as one's thinking about a triangle involves an image at all, the image is to be *taken* to "equally stand for and represent all rectilinear triangles whatsoever, and is in that sense universal". Berkeley innocently concludes, "All of which seems very plain and not to include any difficulty in it."[2] This is fine so long as we forget that the whole point of the theory is to give an account of *what it is* to take a sign in one way or another, so that once the proposed intermediary, in this case images, is shown to need this supplementary comment, there is no theory left. It is as though I accept a challenge to make a film illustrating the truth that all triangles have some property or other. I can show long, fat, right-angled, obtuse, isosceles triangles; I can blur my images, I can superimpose some upon others. But I cannot do anything which suggests that these exhibitions are to be taken to be representative of all triangles whatsoever. I can only rely upon the audience to "catch on". Or, I can add the *words* 'what is shown here applies to all triangles'. But images were introduced as the very intermediary to explain how we understand such words in the first place. So they cannot now rely on words for help. And if we rely on the audience to "catch on" we still lack any explanation of what it is to do that. It can't be merely rehearsing the film just shown, and it cannot be just repeating some set of words, since words need understanding in one way or another.

Probably it is obvious, once pointed out, that gazing at a public picture of a thing is not the same as thinking of the object or features of the world pictured. A picture can prompt one to think of many matters, and ones which resemble or fail to resemble aspects of the picture itself in any variety of ways. The same is true of mental imagery. This is not to deny that it may be useful, as well as pleasurable, to turn over images of things as one does one's thinking. An image can indeed be taken to represent any triangle, or any man, or any unemployed contemporary teenager, or whatever, and the presence of a compelling image, in the head or on paper, can help all kinds of thinking. It is just that the presence of the image is not sufficient for the thinking to be going on. Nor does it logically determine the character of any thinking that is going on.[3]

---

[2] Berkeley, Introduction to the *Principles of Human Knowledge*, §15.

[3] I do not want to claim that imagining is *only* a matter of the presence in the mind of representations. Images may themselves be intrinsically representational. They are directed at the world. But then we cannot use the fact that they are like this to explain how anything *can* be like this. In the tradition I am attacking, the pictorial quality of images was held to explain this.

The insufficiency of images is evident again if we turn from thinking about things and features of things – thinking about triangles or men or climbing hills – and thinking *that* something is the case. A scene is not itself an assertion or judgement to the effect that something is so. Neither is a picture, however naturally is might come to us to make some judgements in the presence of some pictures. We need not even accept that any state of affairs obtains which in any way resembles what is depicted. And to judge that one does obtain which in some way resembles what is depicted demands interpreting the picture: selecting features, generalizing, abstracting, *conceptualizing*. Finally, an inability to image some scene is not the same as the inability to make a related judgement: if I ask you to imagine a bed without an attractive member of the opposite sex in it you may, temporarily, be unable to do so. But you do not temporarily lose your ability to understand, and believe, that there are such beds.

How general is this argument? We started only from the need to take words in one way or another, if we are to understand them. This became the need to have a way of representing to ourselves what it is that they stand for. This became the need for the intrinsically representational medium, in order to halt the regress which develops if there is the possibility of taking the representations in one way or another. Images are suggested as a plausible kind of candidate, for their connection with the appearance of things, which they literally *re-present*, is especially natural. But even they are not good enough, for a picture too needs definite interpretation, and its presence is not sufficient to guarantee any particular way of taking it. Perhaps then nothing can fill the role: *no thing can halt the regress of interpretations*. So where has the argument gone wrong? We can come at this by seeing why images, at least, cannot be *necessary* for thinking either.

Wittgenstein puts the case against the role of images in a theory of understanding like this:

If I give someone the order "fetch me a red flower from that meadow", how is he to know what sort of flower to bring, as I have only given him a *word*?

He imagines someone using the word to determine a mental

picture of a red flower, or even a red square on a physical colour chart which he carries about, and then finding a flower which matches it:

> ... But this is not the only way of searching and it isn't the usual way. We go, look about us, walk up to a flower and pick it, without comparing it to anything. To see that the process of obeying the order can be of this kind, consider the order "*imagine* a red patch". You are not tempted in this case to think that before obeying you must have imagined a red patch to serve you as a pattern for the red patch which you were ordered to imagine.[4]

The point is not just that we do not feel any such second-order pattern. It is stronger than that. The image cannot be necessary to understanding the order, because it can only figure in an explanation if we understand that *it is the right image*. But that is just as blankly mysterious as understanding that you have the right flower. Knowing which is the right kind of flower is not explained by knowing that the flower matches some given pattern, unless we also know that it is the right kind of pattern. But recognizing patterns to be the right ones is no easier than, or different from, recognizing flowers. The point is the more vivid if we take a colour term which is slightly unfamiliar: magenta, or puce. If I ask you to pick me a puce flower, you may imagine various shades. But if you do not know which of them is puce, you cannot obey me, except by luck, by matching a flower to a particular shade. On the other hand, if you *do* know which of them corresponds to puce, then you know which flower does in the same way – whatever way that is. So the detour via intermediary images is useless. And this point has wider applications. For any dog-legged theory faces the objection. We need to know that we are interpreting the words via the right intermediary. But knowing that we have used the right intermediary for a word is no easier than knowing that we are using the word itself to apply to the right kind of thing.

What then was wrong with the original argument? The little transition from 'we need to take words in a particular way, if we understand them' to 'we need a way of representing to ourselves what they stand for' must have played us false. A representation is too much of a *re-presentation* – a mental presence which maps

---

[4] *The Blue and Brown Books*, p. 3.

onto the real world according to some method of projection.
And as we have seen, introducing any such thing is apt to be just
a shuffle. The one problem, that of interpreting words to stand
for aspects of the world, becomes replaced by two: that of
interpreting words to connect to the right aspects of one's
mental scene, and that of interpreting aspects of one's mental
scene to stand for aspects of the world. The flaw is easy to see:
indeed, there is nothing very controversial in the arguments
which have just demolished the type of theory. But the conviction that there *must* be an intrinsically representative medium,
for otherwise there is no account of what it is to understand
words, is very strong. It is as though we can envisage no other
model of what it could be to understand words, except one that
more or less surreptitiously regards such understanding as a
matter of mapping the words into some other representative
medium, whose powers are conveniently left unexamined.

In Book III of *Gulliver's Travels* Swift describes the language
school of Lagado, which is occupied in making men *use* in
language only the very things they are to talk about: ". . . since
words are only names for *things*, it would be more convenient for
all men to carry about them such *things* as were necessary to
express the particular business they are to discourse on."[5] Swift
imagines the Professors of Lagado as pedlars, carrying the
objects of their conversations on their backs and just showing
them to each other in place of speaking. In effect a dog-legged
theory applauds this ideal, and only avoids the absurdity first
by making the *things* mental and secondly by magically endow-
ing them with a power of pointing beyond themselves.

[5] *Gulliver's Travels*, p. 151. Swift's thrust is directed against the linguistic pretensions
of the Royal Society. Late seventeenth-century thinkers were convinced that stylistic
faults and faults of language had impeded all scientific progress. The Society
maintained, in the words of its historian Thomas Sprat, "a constant Resolution, to
reject all the amplifications, digressions, and swellings of style: to return back to the
primitive purity, and shortness, when men deliver'd so many *things*, almost in an equal
number of *words*" (*History of the Royal Society*, p. 113). Of course, in so far as this is just a
plea for plain speaking or purity and clarity in prose style, it is perfectly just. But Swift
must have sensed an underlying delusion that the presence of things themselves, or
even pictures of them, made the *best* kind of judgement, whereas of course in reality it
makes no judgement at all. I owe the reference to Sprat to Professor Hermann Real of
Münster: a description of the stylistic preoccupations of the early Royal Society is given
in 'Science and English Prose Style in the Third Quarter of the Seventeenth Century'
by R. F. Jones (reprinted in *The Seventeenth Century* by R. F. Jones).

3. *An Innate Representative Medium?*

It might be thought that all this affects only some old mistake, committed perhaps by Aristotle and Locke, Hobbes and Hume, but transcended in the twentieth century. But here is Jerry Fodor, a founder of one of the most influential recent approaches to language and language learning:

Learning a language (including, of course, a first language) involves learning what the predicates of the language mean. Learning what the predicates of a language mean involves learning a determination of the extension of these predicates. Learning a determination of the extension of the predicates involves learning that they fall under certain rules . . . But one cannot learn that P falls under R unless one has a language in which P and R can be represented. So one cannot learn a language unless one has a language.[6]

Instead of taking this as a *reductio ad absurdum* Fodor takes it to prove the existence of an innate language, a "language of thought", in which we initially represent (that word again) what might be being signified by the word of the language we are trying to learn. Thus if learning the word 'carrot' in English, the baby's "cognitive system" forms various hypotheses, expressed in this innate language, about what the term might mean: he thinks, unconsciously, to himself that perhaps 'carrot' applies to all and only things which are R. Eventually he hits upon the right rule, R. This is what Fodor means by rules determining the extension of a predicate – i.e. rules which determine the things to which it applies. The language of thought in which these infant hypotheses are framed cannot of course itself be learned – or at least if it is, there must be a preceding language in which its predicates and possible meanings for them were represented, and to stop the regress we might as well stick at one language of thought. But although unlearned, it can be part of our innate equipment.

It is a pretty impressive part. For by the argument we can never come to understand a term unless we can as infants express its rule of use to ourselves in our innate language. Unless the infant has innately the resources to describe what a Romantic sonata is, or a chivalrous gesture, or a carrot, or a

6 *The Language of Thought*, p. 64.

bonfire, he will never learn. For his only strategy is to map the English terms, which express these notions, onto his old vocabulary: he represents to himself what the terms mean in his innate system. The re-presentation could go in stages: he might define a Romantic sonata or carrot in different words of English, and then use a previous representation of those in his innate language. To make this seem remotely plausible one needs startling confidence in "decompositional semantics": in other words, in analyses and definitions which reduce such complex notions as that of a chivalrous gesture or a carrot, into concepts and ideas which might plausibly be thought of as an innate endowment, and common to all mankind, regardless of variations in experience, knowledge, and culture.

The analogy which inspires this school of cognitive psychology is that between the processing mechanisms whereby a person comes to understand and use the vocabulary he does, and the inner workings of a computer. Fodor's view is that the internal system of representations is like the "machine language" of a computer, the physically realized bits which represent inputs of data and instructions, and upon which the machine effects its transformations, before retranslating some end stage of these internal processes back into a surface display. Part of the surface instruction to a machine – say, typing '7' at some point – effects a modification of the subsequent process, until an answer emerges which contains some feature which is itself a function of the original input: e.g. '14' if the subsequent instruction was '× 2'. What is present to consciousness is like the computer's visual display. The underlying operations go on in a different medium, inside. And this medium has to be rich enough, structured enough, to be able to 'represent' any of the data and instructions upon which the computer operates.

It is no objection to this analogy that the underlying processes are supposedly complex, and yet hidden from consciousness. Psychologists are very familiar with the need to postulate just such kinds of processes. For instance, it is quite clear that the visual cues which cause us to interpret a visual scene in a particular way – such as containing objects of a given size at certain distances – are complicated, and largely hidden from our consciousness. It takes a good deal of experiment to even begin to separate them and to generate a theory of how the eye and brain respond to the stimuli impinging on the eye. As we saw in connection with Chomsky (1.5), thinking of the causal process as analogous to the transformations from one state to another of a computing mechanism is not something which can be fruitfully criticized from the armchair: it is a matter of scientific judgement whether causal theories of our abilities inspired by the computational analogy prove their worth.

But it is a matter of philosophical argument to see whether the elements of a computing system can be regarded as items whose own representative powers actually explain, or even play some part in explaining, what it is for us to understand our own terms in particular ways. One thing is certain. There is no sense in which elements of a chemical or electrical system intrinsically represent aspects of dogs or carrots. The elements of computational mechanisms are just that: elements of a causally complex structure which determines various outputs given various inputs. The elements play a role in this "horizontal" transition from state to state. But they do not also have a God-given "vertical" connection with the world outside the mechanism, in virtue of which their mere presence suffices to explain how we understand our words. As we have already seen, this was not even true of images, which at least appear to have some natural connection with the states of affairs they represent. It is quite impossible to see how one element of a chemical or electrical system could in and of itself represent an aspect of a carrot, any more than the fall of a box of paper tissues could in and of itself represent the sinking of the Titanic. Thinking otherwise would be like explaining how numerals refer to numbers by unscrewing a computer, finding some modification in the circuits which nurses an input of a given numeral through the computations, and concluding that the numeral '7' represents the number 7 because the numeral is translated into *that* modification of the circuits and *that* intrinsically represents the number 7.

However, although the internal elements have no intrinsic powers which enable them to explain, by their mere presence, our understanding of terms, they may have some other role to play. We *can* speak of a modification of some mechanical or biological system representing one thing or another. We *can* impose the vertical connections, just as I can impose the instruction that the movement of the box of tissues is to represent the sinking of the Titanic, e.g. for the purpose of some game, or some description of events. We can give some modification of the machinery the significance we want. Since we take the visual display which is the output of some device in a certain way – e.g. as referring to the number 7 – we can interpret the modifications of the system which underlie this production in various ways as well. However, if that is all that could be said, we wouldn't be much further advanced in understanding what it is for us ourselves to take terms in one way or another. We would just know that since we do so, we can also impose a representative function on other things as well. That is hardly news. Our own understanding is left, like a frog at the bottom of a mug, simply staring. It powers our ability to see other things, such as elements of internal systems, as having a representative role. But the whole point of a dog-legged theory is to reverse this direction, so that the representative nature of the intermediary elements plays some part in explaining our own understandings.

There is, however, one further possibility. Might we discover that as a matter of contingent, scientific, fact, there are such elements which have representative powers? The problem then is still to get some conception of the kind of fact this might be. Perhaps inside our heads there are structures which because of some fact or other actually do play a representative role for us; perhaps words have their significance because they are mapped into these structures, in some natural and unconscious transformation. This scientific version of a dog-legged theory cannot be ruled out of court. But its immediate appearance is not all that promising. For it shares with the absolute starting-point of the enquiry the need to see the *kind of fact* that is missing: the element of organization, or function, or whatever it might be which makes it true that a given internal structure has a given significance, which it transmits to words which are transformed or mapped into it. But why shouldn't the missing kind of fact which endows it with its representative powers *directly* infuse ordinary straightforward language with its significance?

For example, suppose we are attracted to a kind of functionalist account. Our brains steer us around the world whose properties impinge upon them. An element represents something, such as a carrot, if it plays a certain part in this system. Very crudely, we could imagine the system activated by certain stimuli, and itself mediating various reactions, from simple salivation to other things more oblique, themselves dependent upon other states of the system which in a similar way correspond to other beliefs and desires we have. The missing fact is here identified as *functional role*. It is clearly an attractive avenue to follow. But then, why not follow it by thinking of the functional role of the good old words of our ordinary language? We can ask whether it is their function in steering us around the world which makes it true that they have the significance they do for us. The transformation into elements of underlying machinery is then part of a *causal* explanation of how this functioning takes place, but not part of a *philosophical* account of what the functioning actually is. The causal explanation is of course highly interesting. But in principle it could be very different while the functioning remained the same (for instance a biological bit of the mechanism which starts to malfunction might be replaced by a silicon chip, with entirely different microstructure, but capable of yielding the same outputs from the same inputs). In the current jargon, systems may function in the same way, but have "variable realizations". My pocket computer may have quite different underlying circuitry from yours. My head might, too. So in the first instance we would do better just to explore the functional role of ordinary, overt uses of words and language. The bits inside are interesting but, as far as understanding goes, mere machinery.

What then was wrong with Fodor's argument? The mistake came in the one misleading sentence: "One cannot learn that P falls under R unless one has a language in which P and R can be represented." Fodor sees this as following from the need to learn rules which determine the kinds of thing which fall under predicates. Learning what things can be truly described as carrots or dogs or Romantic sonatas can be described as learning a rule of correct application of the terms. Now the infant might, like the man with the colour card who uses it to search for a red flower, or like a man learning a second language, already have a way of representing (that word again) to himself the *kind* of thing a carrot of dog or Romantic sonata is, and have a way of translating the English word into his own idiom. I have

already criticized the powers this account attributes to the
innate idiom. But even if the infant *might* have done this, there is
no reason at all to suppose that he did. William James described
the infant's world as one of a "blooming, buzzing confusion".
Out of that confusion patterns begin to separate and order
begins to form: we begin our acquaintance with sounds, tastes,
colours, shapes, and with the reliable recurrent things which
make up the landscape we live in. With joy or sorrow, we make a
first acquaintance with dogs and carrots, and grow into an
appreciation of what a Romantic sonata, or a smile, or an
electron, is. Growing into such an appreciation needs an
acquaintance with things. Without this acquaintance it is not
even possible to think of anything as a carrot, or as a Romantic
sonata. With the acquaintance comes not only an appreciation
of what words actually mean, but of the kind of thing they *could*
mean. Acquiring the concept needs learning that there are
things which persist in time, which have various clusters of
properties, and it requires becoming able to distinguish those
things from others on the basis of these properties. Without this
knowledge terms cannot be understood. Hence, they cannot be
understood by translating them into a medium which *itself*
represented things in advance of the knowledge.

To meet this obvious point the language of thought theorist
must think of the language as itself growing, in its semantic
powers, as the infant increases his appreciation of the world,
and his ability to cope with it. But this is then a matter of some
inner states *acquiring* representative powers. And this then is *not*
a matter of them being mapped onto some other states which
already have those powers. Because if it were, the argument
would repeat itself at this level. So Fodor cannot maintain that
learning requires a previous ability to represent what is learned.
And if this cannot be maintained in full generality, there is no
reason to postulate an "inner code" at all: we do just as well by
trying to think of what it is for ordinary words of a public
language to acquire their representative roles, and to abandon
any attempt to understand this by thinking of them as translated back into conveniently powerful innate media.

The account of learning which I have been attacking has
affinities with the famous episode in Plato's *Meno*,[7] when

[7] *Meno* 80d ff.

Socrates takes a slave-boy through a geometric proof, and concludes that since he has come to appreciate something new he must in some sense have understood it all along. The infant is a "little linguist" or, as we might call it, a cognitive imperialist: he brings a complete stock of concepts with him, and cannot comprehend any influx of experience or learning which would expand it: anything he learns he does so by translating it back into a home medium. Learning becomes just a matter of associating new terms with ones already playing the same representative role. To avoid this seductive idea it is essential to remember the argument just given. Suppose we accept some provisional equation between a word's having a meaning for some subject, and it playing some causal or functional role in the way he behaves. Then the reason for avoiding an innate language of thought becomes stronger. For a person functions differently in a world of carrots and Romantic sonatas than he would in a world without them: functional organization itself grows, adapts, and changes with an appreciation of the world. Before the infant adapts to the world, nothing can play the role: hence, coming to understand a language cannot be understood as translation back into a home medium, with elements representing things in advance.

4. *Radical Interpretation: Manifesting Meaning*

So the attempt to understand meaning by a dog-legged approach fails. But what other ideas can we use? Perhaps the most promising is to stand back and think about the way we attribute meaning to the utterances of other people. The idea is to think about what meaning is by thinking about how we detect it. This is the approach dramatized in the person of the radical translator, or radical interpreter.[8]

Next, perhaps, to the works of Wittgenstein, the most influential book in modern philosophy of language has been W. V. Quine's *Word and Object*. In chapter II of this great work Quine introduces the figure of the *radical translator*. This character has the task of discovering which language is spoken by some group of speakers amongst whom he finds himself. His position

[8] There is a distinction between interpretation and translation, but that is for later. See 3.1.

is radical in the sense that he is to have nothing by way of collateral information to go on. He has no information from persons who have already interpreted the native language, or from similarities of native vocabulary or syntax with other known languages. In the radical position it is simply and purely the *use* the natives make of their terms which is to provide the data for the interpretation or translation. The point of introducing someone in this position is to isolate the nature of the evidence available to him and the nature of the theorizing which he must base on that evidence. Such a "rational reconstruction" of the procedures of the outsider is then intended to illuminate the concept of meaning in a classic way: by seeing how *we come to know* that a group means such-and-such by their utterances, we improve our knowledge of *what it is* for them to mean such-and-such by their utterances.

The concepts we have already met enable us to ask some questions about this idea. Firstly, we have learned to be sceptical about the value of some dog-legged approaches to meaning. Is this just another such approach, but one in which the native speech is understood to be meaningful just in so far as it is interpreted back into some other medium (the one the interpreter brings with him) about whose meaningfulness we don't ask? Secondly, notice that the goal of assigning meanings to the sentences of a group is the goal of coming to *understand* them. To call someone who is doing this from scratch a radical translator or interpreter already seems to imply a distinct conception of the task. It implies that understanding is gained by translation back into a home medium which the outsider brings with him. Like Fodor's infant an interpreter is a cognitive imperialist, who imports his own compound of categories and concepts, beliefs and principles, into which he retreats while he ponders the significance of native carryings-on. But since we have already found that not all acquisitions of understanding can be regarded as reinterpretation back into an antecedent medium, will it be legitimate to consider questions about meaning by considering a situation where this is the only method allowed? Thirdly, the radical translator first flourished when the philosophy of science was relatively confident of "rational reconstructions" of scientific method. These would provide some ideal description of the data and the use made of them in the proper evaluation of scientific theories. But this confidence has largely gone. Writers now are much more inclined to stress the creative, non-rational elements in our reaction to things, in our selections of "data" and our ways of using what we select. So we will need to ask whether there is any prospect of an objective and adequate scientific description of the procedures of interpretation.

Our immediate problem in this chapter is the possibility of meaning: how are we to conceive of the way in which a physical, natural world contains anything as strange as the fact that one thing can think of others? How do the facts (about physical systems, or natural, behaving animals) determine or permit the facts about thought and meaning? This is a rather different question from how *we*, in the guise of radical interpreters, determine the facts (about some group's meanings). In fact, it is crucially different, inasmuch as if we take our own intentional powers for granted, the second question might have a relatively simple answer, while the first question was untouched. I, thinking of Henry VIII, can interpret you as doing so too provided that you . . .; I might fill out such a claim with a plausible description of the kinds of thing which would lead me to so interpret you. Yet my own understanding would remain quite inexplicable. In short, we might know how *we* determine the facts without, as David Lewis put it, knowing how the facts determine the facts.[9] This would be through taking our own powers as simply given.

Quine's problem was not the possibility of meaning, and it need be no criticism of the use he makes of his radical translator that he would mark only a dog-legged approach to this problem. (It will be a matter of judgement to see how far this incompleteness worries us. Part of the point of my original metaphor of a triangular landscape is that philosophers differ not only over which landmarks to climb to, but also over how good is the view from any given one.) Quine was concerned with the extent to which dispositions to verbal behaviour uniquely fix the meaning of native remarks: his concern was to argue that they do not, so that speakers sharing identical dispositions to say things might nevertheless not mean the same by their remarks. Quine used this conclusion to destroy the

[9] David Lewis, 'Radical Interpretation', *Synthese* (1974).

scientific respectability of any concept of meaning. He intended to establish the conclusion by considering the way in which two different translators could properly come to assign quite different meanings to the sentences of the natives they observe. My second worry, about the cognitive imperialism implied by conflating coming to *understand* a language with *interpreting* it into a home medium, is relevant to this strategy. For if two different radical translators bring with them different home media – if they have different conceptual schemes to some significant degree – then we might expect that they will end up regarding their natives as saying different things. But this will not make unscientific the idea that there is a definite single thing which the natives mean. There could be a fixed and definite fact about what a native sentence means, even if differently reacting interpreters miss it in various degrees. An interpreter may be unable to understand native speech without first dropping his own preconceptions, and then learning to appreciate things their way.

The distinction between interpretation back into a home medium, and understanding, affects uses which other philosophers than Quine have made of the radical translator. Donald Davidson has influentially argued that we can make no sense of fundamentally divergent conceptual schemes. Davidson knows, of course, that there can be languages of different expressive powers in particular areas (Eskimos with fine and untranslatable distinctions amongst kinds of snow; Arabs and camels; scientists and the language of theories which they alone understand). But he believes that:

We can be clear about breakdowns in translation when they are local enough, for a background of generally successful translation provides what is needed to make the failure intelligible.[10]

The idea is that we can tell when a group is expressing ideas which are new to us only after we have become good at translating them in general. Davidson wants this point to sustain the conclusion that we can have no conception of what it might be for a group to have a language which expresses concepts and beliefs radically different from ours – too different to provide the

[10] 'On The Very Idea of a Conceptual Scheme', *Proceedings of the American Philosophical Association* (1973).

backdrop of shared thoughts which make mutual translation generally possible. Such an argument relies on a principle of verification – an inference from the fact that we cannot *verify* that something is the case to the conclusion that we cannot conceive as a genuine possibility that it *might* be the case. By this principle an hypothesis which cannot be verified marks no intelligible possibility. But although verificationism surfaces in many forms, the current consensus would be that it is dangerous to rely upon the principle. This is especially so when a general theory or way of looking at things allows unverifiable possibilities, but itself contains a way of explaining just *why* they are unverifiable. And it is of course explicable – trivially so – why we cannot verify that a group possesses a radically different conceptual scheme from ours by interpreting them in our own terms. Such an interpretation would be given by saying, in English: 'they think that . . .', where the dots are filled out by an English sentence. And this form of report can only describe thoughts which English speakers can have. But this does not suffice to show that the existence of a divergent scheme cannot be verified by any means at all. Couldn't we verify the existence of such a scheme not by translating it, but by coming to understand it?

Consider the following analogy. People enjoy some pretty dreadful sounds, but not any old production of sound counts as making music. To interpret a group as making music we try to recognize *our* notes, intervals, harmonies, rhythms, and so forth in the noises produced. So if anything counts as making music it must use notes, etc. recognizable to anybody else: there can only be one musical scheme!

This argument is flawed because it ignores the possibility of working our way into a different musical scheme: going native, and learning to appreciate quite different structures of sound as genuinely musical. This is what is done by people who, for instance, embrace the Scottish bagpipes. But there is an interesting point about the sense in which they verify that these things do indeed provide music. For an outsider who refuses to learn can consistently regard the learner both as losing his power to tell whether an activity counts as making music, and also as regrettably spending his time doing this other thing. People who go native are always suspect: to any good, old-school imperialist, the fact that such a fellow finds untranslatable concepts in native thoughts just confirms what a crackpot he is. The verification is itself relative to an understanding.

This is inevitable and applies to any family of concepts. There is, for example, no telling what someone means by tenses, which does not demand appreciating the passage of time; no telling what someone means by moral language, which does not demand a moral understanding; and so on. There is no way of "manifesting" what is meant by terms from these families to anyone incapable of the kinds of judgement they make. The situation is extremely clear if we consider an advanced theory, such as high-level physics. A physicist can only show what he means by spin, charge, field, and so on by having the learner come to understand the overall theory. There is no likelihood that the learner has *any* terms into which such notions can be translated before doing this. So it is the verification of the learner, not the translator, which counts, and Davidson's argument fails.

The third query which I raised about the device of the radical translator concerns the prospects for a rational reconstruction of his method. Pessimism would predict only very bland results: that the translator must use his observation of native dispositions, and his own understanding of things, in order to come to see the natives as sharing similar beliefs, thoughts, and meanings. More detailed accounts of the scientific way of doing this might be misguided even in principle: rather like manuals for telling how to use purely physical descriptions of facial muscles and geometry in order to verify whether someone is smiling. The trouble with such a manual would be that it is unusable: if someone's unconscious "cognitive system" does not deliver an immediate judgement of whether an observed person is smiling, a conscious calculation is unlikely to help. This is not however to deny that the unconscious cognitive system (the same thing that enables us to make immediate, non-inferential, unargued judgements of spatial size and distance, direction of sounds, etc.) may react to geometrical and muscular features in coming to a verdict. So there is room for a science of which features do determine such a verdict: similarly, is there not room for a science of the features of behaviour, with words and with the world, which determine verdicts of what words mean? In effect this is the science of what in chapter 1 we called the external problem of competence (1.4).

Philosophical preconceptions very quickly dominate this embryo science. The basic preconception which Quine brings to the issue is behaviouristic: the understanding of a sentence should at bottom be a matter of a disposition to respond to kinds of stimulus. So the initial procedure for the radical translator is to note the kinds of stimulus which prompt an affirmative reaction to a sentence, and the kinds of stimulus which do not. It is the actual presence of a situation in which, say, there is a rabbit visible, and the disposition of speakers in that situation to affirm 'rabbit!', which affords the prime datum – the prime way in which a sentence connects with its interpretation. The capacity to use a sentence in full understanding is basically a disposition to respond appropriately to situations which do, and to ones which do not, exhibit whether it is true. The basic image is one of confrontation with situations in which the correctness of some response can be immediately recognized; the interpreter then starts his task by himself correlating the situations and the sentences whose truth they guarantee. Difficulties in this model fall under two headings: first of all, whether there are any sentences at all to which it is appropriate, and secondly, how we extend it to sentences to which it is not appropriate. These last clearly include sentences about the past (we cannot exhibit our understanding of past-tense statements by making the right reaction when confronted with past circumstances, since we are never so confronted), future, spatially distant states of affairs, states described in theoretical terms, and indeed any state of affairs whose "recognition" involves using networks of other beliefs, principles, and concepts. Many philosophers would say that *no* sentence can be thought to have its own individual footing in experience: even recognizing a "stimulus" as indicating a rabbit implies grasp of a framework of linked concepts (that of an individual animal, persisting through time, in a world of things spatially distant from the observer). So there arises a general bias towards emphasizing the "holistic", anti-foundationalist nature of all verification.

This fundamental issue in epistemology is pursued a little further in chapters 5 and 7. The present point is that it makes a crucial difference to the way we have to regard translation. In so far as we sympathize with the holistic theme, we will deny that our grasp of any sentence is a matter of a disposition to affirm it in any set range of situations. All that will be true of someone who understands even such a basic sentence as 'there are rabbits about' is that he should be disposed to assent to it when he *believes* that there are rabbits about; but there is no limit to the number of other beliefs, ways of confirming this, contrary interpretations of things, and so on, which he might have, and which would make a difference to the actual range of circumstances in which he *does* believe this. Thus if I hold the dotty belief that the Russians have little rabbit-formed spies everywhere, I will not assent to 'rabbit!' just when you do. My "stimulus meaning" – the class of situations prompting assent to the utterance or dissent from it – is different. But I could nevertheless mean the same as you do by the term. It is indeed because I mean what is normally meant that I say that there are so very few rabbits about. As epistemologists move away from the idea of a purely ostensive guarantee of the truth of anything, so philosophers of language move from the idea that it is in such a confrontation that we find the fundamental word–world relationships that bestow meaning. The shift is away from a model in which the radical translator starts with a privileged range of affirmations which relate directly to a range of stimuli, towards one in which he works his way into a whole block of meanings, beliefs, thoughts, and principles by following the general policy of attempting to see native thoughts as overall intelligible and rational.

This shift marks the basic division between Quine's attitude towards radical translation, and the later conception of it in the hands of Davidson.[11] I return to this concept in the context of systematic descriptions of natural languages in chapter 8. Another highly influential recent philosopher whose work takes a slightly different complexion in the light of this shift, and of the earlier points in this section, is Michael Dummett. Dummett has emphasized that we must see meaning as something which is capable of being *manifested in the use* we make of an expression. What he says here of mathematical expressions is intended to apply quite generally:

[11] Notably in 'Radical Interpretation', *Dialectica* (1974).

The meaning of a mathematical statement determines and is exhausted by its *use*. The meaning of such a statement cannot be, or contain as an ingredient, anything which is not manifest in the use made of it, lying solely in the mind of the individual who apprehends that meaning: if two individuals agree completely about the use to be made of the statement, then they agree about its meaning. The reason is that the meaning of a statement consists solely in its role as an instrument of communication between individuals, just as the powers of a chess-piece consist solely in its role in the game according to the rules. An individual cannot communicate what he cannot be observed to communicate . . .[12]

Manifestation is primarily a relational matter. A man may manifest marvellous musicianship by blowing the 'Pibroch of Donald Dubh' if the hearers are capable of appreciating it, but he may not manifest anything to me by his performance. So what kind of *manifestee* is appropriate to Dummett's requirement? The last sentence suggests one who is capable of making observations, but no more. But let us suppose that some things lie outside observation: the past, or other peoples' sensations, or sub-atomic particles. Then it is clearly not a sensible requirement that a man should manifest his understanding of these things to someone who himself is capable of *only* making observations. Since this audience is incapable of thinking beyond the present, or beyond other peoples' behaviour, or the world of macro-objects, it is incapable of appreciating that anybody else is either. Such limited observers make poor audiences. The *only* reason for respecting them is the same as Quine's: the idea that the understanding of a sentence has to be the disposition to do the right thing in the right range of empirical circumstances, for then *nothing can count* as manifesting understanding *unless* it is visible to a passive observer. But the very word 'manifest' reveals the doubtful nature of this requirement. Like 'display' or 'reveal' it has highly visual overtones: I cannot display or make visible the past events I talk about, the future ones, my own pains and thoughts, let alone electrons or numbers: taken literally the requirement that you should be able to manifest meanings would suggest Swift's image of people only able to communicate about whatever they can carry with them.[13] A

---

[12] 'The Philosophical Basis of Intuitionistic Logic', in *Truth and Other Enigmas*, p. 217.   [13] n. 5. above.

better expression of Dummett's idea would be that the meaning of a statement cannot be, or contain as an ingredient, anything that cannot be *understood* or *known* from the use made of it. And then, for instance, the question of whether the meaning may be a function of something lying beyond observation will hinge upon what we say about our knowledge of such matters. There will be no swift argument from lack of manifestation which will settle that.[14] This recasting makes it plain how if we pursue meaning through either the device of the radical interpreter, or (which is essentially the same thing) through considering how we make meanings known to each other, it takes a whole theory of knowledge to sustain any conclusions.

I have sketched three reservations about the *persona* of the radical translator, considered as a device for improving our understanding of meaning. Firstly, if it is the very possibility of meaning which puzzles us, he suffers from the same objections as other dog-legged approaches: the interpreter's own understanding underwrites his interpretation of theirs – but what funds it itself? Secondly, since we must draw a distinction between translation (or interpretation back into a home medium) and understanding, it is what is involved in the acquisition of understanding which should really interest us. Otherwise we risk importing unjustifiable restrictions on what the interpreter himself brings with him. Thirdly, the prospects for a scientific reconstruction of the procedure of interpretation are not wholly good, and the form we impose on this procedure is likely to reflect controversial doctrines in epistemology. None of these reservations deny some use to the device: indeed we shall see in chapter 8 how it can be used to further some aspects of our understanding.

The attack on dog-legged theories, both overt and disguised, was one of the central achievements of the later Wittgenstein. But he wrestled constantly with the problem of the kind of thing

---

[14] Although I have taken this passage from Dummett as an example of a dangerous mistake, it must not be supposed that the mistake infects his whole philosophy of language. But it is significant that Dummett is a staunch advocate of the priority of the philosophy of language *over* the theory of knowledge, whereas at this crucial point, it is an error in the theory of knowledge which needs correction, and only a better theory of knowledge which could provide it. An excellent discussion of this is E. J. Craig, 'Meaning, Use and Privacy', *Mind* (1982).

meaning is, and how it is possible. It is his approach to the problem that I now introduce.

Notes to Chapter 2

2.1 Some of the problems surrounding Locke's use of the term 'Idea' can be gleaned from the collection *Locke on Human Understanding*, ed. I. C. Tipton, especially section III.

What is in effect the regress or elephant problem is presented in Jonathan Bennett, *Locke, Berkeley, Hume: Central Themes*, ch. 1.2.

2.2 The whole phenomenon of imagining needs very careful and extended attention. As well as the Wittgenstein quoted in the text, the two volumes *Remarks on the Philosophy of Psychology* are excellent. But the work of Wittgenstein in this connection is better studied alongside chapter 3, where his own puzzles with meaning are developed. The reader might also try:

Gilbert Ryle, 'Imagination' in Gustafson (1964).
H. Ishiguro, 'Imagination' in Williams and Montefiore (1966).
R. Scruton, *Art and Imagination*, chs. 7 and 8.

The place of imagination in perception is mentioned in chapter 7 below, and the role of imagination as an adjunct to passive observation, if we are to form any conception at all of our world, is developed a little there.

2.3 The idea of an internal language of thought, "mentalese", has recently been very popular, notwithstanding the kind of argument given in the text. Readers might consult:

G. Harman, *Thought*, ch. 6.
D. Dennett, 'A Cure for the Common Code' in *Brainstorms*.
H. Field, 'Mental Representation', *Erkenntnis* (1978).
J. Heil, 'Does Cognitive Psychology Rest on a Mistake?', *Mind* (1980).

The text here does not consider all the arguments that might be used in favour of giving inner states some representative power. But I believe that similar considerations stand in the way of any such theory.

2.4 The methodology of the radical interpreter, and the conclusions to be drawn by considering him, have generated an enormous literature. This is partly because of the startling nature of the conclusion that Quine himself drew: that translation is indeterminate (and, since there is no truth about meaning which is *beyond* an interpreter, so is meaning). As well as references in footnotes, the reader might consult:

N. Chomsky, 'Quine's Empirical Assumptions', in Davidson and Hintikka (1969).

W. V. Quine, 'Reply to Chomsky' (ibid.)

— 'On The Reasons for Indeterminacy of Translation', *Journal of Philosophy* (1970).

R. Kirk, 'Underdetermination of Theory and Indeterminacy of Translation', *Analysis* (1973).

C. Boorse, 'The Origins of the Indeterminacy Thesis', *Journal of Philosophy* (1975).

S. Blackburn, 'The Identity of Propositions', in Blackburn (1975).

The requirement which Dummett has insisted upon, that meaning be something which is manifested in the use made of an expression, has given rise to a large but difficult literature. As well as the article by Craig (chapter 2, n. 14 above), the following might be useful:

C. Wright, *Wittgenstein on the Foundations of Mathematics*, esp. Pt. 2.

P. Strawson, 'Scruton and Wright on Anti-Realism', *Proceedings of the Aristotelian Society* (1976).

C. McGinn, 'Truth and Use', in Platts (1980).

There are references to Dummett's revisionism about logic under 6.4 below. The next chapter, which relates meaning to dispositions, is also relevant.

CHAPTER 3

How is Meaning Possible?

Frankly, it is not my words I mistrust, but your minds.

Joseph Conrad, *Lord Jim.*

1. *Describing: Three Ways of Being Odd*

In the last chapter I went through some arguments against supposing that we understand words by connecting them with a directly representative "presence", carrying its own lines of projection onto aspects of the world. We discovered the negative point, as I shall refer to it, that no thing could halt the regress of interpretation. Our conception of what it could be to have a thing, including a diagram, model, or picture, present to the mind, allows for different ways in which the thing could be taken or understood, and this defeats the purpose of the theory, which is itself to explain what it is to take signs one way or another. This negative point means that we must cast around for some other way to come at the phenomenon of meaning.

So far the discussion has been extremely general. Now, however, we specify a little more the kinds of word whose understanding concerns us. This chapter centres upon straightforward, simple applications of predicates to things: the description of things as red, blue, buses, heavy, expensive, and so on. We can apply these terms all right! And we know what we mean when we do so. Our ability to follow principles of application for predicates is our ability to use universals: to classify, think, and judge at all. The difficulties philosophers have found in understanding this kind of ability are not entirely easy to feel. Fortunately however, there are modern ways of approaching these problems, developed more or less simultaneously, and independently, by Wittgenstein, Russell, and Nelson Goodman.[1] Together they put immense pressure upon our understanding of what it could be to assign a meaning to a predicate.

[1] References in notes to this chapter.

Imagine, then, a man going about applying some predicate –
say 'round' – to some things, and withholding it from others. He
gives the appearance of judging that things have some property
or other, which he expresses by means of this term. Perhaps he
means that these things are round – he might seem to go through
the right procedure to make this his judgement: he assesses
distances from the edge of the thing to what we should deem the
centre; sees whether such things roll evenly, and perhaps does
other tests. He seems liks a man judging whether things are
round. Now we imagine that he comes upon a new thing – a
thing which is quite obviously square. He considers, and he
says, 'It's round.' He applies the term! Naturally, our first
thought is that he has made a mistake – he has said something
which he ought not to have said, something false or incorrect.
But two other hypotheses are possible. Perhaps he meant something different by the word – some property which was possessed by the initial set of things to which he applied it, but is also
possessed by this square thing. In the terms of chapter 1, his
actual language is one in which 'round' means something other
than – round. Finally, perhaps he means *nothing* by his term. He
is just going through a *parade* of making a genuine judgement
as children may sometimes parrot adult judgements without
really understanding the terms used in them. So we have three
kinds of hypothesis: that he makes a mistake, that he means
something different, or that he means nothing at all. What
determines which hypothesis is true? What kind of fact is it,
which is ultimately the fact in virtue of which one of these
hypotheses is correct, and the other two not? For we cannot
doubt that on many occasions one *is* correct and the other two
are not, although which one varies from occasion to occasion.
Mostly, of course, we think that the first is true, because we are
used to believing that people mean *something* by what they say,
and that mistakes are more common than different usages,
particularly of a common word like 'round'.

It will be convenient to have titles for the three hypotheses. In
the first, the man means what we do by his term, but makes a
mistake. He uses it in accordance with the same rule, or, to put
the same thing another way, expresses the same concept or
same judgement. That indeed is *why* he is wrong, and says
something incorrect, false. Call this the *right-rule* view. In the

second, the man takes the term in a surprising way: he uses it in accordance with some deviant rule, meaning that some of the things which he calls 'round' are what we would also call round, but that others are not. Call this the *bent-rule* view. The last case is that of someone who gives an appearance of applying words to things in accordance with some meaning given to them, but is not really doing so. His sounds are just sounds, capable neither of correctness not incorrectness, because no rule exists to determine whether a particular "application" of the term is right or wrong. Since an utterance cannot be incorrect, neither can it be correct: no judgement is made. Call this wooden utterance of a term, in which no rule exists to determine significance, the *no-rule* view.

It comes naturally to say: the man himself knows which of these hypotheses is true. So whatever fact it is, which makes one of them true and the others not, it is accessible to him. Perhaps he can introspect it, and make us aware of it in the same way that he can make us aware of other mental facts about himself. *He* knows whether he is making a judgement, and which judgement it is. Whereas we, perhaps, might be less good at judging which of these hypotheses is true, and might get it wrong. On occasion this is how it is. For example, a child might show enormous concentration in writing down an apparently random series of numbers. We might suppose that his production of a numeral is a random event and that the series is not being determined by any rule – just as a lunatic might cover pages and pages with formulae in the belief that he is a mathematician doing great calculations, but signify nothing. The child on this hypothesis has in mind no rule determining a series: his writing one numeral after another is wooden. Nothing counts as correct or incorrect. But the child (like the infant Gauss is said to have done) might surprise us. He might explain which series he is expanding, and show is that he is doing it rightly. We change our mind, and admit that there was method in the madness after all. On a given occasion we might not be sure whether this was going to happen or not. When we don't know, the irresistible image is of something in the child's mind, accessible to him, but only guessed at, perhaps fallibly, by us. We imagine that if we could, as it were, lift off the mental lid – if like God we could look into the glassy essence of the mind – we would then know, just as the child does, which of the three hypotheses is true.

A great deal of the work of the later Wittgenstein is devoted to showing that this picture of the situation is false. One of his main arguments is the negative point of the last chapter. How do we envisage the subject's own knowledge of his meaning? What does the introspective candidate find as he considers his own mind, which tells him determinately which hypothesis is true? Perhaps pictures, or formulae, or definitions of terms. But the presence of any such thing *cannot be the fact* which determines which hypothesis is true. For any such thing can be taken in different ways. Of course, the presence of an image, or of words framing a definition, or some other presence, might give the candidate confidence that he knows what he means, that one hypothesis out of the first two is right. But it doesn't *make* any particular hypothesis right. It cannot of itself constitute the missing fact, because of the problems of the last chapter, summed up in the negative point. No thing can halt the regress of interpretation, for any thing can be taken in different ways, or in no way at all. Images or words may flit through the candidate's mind, but leave him using the word meaninglessly.

It does not follow that the subject himself is *not* an authority on whether he means anything, or if so, what. All that follows is that we need some different approach to this kind of self-knowledge. It must not be conceived of, as knowledge so often is, as an acquaintance with any kind of presence, mental or otherwise. But that leaves other possibilities. The child in the above example may rightly have perfect confidence that he is genuinely calculating, and that his placing of one number after another in his series is not wooden; he may know this at a point at which an outside observer would not know it. This is not in question: it is the introspective picture of how it can be true which the negative point attacks. Perhaps the candidate knows what he is doing in whichever way we know what we intend or what would please us. The case of the lunatic shows that such confidence can be mistaken, but of course often it is *not* mistaken.

One way in which Wittgenstein pursues the negative point is particularly compelling. He considers someone who understands correctly a simple numerical operation, such as developing a series by adding 2 to the preceding number. We could all do this, and a learner, after a little instruction with a small sample of such sums, might "catch on" – perhaps in a flash he might come to see what is meant, and then know that he can continue the series correctly, indefinitely. Again, the fact is not in question. And it might seem particularly tempting to think of it in terms of the sudden presence to the mind of a display, a revelation of what is required. But further thought shows that this cannot be right. For consider a later application of the understanding: when the learner writes, say, 188 after 186. If the right-rule view is true, the learner means something which makes it incorrect for him to write anything but this. If he put down 193, he would be wrong. But suppose the second view was true, and the learner had taken our instruction in an unintended, queer way: perhaps he caught on to the bent rule 'add 2 up to 186, and then add 7'. This is a perfectly good instruction – we could programme a computer to follow it, and we might have a purpose in doing so. Now ask: what display in the mental life of someone determined the fact that he took the instructions one way or the other? Not a display of *all* the numbers, because there are too many of them. It would be a pure accident if, in considering the instruction, someone actually thought of *this particular* application. Perhaps a display of some other words: 'Do what was done in this initial sample, whenever *any* number is proposed.' Such a display might occur, of course. But suppose the learner had, in some bent and remarkable fashion, taken the instruction to introduce the bent function 'add 2 up to 186 and then add 7'. Why shouldn't just these words also go through his mind? He could think of himself as "doing what was done in the initial sample whenever any number is proposed". That is, compute *this* function whenever any number is proposed. So the presence of these words does not seem to separate the right-rule learner from a bent-rule learner.

At this point a great variety of issues start to clamour for attention, and it is difficult to preserve a sense of direction. In particular many philosophers see here an opening into a relativistic, conventionalist, view of our own classifications. To *us* it seems absurd and almost incomprehensible that someone would actually take the instructions and the initial sample in this bent way. Why should he get the idea that there is such a gross singularity just at 186? Why didn't he enquire about it?

But might it be that we are here imposing our own, accidental perspective? From the point of view of this bent learner, going on to add 7 after 186 *is* going on in the same way. It is our "similarity space" which, allegedly, he finds bent. Since it came naturally to him to think of the relation between 186 and 193 as like that between 184 and 186, he finds our tendency to insist on 188 as the right successor highly deviant. This conventionalism is sufficiently important to deserve a section to itself. But that is in part a digression from the main issue about meaning. The main issue is not whether there is an element of conventionality in taking the instruction one way or another. The main issue is to obtain some conception of *what it is* to take the instruction in any way at all – in other words, to find out what makes true the right-rule view, rather than the bent-rule view, or the no-rule view. Still, it may help with that problem to think a little further about bent classifications.

2. *Bent Predicates: Wittgenstein and Goodman*

What are we to make of the possibility, if it is one, that some-body takes our instructions, and an initial sample of cases, to introduce a rule of application of some term, but a bent one? It will help to have some examples in mind.

'Add 2'	Bent-rule:	Add 2 up until 186, then add 7.
'Red'	Bent-rule:	A thing is to be called 'red' just if it is observed before 1 January 1986 and is red, or is not so observed, and is yellow.
'round'	Bent-rule:	A thing is to be called 'round' just if it is one of an initial sample, and has the shape defined by a point, travelling equidistantly from a fixed point, or does not belong to the sample, and has four straight sides of equal length, at right-angles to one another.

There is nothing intrinsically wrong with the bent rules. They define perfectly good uses for terms. As I have already remarked, a computer programmed to recognize shapes, if it can determine which things are in the original sample, can give verdicts according to the last rule. Things like canaries which are only observed after 1986 has begun will be properly called 'red' if that term is used in accordance with the given rule – red[BR] (red-bent-rule), as I shall index it. The bent rules describe meanings which words *can* take: indeed the words used to express them together define them. The curiosity is that terms such as red[BR] and round[BR] apply quite properly to the sample of objects which a learner of our ordinary vocabulary will have been shown. So it seems that there could be nothing improper in the learner taking our instructions to introduce these bent meanings. But if he does so, one fine day he will apply the terms in accordance with his understanding to quite astonishing objects – yellow or square objects. In the numerical case he will continue the series in a dramatically devious way.

The bent learner can be thought of graphically in the following way. We can imagine the dimension of colour, shape, or arithmetical addition functions (add 2, add 3, . . .), arranged vertically on the side of a graph. Increase in time (or in number) is plotted along the horizontal axis. We would plot continuities like the line C, and kinks and changes with a line like K in Fig. 2.

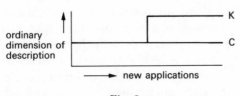

Fig. 2

The bent learner has got hold of a "dimension" of properties which reverses the picture. The state of affairs represented to us by C appears to him as a kink; what appears to him as a simple straightforward continuity is the state of affairs which appears bent to us. So his graph is like Fig. 3. Thus, our dimension of arithmetical plus-functions represents someone who adds 2 up to 186 and starts to add 7 after 186 as bent; but the **BR**

dimension represents him as going on the same way, and some-
body who continues to add 2 after that point is represented as
kinked. Of course, there is an indefinitely large variety of possible bent dimensions in addition to the examples chosen. They
can be created quite automatically.

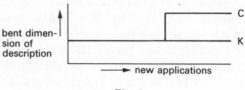

Fig. 3

Goodman used the possibility of these bent dimensions to
cast a new light on the classical problem of induction.[2] This
problem queries our right to take observed regularities in things
as representative – as likely to continue or to have continued in
regions of space and time beyond our actual acquaintance.
Thus we suppose that things tomorrow will be pretty much the
same as things today, and that where they are not the operation
of underlying similarities is responsible for any particular
changes. We do not expect objects to gratuitously change
shape, colour, size, and weight; we do not expect physical
constants to suddenly vary, forces to spring up and die down.
Our whole lives are premised on the stability of the natural
world in myriads of respects. But now take a dimension in
which, in given circumstances, we expect stability. We can then
mechanically define a bent dimension of predicates governed
by bent rules, with the feature that if things stay the same in our
respect they change in the bent respect, and vice versa. For
example, take the bent predicate red^{BR} mentioned above; we
would expect new rubies, mined after 1985, to be red; we would
expect new wounds to give red blood. If so, they are not, like
rubies and drops of blood observed before 1986, red^{BR}. Since
they issue after the crucial date, they would be red^{BR} only if they
were yellow. Now why do we prefer redness to red^{BR}ness? What
makes us think we have got hold of a similarity which nature

² *Fact, Fiction and Forecast*, ch. IV.

will herself protect, whereas some unfortunate who catches on to a bent rule will get a nasty shock in the dawn of 1986?[3]

Goodman himself, and many philosophers influenced by him, saw nothing but linguistic convention to hold onto. We do speak a language which sees redness as simple and red^{BR}ness as bent; we could have spoken a language which placed them the other way round. But since we do and have used the former, we are in the habit of expecting things to continue red and of regarding any other prediction as irrational. We ourselves would look just as irrational from the perspective of a community which "entrenched" a predicate following the bent rule. It just so happens there are no such communities. This answer of course presupposes that there is some fact making it true that we mean the one thing and not the other by our terms. In other words, it brings us no closer to solving the problem of how it is possible to mean a determinate thing by a term, which loomed in the last section. It still leaves it possible that we form a wooden community, there being no truth that any of us mean one thing and not another by our predicates. Or perhaps we form what we call a mutually bent community, in which individuals have taken their training and the initial samples in different ways, formulating different rules which may suddenly dictate divergent applications, to our mutual consternation. But let us put that on one side. It is still true that our preference for our rules and not their bent counterparts is hard to regard as a product of purely conventional arrangements. For it is incoherent, in a way which I shall later elaborate (chapter 7), both to be confident that, say, future blood samples will be red, but also to regard that confidence as the outcome of an arrangement which we merely happen to have hit upon, out of a selection of equally attractive arrangements. If the opinion had such an insubstantial ancestry, so disconnected from the way things are, it had better not be trusted. In other words, if Goodman's were the ultimate answer, we would have no defence against total scepticism about whether the world is stable in any of the respects which we rely upon. Butter might be red tomorrow,

---

[3] There are sciences where this kind of question matters. Econometrics is bedevilled by the fact that many equations or models of what varies with what in an economy may fit initial segments of data, but diverge in their predictions of what will happen when things change.

and blood yellow; either might sing to us or cause golden eggs to come out of thin air.

A slightly more substantial answer would be that nature looks after our groupings, ensuring that our natural dimensions of classification are ones which are stable. Perhaps an evolutionary explanation works, so that time and selection weed out groups with a tendency not to latch onto the right groupings, not to "carve nature at the joints". This answer restores the coherence which seems lacking in a pure conventionalism: we might reasonably retain confidence in a prediction if we felt that a history of pressures which selectively favour the successful had brought it about that we have that confidence. But the answer has its problems: a group using red[BR] would have done just as well as us until now. It is only in 1986 that they will get their come-uppance. The evolutionary story might actually predict that there would be a multiplicity of predictions at any time, since only the pressure of the *future* redness (or red[BR]ness, as the case may be) of things defeats bent-rule-followers. Surely liberal nature would have grown some?

At this point we might begin to suspect the way we are looking at the issue. How credible is the possibility of these bent-rule-followers? Perhaps we can't ultimately make sense of the stories. For instance, consider again the deviant interpretation of the arithmetical rule: add 2 up to 186, then add 7. What else is true of the learner who takes this rule in the bent way? Does he think that he is *going on in the same way* when he adds seven bricks to a pile to which he was previously adding two at a time? What if he can carry two bricks but not seven? Does he not notice the difference: is he not aware of the shambles he gets into? Does the round[BR] operator not notice that wheels "like" the ones he was initially shown do not roll, but meet flat planes sometimes at a point and sometimes along a line, and so on? Worse still, these people normally notice what we would consider to be similar deviations. If the foreman tries to load the bent bricklayer with seven bricks after he has added 184 bricks he protests: this is not going on in the same way. But two bricks later, it is. Again, the bent interpreter of 'red' is normally aware of the sudden emerging of a yellow member of a class whose members were hitherto red. It is only if the yellow arrival times its entrance for midnight 1985 that he regards everything as "going on in the same way". I do not myself believe that we can really conceive of this kind of sensibility. Certainly we would in practice cast around for other interpretations of these people: perhaps they are blind to certain changes; perhaps they suffer from mysterious lapses of memory; perhaps they aren't really talking about numbers, shapes, and colours at all, but have other features in their minds, features of which we are not aware, and cannot define even in a bent way. In this respect, we do not inhabit the same world.

If this remains just a point about what we would do, it suggests cognitive imperialism. *We* would find it difficult to imagine someone who takes the bent rule to be straight; *we* would be mystified by his words, would be inclined to reinterpret him, and charge him with blindness to various differences of things. But perhaps that is just us, locked into our own capacities and "similarity spaces", with our own particular imaginations, natures, or conventions. If this is all that can be said, then from a more objective standpoint, the bent-rule-follower is not only possible, but there is no sense in which we are doing something properly, which he is doing badly. We couldn't regard ourselves as having locked onto the *real* similarities amongst things, or the right way to classify things, about which he is mistaken. There would only be correctness relative to a scheme of classification. This is the position in the theory of universals (that is, of rules governing predicates) we know as *nominalism*.

Can we really see these problems with the bent-rule-followers as the outcome of some contingent, parochial, fact about ourselves? This is not as simple as it looks. We can press the difficult questions. For example, the bricklayer responds very differently if the foreman loads him with seven bricks after he has added 184 bricks from how he responds after he has added 186. It follows that he must know how many bricks he has added. Equally if this bricklayer is watching a film about such an episode he doesn't know whether the man is going on in the same way unless he knows how many bricks he has already added. There seem to be three possibilities. Perhaps the bent-rule-follower knows these things in some mysterious, innate, way. But then he is not separated from us by mere conventions, or even by normal differences of receptivity: he is separated by total mystery! The second possibility is that he knows these things normally: when he is loading bricks he keeps track of the number he has added, and if he loses track he doesn't know how to keep on the same way: coming in the middle of a film he cannot describe whether the colleague adds two bricks at a time, since he cannot tell when he passes 186. But that just shows that he is using this number to mark a difference: he needs to know whether the *different* thing which happens after it happens at the right point. This destroys the intended symmetry with us, that he should think of everything as going on the same way. We don't need to be aware of how many bricks have already gone to know whether the man continues to add two at a time. Finally, perhaps there are no signs of normal or abnormal knowledge. It is just that after 186 he struggles with seven bricks and shows *no* awareness that anything is different. To him it is as though everything is the same. But how can this be? This bent-rule-follower *fails* to perceive what we regard as differences, if they happen at the right point. But that's just failure. How does it transmute into the picture of someone who is genuinely making different judgements, following a different rule? It builds an image only of someone who forgets what he was doing at a particular time, or is unaware of much of what is going on: if we generalized this alternative over a good number of normal predicates (so that the man shows the same insensitivity to changes of shape, weight, colour, number, . . .) we simply end up with someone who does not know the world about him.

All these are things which *we* say! Well, they are of course. But before this rekindles the nominalist flame, we might reflect that since they are things which we say, we ought also to say that we can make no sense of the possibility of a sensibility, a way of perceiving and classifying things in the world, which naturally operates in terms of the bent dimensions. Bent predicates are important in the philosophy of language (and, of course, in the philosophy of induction, and for that matter in any branch of philosophy where similarities and differences are important, such as ethics or the philosophy of mind) because they offer a way of filling out the vision that our descriptions are in some way arbitrary, conventional, parochial to us. If the filling does not help the vision, then something else might in principle do so, but it remains true that the introduction of bent predicates does not do the work which was expected of it.

Let us return to the bent learner. All this does not mean that he is impossible. It only means that if he caught on to the bent rules he would have to do *more* than simply go astray at 186 or the beginning of 1985, or wherever. He would need to show some awareness of the bend in the function he takes '+ 2' to express or in the class of things properly described as 'red' or 'round'. If he did catch on in the bent way he might, for instance, argue with a foreman who asks him to add bricks two at a time. He would point out how unreasonable this would be after he has added 186 bricks. Society's amazement at his difficulty would bring to light the odd way he took the explanations, and we would expect some simple account of what went wrong, and expect to have a reasonably clear remedy, explaining again what the foreman intends. What the learner cannot do is *both* take the initial samples and explanations in the bent way, *and* show no awareness of the bend, for by the above arguments we only deceive ourselves if we think we can make sense of that. It follows too that we can make no real sense of the possibility that *we*, now, might form a mutually bent community, so that having latched onto quite different rules of use of terms, we are poised to diverge in mutually unintelligible ways when presented with new things to describe. I can certainly eye my fellows askance in a number of ways. I can mistrust their judgements, their memories, their real grasp of any principle for applying terms. And on occasion someone may get hold of the wrong end of the stick; if he is brighter or less bright than others he may perceive similarities between things compared with which other differences are unimportant, or perceive differences where we see only similarity. This can lead to scientific reforms and advances, for although these mistakes and dissatisfactions may at a time be undetected, they are in principle detectable. They involve different dispositions and ways of talking and acting, in advance of different occasions of application of a term.[4] So since my companions show no undue interest

---

[4] This is a point on which I diverge from Saul Kripke. In his superb discussion of this (*Wittgenstein on Rules and Private Language*) Kripke denies that dispositions uniquely fix the question of whether a person is faithful to the right rule or a bent rule; in other words, a bent-rule-follower need not have different dispositions. For a discussion see my 'The Individual Strikes Back', *Synthese* (1984).

in 186, no undue fear lest next year's motor cars will have round wheels, no concern to lay in a stock of observed, yellow, bandages to match 1986 blood, I know them not to interpret the words in the bent ways defined. But are we entitled to talk of intended meanings at all? Does the wooden, no-rule picture, the third hypothesis, now come into its own?

3. *Wooden Communities: Uses and Ways of Life*

This is the central problem of the later world of Wittgenstein. Until paragraph *198 in the *Investigations* he develops what we have termed the negative point: 'any interpretation still hangs in the air along with what it interpreted, and cannot give it any support.' The existence of a rule governing the application of a term is not created by the existence of further substitutes for the term, for they pose the same problem. Wittgenstein then squares up to the threatening paradox, that the wooden picture is inescapable, and that nothing can create the existence of this rule. A man who calls a taxi a bus or a banana red would be no more wrong that us; just different. His training gives him one kind of disposition, ours gives us another. In neither case can the contents of our minds provide a rule determining whether what we are saying is correct or incorrect. Any course of action (i.e. any application or withholding of terms) can be made out to "accord" with what went before, as the example of the bent learner shows, and this just means that there is no right or wrong in our sayings, and therefore no judgements are made.[5] Wittgenstein's answer to this wooden picture is well known. He wants to connect the fact of a term being governed by a genuine rule, determining correctness and incorrectness of application, with its *use*, with a *custom*, a *technique*, a *practice*, with the fact that the word is embedded in the "language games" and "form of life" of a community of people. So how do practices give rise to meaning, when it looked impossible that anything would?

One suggestion is this. There is indeed nothing but the

[5] The example of a pocket calculator may help. Suppose such a machine with the oddity that although it adds 2 correctly to numbers before 186, when instructed to do so for numbers above that, it adds 7. It computes the bent function correctly, the straight one incorrectly. But in itself it just shows numerals, and there is no correctness or incorrectness about it. Only from some outside point of view is there a truth that it is functioning well or badly.

continuous flow of utterance, and the continuous play of dispositions, which seemed to allow nothing better than the no-rule view. But after all the dispositions include tendencies to correct, criticize, and adjust deviations. So in a *community* a deviant who calls a taxi a bus, or a banana red, is criticized. His behaviour will give rise to inopportune actions on the part of other people. Taking his utterance as they naturally would, they will go wrong. If the man appears normal in most respects then they say he spoke falsely; if enough of his classifications are out of step with the rest of the group's they find him unintelligible. (They may speculate about the possibility of bent-rules, suggesting that he takes his terms in some genuinely different way. But for the reasons I developed in the last section, they are unlikely to make much of that.) The point is that the *normative* aspect of meaning – the fact that some applications of terms are *incorrect*, and that the rules prescribe what kind of thing is *correctly* described as what – emerges from mutual pressures towards conformity.

On this view a community, in its language-using practice, is like an orchestra without either conductor or score, but with a tendency to turn on players whose notes are discordant with a democratic attempt at harmony. The negative point is supposed to prevent us from believing that each individual player has his own score – his own private instruction how to describe things, which gives him a standard for applying terms.[6] If we take this orchestral metaphor seriously it implies that the lone individual, considered quite apart from any surrounding group, could not mean anything by his terms. The wooden, no-rule view would be inevitable, for nothing exists to give the solitary speaker standards of correctness. Suppose he faces a square and describes it as round. This seems right to him, and what else is there to create a standard by which he has made a mistake? "Whatever is going to seem right to me is right. And that only means that here we can't talk about 'right'."[7]

This is the heart of the famous anti-private language argu-

---

[6] Idealists who were sensitive to these considerations (including Kant and T. H. Green) tended to see the standard for description as laid down by the infinite or absolute mind in which we each to some extent participate – corresponding to the antecedent instruction of a composer. This theory is not attractive: what voice tells me how to take the instructions of this mind? Why should I listen to it? And how did *it* get off the hook?

[7] *Philosophical Investigations*, § 258.

ment in the later Wittgenstein, which I explore further in the next section. But the orchestral metaphor looks dangerously unconvincing if it is supposed to have such a strong consequence. Remember that the initial suggestion was that the existence of a technique or practice in which a term is embedded is the magic ingredient which creates a meaning for it. It needs to be argued that the technique or practice which is necessary to create meaning has to be *public*. Why shouldn't the solitary individual embed terms in instructions to himself: instructions which contrive to give him a technique, to cope in some way or another with his world, although there is no pressure from surrounding speakers creating standards of correct ways of taking those instructions? It is easy to go through the thought-experiment of coming across such an individual. A solitary individual growing up in perfect isolation – a born Robinson Crusoe – might give all the appearances of following rules, including linguistic rules, and of having a practice which embodies a distinction between correct and incorrect performance. Indeed we can imagine cases in which we simply have to say this. An example due to Michael Dummett is that of a born Crusoe who over the years evolves a technique for solving a Rubik's cube washed onto his island. There is no way of regularly doing that by chance. You have to follow rules. Perhaps to help himself he creates symbols reminding him of what to do at various points, and appeals to these on the way through the cube; with these symbols he can do it, and deprived of them he cannot. Clearly he has the *practice* or *technique* which entitled him to be regarded as meaning various determinate things by these symbols.

Wittgenstein's followers have tended to divide on the issue of whether his solution to the problem of meaning denies meaning for born Crusoes or not. The difficulty is that if the argument does deny it then, as I have just suggested, it seems unconvincing (consider what else he might do to show us that he really means things by his signs and symbols, or follows countless rules in his practices); on the other hand, if he is allowed to be a rule-follower, the orchestral metaphor ceases to embody any solution to the problem. A compromise is suggested by Saul Kripke. He points out that we might indeed think of Crusoe as following rules, but all that follows is that *if* we do so, we are "taking him into our community and applying our criteria for rule following to him".[8] But it is not clear what this means, nor whether it gives the community any particular prominence in the creation of meaning. An orchestra coming across a solitary player, concentrating hard and making noises, might well say that *if* he were with them, he would be doing well or badly making these noises. But on the "democratic harmony" theory, they could not say that he *is* doing well or badly since in isolation there is nothing for him to do well or badly. The problem Crusoe poses is that he *does* have a practice (follows a tune) *regardless* of how we or anybody else think of him. Of course, Kripke is right that when we say this we apply our own criteria for rule-following to him; it is our judgement that he is following a rule. But this does not bring our community or any community far enough into the picture. It would be *our* judgement that an island has a tree on it. But whether an island has a tree on it is quite independent of how we or any community describe it, or even of whether any community exists to describe it. On the face of it, the situation is the same with the solitary intelligent Crusoe, in which case he has rules, meanings, standards for applying terms in his own solitary state, and with no reference to any community.

The problem with Crusoe shows that we must not fall into the common trap of simply equating practice with public practice, if the notion is to give us the heartland of meaning. It will need arguing that, contrary to appearance, the practice of isolated individuals cannot count. In any case, if the practice of an individual in isolation is not enough to create the fact that his words have meaning, how is the practice of a lot of us together to create the fact that *our* words have meaning? We talked earlier of the norms which arise from mutual pressures towards conformity in description. But how exactly does group conformity relate to understanding a predicate? In the orchestral analogy, a player knows whether he is wrong by listening for concordance with the group, and nothing else matters. But when I judge something to be red I am certainly not offering a shorthand for the more elaborate judgement: 'this is what most members of my group would call 'red'.' This can be no general solution to the problem of the meaning of predicates. For to

[8] Kripke, op. cit., p. 110.

make this judgement I need to understand the more complicated predicate 'what most members of my group would call
'red'.' This predicate allows just as much for bent rules and no
rules. If we apply the equation once more we get: 'This is what
most members of my group would call 'what most members of
my group would call 'red'''; and we are off on a regress. Any
predicate 'P' transforms into '$P*$': 'what most members of my
group would call 'P' ': this transforms into '$P**$', and so on.
There is no solution to our problem here. The more complex
predicates are not even synonymous with the bases from which
they derive, for it need not be true that most members of my
group call things which are X, 'X'. They may make systematic
mistakes. And in any event, it is no easier to conceive of the
fugitive fact, that we are genuinely guided by principle, when
we think of the more complex predicates, than when we consider the simplest ones. So the orchestral analogy cannot be
taken this way.

The point also damages another analogy in which the
practice of a community gives rise to certain kinds of fact. This
is the analogy with the conventions which underlie *money*. Pieces
of paper can be of no value to an individual in isolation. But the
practice of a group of individuals can *create* the fact that their
pieces of paper have value to them individually. (Paper money
astonished Marco Polo when he visited China.) The analogy is
short-winded: the value to me of a banknote is *directly* a matter of
what other people will do for it. But in applying a word I am not
directly concerned with the reactions of other people. I do not
generally consider their assent or dissent to be the final court of
appeal on whether I am right. I am directly concerned with
whether a thing is red or round or whatever, which is a quite
separate issue from whether people describe it as such.

The democratic harmony view is responsible for the relativism which is frequently associated with the later work of
Wittgenstein (quite against his own intentions). An individual
player in the orchestra may go wrong. But how can the orchestra
itself do so? There seems to be no external standard by which it
can be deemed to be doing well or badly. The standard for
correctness in description seems to have shifted, as it were, from
conformity with how things are, to conformity with each other.
If I live in a community which calls the earth flat, is not this just

one more element of the dance, on which I ought not to get out of step? There are actual illustrations of the way in which the emphasis on practices and customs introduces this danger. Suppose a group has a religion. Part of the religious practice will be to say certain things – that the God or Gods are thus-and-so, that various actions need doing, various doctrines are true. The practice is to say these things; perhaps the practice stands the group in good stead practically or emotionally. Saying the things is an action: if it works, how can it be criticized? The natural opposing thought is that if in these sayings they *intend to describe* what the world is like, then they may be wrong. But remember that it is the nature of the practice which is being held to determine what the intentions are, not the other way round. It is not their mental lives which determine the correct-ness or incorrectness of saying that God is thus-and-so, but the nature of their customs, techniques, ways of life. So they derive the powers of these sayings from their role in their customs. And then there seems to be no room for an ingredient of meaning which makes it possible for the sayings to be *false*.

If this conclusion were right, it would best be taken to show that the notion of a practice is an insufficient source of standards of correctness, that is, of rule-following and of mean-ing. If practices do not lift sayings into a *normative* dimension[9] in which they are susceptible of falsity, and hence of truth too, they are not filling the role which is demanded of them. The example illustrates that we cannot glibly announce that the concept of a custom or practice obviously has this power: it is going to be difficult to picture the emergence of truth and falsity out of customs and practices, just as it is difficult to picture the emerg-ence of meaning out of any amalgam of mental and physical facts. But the descent into relativism can be avoided. If the *only* ingredient in the practice were to say the words, then it is indeed hard to see why they should be taken as expressions of belief, and susceptible of truth and falsity. And we have already learned to doubt the authority of the person using the words: it is not clear that he will have privileged access to whether they express a belief, or serve some other role.[10] However the

---

[9] This normative aspects of things is stressed in Kripke.

[10] Suppose you say to yourself 'I believe in life after death'. Do you know that this expresses a belief? Why not suppose that it expresses an attitude, or vague emotion?

practices may have many strands: the words used in religious ceremonies also occur elsewhere; the sayings are subject to the same kinds of criticisms and doubts as others, perhaps the commitments they express influence people in the same kind of way as other beliefs, and so on. The idea will be that a saying expresses a judgement if the practice involves taking it as expressing a judgement, which itself involves *procedures* of assessment, acceptance, and rejection. This, at least, ought to be Wittgenstein's answer. Ironically it follows that the major industry of taking his later work to release religious faiths from arguments concerning their likely falsity, is misdirected. The price of the release is that the sayings no longer express beliefs, for without the controls which are part of a genuine judgemental practice, language is just on holiday.

Crusoe showed that it is not clear what the word 'public' is doing if 'public practice' is regarded as the source of standards of application of terms. The religious example shows that it is not very obvious what counts as a practice either. In particular, we must be careful over what counts as *identity* of practice. In the last section I introduced the possibility of a mutually bent community, in which each individual had taken his initial exposure to terms in a different way. I urged, against nominalism, that although an individual could catch onto a bent rule, we could make no sense of his both doing this and failing to appreciate the bend. And this appreciation would display itself in different dispositions, or practices (the bricklayer who is asked to carry bricks up two at a time). Suppose, however, that I were wrong about this. In that case a *concealed* mutually bent community would appear to be a possibility, in which the apparent identity of practice at a time is a cover for different individual ways of taking terms, each supporting its own standard of future application. Each member of the orchestra would be resolutely following his own conception of how the theme should go, and the harmony in the first few bars would be a matter of luck. If a concealed mutually bent community is a possibility, then their common practice at a point seems to be no source at all for standards of future correctness. At a point of divergence the individual carries on one way, and others carry on other ways. There is just nothing to say who is "right", since their preceding practice allows for this diversity:

their tunes can be continued whichever way they see fit. The orchestra is in no position to criticize any individual player, since the democracy is no longer speaking with one voice.

Of course, we do not believe ourselves to form a concealed mutually bent community, partly because we believe in the common nature of mankind, and partly perhaps for the anti-nominalist reasons I developed in the last section. Wittgenstein might be seen too as denying the mere possibility of such a community. It gives each individual a conception of the right way the tune should go, or in other words his own previous intention to use a term in some specific, determinate way, and this intention exists and determines a standard for truth in his judgements entirely without reference to other people. This is in many commentators' eyes exactly the idea which Wittgenstein opposes, substituting instead either the democratic harmony view, or some close cousin which we come to later.[11] But it is still at this stage unclear why he can oppose it. Certainly the negative point warns us off one particular conception of this individual intention. If the individual has this determinate intention, and knows what it is, this is not made true by the presence to his mind of a particular display. But on the face of it that leaves other possibilities. Crusoe may know how he intends to use the symbolism which determines the way to solve Rubik's cube not just because particular pictures come into his mind, or other symbols, but because he does something which counts, for him, as according with the rule, and something which does not, if he makes a mistake. He has his own practice. Similarly we naturally think of the child of the last section, who has a rule for developing a series, as aware of how he *should* go on *by his own lights*. It is this determinate intention which gives him standards of correctness and incorrectness, and generates the truth that he means something, and is not, like a wooden child, merely writing numbers one after the other. This natural picture is not destroyed by the negative point. That only attacks one conception of what it is to have a determinate intention (it is to have some presence in the mind) and how we know of it when we have one (by introspective awareness). It is not by itself strong enough to suggest that no conception of the difference between

[11] See Crispin Wright, *Wittgenstein on the Foundations of Mathematics*, pp. 20 ff. for a good discussion of this.

the solitary understander, and the wooden individual, is possible.

The upshot is that it is no easy matter to make public practice or custom into the magic ingredient which would turn the wooden picture into the full one. The negative point offers nothing strong enough to oppose Crusoe's claim to be using and understanding a term, and to know its meaning through first-person knowledge of his own rules, intentions, and procedures. The negative point only shows that this knowledge is not to be thought of as a simple matter of the presence of some display in the mind.

My Crusoe would have invented a fragment of a personal language – an "idiolect". Now the fact that he is possible should not be taken to imply that a linguistic community may be regarded as a group of individuals, each with their own idiolect, but amongst whom, because of their need to communicate, there arises a pronounced similarity of idiolect. This conformity would be in a sense accidental: the fact making a word mean what it does in an individual mouth would be entirely a fact about the speaker, and a fact upon which he would be the authority. Whereas in an actual linguistic community we recognize independent authority. What a word means, and what a person has said by using words, is a socially fixed matter, and often does not accord with a speaker's own understanding, or lack of it. If a man says that he has an elm in his garden, or that his father has arthritis, he may have a very poor understanding of his own saying: he may understand no more than that he has some kind of tree in his garden, or that his father has some kind of ache in his joints. He may himself be quite unable to tell an elm from a beech, or arthritis from rheumatism: nevertheless we will not hold him to have spoken truly if he has a beech in his garden, or if his father has rheumatism. We enforce what in the next chapter I call deferential conventions, meaning that we recognize community authority, and expert authority, in providing the actual sense of words (4.6). We emphatically do not allow that someone has spoken truly because in his private idiolect 'elm' covers beeches as well. The reason why we do not allow this is that it threatens the social utility of language: we need social norms towards confirmity of usage if we are to rely upon the messages made with words. Otherwise we could not reliably tell what is to be understood by the utterances of an individual.

Although this point is undoubtedly correct, it must not be overstated. It does not deny that an idiolect could be a self-standing language. It leaves it open whether an isolated individual might have the determinate intentions or procedures to afford a sense to his terms quite without any question of deferring to the authority of anyone else. For example, if the meaning of a term were thought of along verificationist lines, as the kind of procedure or experience which determines whether a term applies, then an individual might himself invent and fix such a procedure or such an experience (but see next section). It is just that such an individual can never rely upon there being a determinate meaning to a term when he does not himself know what it is. He thereby differs from members of linguistic groups, who defer to others, as in the elm and arthritis example. I am here dissenting from Dummett's treatment of this issue.[12] Dummett correctly takes the way we bind ourselves by deferential conventions to show that "there is no describing any individual's employment of his words without account being taken of his willingness to subordinate his use to that generally agreed as correct". This is true. But he continues: "That is, one cannot so much as explain what an idiolect is without invoking the notion of a language considered as a social phenomenon." This is not true, or, if it is it needs a different support. For it is not equivalent to the first claim: it implies that an individual cannot do for himself what a society can do together (provide meanings for terms), whereas the first claim says only that an individual will not actually have done that, but will be bound by social facts which he will recognize, or ought to recognize, and which can split his actual meaning from his own understanding. The stronger claim needs the idea that meaning *has* to be social, and this goes beyond saying that it actually *is* social.[13]

The essence of the matter is that there seems to be no impossibility in an individual creating and abiding by his own rule of use of a term. But if an individual cannot do this, the fact that he is surrounded by others seems a doubtful source of help. The

---

[12] 'The Social Character of Meaning', in *Truth and Other Enigmas*, pp. 424–5. Also 'What is a Theory of Meaning?', in Guttenplan ed., *Mind and Language*, p. 135.

[13] I discuss deferential conventions further in chapter 4.

fact that there are lots of individually wooden people, forming a public group, is not itself calculated to suddenly transform them into a non-wooden community, sharing genuine identity of concepts, with real rules of application.

Crusoe's idiolect is not a private language, in the sense which that phrase bears in Wittgenstein's most famous development of these thoughts about meaning: the anti-private language argument. Crusoe's practice, for instance with his signs which help to solve the Rubik's cube, is only accidentally private. If Man Friday arrives, there is no reason why he should not be taught the same procedures and rules. But the private language which Wittgenstein opposes is private in a stronger sense. Its terms are given their meanings by reference to private episodes, such as sensations. We must now consider Wittgenstein's arguments against such a language, and the place of those arguments in philosophy.

4. *Privacy and Practice*

So far in this chapter we have tried to find what makes it true that either (i) a person is using a word in one definite sense, or (ii) he is using it with a different, bent interpretation, or (iii) he is not using it with a sense at all, but is merely parading the term under the impression that he is doing so. *Some* fact must determine which of these is true. We have accepted the negative point, that it is not a display to the mind which does it. We have cast doubt upon the idea that the actual presence of a communicating group is essential: whatever fact it is which marks the difference, it seems possible that an individual should satisfy it by himself. In this way his earlier self can transmit information for his later self to profit from, just as different members of a group can. In effect we are left with a pair of suggestions (not necessarily exclusive): it is the existence of a *practice* or *technique* which makes the difference, or it is the existence of a determinate intention, known to the speaker in whichever way we know about our own intentions, which makes the difference.

As is often the case in philosophy, a good way of exploring these ideas is to see what they rule out. The anti-private language considerations aim at this conclusion: no language can contain a term whose meaning (or sense) is constituted by a connection the term has with a private item, which lies, or lay, solely in the mind of the individual who understands the term. We can call the doctrine that rules out such a term, "semantic externalism".[14] It is a doctrine about the terms of any language at all, including ours. It tells us that no term of any language, including terms like 'pain' 'tickle' 'experience as of seeing red', have their meanings fixed by a certain kind of connection. The importance of this claim is that the reverse doctrine is so tempting. It is tempting to say that I know what a term like 'pain' or 'burnt taste' means from my own case. Under some circumstances I have a certain kind of experience. Others, supposing that I have it because of my situation or my reactions, teach me to use some word to apply to it. I absorb their teaching by giving myself a private ostensive definition: I focus upon the sensation, say a pain, and promise to call just that kind of sensation 'pain' in the future. It is the fact that I use the term in conformity to that rule which identifies its meaning. The rule fixes the connection between the term and the private sensation, lying solely in my mind. Semantic externalism opposes this model. By opposing it, the doctrine threatens whole clusters of ideas in the philosophy of knowledge and the philosophy of mind. It stands against the thought that our best or fundamental knowledge is of the contents of our own minds. It stands against the whole Lockean model of language, whereby the immediate significance of a word is an Idea in the mind of the person who apprehends it: what Locke believes to be true of all words, semantic externalism believes to be true of none. It eventually alters the whole conception of the privacy of our own experiences and sensations, although the consequences here are indirect, and need a little explanation.

Semantic externalism says that terms like 'pain' do not have meanings which are constituted by their connection with a private item. Now we might decide that pains, experiences, sensations, are precisely items of this proscribed private kind. In that case the doctrine forces us to revise the idea that it is through a connection with such things that any words have their meanings. Alternatively, we might suppose that it is quite certainly through that connection that the words have their meanings. What could be more certain than that the word

14 I borrow the term from E. J. Craig.

'pain' means what it does because of its connection with *pain*? In that case we are forced to revise our philosophy of mind. Pains, sensations, and experiences then cannot be items of the proscribed kind, and we must seek an account on which they are not items of private acquaintance, but are thought of in some other way. On the first alternative the private language argument, and the semantic externalism which is its conclusion, remain doctrines about meaning. We can think of minds in a traditional ("Cartesian") way as private repositories of experience, sensations, perhaps intentions, of which the subject has a privileged acquaintance. But our ideas of what gives the meaning to terms like 'pain', 'experience of seeing red', and so on, have to be altered. On the second alternative it is the conception of privacy itself which is threatened.

The first alternative seeks to reconcile Cartesian privacy with semantic externalism. Its strategy is to distinguish between the *sense* or meaning of a term like 'pain', which is not given by its connection with the private experience, and its *reference*, which may yet be the private content. But although the sense/reference distinction is quite legitimate (see chapter 9) it cannot effect this marriage. The distinction is at its most visible when we take phrases which can be fully understood (i.e. whose sense can be fully apprehended) when it is not known to whom or what they refer. Thus I perfectly understand many sentences containing definite descriptions ('the person who committed this crime'; 'the richest man in the world') although quite ignorant of who or what it is that they refer to (see 9.1). This is why I can understand and obey instructions like 'Look for the person who committed this crime', or statements like 'Economists do not know who is the richest man in the world'. The sense of these sentences is a function of the sense of the individual words occurring in the descriptions, and this is quite independent of whether x or y is the person who committed the crime, or the richest man in the world. But 'pain' does not function like this. There is no understanding of the term by people who do not *know what pain is*. It is through knowing what pain is that we come to understand pain ascriptions, whereas it is not through knowing who is the richest man in the world that we come to understand sentences using the description. Because of this we cannot separate out two processes: learning the sense of the term 'pain', perhaps compatibly with semantic externalism, and *then* learning to what it refers (the Cartesian private item). Rather, it is by knowing what pain is that we come to understand the term, and what it means to apply it. If this knowledge is essentially knowledge of a privately shown item, lying solely in the mind of the subject, then semantic externalism is refuted.

For this reason, the second alternative is more promising: if we accept semantic externalism, we must revise our whole conception of the privacy of the mental, and our knowledge of the contents of our own minds. But what is there to be said for semantic externalism? What is the force of the anti-private language considerations?

Let us consider a proposed case of private ostensive definition. A man has a certain kind of sensation. This sensation has a "phenomenal quality" which is known to him alone: *he* is aware of it, just by having it. He can attend to it, like it or dislike it, relish it, and, let us suppose, christen it. By this christening he (purportedly) provides himself with an *intended rule*: in the future call only *this* kind of sensation, '*S*'. This rule would determine what is correct application of the term '*S*' and what is incorrect. A later sensation with its own definite phenomenal quality would be rightly called '*S*' if it falls within the intended range of the term, and wrongly called '*S*' if it does not, but the subject mistakenly takes it to do so – perhaps by forgetting the actual nature of the original example. To use one of Wittgenstein's metaphors, the intended rule provides a measure or yardstick to lay alongside a new sensation, which will then conform with it or not, as the case may be. Let us say that a man is *faithful* to the original christening if there was an original episode of ostensive definition of this kind, which gave him a definite intention to call only sensations of a certain kind of quality '*S*', and if the man later uses that intention as a rule which allows some sensations to *be* '*S*', and disallows others. Wittgenstein's endeavour is to show that there can be no such truth as this: no truth that a man is (or is not) being faithful to the original episode of this kind. The appearance must be a sham, and hence the idea that a man is later *judging* a new sensation to be '*S*', or not to be '*S*', is also a sham. For genuine judgement demands faithfulness to a pre-existing rule.

Otherwise the later occasion shows nothing but the man making a new *decision* (I'll call this '*S*'/I'll not call this '*S*'). Such a decision would not be responsible to anything that happened previously. Hence it would not be correct or incorrect, and it cannot be regarded as the making of a judgement. For judging is something which is essentially capable of being correct or incorrect. In this case, according to Wittgenstein, nothing previous created a standard whereby this can be so. Once again: "whatever is going to seem right to me is right. And that only means that here we can't talk about 'right'."

Why can there be no truth that a man is being faithful to an intended rule, whose content was fixed by the first sensation? When the later case arises he might say, "Ah, here is an '*S*' sensation again, and he has the *impression* of the term '*S*' having a definite sense, so that this remark makes a judgement. But being under the *impression* that you are following a rule is not sufficient to be *truly* following a rule. We have already met the no-rule hypothesis, or possibility of a subject who thinks that he is following a rule when he applies or withholds some term, but who is like a lunatic covering pages with "sums", or like the man whom Wittgenstein considers in § 237 of the *Investigations*, who intently follows a line with a pair of compasses, with one leg on the line, and the other following at a distance, but at a distance which he constantly alters by opening and shutting the compasses as he draws the points along. This man may think he is tracing a path defined by the first line, but not be doing so. For since nothing would be a violation of this rule, the hypothesis that there is a rule is mere show. A rule must allow some procedures and disallow others.

In the public case the "wooden" individual, whose use of a term is not rule-governed, can be detected, because his practice is eventually different from that of someone making genuine judgement with the term. The lunatic's "sums" form no part of the practice of an applied mathematics (if they do, we might revise the opinion that there is no method in them). But in the private case, only the subject himself is an authority on whether his applications of the term conform to an intended rule. So Wittgenstein can ask what, in the private case, is the distinction between (a) someone who is genuinely faithful to a pre-established rule, which determines correct and incorrect appli-

cation of 'S', and (b) someone who is disposed to use the term
under the illusion that he is following a rule determining its
application?

At this point one is inclined to concentrate upon the
phenomenology of the matter. Give yourself a sensation,
remember it, and ask whether a later sensation is the same or
different. It seems a well-formed, well-understood question, at
least if you take care to specify various respects of sameness, like
intensity, or felt location. But there is a possibility, even if it
is one you are likely to dismiss, that you later misremember
what the original sensation was, and hence misapprehend the
intended rule it was used to introduce. You have then the new,
candidate sensation, and a memory of the intended rule, fixed
by the old exemplar. But the memory would be deceiving you.
It would lead you to think that the new example is very like the
old, and deserves the same name, when in fact it is quite
different. Let us call this possibility (c).[15]

If Wittgenstein is allowed to use the verification principle, he
is well placed to attack the idea that there is a real distinction
betwen (a) and (b) and (c). For anything the subject does or
experiences at a moment, or himself says, is compatible with
each hypothesis. And the public is in no position to tell which is
true either. No third person can tell whether the later sensations
are really like the first, or really different, or whether the subject
is really following no rule at all in what he calls 'S'. If there is no
verifiable difference between the three hypotheses, then by the
verification principle there is no real difference between them.
But for the term 'S' to be meaningful there must be a difference
between them, for it must be rule-governed and permit of
incorrect application.

What is much more doubtful is whether Wittgenstein can
reach this conclusion without relying upon a verificationist
step. Many writers suppose he can.[16] They think that the
challenge to say what *makes* the difference, in the private case,
has its own force. It is not just a question of how we might tell

[15] "Always get rid of the idea of the private object in this way: assume that it
constantly changes, but that you do not notice the change because your memory
constantly deceives you". *Philosophical Investigations*, II, p. 207.
[16] e.g. A. Kenny, 'The Verification Principle and the Private Language Argument',
in O. R. Jones (1971); C. Peacocke, 'Rule Following: the Nature of Wittgenstein's
Arguments', in Holtzman and Leich (1981).

which one is true, but of whether we have any conception of what would *make* one of them true. The challenge is to state this, and it is alleged that the would-be private linguist has no answer.

The challenge needs quite delicate handling, or it threatens to destroy public language as well. That is, in so far as the individual has difficulty in meeting it, it is also possible that a group does. We have already seen how hard it is for a group to defend themselves as being genuine rule-followers, sharing an identity of concept, rather than a mere number of wooden individuals, or a mutually bent community holding quite divergent interpretations of shared predicates. But even if we waive this problem, perhaps because we draw on the idea of a practice, or technique with a term, which saves the public, the prospects for the challenge are not all that bright. This is because it is rather hazy whether the challenge, to show what makes the difference, can legitimately be met just by repeating the description of the three cases. Suppose the private linguist defends himself by saying: "We already know what makes the difference. In the one case there is a rule, and it is determinate whether an application conforms to it; in the second case there is merely illusion; in the third case there is a misremembering of which rule was established. If there is a challenge to verify these hypotheses, then unfortunately it cannot be met. But that is often the way with sceptical challenges, and does not disturb the genuineness of the distinction." The challenger will impatiently reply that this is not good enough: he wants to be shown what the distinctions *consist in*, in the private case. But what does this mean? Perhaps only that the distinction should be drawn in other ways, themselves making no mention of intentions, or rules, or fidelity to a pre-established sense. But why should this request be legitimate? A distinction made with one kind of vocabulary often cannot be captured except by using that vocabulary: the distinction between red and green is essentially a distinction of colours, and cannot be shown to "consist in" some difference which does not refer to colours. The distinction between happiness and pleasure is a psychological distinction and cannot be made except in terms from that theoretical vocabulary, and so on. Notice too that by urging the negative point, Wittgenstein has already led us to think of intentions as irreducible, in the sense that the issue of the intentions with which a person uses a term is never just the issue of which display he has before his mind.

So Wittgenstein's challenge is objectionable if it presupposes that the distinctions between (a), (b), and (c) must be capable of being drawn in other terms. It is also objectionable if it threatens public language as much as private language. Following Kripke we can put Wittgenstein's challenge in the garb of scepticism: this sceptic denies that anyone can *know* whether, after an attempted private ostensive definition, and attempted further use of the term, it is really (a), or (b), or (c) which is in force.[17] But then we have already discovered the scope for equivalent scepticism in the public case: the sceptic who wins against the private linguist looks well set to win against a public group when, corresponding to the three hypotheses in the private case, he asks whether the right-rule view, or the no-rule view, or the bent-rule view, is the true one. If the moral of the rule-following considerations is that we, the public, cannot meet this challenge except by insisting that we do know what we mean, and that we mean the same, and know this by knowing our intentions, then the would-be private linguist can avail himself of the same liberty.

If the would-be private linguist sits tight on his claim to have a determinate intention in calling a new sensation '*S*', the only way forward is to concentrate upon the notion of a practice, or technique. Suppose we accept that understanding a term is possessing a skill with it, and that this skill is to be thought of as a kind of technique or ability. All terms of a language must be associated with such a technique. Then perhaps there is argument to show that the term '*S*', introduced by private ostension, equips its user with no genuine technique at all. It forms no part of a practice whose proper pursuit stands the user in good stead, and whose improper pursuit leads to errors and disappoint-

---

[17] One must be careful of framing these issues around the figure of a sceptic. Wittgenstein's point is never to arrive at a conclusion of the form 'so we don't know whether . . .' His aim is to alter our conception of the facts we take ourselves to know: the aim is metaphysical. But his means to such conclusions may use sceptical dialogues as an integral part: *if* this conception of the facts were the right one, *then* we wouldn't know such and such, but we do, so we need this other conception of the facts. Again, I discuss this further in 'The Individual Strikes Back'.

ments. At first sight this idea seems promising. For precisely because there is no verifiable difference between (a) and (b) and (c), it seems that a "mistake" in applying 'S' is utterly inert. Let us adopt the standpoint which Wittgenstein is attacking for a moment. Imagine two prospective private linguists, each giving themselves what is in fact the same ostension, and coming away with the same intention. One has a better memory or better luck than the other, and only applies 'S' thereafter to cases which do fall within the range of the original intention. The other is fickle and faithless and often applies 'S' to cases which should have been excluded. How is it that one does well and the other does badly? What cost does the errant linguist incur? Apparently, none whatsoever. And if this is so it suggests that there is no real failure of a technique or practice here. A technique is essentially something which has consequences, and whose failure can let us down. So the hypothesis that the would-be private linguist is really operating a technique seems to be pure show. The normal surroundings and stage-setting of the technique of judgement are missing: he is like a man driving an imaginary motor car, or playing an imaginary piano. Consequently it cannot *matter* whether we regard him as a case of (a) or (b) or (c).

The obstacle to this range of thought is that it is we who introduced the S-classification as an isolated and inert incident, with no consequences for good or ill. But suppose on the contrary that the private linguist's performance *is* part of a technique which he is forming, testing, trying to render reliable. The technique is to bring order into his life. By correlating the recurrence of one experience with the recurrence of others of related kinds (warmth – pain! visual experience x – tactile experience y, etc.), the private linguist can begin to find order in his subjective world, and an ordered subjective world is a nice thing to have, since without it we can have no understanding of ourselves as conscious of an objective or spatially extended world. So the enterprise to which the classification of private experience belongs can be a serious one, and it can go well or badly, and it can matter to the subject why it is going badly. If, for instance, S which is usually followed by R is on some occasion not so followed, the private linguist may doubt their general correlation, or doubt either or both of his classifications. And it can be a serious matter to decide where the failure lies, and to accommodate future classifications and expectations around it.

In this circumstance there is no reason at all for the private linguist to take the attitude that whatever seems right is right. He may do better to take the attitude that his memory is not totally reliable, that it is easy to fail to notice genuine differences between '*S*' and sensations like '*S*' but importantly different in what surrounds them, and so on. Judgements of recurrence take their place as corrigible in the light of subsequent experience. The moral will be that there is a point to discriminating the private linguist's performance as genuine judgement, capable of truth or falsity in the light of pre-established intentions, only when the performance is part of some general technique of belief-formation. It would then follow that beliefs have to come in populations, but not that believers do. The would-be private linguist's title to think of himself as a believer would be derived from his title to think of himself as a theorist, attempting a whole set of views about the order of his mental life.

A philosopher impressed by the challenge to make the distinction between (a) and (b) and (c) will still complain. Perhaps we can suggest why the private linguist may pointfully take the *attitude* to himself, that he is making genuine judgement. He need not take the attitude that anything that seems right will be right, nor that his dispositions to call things '*S*' answer to no previous intentions. They have the crucial normative dimensions of correctness or incorrectness. But, the opponent will ask, how is this attitude justified? If there is no *fact* of correct or incorrect applications of the term '*S*' to a new sensation, then surely the attitude itself involves a delusion. It is not enough to say that a private linguist (or public group) may dignify or compliment himself on being a rule-follower or on making judgements which have a genuine dimension of correctness: the compliment must not be empty. There must be a fact of the matter whether he is one or not. And we still have no conception of how the original episode reaches out, as it were, to constrain the proper use of '*S*' on any subsequent occasion.

I do not think that it is true to the later Wittgenstein to pursue the challenge this way.[18] Firstly, Wittgenstein is on the side of those philosophers who query the borderline between genuine

[18] This is another point of difference from Kripke.

beliefs (in *facts*, with *truth-conditions*) and other kinds of commitments (such as possession of attitudes, or acceptance of rules). The error of his earlier philosophy was to exalt a simple, single conception of a fact (as in effect a spatial array of objects), and to make no room for truths expressed in terms which do not refer to such spatial arrays: for instance, truths about causal relations, about psychology, about the will, or about ethics. The later work is acutely conscious of the way in which our difficulty in conceiving of psychological facts arises from a spatial or physical model of what a fact must consist in. This is why we find our ability to think of absent things or to form intentions which cover cases which we have not thought of, so mysterious. But the characteristic tone of the later work is one of toleration towards different vocabularies, even when we "have no model" of the truths they describe.[19] A pertinent example is Wittgenstein's famous reaction to the talk of the belief that another person is conscious: "My attitude towards him is an attitude towards a soul. I am not of the *opinion* that he has a soul."[20] The belief or attitude is not a belief *in* a certain fact (a spiritual interior to the animal, or a ghost in the machine), but is something whose content is given by my reactions to the person, ways of behaving and dealing with him. Against this background it would not be appropriate for Wittgenstein to insist that the private linguist can *only* take up an attitude towards his own classifications (the attitude that they answer to a previous rule or intention), but that there can be no *fact* about whether they do: the justifiable attitude is just the kind of thing to give content to this fact. (I offer my own exploration of the attitude/belief distinction in chapter 6.)

When the would-be private linguist classifies a new sensation as '*S*', he thinks of himself as laying it alongside his rule. The rule came into his possession after the private ostension; its content is given in his intention which was formed on that occasion, to call only things like the original example by the term. Wittgenstein's brilliant strategy was to shrink this alleged

---

[19] *Philosophical Investigations*, §192. Cf also the discussion in *Remarks on the Philosophy of Psychology*, vol. 1, when Wittgenstein says of expressions of intention: "Yes, and such use of language is remarkable, peculiar, when one is adjusted only to consider the description of physical objects" (§ 1137).

[20] *Philosophical Investigations*, p. 178.

comparison down to a point, leaving nothing but the new sensation, and a bare disposition to say '*S*' or not. The previous history drops out from the use of the term, for everything about that use could be the same whether or not your memory is utterly deceiving you about the character of the original example (case (c)), or whether you are only under the impression that you are really guided by the nature of the original example (case (b)). The difficulty is to destroy our stubborn conviction that we are right to believe ourselves to be in one category and not in either of the others. Broadly speaking there are two possibilities. Wittgenstein can put on the garb of a sceptic, and allege that we do not know the nature of the previous episode, and the intention which it was used to form. Or, he can raise the metaphysical or ontological charge that we have no conception of the fact that we are genuinely guided by the previously formed intention. Either way, the issue is likely to remain inconclusive. The sceptical charge is too near to blockbuster scepticism, which would destroy our knowledge of anything, especially of public meanings. The ontological or metaphysical charge is too near to insisting that there should be a fact of our being guided by a previous intention which can, as it were, be laid out to view in the form of an image in the head or other guide. This is just what the negative point attacks. And then, if the private linguist refuses to try to force his fact into this kind of shape, it is hard for the later Wittgenstein to deny his right to do it.

5. *Exercising Mental Concepts*

Even if the anti-private language argument is inconclusive, it does a tremendous service in the theory of knowledge. It entirely subverts the idea that our knowledge of our own meanings, derived from the acquaintances we have with our own mental lives, is a privileged, immediate, knowledge, beyond which lies only sceptic-ridden insecurity. This Cartesian picture, according to which my knowledge that my present sensation is green, or hunger, or a headache, is peculiarly incorrigible, is, I believe, overthrown by the realization that the only "incorrigible" element is the single point, the present sensation; any enterprise of judging it to be one thing or another involves bringing it into contact with a rule or previous intention, and hence brings the possibility of misidentification of what that was. But this does not entail that there could be no such judgement. It only entails that it has no unique immunity from error.

There is one further aspect of this difficult area which needs mentioning. I characterized semantic externalism as the denial that the meaning of any term can be "constituted by its connection" with a private exemplar. The same thought is sometimes put by denying that it is "from our own case" that we learn the meaning of sensation terms. The alternative account of the meaning of such terms is likely to stress public criteria of their applicability. To understand a sensation term requires knowing what kind of situation or what kind of display would make it appropriate to attribute the sensation to a third person: it might also demand knowing that people can sham, or be hypnotized, or whatever, into appearing to have sensations when they do not. But this, it is suggested, gives no ground to Cartesian privacy. It only shows that our public evidence is inconclusive or "defeasible" by further public evidence, which could arise if peoples' motives for shamming, or queer state of hypnosis, were removed.

Accuracy demands a little suspicion of some of this. There is at least room for a theory which admits that it is not *wholly* from one's own case that one understands a sensation term, or that the meaning of such a term is not *wholly* a question of its connection with the private example, but also insists that it is *partly* from one's own case that one understands the term. That is, a full grasp of sensation terms would require knowing what the sensation is like (privately), and realizing that other subjects might or sometimes do possess it too. It might also require understanding the kind of evidence which justifies the belief that they do. It is an awkwardness of the anti-private language argument that it seems to rule out even this diluted semantic internalism. It is so strong that it leaves *no* role for the internal examplar. For the subject can only be under the impression that his own example of the sensation plays any role at all in identifying a rule of application, and this impression is, supposedly, not enough to make it true that it plays a role. And nothing else can make that true either.

Even dilute semantic internalism faces or raises difficulties. So far I have concentrated upon what we can call a "vertical" version of the private language argument. This considers one agent and his relation to his past states. But there is a "horizontal" aspect of the argument too. This questions whether dilute semantic internalism can allow any sense to the thought that some other subject has the same kind of sensation as oneself. To make the problem vivid, imagine someone arguing that he does indeed get the concept of pain from his own case; his own case enables him to tell when there is pain about, which is to say, when *his* body is injured or he is affected in some unfortunate way; hence no other events are associated with pain at all. *Your* injury is just not the sort of thing which causes this sensation. *He* never feels it when *you* are injured. The concept of sensation is exercised "vertically" as it were: in the one dimension of my own feelings.

The challenge is to explain how, *if* our basic use of the concept is in our own case, we can ever come to exercise it in full generality. How do we understand that we are each just one of the many creatures which equally have sensations (even if we then go on to wonder how like our own those of our fellows might be)? This kind of challenge is of great importance in philosophy. For example, Berkeley anticipated Hume in finding it hard to understand how we gained a concept of causation by acquaintance with the ("passive") flow of events in the world which we sense. He proposed instead that the origin of the idea lies in our knowledge of our own agency or exercises of will.[21] But (as he realized) that makes it impossible to see how we can properly describe non-mental things as causing anything. Again Hume describes the origin of our idea of justice in the need for a scheme or system of rules whereby we can gain reciprocal advantages from one another: there is a problem then whether he can make sense of our idea that we have a duty of justice to future generations, or animals, who cannot reciprocate.[22] We could put the challenge by asking why, on these theories, the term in question is not ambiguous, meaning one thing in the home case (from which we get the idea) and another thing in the further cases. How can it be the *same*

[21] *Principles of Human Knowledge*, § 25.
[22] *Treatise of Human Nature*, Bk. III, Pt. II, Sect. 1.

concept, which is exercised in the home case and in the further cases?

If the challenge were just one of explaining the genesis of our understanding, it would seem feeble. We might reply that it just comes naturally to us to extend the concept from the one kind of case to the other. But the real challenge is to say why it is the same concept in each case. Is it responsive to the same kind of evidence or argument; do we appreciate its consequences in the same way? In the current example a dilute semantic internalist cannot just say, for instance, that in my case I recognize and remember my private exemplars, but in your case I exercise the concept of pain by, for example, caring about you or reacting with emotion when I judge that you are in pain.[23] He must go on to *connect* these two exercises: to show why it is appropriate to talk of *one* concept which I apply equally to you and to me. However there are steps towards meeting this demand which the semantic internalist can take. He can point out that many of the things I know (or believe) about my own pains I also believe about yours: that it is no accident that this kind of sensation makes me behave in this kind of way; that there are ways in which I can conceal sensations, that sometimes I cannot, that there are ways for you to behave towards me if you believe me to have a sensation and also have various attitudes towards me, and that these are ways I behave towards you in the light of the same beliefs. In other words, I can judge so that my sensations and yours are subjects of similar predicates and claim that the same concept is involved just because of that. It would, I believe, be extremely hard to phrase the demand or challenge so that this kind of answer does not meet it. Consider this parallel: people think it makes sense to ask whether numbers are *objects*, but how can the question even make sense when the notion of an object is at home in talking of ordinary spatio-temporally located and bounded, solid and visible things? Answer: because (perhaps) we say enough about both numbers and more ordinary objects to explain the common term (they are equally referred to, counted, known about, independent of us . . .)[24]

So semantic internalism can attach a meaning to the view

---

[23] Although curiously this is at least a part of Wittgenstein's own thought.

[24] So we do have identity of meaning, or only similies or metaphors? Numbers are like objects in that . . .; unlike them in that . . . See more on this in 5.7.

that other people have sensations like ours. This leaves the question of whether we know that they do, and how we rebut scepticism about their similarity to us. But that takes us too far from the philosophy of language. The present verdict is that the private-language considerations seem at best inconclusive. There is no compelling reason why there cannot be a practice of judging that our own private sensations are thus-and-so. And the intention with which we apply the classification may, so far as the argument goes, be identified by private ostension. There is equally no compelling reason why such a practice should not also serve to identify (part of) the meaning of our public sensation terms. The two elements of meaning which we have been forced to make prominent in coming to this conclusion are, firstly, the relation between meaning and intention, and secondly the relation between meaning and a whole practice of coping with the world. I propose to pursue the first of these in the next chapter, and the second infuses the next part of the book, in which we consider ways in which we judge the world, and the kinds of truth they deliver.

Notes to Chapter 3

3.1   The central references for this chapter are:

> L. Wittgenstein, *Philosophical Investigations* §§134–230.
> N. Goodman, *Fact, Fiction and Forecast*, ch. IV.
> B. Russell, *Human Knowledge, its Scope and Limits*, pp. 422 ff.

Russell makes only passing reference to bent rules. Goodman uses them to shed new light on the problem of induction, but bent rules and no rules are used to cast their shadow over meaning by Wittgenstein. Easily the best commentary to date is Saul Kripke's, referred to in the text (n. 4 above).

"It does not follow that the subject himself is *not* an authority . . ." It is vital to see that Wittgenstein is not denying that there is such a phenomenon as rule-following (nor that there are facts about which rule is in force, not that it is true or false that there are rules in force). The whole debate is about the conception of these facts that we can obtain. Even the best modern commentators (including Wright and Kripke) do not bring this point out fully enough; they leave it uncertain whether we can properly allow facts of this kind. They have a good excuse, because we have here a classic philosophical problem: a critique of one conception of a kind of fact is so powerful that it leaves people unsettled whether we can any longer go on saying the things we used to say about the area. This predicament is discussed further in 5.1 and 5.2.

3.2   "A slightly more substantial answer . . ."
Although I say enough in the text to register my disagreement with both conventionalist and naturalistic approaches to Goodman's problem, a fuller discussion would bring in much more. I discuss the paradox with reference to induction in *Reason and Prediction*, ch. 4. Important discussions of Goodman's paradox include:

> S. Barker and P. Achinstein, 'On the New Riddle of Induction', *Philosophical Review* (1960).
> J. J. Thomson, 'Grue', *Journal of Philosophy* (1966).
> P. Teller, 'Goodman's Theory of Projection', *British Journal for the Philosophy of Science* (1969).
> S. Shoemaker, 'On Projecting the Unprojectible', *Philosophical Review* (1975).

See also 7.7

3.3   "A compromise is suggested by Saul Kripke . . ."
I give a more detailed discussion of Kripke's views in 'The Individual Strikes Back', *Synthese* (1984) (this volume, edited by Wright, also contains relevant papers by J. McDowell and C. Wright).

". . . taking his later work to release religious faiths . . ."
There is a trenchant discussion of post-Wittgensteinian views of religion in J. Mackie, *The Miracle of Theism*, ch. 12. It is, in my view, very uncertain whether the stress of religion as a human phenomenon, giving vent to human needs and feelings, actually conflicts with the view that religious beliefs are real beliefs, capable of truth or (usually) falsity.

3.4   Any selection out of the huge exegetical and critical literature on the private language argument is bound to be fairly arbitrary. Treatments which should profit students, in addition to those already mentioned, include:

> A. J. Ayer, 'Could Languge be Invented by a Robinson Crusoe', in O. R. Jones (1971).
> R. Fogelin, *Wittgenstein* (The Arguments of the Philosophers), chs. XII and XIII.
> J. J. Thomson, 'The Verification Principle and the Private Language Argument', in O. R. Jones (1971).

C. Peacocke, 'Rule-Following: The Nature of Wittgenstein's Arguments', in Holtzman and Leich (1981).

But the best modern discussions, triggered by Kripke, seem to me to be nearer to the real heart of Wittgenstein's problems.

"I do not think it is true to the later . . ."
I here agree with two other writers who have explored Wittgenstein's later conception of fact:

P. Winch, 'Im Anfang war die Tat', and
B. McGuiness, 'The So-Called Realism of Wittgenstein's Tractatus', both in Block, ed. (1981).

3.5 "horizontal" and "vertical"
This adverts to the extensive literature which believes Wittgenstein to have subverted the familiar argument from analogy for other minds. The idea is that we cannot learn what pain is, in our own case, and then as much as *understand* what it could be for someone else to be in pain; hence we cannot argue by analogy with our own case that other, similarly behaving bodies belong to subjects with similar mental experiences: we cannot understand what this means. A good collection on this problem is *The Philosophy of Mind*, ed. V. C. Chappell, especially the editor's introduction, and the papers by Malcolm and Strawson.

I am very conscious that this section suggests more profound problems than it manages to treat. It is probably fair to say that the philosophical community, at present, is involved in a general shift away from supposing that anything is ever learned in our own case – this being supposed to involve a "Cartesian" conception of mind, whereby the contents of our own minds are immediately present, private showings, whose nature wholly determines our thought. The whole difficulty is to separate what is right about the direction, from what is wrong, or questionable, about the individual theses which people have taken to support the direction. Although I am sceptical of some of the arguments from the philosophy of language which have been used to support the shift, I have no settled opinion on the shift itself (the time will come when people begin to ask what was *right* about Cartesian intuitions in the philosophy of mind). In this work I am only concerned with the arguments as they emerge in connection with understanding and meaning. This is also evident in chapter 9, where in order to avoid a Cartesian, or even solipsistic view about the nature of thought, philosophers have been led to defend unduly implausible views about reference and thought.

CHAPTER 4

Conventions, Intentions, Thoughts

> "I saw you take his kiss!" " 'Tis true"
> "Oh Modesty!" " 'Twas strictly kept:
> He thought me asleep; at least I knew
> He thought I thought he thought I slept."
> > Coventry Patmore,
> > > "The Kiss".

1. *Grice's Approach*

What change is involved when someone comes to possess a language? What is the difference between linguistic and non-linguistic creatures – what difference are we looking for if we debate whether whales or chimpanzees really use language? The last two chapters may leave us dissatisfied with an answer which merely cites thoughts, and describes language mastery as an ability to display those thoughts to others. We might sympathize with the idea that somehow the practice of transmission, and the grasp of symbolism with which to do it, actually creates our ability to have the thoughts. But this remains mere speculation, unless we get a better focus on what it is to have a language anyway.

The classic paper introducing modern attempts to analyse communication was written by H. P. Grice.[1] Grice's approach has been much debated, rejected, altered, and improved upon. The basic ideas can be appreciated without following many of the elaborations which have emerged, and I shall in any case be attempting to show why many of the complexities which abound in the literature are misconceived.

Grice presented his analysis as an attempt to locate a notion of "non-natural meaning" – the kind of meaning a sign or action or utterance may have, not because it is naturally a symptom of something else (in the sense that red spots mean measles, or

[1] H. P. Grice, 'Meaning', *Philosophical Review* (1957).

clouds mean rain), but because it is somehow *intended* to signify something. Thus I might present you with the head of John the Baptist, intending to show you that he is dead, or draw a picture of Mr. X being intimate with Mrs. Y, intending to show you that this is how they are; or I might throw a bucket of water over you, intending to suggest that you leave; or open a window, intending to have you look out and see that it is raining. Suppose then an action done by one party (the *utterer*, although the action need not at this stage involve language) and directed to another (the audience). The primitive basis, then, is an utterer doing x with the intention that the audience comes to believe something, or comes to do something. Call such an action an AIIB – an Action Intended to Induce Belief. (Following most writers, I shall concentrate upon transmission of belief for the moment, leaving commands, etc. until later.)

Now an AIIB may aim at inducing belief that p without signifying or meaning that p. It seems stretched to say that by opening the window I meant that it was raining. But it seems all right to say that by drawing Mr. X and Mrs. Y, I meant or communicated that they were on certain terms. So what is the difference? Grice effectively located it in the way the transmission of belief works. In the window case the audience may take the fact that the window is open, or the fact that I evidently want him to look out, as a reason for looking out, and having done that he sees the rain and acquires the belief. But it is not important to this process that at any point he should realize that I intend him to believe that it is raining. By contrast, when I draw the picture, unless the audience realizes that I do so with the intention of getting him to think that the couple stand in a certain relation, there is no likelihood that he will then come to believe that they do. In other words, the mechanism of getting the audience to have the belief involves in this case the audience recognizing that this is what is intended.

We can appreciate the difference in this way. Suppose you and I are in what I shall refer to as the "one-off predicament": I need to get you to believe something, p, and I can rely upon no shared language. (The point is to build an account of what it is to have a shared language, so we obviously cannot help ourselves to its properties at any stage.) In the one-off predicament I must come up with an AIIB. One such would be engineering a natural sign that p. For instance, if there is quicksand about, I might rig up a device for dropping a stone in front of any traveller; the stone will sink and the traveller realize that there is quicksand ahead. If I am a brain surgeon I might be able to directly modify the audience's brain, so that they then believe that p. But the scope for this direct action is limited. Now in the one-off predicament there is only one other way of proceeding. I have to do something which you are likely to take in one specific way. The natural way to do this, given the ways we interact with other people, is to perform some action with the intention that you realize why I am performing it. I might, for instance, draw a skull on a post, hoping that you come along, see the skull, ask yourself why someone should draw that, and become alerted to the quicksand. I would rely upon your perception of my intention, for there is nothing else to rely upon. And we can imagine ways in which that reliance would be well placed, although they involve rather primitive messages. This is because unless we have shared habits of ways of taking utterances or actions, it is not so easy to do anything which you are *likely* to take in any one specific way.

Let us call an action intended to induce the belief that p, and relying for its effect upon the audience appreciating that this is the intention behind it, a Gricean AIIB that p ($GAIIB_p$). Then we must certainly applaud Grice for suggesting a mechanism to be used in one-off predicaments. But what is the next step? The line which Grice himself inaugurated is to ask whether a $GAIIB_p$ means that p, or whether by such an action the *utterer* means that p; or even says that p, or communicates (if successful) that p. The promise is this. If we can wrap up a nice condition for an action in a one-off predicament meaning that p, then we can expect it to be a short step to saying what it is for an action or utterance to mean in general that p (in the mouths of some group, say). It would be, roughly, for them to have it as a habit or convention that the action is performed with the intention of inducing the belief that p, relying upon the Gricean mechanism. Regular meaning would be fossilized one-off meaning.

This direction of explanation is called "linguistic nominalism" by Jonathan Bennett although the title is a trifle misleading. (It has nothing to do with nominalism in the theory of predication.) We should notice one very odd feature of it. In the one-off predicament I have to rely upon Grice's mechanism – that is, your recognition of my intention in uttering – because there in nothing else for you to go on. But evidently this is no longer true once we have habits of taking utterances one way or another. If I have to gesture or mime or otherwise invent a performance I must hope that you appreciate why I am doing it. But once we have methods of communicating into which we have been trained, perhaps I need not care at all if you recognize my intention in uttering. It would be enough if you heard my words, because you will have been trained to take them in a certain way, and so taking them, you will understand me. Since this is so, linguistic nominalism has a powerful rival. This rival would avoid importing conditions on one-off communication into the full, general case of shared communication through language. We could thank Grice for his insight into the one-off predicament, without in any way supposing that the complexities which enable people to resolve it must always be present, even when they have shared habits to rely upon, enabling them to bypass the complexities. In other words, conventions or habits would not need to fossilize complex Gricean conditions – they would supplant the Gricean mechanism, which is only needed in their absence. Where x is the $AIIB_p$ the difference is between:

$$\text{one-off } AIIB_p(x) \longrightarrow \text{one-off } GAIIB_p \xrightarrow{\text{fossilized}} \begin{array}{l}\text{regular meaning} \\ \text{of } x \text{ that } p\end{array}$$

which is linguistic nominalism, and

$$\text{one-off } AIIB_p(x) \xrightarrow{\text{fossilized}} \text{regular meaning of } x \text{ that } p$$
$$\quad \longrightarrow \text{one-off } GAIIB_p$$

The second route represents the idea that if a way of inducing belief becomes fixed in a community, that might be enough for it to be said to mean that p, even without considering the complex intentions which would be needed to communicate that p, were the regular habit not already extant.

From the second standpoint, linguistic nominalism is like imagining the psychological complexity of a situation in which two non-communicants manage something – say to pass each other on an appropriate side of the road. This would involve, perhaps, a guess at the other's intentions, or at his beliefs about one's own intentions, or even at his beliefs about one's beliefs about his own intentions. And then the total psychology of this situation is supposed to be fixed when there is a convention or regular habit of taking one side of the road rather than another. Whereas it is far more plausible to say that the habit or convention *supplants* the need for such beliefs and such intentions.

2. *Openness and Communication*

However, there quickly arose another reason for being interested in Grice's higher-order intentions (intentions that intentions be recognized). Although this has a place as a sheer mechanism, being the only hope of people in the one-off predicament, it quickly came to seem more integral to meaning. For philosophers soon pointed to cases where Grice's conditions may be met, yet where various kinds of deception and concealment were involved, with the utterer intending to bring about a misapprehension on the part of an audience. These seemed to destroy some ideal of full *openness* in communication. And they also seemed best avoided by demanding more and more high-order intentions – intentions that other intentions be recognized. So there is a coincidence of reasons for adding higher-order intentions to an analysis of communication. But the matter soon became extravagantly complex.

For instance, Strawson described a case in which someone intends by a certain action to induce in someone the belief that p:

He arranges convincing-looking 'evidence' that p, in a place where A is bound to see it. He does this knowing that A is watching him at work, but knowing also that A does not know that S knows that A is watching him at work. He realizes that A will not take the arranged 'evidence' as genuine or natural evidence that p, but realizes, and indeed intends, that A will take his arranging of it as grounds for thinking that he, S, intends to induce in A the belief that p. That is, he intends A to recognize his (first) intention . . .[2]

A, the audience, is intended to argue that S would not be trying to arrange apparent evidence that p for him, unless S intended to get him to believe that p, and, if he trusts S on this matter, he

[2] "Intention and Convention in Speech Acts", *Philosophical Review*, 1964.

will then come to believe that p. But, Strawson urges, this is not a case of attempting to communicate that p by an action. The action does not mean that p.

Strawson believed that what was missing was a further intention. The speaker or utterer should, if he is to mean that p by his action, intend the audience to recognize his intention to get the audience to recognize his intention to think that p. This is not easy to keep tabs on. Furthermore, there is no end to the possibility of more and more complex kinds of deception. I may want you to believe that p, but also want you to think that I want . . . something else. There is then some deception or exploitation of a mistake involved, and this, perhaps, destroys some idea of openness in communication. In good cases of communication we want everything to be above board. It began to be speculated that we need limitless strings of intentions to really communicate.

But linear strings of higher-order intentions are not the best way of ensuring full openness. Such strings can exist all right. Take a case of Nagel's:[3] in a restaurant I try to attract the attention of a pretty woman. I want to look at her. I want her to see that I want to look at her. I may want her to see that I want her to see that I want to look at her. Or, take a blacker case. You do something which slightly offends me. But you in turn may be substantially offended by my offence. When I realize this, I may become grossly offended – you have no business judging me like that. And this, to you, may be the last straw . . . A common way in which trivial causes generate desperate hostilities.

But in the restaurant is it really plausible to say that when our eyes meet in full mutual awareness, I (and she) have an endless stock of wants? The ideal of full openness is more simply captured if we just add the want that nothing about my wants be concealed. This rolls the rest of the linear regress into one want, which is a good deal more economical. Thus I want to look at her, want her to look back, and want nothing of my wants to be unknown to her. I *may* have more complex wants as well, but the openness is captured in this last want.

If we cannot shut the regress off with such a clause it becomes quite unclear whether there could be a "natural kind" which it

<hr />

[3] T. Nagel, *Mortal Questions*, p. 45.

defines. Take, for example, the seventh or eighth order in 'I intend that the hearer recognize that I intend that he recognize that I intend . . .' How could it have mattered to us that just *this* condition enter as part of a definition of meaning? Why should nature have built us to regard this as part of an important condition, so that were just it absent we should no longer allow the action as a case of meaning something by an action? Most people cannot understand the condition (try to think of a case where just it fails, although the sixth-level intentions are present). The verse at the beginning of the chapter probably stretches most people quite far enough. In fact, the only division which matters to us is that between cases where an utterer wants everything to be open, and ones where he is intending some kind of concealment.[4]

We can appreciate what I am proposing like this. Suppose some bunch of intentions, *I*, is produced as an account of what it is for an action to mean something in a one-off case. The linear regress gets under way because someone then imagines a case where the utterer has *I*, but is indulging some higher-order concealment or deception. To meet this someone suggests adding further intentions (e.g. that each of *I* be known to the audience). This gives *I*+. The argument repeats itself, yielding *I*++; *I*+++ . . . But soon the bunch loses all contact with any normal interests or capacities for forming intention, and the analysis grinds to a halt. Suppose instead that we include in the initial bunch the *intention that all intentions be recognized*. Then anyone possessing *this* bunch has no opportunity for further concealment: he has an intention which itself closes off higher-order chicanery. So we could offer a simple concept of an *open* Gricean AIIB$_p$. This would be an action (i) done with the intention of inducing in an audience the belief that *p*, (ii) relying for success upon the audience's recognition of this intention, and (iii) performed by a speaker who wants all his intentions in so acting to be recognized.

It is hard to find in the literature, but I suspect that philosophers have avoided this simple concept in favour of the linear complexities because they are morbidly afraid of paradoxes of self-reference. And in condition (iii) there is an

---

[4] To avoid misunderstanding I should point out that in this chapter I intend no difference between 'wants' and 'intends'; they are stylistic variants.

element of self-reference: in (iii) there is a want which falls within its own scope. The totality of wants which the speaker wants recognized will include that very want. To understand this, imagine a certain kind of love affair. I want you to know *everything* about me. And everything includes, especially, the fact that I have this want. If you didn't know that about me, you might suspect me of concealment, and I wouldn't want that. There is no paradox here, and no regress either. One might think: well, isn't there an element of vacuousness: imagine someone whose *only* intention is that all his intentions get fulfilled? What does he do? But *his* problem arises because there is nothing else in the totality. When there is something else, the self-respecting want or intention is quite intelligible and, as the love affair shows, quite common.

Do open GAIIBs form a natural kind? We can see how an open Gricean performance would be what we should expect in a one-off case: it is the honest informant's natural action. But I am not convinced that it is a good idea to pursue whether such actions have *meaning*. For that notion is only at home in systems of communication, and our intuitions or decisions about whether it applies are apt to be hazy in one-off cases. Suppose, for instance, I want to communicate to you that Sam and Janet are arriving in our restaurant: I do this by whistling the first few bars of "Some Enchanted Evening", knowing that you know the joke (Sam and Janet evening . . .) relying upon you understanding why I am whistling, and desiring to conceal nothing. Does my whistling then mean that Sam and Janet are entering the restaurant or is this not a case of meaning at all? Personally, I have no strong attachment to either answer. I believe that it is a bad question to concentrate upon. By whistling I intended to communicate that they are, and perhaps succeeded. Why go on to query whether, since that is so, my action meant that they are? (We shall see further at the end of the section 4 why this is a bad question.)

The success of an action in a one-off case can become entrenched, so that a group comes to possess a reliable and regular way of signalling and transmitting information. If linguistic nominalism is right it is an open GAIIB which becomes regularized. For an action x to mean that p would be for it to regularly, or habitually, or conventionally (i) be made with the intention of inducing belief that *p*, (ii) rely upon the audience's recognition of the intention for success, and (iii) be performed by a speaker who wants all his intentions in so acting to be recognized. But I have already suggested that clause (ii), so important to the one-off case, loses its point when the speaker, instead of relying upon Grice's mechanism, can rely directly upon the habits of his audience. Furthermore the third condition, useful as it is in defining the honest communicant, seems curiously irrelevant here. For on the face of it a community might entrench a meaning, communicating that *p* when they say or utter *x*, although *habitually and regularly* when they do so they have devious intentions, concealments, and stratagems up their sleeves, falling short of openness. For example, there is no regularity or habit or convention that when a young man says "Of course I'll respect you in the morning" he wants all his intentions in saying it to be open to view; in fact (as a matter of statistics) the sentence may be used mostly by people with various deceptions in hand; yet for all that his utterance means that he will respect the girl in the morning, and this is what he has said. We must not confuse questions of morals with questions of linguistic convention.

So I prefer a version of the second route, according to which all that needs to be regular, habitual, or conventional, is that a particular action be usable to induce the belief that *p*. The detour through Grice's mechanism and through openness does not, in my view, yield anything which belongs to the essence of linguistic meaning. But to see how such an analysis might proceed we need first to understand the place of convention.

3. *Convention*

Convention is a concept which has suffered varying fortunes. In the positivist high summer, it seemed plausible to explain many features of our intellectual lives as the outcome of convention: this was a convenient way of removing the mystery from commitments which seemed to escape reduction to brute experience.[5] But then under the influence of Quine the idea that we could separate out any particular truths about language as due to convention became doubtful. Certainly, groups have the habit

[5] This is explained further in chapter 5.

of taking utterances in particular ways. But calling such habits conventional seemed to imply a ludicrous historical claim. Imagine a primitive group sitting around and agreeing to take various words to refer to various things. To do this they must have a way of referring both to the new words, and to the things. So forming a language by agreement presupposes having a previous language, of equal or greater power, and this puts a vicious regress in front of any such explanation either of the origin of language or of its essential nature. It is exactly like the regress in imagining a historical meeting in which people contract into the recognition of promises: what happens at a meeting can only be *contracting into* something if the institution of promising is already current.

Convention was rehabilitated in a beautiful study by David Lewis.[6] Lewis separated out the claim that a regularity is conventional in a group, from the claim that it is explained by historical agreement. The core of his analysis is the notion of a regularity (such as driving on one particular side of the road, or meeting at some particular spot, or meaning some definite thing by a particular word) which benefits each member of a group. This happens when a group has a problem of *co-ordination*: it is best for each of them if they follow the same regularity, and they each have an interest in co-ordinating themselves so that they do. But compared with the need to co-ordinate somehow, it may not matter much, or at all, *which* regularity they hit upon. It may not matter where we meet, so long as we meet, or which side of the road we drive on, so long as we all drive on the same side. Now any number of things might explain how some particular regularity, out of a number of possible candidates, becomes a group's preferred solution to a problem of co-ordination. It may strike them as obvious, or be handed to them historically, or be a solution they shuffled towards in a number of attempts to get their acts together. But once a regularity has become the selected one, it will be conventional if people conform to it, and expect others to, and if this mutual expectation is at least part of the reason why they do so as opposed to doing something else. Were I to cease to expect other people to drive on the left (in England) I would lose my reason for driving on the left. Were I to cease to expect you to meet at our usual place,

6   David K. Lewis, *Convention: A Philosophical Study*.

I would lose my reason for going there. The same is true of you. A convention would break down if these expectations began to be disappointed, and we lost any way of re-establishing co-ordination. So Lewis's preliminary definition is:

> A regularity R in the behaviour of members of a population P when they are agents in a recurrent situation S is a convention if and only if, in any instance of S among members of P,
> (1) everyone conforms to R;
> (2) everyone expects everyone else to conform to R;
> (3) everyone prefers to conform to R on condition that the others do, since S is a co-ordination problem and uniform conformity to R is a solution to the problem. (Lewis calls this a co-ordination equilibrium.)[7]

This analysis captures the idea that a regularity may be conventional regardless of how it emerged. What is important is the explanation of why it continues. The continuation is to be dependent upon people's preferences, in particular their preference for some co-ordination with others, and secondly their expectation that the others will do a particular thing – drive on the left, wear certain kinds of clothes, row together if they are jointly managing a boat, and so on. I shall rephrase Lewis's own definition, to bring out this place that explanation has:

(CON)   A regularity is maintained as a convention among P if and only if all or most members of P conform to R, and (at least an important part of) the explanation of why they do so, as opposed to conforming to any equally serviceable rival, is that they each expect the others to do so, and each prefers to do so if the others do.

The definition CON has a number of nice properties. It allows the conservative idea that conventions are essential and respectable, for some co-ordination problems (driving on the same side of the road) simply have to be solved. It allows the romantic idea that there can be too many conventions in a society – people may wish to co-ordinate (e.g. over dress) because they have been brought up so to wish, and things might have been better if they hadn't. The definition allows us to meet

[7] Ibid., p. 42.

a desideratum first mentioned by Tyler Burge (in criticism of a later complication which Lewis introduced), which is that the status of a regularity as conventional or otherwise should be something about which discoveries can be made and about which people can be ignorant or mistaken.[8] People might think, for example, that English word-order is not conventional, but is explained by the way in which thoughts arrive. More seriously there is controversy as to how far the grammar of languages is conventional, and how far it should be regarded as "wired in", so that we have no option but to adopt languages which obey it. There is controversy too over whether some features of our descriptions of the world – such as the imposition of a particular geometry on space – are explained by the facts or are due to conventions of description. The definition explains well what is at stake in such disputes, and why they might be difficult to resolve.

However, this very feature caused Lewis to complicate things. Suppose you and I have the habit of meeting outside the Town Hall for lunch. I have to travel to get there, but do not mind because I believe that you work there and cannot very well travel anywhere else. You believe the same about me: we are each under a misapprehension. Nevertheless, we are each there because we expect the other to be there, and prefer to be so if he is. Is it fair to say that the meeting at the Town Hall is maintained as a matter of convention? Notice that *we* would each deny that it is. If the truth came out we would also be likely to say that the arrangement was due to mistake rather than convention. We don't *have* the convention of so meeting. Lewis responds to this kind of case by adding the imposition that the population P should know the status of the regularity – not only that, indeed, but know that the others know it as well, and know that the others know that the others know it . . . In fact, there is the same kind of regress that Grice and his followers met, and again the basic idea is that everything should be above board. We can say, when nobody is mistaken or ignorant about the status of a regularity, or about anyone else's awareness of that status (and of the fact that everything about it is recognized by everyone), that we have an *overt* convention. Lewis restricted the term convention to overt conventions. But I think that

[8] 'On Knowledge and Convention', *Philosophical Review* (1975).

Burge is right, and that it is correct to call things like word-order conventional even if their status is something the population does not understand. To analyse language we probably need the concept of a non-overt convention: there will be conventions in our use of terms which require complicated and even technical description, which ordinary speakers will not be aware of.

Asserting that a regularity is conventional means showing that we need to co-ordinate on some feature out of a choice of equally serviceable ones, and that the reason we adhere to one is, at least in part, that we expect others to do the same. In chapter 7 I shall use this analysis to address some recent proposals in the theory of knowledge; other problems which benefit include that of how conventions can give rise to norms – duties to conform, or laws establishing conformity. As far as language goes, Lewis's work enables us to see how attaching a particular meaning to a particular sentence or feature of a sentence *can* be conventional. This does not, for instance, involve claiming that anyone ever decided or consciously arranged that it should be so. Nevertheless, caution is still in place. For even if we decide that language actually is a system of regularities which each has a conventional status, this may not tell us much about whether it *has* to be so. For instance, it would not immediately entitle us to rule out a private language because one individual has no problem of co-ordinating with himself. And it would leave the possibility of groups whose linguistic regularities are "wired in", so that they naturally take certain sounds to have certain meanings; the regularity would not have the conventional status, but it might be arbitrary to deny that they have a language and genuinely attribute meaning to the features. In other words, Lewis's work does more to show how semantic regularities *can* be conventional than it does to show that they *must* be. Yet the former achievement was remarkable. And, inevitably, it gives rise to difficulties.

4. *Force*

Which kinds of habits or regularities in our use of signs might be regarded as conventional if CON is right? The simplest suggestion is that we might take an utterance of a certain sentence, and regard it as a regularity with the conventional status, in a group, that the sentence is uttered only with the intention of inducing belief that p. But this will not do, because sentences may be uttered with all sorts of intentions without flouting any linguistic conventions. This is because in two ways speech is too flexible an instrument for such connections to be rigid. Firstly, confining ourselves to straightforward assertion, I can properly assert that p although I know that my audience already believes that p (I want to associate myself with them, perhaps), or although I know that they will never come to believe that p (I want to define my difference from them, perhaps). Secondly, a sentence can be uttered in other ways or other contexts than those of assertion. In particular, sentences may be put into indirect contexts, where their presence indicates no kind of commitment to their truth. I may assert 'the cat is in the garden', but I may also say 'if the cat is in the garden you will not see any birds' or 'when the cat is in the garden it sleeps over there'. In each of these the subordinate utterance of 'the cat is in the garden' indicates no commitment – nobody is saying that the cat is in the garden, or trying to induce belief that it is. Yet the sentence means what it always means.[9]

The problem is this. Suppose we aim for an analysis of what it is for a sentence S in the mouths of some group to mean or say that p. We want to profit from Lewis's work, represented by CON, and see this as a matter of a conventional regularity. But then we need to say quite what is the regularity. We cannot hope for anything as strong as 'regularly and conventionally, when they utter S they intend to induce belief that p', because of these two kinds of flexibility. On the other hand, we cannot put a term like 'means' or 'understands' inside the description of the regularity. Something such as 'regularly and conventionally, when members of a group utter S they mean/are understood to be saying . . . that p' leaves untouched the problem of what it is for a term or sentence to mean something.

The natural way forward is to identify some basic functions of utterance, and to identify the conventional regularity in terms of those. Perhaps it is plausible to see language as a development of animal signalling systems, whose prime evolutionary purpose is the transmission of information, enabling one animal to use a display by another as itself a sign of something. So

[9] This phenomenon is of great importance later: see 6.2.

imagine an action habitually taken by a group as a signal that *p*, and let us say that someone performing it is *displaying* that *p*. What is displayed need not be a belief of the utterer. An appropriate utterance will display that a house is on fire or that the fish are rising. Usually it will also be a sign that the utterer believes it, because in normal circumstances we can only reliably transmit information we believe to be veridical. But we shall see in 4.6 that speakers may be taken to display information which they do not properly understand. Now among self-conscious human beings (perhaps unlike animals) an agent will be able to go through a display for all sorts of reasons: to transmit information, to mislead, with no hope of transmitting belief, as a ritual, and so on: if he does so he may be liable to the penalties attending carelessness or deception. But for the two reasons mentioned, utterance of a sentence will not count, in and of itself, as a display. Only the utterance of a sentence with a definite *force*, which itself will need some indication, would count. Thus 'the cat is in the garden', said solemnly, in the right context, may betray signs that it is intended to be taken as a sign that the cat is in the garden, and that the utterer believes that it is. Said with other intonation, or in other contexts, it would not be so taken.

An utterance usually works as a sign of the truth only via the fact that it is a sign that the utterer believes that it is the truth, and is in some kind of position to know, or to have his belief taken seriously. So it is initially tempting to concentrate upon the central case, in which an agent is taken to display his own belief. The kind of conventional regularity which might then exist would be identified in terms of making an utterance with signs of basic assertive force. The conventions will be twofold; firstly, that the signs (such as tone of voice, or presence of the indicative mood) are signs of this assertive force; secondly, that the particular utterance, say of a sentence *S*, correlates with the belief that *p*:

It is a conventional regularity in group *G* that one utters *S* with indicators of assertive force, only if one intends to display belief that *p*.

Do such conventions exist? Someone uttering something will

standardly include an indication of the way his utterance is to be taken – as a command, or a sincere expression of belief, as a question, ironically, and so on. But it is not at all clear that such indicators are standardly indicators of his *intention* in uttering. For there is still that first kind of flexibility. I can assert something, or command it, with all kinds of intentions: I can command something with no intention of being obeyed, for example (an authority may issue something with all the conventional signs of command but with no intention of being obeyed, because it has to, or it's the done thing to do: "students shall not drink in public after examinations", etc.). These are not cases in which convention is flouted. Things are properly said or commanded, with the most diverse variety of intentions.

There has been a tendency to think of this as the end of the road for a convention-belief approach to meaning. By contrast, some writers have urged the "autonomy" of semantics, meaning that the only reliable truth about utterances is that they have meaning (words refer, or sentences have truth-conditions), and that there is no way of seeing such facts as reducible to the conventions and intentions current in a population. But this is defeatist: *something* about a population makes it true that their sentences and terms have the semantic properties they do – that they speak one language (in the sense of 1.4) and not another. And there is still plenty of room for finding what it is. For even if we abandon conventions concerning the intention with which a kind of performance is to be made, there are others.

I believe that the basic convention with which a linguistic group binds itself is that someone who makes an utterance with an appropriate indication of its force *may be taken* as having displayed that something is so. This does not mean that it is regularly sensible to take people to actually believe what they say. But it means that they become *liable* to being treated as having displayed that *p*. An utterance with an indication of assertive force is then an act which renders a speaker liable to a certain kind of consequence: it gives others in the group a right to regard him as a displayer of a fact; his intentions in so acting do not themselves influence this social liability. He may have spoken foolishly or carelessly or dishonestly or with the most devious and complicated intentions, but still be open to the same attitude from others. We can frame this kind of convention like this:

> It is a conventional regularity in group G that someone uttering S with an indication of assertive force, may be regarded as having displayed that p.[10]

I shall say that when this is true a group conforms to an S/p regard-display convention. Such conventions are defeasible; they can go out of force (for instance, if the context is one of play-acting, or the utterer is a child), but this is no argument that they do not normally hold.

There is no principled reason, that I can see, why a group should not conform to such a convention.[11] If they do, is it right to see them as speaking a language in which an utterance (or sentence) S says that p or means that p? My answer is: nearly. To appreciate how nearly, we need to draw in one more strand, which is the place of system and composition in language. Meanwhile, there is one comment to make about the difference between S/p regard-display conventions, and ones which try to link utterances with intentions, or beliefs.

S/p regard-display conventions are social. The regularity in a group defines a way in which they may regard someone who makes an utterance. This is not in itself a defect; on the contrary, it avoids the problem over the flexibility of intention, and accords with many features of the social nature of language, and particularly of the way in which a group is an authority over what has been said (see the end of the next section). Nevertheless, it opens up a problem. For suppose that with certain provisions we came to regard a system of S/p regard-display conventions as sufficient for a language. We would naturally be eager to see if it is necessary as well to lay claims to having defined just what it is for a group to have a language in which S means that p. But this would be presumptuous. For there has been no serious argument that a person could not (systemati-

---

[10] I have here identified utterances by the sentences they involve. This is a simplification. The rule for sentences containing indexical expressions like 'I', 'here', 'now' require recovering what was said not from the sentence, plus rules of language, but from the sentence, plus context, plus rules of language. So S/p regard-display conventions are an approximation, but one which does not affect the points of this chapter. See 9.1.

[11] And to similar ones for utterances with other forces.

cally) voice his thoughts *without* being a party to any such system of conventions. Still less has there been any argument that unless someone is party to such a system he cannot have thoughts, or thoughts of a certain complexity, at all. In other words, although membership of a group which abides by such conventions might be *enough* for speaking a language, it may also be *more* than is required if language use is also to be seen as somehow itself creating thought. I return to this at the end of the chapter. Meanwhile, what of system in language?

5. *The Place of System: Homeric Struggles*

We have moved some way from linguistic nominalism, and from the cycles of Grice's mechanism and higher-order intentions. But Grice's work has been subject to a fairly persistent kind of criticism which might embrace this approach too, and indeed any attempt to understand meaning in terms of some amalgam of intentions, conventions, or beliefs. The criticism I have in mind has two connected prongs. The first is that any such approach ignores or distorts the compositional character of language. The second is that because of this it fails to give any theory of how we come to understand a language – fails to address the question, which is dramatized in the radical interpreter, of how it is established that a sentence or word means any particular thing.

The first kind of objection is voiced by Mark Platts. He is talking about Grice's own theory, but the point, if good, would apply to any convention-belief theory of meaning:

On Grice's theory, sentence-meaning is defined in terms of the intentions with which the sentence is uttered, along perhaps with the response standardly secured in an audience by that utterance. Now, as an account of the meanings of sentences in natural languages this will not do for a simple reason: the majority of such sentences . . . will never be uttered . . . what then can Grice say about these unuttered sentences?

He goes on to point out that if Grice simply mentions the hypothetical intentions, with which these sentences would be uttered, he must admit some constraint upon what these would be, and continues:

Generally the constraint upon the hypothetical intentions with which a sentence can be uttered, and upon the audience's response to such an utterance, is precisely the meaning of the sentence . . . If this is correct, the attempt to define the meanings of unuttered sentences in terms of hypothetical intentions and responses is hopeless: for it presupposes a prior notion of sentence meaning.[12]

This is a forceful expression of the autonomy of semantics. But it is confused. It is certainly true that although a speaker will at any time only have understood a certain set of sentences which he has been exposed to, he is equipped to go on and understand new ones, and will standardly do so in just the way other speakers would as well. That is fortunate. But it is not some mysterious thing, the meaning of the new sentence which "constrains" the speakers and explains this identity in psychology. By analogy, consider numerical codes which interpret digits and sequences of them making up numerals in the standard arabic way as far as enormous numerals, and then go on to diverge (e.g. if there are more than 53 digits in a sequence, then it refers to $n + 7$, where n is the number assigned to it in the ordinary arabic interpretation). Something has brought it about that I conform to the ordinary interpretation of these numerals, rather than those they get in these bizarre codes. But it is not possible to explain that by saying, "well, that's what the numeral *refers* to". The point is precisely that it *could* refer to all kinds of different numbers. There is no such thing as its reference, in advance of a common habit of taking it to refer to one number rather than another. *Nothing* constrains a group to fall into one such habit rather than another except their training and the way they find it natural to take that training. This results in us, for example, using ANN (see chapter 1) rather than a possible Goodman-style bent competitor, which diverges at advanced points. The same is true of a fully-fledged language. It is our habit of taking new English sentences in definite ways which itself creates the fact that they have definite meanings. Every theorist recognizes that it is our trainings and our psychologies which explain those dispositions. And there is no reason why the dispositions should not themselves be S/p

---

[12] Mark Platts, *The Ways of Meaning*, pp. 89–90. Chomsky charges Lewis with the same problem: conventions are finite; language runs beyond them (*Rules and Representations*, p. 83).

regard-display habits with the status of conventions, or be describable in any other way a convention-belief theorist proposes.

How then should we understand the fact that our conventions apply to unusual or unspoken sentences, even when there is no common habit of taking them one way or another, since they are not commonly put forward at all? Obviously, we perceive in new sentences old words (or subsentential elements, such as inflexions) in familiar grammatical patterns. Now one of the merits of a convention-belief approach is that it concentrates upon the total act of communication – the whole desire or belief communicated by a whole sentence. (This need not necessarily be a grammatical sentence. An infant's single word may be intended as and be taken to communicate a belief or a command.) The presence of a word is subsidiary – a word is something whose presence is a meaning-determining feature of a sentence. If we like we can illustrate this in the figure of the radical interpreter. His initial hypothesis is that some native utterance communicates some whole judgement or command – that p. From a number of such hypotheses he can start to extract the features which recur and whose presence seems to be determining the interpretation to be given to any sentence; once this is done he can predict the way in which new sentences will be taken. A convention-belief approach will see the second stage as one of correlating recurrent *features* of utterances with recurrent *features* of beliefs which natives seem to be displaying. The presence of the word 'fish' may indicate, for instance, that the speaker is displaying a belief about fish. Once there is regularity in the features of sentences which indicate features of beliefs, there is the possibility of using those features in new combinations to display new beliefs, and we have the elasticity of language.[13]

Here, then, we have the place of system according to one

[13] See Jonathan Bennett, *Linguistic Behaviour*, §§65–7. Bennett's proposal is misunderstood by B. Harrison, *Introduction to the Philosophy of Language*, who thinks that it fails to protect a proper distinction between a complete utterance, and a meaning-determing feature of one. But the only argument that supports this is that the interpreter may go wrong on occasion. He may mistake one utterance with two words for two utterances of one word, each conveying a separate message, or vice versa. Of course, there is the possibility of such mistakes, but increased acquaintance with a language irons them out. There would be trouble for any approach to language if it could not say what the mistake amounts to, but the convention-intention approach does this nicely.

natural view of language. It too has a number of nice consequences. As foreshadowed in chapter 1, it suggests a strong
interdependence between syntax and semantics. That is,
identifying the words in a sentence and the recurrent patterns of
composition is secondary to understanding, in the sense that
isolating particular words and particular grammatical
structures in a sentence is itself a matter of charting the features
whereby its meaning is generated. When we say, for instance,
that the sentence 'the police apprehended him' contains neither
the word 'lice' not the word 'hen' we are denying that its
meaning is in any way a function of the difference in beliefs
(making their topic lice or hens, respectively) which these
words conventionally make. This is easier to see if we think of
spoken language, where a skill at hearing which words are said
only comes after practice at understanding total utterances,
and learning to hear recurrent features of them. This is why
foreign speech is initially mere noise.

6. *Deferential Conventions*

If a convention-belief approach thinks of the systematic nature
of language like this, does it suggest any elaboration or modification of the idea that meaning is a matter of S/p regard-display
conventions holding in a group? It gives us scope to play the
individual sentence against the system. That is, an individual
sentence might start to be used and regarded as though it
displayed that p, when its composition and the effect of its
elements on other sentences would lead us to predict that it
would be used to say that q. Sometimes this divergence can
become institutionalized, and then we might talk of different
meanings of the terms involved, or metaphorical or other uses of
expressions. Sometimes too the convention or habit in play in a
group seems less to relate to the *actual* use of a term, and more to
relate to the kind of authority they *defer* to, in order to determine
what was said. For instance, if I use an unfamiliar term there
may be no direct evidence of a convention that someone using it
is regarded as saying such-and-such; the convention is that
someone using it is taken to say whatever the Oxford Dictionary
or some other authority describes him as saying. If I tell you
that Fred went punting with a quant the only habit of interpre-

tation in my group that I can rely upon is that they use the dictionary to identify what I can be held to have said (that Fred went punting with a pole suitable for use in mud).

Such deferential conventions have come into prominence recently under the heading of the "linguistic division of labour" (Putnam's phrase). This means that a speaker may use a word in substantial ignorance of its real meaning. Nevertheless, he counts as saying that . . ., where the content is given by that meaning. To use the example mentioned earlier (3.3), if I make an assertion by saying the sentence 'Fred has arthritis', I count as saying something quite specific about Fred and the degeneration of his joints. And this is so even if I myself think vaguely that arthritis is any old rheumatic feeling, or pain in the leg, or whatever. As a group we defer to medical authority in defining what does and does not count as arthritis, and I will be held to have said whatever it tells me I said – thus, I spoke falsely if Fred has a vague rheumatism, but does not have the disease doctors know as arthritis. And this is so regardless of my own understanding of what I was doing. Using such a term is rather like picking up one of those government-stamped pieces of paper that some countries go in for. By writing on it, you might suddenly find that you had done something which you had little or no intention of doing, or did not understand yourself to be doing.[14]

Deferential conventions open up interesting possibilities. For it could be that a group institutionalizes two different ways of expressing beliefs. You may intend to communicate that p, and choose one form of words, with the consequence that you speak truly if one kind of state obtains. But you might choose another form of words – more official notepaper, as it were – and count as speaking truly only if some rather different decision procedure (like the experts' agreement) goes your way. The content of your remark, so judged, and the content of your understanding of it, will then be divergent. This needs careful application to problems surrounding our understanding of names (chapter 9).

Naturally there is room for all the different elements to clash.

[14] I intend this analogy quite closely. S/p regard-display conventions have a normative element. They define how a group *may* regard someone. Saying something is like performing an act with legal consequences.

The intention of the utterer, the meaning of his remark as predictable from its methods of composition coupled with the way the group regards the utterances with the same elements, and the meaning as it is or would be certified by conventionally deferred-to authority, can all be different. Hence, in particular, the juristic art of interpreting statutes, whose words so often belie the intentions of those framing them. Those who framed the rule prohibiting spilling of blood on the streets of Bologna were embarrassed to find a surgeon charged with the offence; a patriotic British statute prohibiting residents in an alien country from inheriting estates, passed during the Second World War, was not intended to cover British prisoners-of-war temporarily residing in Germany. One advantage of the convention-belief approach to meaning is that it enables us to appreciate such difficulties as both understandable, and inherent in the use of a systematic language. That is, the difficulties do not only arise because of some primitive faith in a fixed "real" meaning of a term or utterance standing opposed to ordinary usage of it; they do not only arise if we forget that we are the masters of our own language. They arise because whatever we intend to display, we cannot always remember the deposit of usage which will allow our words to be taken to display something else. And then too there is scope for different attitudes to different elements of the jungle (whether etymology is relevant to identifying what a term should now be taken to mean, for instance): the stuff of law-courts and correspondence columns. The philosopher's contribution to all this is to show that we all stand on the same raft of conventions and higher-order conventions; that these count as in force only ultimately because we have habits of taking each other in definite ways; and that there is unlikely to be just one "right" way of regarding the construction of the raft. (The other contribution is that there is no principled way for meaning to stand fixed when beliefs change, and we see more of this in the next chapter.)

The natural way to incorporate this into the results of the last section is to talk of a suitably vague system of conventions:

(RD)   A sentence S means that p in the language of group G if it is a regularity, or the consequence of a system of regularities, with the status of a conven-

tion that one who utters S with basic assertive
force may be regarded as having displayed that p.

A language becomes in effect, a *system* of S/p regard-display
conventions. Of course, although for simplicity I have concentrated upon display of belief, a similar approach would also
cover such things as commands and questions. A sentence
would be a command to bring it about that p if there were the
same type of conventional regularity that someone uttering it
with basic imperative force might be regarded as having commanded that p, and so on for other forces.

In his famous inaugural lecture in 1969 Professor Strawson
identified two sides in what he called a Homeric struggle in the
theory of meaning.[15] One side sought to develop a convention-
belief approach to language. The other side believed that this
was unnecessary or even misguided, and hoped instead to
illuminate meaning by developing formal semantics for natural
languages and by showing (through the person of the radical
interpreter) how a formally described language can be
attributed to a group. Strawson himself hinted that the cause of
hostilities was obscure, although many writers over the last
decade have been eager to join one side and belittle the other.
By now I hope to have deflected most of the popular objections
to a convention-belief approach: these have included the
alleged difficulty over composition and the unuttered sentence,
the unattractive complexities of Grice's own regress, the realization that meaning sits some distance apart from the intentions of an utterer, the belief that all conventions have to be
overt, and the charge that the approach yields no theory of how
we come to know about the meanings of remarks – no procedure
for the radical understander. The answer to this last charge
emerges from the place of system: to understand a language
demands coming to know what whole utterances mean, and to
be sensitive enough to how the meaning arises to be able to
predict the way new ones should be taken.

In so far as the other side in Strawson's Homeric struggle
have offered any account of what makes it true that utterances
mean what they do, or that words refer and sentences are true or
false in various circumstances, they have relied upon the right

[15] P. F. Strawson, 'Meaning and Truth', in his *Logico-Linguistic Papers*.

method for the radical interpreter. The idea is that if his ideal way (W*) of attributing a language to a population results in his regarding them as speaking one in which S means that p, then it is true that S means that p. The meat of the proposal (which is otherwise purely programmatic) comes when W* is better described, and in particular if the relation between S and p which it certifies can be described in terms which avoid the notion of meaning. Thus, following Davidson, many theorists favour a formula which substitutes truth for meaning:

(W*L)   A sentence S means that p in the language of group G if W* would result in a radical interpreter assigning to G an abstract language whose systematic semantic description yields a theorem stating that S is true if and only if p.[16]

This is just a rough outline, and the approach demands many subtleties. I discuss it much further in chapter 8. Meanwhile it is important to point out that as a focus for a Homeric struggle the two offerings RD and W*L suffer from a major defect. This is that they are perfectly compatible. Both will be true provided that W* and the systematic description mentioned in W*L pick out those S/p pairings of which the regard-display conventions described in RD hold. And why should they not? Indeed, why mustn't it be regarded as an essential condition on the adequacy of W* that it should do just this? The upshot is that although there is much more to say about particular proposals for filling out each analysis, there is no reason to see them as essentially in opposition. They offer no invitation to philosophers to form rival schools (philosophers, however, need few such invitations).

7. *Thought Again*

It is pleasant to be a member of a group with an established system of regard-display conventions; pleasant no doubt to be a member of a group which a radical interpreter (2.4) regards as making utterances with definite content (at least if he is right).

[16] Davidson himself does not favour the idea that any such formula *analyses* the notion of meaning ('Radical Interpretation', pp. 324–5). But it clarifies or elucidates or somehow makes progress in understanding the notion.

But unless we can get a fuller view than this, it makes it seem as though mastery of a language is merely a matter of being able to transmit information, and to prompt action, and to become receptive to the transmissions of others. And this does not touch the question of whether there is any more intimate connection between language and thought – in the limit, whether having the mastery of a language creates the capacity to think, or at least to think at a certain degree of complexity.

In chapter 2 we met the difficulty of understanding what it is to take words, or any other symbolic elements such as images, in a given way. The vague answer is that it is to *use* them. So suppose someone argued: a creature is not thinking of (say) an absent state of affairs unless it has something present to mind *and* takes that thing in a definite way; its so taking the thing is a matter of how it uses it; e.g. what it is disposed to do in the light of its other desires or beliefs. For example, a non-linguistic being might start to think of food. Its doing this would demand its having some counter – an image, perhaps – present to mind, and taking that image in a definite way. This might be, for instance, starting to hunt for food because of it, or even starting to salivate or change physiologically because of it. If this counts as "using" its mental modification in the right way, then there seems to be no reason why only elements of a language, with a conventionally cemented regularity of use, should be given uses by individual animals.

In fact, our ordinary unphilosophical opinion allows thoughts to pre-linguistic and non-linguistic creatures. Babies and animals plan, believe, and anticipate; they may think of various events and states of affairs, and have a variety of attitudes or emotions towards what they think of. At least our best, and often our only, way of describing their doing is to take up this "intentional stance" towards them – that is, describe them in terms of their thoughts and purposes. Now it is a mistake to infer, from the fact that *we* properly and perhaps inevitably invest their doings with such significance, the conclusion that *they* actually invest some elements with significance, taking it to represent absent states of affairs, for example. At least, this is not a mistake only if the fact that we find it appropriate, useful, or even inevitable to describe a thing as thinking, planning, regretting, etc. is sufficient to show that it is *true* that it is doing these things. And that move requires a particular theory of truth (a form of pragmatic theory – see chapter 7). As far as the presence of thought or understanding goes, the danger in the approach is obvious. Even if we decided that the well-tuned interpreter may legitimately describe an animal or a system which is doing various things as thinking about (say) absent states of affairs, he can only do this if he himself can think about those absent states of affairs (in order to relate the original subject to them). What makes it true that he can do this? If the only kind of answer is that a second-order interpreter could legitimately see him as doing so we have a useless postponement or regress – a disappearance theory of mind. Problems of mental power are endlessly shuffled back onto what would or would not be said by an equally or more powerful mind, itself capable of doing all the thinking which is puzzling. This is the dog-leg of chapter 2, again.

In recent years this problem has flared in disputes over the thinking of machines. One school, headed by Daniel Dennett,[17] argues that it is legitimate to take up the intentional stance which describes such machines as thinking (planning, believing) where the content of the thoughts, plans, etc. might be 'I must get my queen out early' etc. Often such machines are only readily describable as the embodiment of a programme which itself needs intentional description (it believes that the best way to achieve a knight and rook ending is . . .). Because a computer is legitimately described in these terms, it is in fact thinking, and conclusions can be drawn about other thinkers, such as ourselves. Another view, taken for instance by John Searle,[18] is that the transition is illegitimate. For any sufficiently complex system yielding some output from a given input can be described, by us, as thinking, if *we* interpret the output (noises, visual displays, whatever) in various ways, but it will not follow that it *is* thinking. Searle's favourite examples include massive arrays of beer cans arranged so that some input (e.g. striking some of them in a certain way) brings about some definite output (e.g. some system of noises or rearrangement or whatever). If the array is delicate and complex, *we* might describe

---

[17] 'Intentional Systems', in *Brainstorms*.
[18] 'Minds, Brains and Programs', Dennett and Hofstadter (1981). 'The Myths of the Computer', *New York Review of Books* (1982).

the input (I asked it what to do with the pawn on queen 4) and the output (it said that I should sacrifice it) *as though* the field full of beer cans is thinking about a chess problem. But that is no argument that it is doing so. Its elements have 'horizontal' connections with each other, but no 'vertical' connections to chess. We impose a semantics, taking its elements to represent chess situations, bits of the world, states of affairs, etc. But *it* takes them in no way at all (compare 2.3 above).

Searle is, in my view, right about this. It leaves it most unclear, however, what does make the difference. I suspect that most of us would think that it is not only legitimate in Dennett's sense, but actually true, that a pre-linguistic baby can think of absent states of affairs, and similarly perhaps for some animals. And we ought to remember that there is no coherent story of how mastery of a language should enable a being to pull off the trick of conceiving of things which without it he could not. For example, if a being lacked the capacity to take a present image or other element to signify a past state of affairs, then this would seem to be a simple restriction on what he can take words to mean, and the sort of language he can learn. Learning to talk, for such a being, would not include learning to talk about the past. For there is a pronounced pull towards seeing a language as secondary to our intentional powers, and not itself explaining them. Of course, if that is right, it is no objection to the convention-belief description of language that it fails to show how language can explain such capacities.

This is one side of the argument. But there is another. Perhaps we have been concentrating upon too big a quarry – no less than a total understanding of our powers of thought. If we take local examples, the interplay between learning to understand and think in various ways, and learning a language, is inextricably close. There is no distinction between mastering physics, and mastering some language in which to express physical laws and concepts. There is no distinction between learning to discriminate finely between various modes of taste, colour, or feeling, and learning a vocabulary with which to express the differences. People who can understand mathematics can use the notations; people who cannot *say* (if only to themselves) what the answers are do not know what they are. A man may be a mute inglorious Milton, or Einstein, just because he never gets around to writing it down or saying what he knows; but he cannot be one, if, were he to try to express what he knows, nothing would happen.

A useful example might be the appreciation of number. Perhaps it is plausible to suggest that a creature with no capacity to use a numeral notation simply could not believe or understand that there are 25 matches on the table (as opposed to 26 or 17). The notation is necessary for the thought. Why might this be? Well, counting is a procedure which requires *some* kind of tally – a process of ticking off something against each element of the set counted. And we might suggest that you cannot appreciate the *result* of the procedure unless you can appreciate the procedure itself by operating it, or being able to operate some equivalent system. So the argument is that understanding the number of the set requires understanding the kind of procedure which certifies it; understanding this requires ability to operate or appreciate the operation of counting procedures; doing that requires being able to take *some* action (the saying of '5', making another notch in a stick, tying a knot in a rope, etc.) as having a certain significance (it is made to locate how many things we have found so far). And that is, in essence, to be using a numeral notation.

If this sketchy argument were generalized, it might suggest an interdependence of the following kind between language and thought. To think and understand that something is the case often involves an awareness of procedures for certifying that it is the case, or more generally for placing its truth in a context of other states of affairs. But these procedures and connections need things to mark where we are – what has been done or remains to be done, what has been established and what has not. It is as though there is no thought without the possibility of movement of thought, and movement of thought needs not so much a linguistic vehicle (inviting the question: why not some other sort?) as a structured map, telling us where we are. But even if this is right, there is no reason to say that the counters telling us where we are must be socially shared elements of a system of regard-display conventions. A man might invent his own way of counting, and use it in complete isolation. And in fact there are cases of people with severe handicaps who cannot hear or use elements of a public language, but who are discovered to have their own private way of expressing themselves.

The relevance of language to thought may be tested by considering the possibility of a totally unstructured language. Suppose a long list of unstructured sounds, and a long list of beliefs or thoughts of some complexity – that Fred is asleep, that there are 25 matches on the table . . . If a group could take the one as *a first language* to express the others, then it will be very tempting to suppose that the competence with the language is simply irrelevant to the mental power enabling them to do the thinking. But is this a possibility? A radical interpreter is unlikely to certify that this is the language of any group, since his favourite device of looking for the systematic effects of subsentential elements draws a blank. He may find, for instance, that a certain noise is made and apparently approved of in some circumstance. But it is a long step from that to supposing that the noise expressed the thought that this circumstance obtains. For circumstances exhibit many things with many features, and it needs work to find out which ones matter to the speakers (is it Fred being asleep, or Fred not being on the farm, or Fred snoring . . . which interests them?) The difficulty is that since their utterances have no structure, there is nothing to work *on* – no feature which can reliably be correlated with the presence of Fred or the feature that something is asleep.

Still, perhaps this is just an interpreter's problem. Can we find a principled reason why speakers, if they can have pre-linguistic beliefs of the right type, could not generate habits and conventions whereby these atomistic sounds display them? It is tempting to suppose that a learner would face the same problem of selection as the interpreter, so that he would never have reason to suppose a given sound to be displaying the belief that *p* as opposed to any of an indefinite number of possible surrounding beliefs. But perhaps the population share the same *feature space*: they naturally carve things in a given way, notice and wish to communicate one aspect of things rather than another. If a particular situation naturally causes a member of this group to form a particular belief and to wish to display it and to interpret others as so wishing, then an utterance made with apparent assertive force will be taken by the learner to be displaying that belief and no other.

However, such a language, if not an *a priori* impossibility, is at least markedly unstable, in the sense that the capacities the population must have, in order to use it as suggested, are the very ones which would naturally bring it about that they do something better. For they must be capable of selecting particular features of situations – say the fact that there are 25 things in a group, or that something is asleep – for attention and comment. But *selecting* such a feature means being capable of recognizing when it recurs, and recognizing the similarity between two different situations in which it recurs (Fred being asleep and John being asleep; 25 matches or 25 children). So the speakers are, as it were, already equipped to produce a feature of speech to correlate with the recurrent feature which they can notice. It would be inexplicable if they did not do this – so much so that we would naturally deny that a system of sounds which had not done it actually expressed beliefs referring to that very feature. If they think in terms of particular things and features, they would naturally need elements of utterances to indicate which things and which features make up their topic.

So a genuinely expressive but unstructured language is intrinsically unstable. Does this settle whether thoughts and beliefs can be understood in the absence of a structured means of expression? Certainly I see no argument that the means must be a fully-fledged language, in anything like the sense of a conventionally fixed system of regard-display habits. And unless we can broaden the tentative suggestion I sketched, over what might be necessary to appreciate the truths arrived at by counting, the assertion that thoughts require language seems to be a promise rather than a result. The way forward would require a convincing description of ways in which acquiring a language *creates* understanding, and this philosophers have not so far provided.

There is of course very much more to be said about this. But provided the reader appreciates the delicacy of the issues, it may be left in order to turn to the third corner of the original triangle: the world, and the way our language, and we ourselves in thought, relate to it.

Notes to Chapter 4

4.1   "... the complexities which abound in the literature ..."
A basic set of readings would include:

H. P. Grice, 'Meaning', *Philosophical Review* (1957).
— 'Utterer's Meaning and Intentions', *Philosophical Review* (1969).
P. Ziff, 'On H. P. Grice's Account of Meaning', *Analysis* (1967).
J. Searle, 'Meaning and Speech Acts', *Philosophical Review* (1962).
— *Speech Acts*, ch. 2.
P. F. Strawson, 'Intention and Convention in Speech Acts', *Philosophical Review* (1964).
S. Schiffer, *Meaning*.
J. F. Bennett, *Linguistic Behaviour*.

But my experience is that the literature is unnecessarily difficult, for the reasons stated in the text.

4.3   "... the autonomy of semantics ..."
This is another of those issues where strong passions soon conceal the issues. Indeed, the autonomy of meaning has become one of the great issues in structuralist and post-structuralist theories of literary criticism. Roughly, orthodox literary critics are supposed to refer back to the intentions of an author, as revealed by their writings; noticing that language is a conventional system, their successors urge that the text itself is an object of study, with no reference at all to the intentions or lack of them which the author may have had. This is not a new idea in literary criticism, but it is a fashionable one. It is expressed in the view that writing (where there is no "authorial presence") is as fundamental a phenomenon in the use of language as is speech – which most philosophers of language have taken as primary. But the debate has nothing essential to do with auditory or written modes of communication, nor with the relative permanence of signal involved in writing versus the transitory signal of speech. It is really a debate about the authority of the speaker versus the independence which his signs have, given their place in public and conventional systems of communication. Unfortunately the issue seems to be taken, by writers following Jacques Derrida, as a licence to take the text in a purely syntactic way, and neglect the conventionally fixed semantic properties of the words – the properties which, whatever else is true of the author and his intentions are ones which explain why he put them down. A rather bemusing debate on this is:

J. Derrida, 'Signature, Event, Context', *Glyph* (1977).
J. Searle, 'Reiterating the Differences', *Glyph* (1977).

Rather more austere treatments of force and convention include:

M. Davies, *Meaning, Quantification, Necessity*, ch. 1.

C. Peacocke, 'Truth Definitions and Actual Languages', in Evans and McDowell (1975).

J. McDowell, 'Meaning, Communication, and Knowledge', in van Straaten (1980).

PART II

LANGUAGE AND THE WORLD

CHAPTER 5

Realism and Variations

The one discovers objects as they really stand in nature, without addition or diminution: the other has a productive faculty, and gilding or staining all natural objects with the colours, borrowed from internal sentiment, raises in a manner a new creation.

David Hume, Appendix 1 of the *Enquiry Concerning the Principles of Morals.*

1. *Oppositions to Realism*

Hume's description of the different offices of reason and taste sets a challenge. How do we tell when we are discovering objects "as they really stand in nature", and when we are doing some other thing, such as projecting onto them our own subjective sentiments? Which side of this divide do we fall on when we describe objects as good or bad, nice or nasty, hot or cold, red or blue, square or round? Echoing Hume the scientist Heinrich Hertz says that "the rigour of science requires that we distinguish well the undraped figure of nature itself from the gay-coloured vesture with which we clothe it at our pleasure".[1] How do we know where to draw this distinction, or what counts as an argument for putting a given saying on one side or the other? This is the issue between realists and their opponents. It takes a bewildering variety of forms, for philosophers have seen it very differently. Realists are contrasted with a variety of alleged opponents: reductionists, idealists, instrumentalists, pragmatists, verificationists, internalists, neo-Wittgensteinian neutralists, and no doubt others. They also form obscure alliances with, and hostilities towards, various views about truth: correspondence, coherence, pragmatic, redundancy, semantic, theories. To swim at all in this swirl of cross-currents we need a better lifeline than any which these mysterious labels provide.

My strategy will be to follow through a variety of possible

[1] Quoted in van Fraassen, *The Scientific Image*, p. 6.

attitudes to some particular area of commitments. This will give us a sense of the options *locally*. But by coming to appreciate local issues, arising, say, in the philosophy of value, or of mathematics, we can work our way into more general problems of realism and truth, and get a sense of why the *global* issues fall out as they do. I prefer this to a top-down strategy, which would approach highly general issues of the nature of truth first, and then apply the results to particular cases, because the general issues are more or less unintelligible unless given particular applications.

When discussing meaning in 2.1 I introduced the possibility of a perspective from which facts about meaning appeared utterly mysterious – a perspective from which the world could not contain any such facts. Similar doubts pepper the whole of philosophy. Hume could not see what kind of thing a causal connection between distinct events could be; mathematical, moral, and aesthetic facts seem suspicious to many people; semantic, psychological, conditional facts invite scepticism, and so on. Once such doubts are felt – motivated in whatever way – a number of attitudes are possible. We might *reject* the whole area, advocating that people no longer think or speak in the terms which seem problematic. Or, we might seek to give a *reductive analysis* of it, advocating that the problematic commitments be put in other terms, and claiming that when this is done the problems disappear. We can try to see the commitments not as beliefs with *truth-conditions* but as expressions of other sorts. We can query whether the commitments are *mind-dependent* – not really describing a mind-independent reality at all, but as in some sense creating the reality they describe. And at each choice-point there will be a jumble of issues and of suggestions about what the debate hinges upon. In particular there can be the attitude which I christen *quietism* or *dismissive neutralism*, which urges that at some particular point the debate is not a real one, and that we are only offered, for instance, metaphors and images from which we can profit as we please. Quietism is a relative newcomer to the philosophical world, owing much of its inspiration to the positivist mistrust of metaphysics, and to the belief of the later Wittgenstein that such problems required therapy rather than solution.

Views about truth will be particularly relevant where we

discuss whether some commitment is best regarded as a belief with a truth-condition, or in some other light. For this contrast seems to hinge upon our view of what it is for a commitment to have a truth-condition, and it is here that the various lights in which truth is put – correspondence, coherence, and so on – affect the issue. Thus, to take a simple example, moral commitments are often thought of as not really beliefs, but as more like attitudes, emotions, or prescriptions: this contrast in turn may look very different if we think of beliefs in pragmatic or instrumental terms rather than in terms of correspondence with facts.

Putting together the positions I have suggested we then get the map illustrated in Fig. 4. But, as I have said, the issue need not be clear-cut at any of these choice-points: there will be different suggestions as to what the decision hinges upon, and, from the quietist, the general disenchantment with discussing the issue at all. Quietism is currently expressed by denials that there is a "god's-eye view" or an "external" or "Archimedean" point from which we can discover whether some commitment is, as it were, describing the undraped figure of nature or imposing clothing. Perhaps we either accept the sayings in a given area, and "from that standpoint" suppose that they describe reality, or we do not accept them, and of course think that they do not. In other words, an overall quietist is only interested in the first choice-point, and ignores the rest. We shall see that this is unduly short-winded. I shall now introduce the various options at greater length.

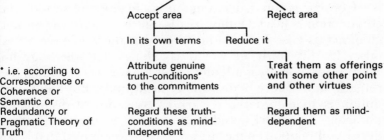

* i.e. according to Correspondence or Coherence or Semantic or Redundancy or Pragmatic Theory of Truth

Fig. 4

2. *Rejection*

We might want to reject a given commitment within an area without rejecting the whole area. We do not accept that $2 + 2 = 5$, but we do, of course, accept many beliefs about numbers. Rejecting a whole kind of commitments is more sweeping. Until relatively recently it seemed to raise few problems. If a remark in some area (e.g. a moral remark) is meaningful it must have a definite content. If it does, either things are as it says they are, and it is true, or they are not, and it is false. If it does not have a definite content it is meaningless, or at least vague and defective on that score. How is there any room for subtlety here?

The only subtleties arise because the neat division between attributing a definite, false, content to a remark and rejecting it in some other way is, in practice, impossible to rely upon. I can introduce the problems this causes with a simple example.[2] Consider the use of the term 'Kraut' as a term of contempt for Germans. If someone describes Franz as a Kraut, I want to reject his remark. Do I say it is *meaningless*? Hardly. I know what I am being asked to think, and it is because I know this that I find the remark offensive. Is the remark *false*? We usually accept an equivalence between 'it is false that p' and 'it is true that not-p'. But I do not want to *say* that it is true that Franz is not a Kraut. That is the remark made by someone who has the contemptuous attitude towards Germans, but believes that Franz is not a German. So I do not want to say that on two counts. So should I say that the remark is true or even half-true? Uncomfortable, again.

One theory would be that the remark is a conjunction: 'Franz is a German *and* on that account he is a fit object of derision.' A conjunction is false if either part is. Since I regard the second conjunct as false I should maintain that the whole remark is false. In this spirit we would say things like 'there are no Krauts', or 'nobody is a Kraut'. This is a way of construing the remark, and thence of disowning the attitude. But a different option is to regard the remark as true, but to disown the phrasing. A parallel would be 'Franz is a *German*' said with a derisive intonation on the last word. Here we suppose that what

[2] In the nature of the case, the following example employs offensive terms with which I do not associate myself.

was strictly said was true but reject the overtone. The convention would be that you only put beliefs about Germans using that overtone (or the derisory word) if you have the contemptuous attitude. If this is the right account then it is in fact true that there are lots of Krauts (although I would not put it that way myself).

Each proposal is "semantically coherent": in other words, a population could properly speak a language L_1 in which the first analysis is right, and the remark is false, or L_2, in which the second is right, and the remark is rejected, although what it strictly says is true. Is there bound to be a fact determining whether English operates like L_1 or L_2? If not, then there is no uniquely right way of expressing rejection of the utterance. Since we are left with a slight sense of discomfort with either of the sharp options, perhaps there is this indeterminacy. The vocabulary belongs to people who accept a certain attitude – that being a German is enough to make someone a fit object of derision. Rejecting the attitude we reject the vocabulary. But if the way the attitude is expressed is indeterminate, it will also be indeterminate whether remarks made by people using it are true or false. In other words, people using a certain vocabulary tend to have clusters of belief, some true and some not, or clusters of attitudes, some acceptable and some not, and tendencies to favour certain inferences, some reliable and some not. But there may be no conventions determining how many of these habits we are endorsing by accepting some remark as true, nor how many we are rejecting by regarding it as false. The overall rejected theory may have distributed its content in no very secure way over the various sentences involved. It will then be unsettled how to express the rejection.

The problem arises in more serious areas. In writing the history of science (or any other body of thought) we want to express what was right and wrong about particular doctrines. But the vocabulary people had may offer no particular way of doing this. Terms will have been used in the context of clusters of beliefs, attitudes, habits of reasoning and inference. Some of these we will accept, and others we will reject. But how could the people have formed conventions determining that some particular thing is the *right* thing to say, in the face of *unforeseen* disruptions of beliefs, attitudes, and habits? There is no cause to worry whether we are speaking L_1 or L_2 just so long as the views and attitudes remain intact. But when they are disrupted, then from the later standpoint it may be indeterminate *which* sayings, expressed in the earlier vocabulary, can be thought of as true, and which as false. For instance, Newtonian mass was a concept central to classical physical theory, and integral to the enormous success and near-truth (as we now see it) of that theory. Unfortunately amongst the things believed in that theory is that the mass of an object is quite independent of its velocity – its rest mass and moving mass are always identical. When this thesis is abandoned, and we consider other sayings of classical physics, such as 'force applied is proportional to mass times change in velocity', it is simplistic to regard them either as definitely true, or as definitely false. They were part of a theory or overall web of belief which involved false views; how much of the falsity is to be read into an individual saying is often indeterminate. The reason we can put up with this indeterminacy is *not* that in any sense we cannot express what the old theory held. We can express it very easily, in our own terms, just as we can say what people think when they describe Germans as Krauts. We do not have to share the views and attitudes in order to know what they are. What we cannot easily or determinately do is describe things in *their* terms (are there or are there not Krauts?) because there is *no unique way* in which the rejected views can be pinned onto individual sayings, and insulated from others. We cannot neatly partition truth and falsity, sentence by sentence, across their individual sayings.

The point deserves attention whenever we consider how to describe our distance from other theories, or webs of views and attitudes. Was there such a stuff as phlogiston? Can a Marxist believe in human rights? Using our terms we can distinguish what was true and false in the beliefs held by phlogiston theorists. Using his scheme of values the Marxist can say what is acceptable and what not so in the (bourgeois) conception of rights. But it is quite hopeless to try to express that distance by allowing that individual theses of the rejected theories express uncontaminated truths, or uncontaminated falsities. That requires *using* the old vocabulary (there are or are not *Krauts*; are or are not human *rights*), and this is something which, from the opposed point of view, it will be undesirable to do.

There is a temperament which would dismiss this as an unfortunate product of the vagueness of ordinary thought, contrasted with some ideal language with the precision to give every remark definite, indubitable conditions of truth and falsity. If we met this ideal, then whatever the changes in belief and attitude, we could always look back and attribute definite truth or falsity to each individual saying in the old terms. But how could such an ideal language be speakable? The significance of remarks has to be one which we are capable of giving them. That capacity is a function of our beliefs, attitudes, of the things we have been exposed to and the habits of thought, reasoning, and inference in which we indulge. We cannot possibly foresee how these may be improved, or what strange possibilities will disrupt them. When they are changed, previous usages will pull in different ways, and there is no reason to expect previous sentences to express individual propositions, isolatable as truths or falsities in the new scheme of thought. To paraphrase Wittgenstein, when we start to abandon a way of thought, the lights do not go out one by one, but darkness falls gradually over the whole.

3. *Reduction*

A different attitude to a theory, which yet shades into outright rejection of it, is that its theses can be accepted, but their content can be expressed in other ways, using a different kind of vocabulary. Thus we might find some particular set of terms awkward or puzzling in various ways; the demand becomes that we can give an "account" – an analysis, or reduction, or reinterpretation – of the things said using them. The analysis supposedly reveals the true or proper content of remarks in the area. For example, if moral commitments appear particularly puzzling, attempts might be made to reinterpret them in some other terms: perhaps 'X is something which ought to be done' means the same as 'X will produce more happiness than any alternative'. The moral vocabulary would then turn out to be just a different way of putting ordinary, natural, or psychological truths. In that case it would import no particular problems of its own – such as ones of what kind of thing moral facts can be, of how we can know about them, or how they relate to underlying natural facts, and so on. If the moral vocabulary demanded a distinct type of moral fact these questions would arise, but since, according to the analysis, it does not, they resolve themselves. We know about what ought to be done in whatever way we know about the creation of happiness, since it is a proposition about this which gives the real content of the moral statement.

Famous positions in philosophy which are based on the claim that analyses and reductions are possible include:

Phenomenalism:	the analysis of propositions about external reality into ones about actual and possible experiences;
Positivism:	the analysis of propositions about theoretical entities into ones about regularities in experience;
Behaviourism:	the analysis of propositions about mental states into ones about dispositions to behaviour;
Logicism:	the analysis of propositions about numbers into truths of (elementary) logic, thought of as describing no especial, abstract, subject-matter;
Naturalism:	the position in ethics already described.

And there are many other local analyses – of propositions about causation into ones merely describing successions of events, of ones about the meanings of terms into ones about peoples' intentions when they use the terms, and so on. Indeed, so many philosophical problems centre around the possibility and desirability of providing analyses of various kinds that in the early part of this century the philosopher's role became identified with this (*analytical* philosophy). Naturally in an empiricist and verificationist time attempts are made to reveal in terms especially close to experience the true content of statements which appear to concern esoteric subjects. The idea behind the verification principle is that the real meaning of any assertion can be found by analysing the difference in sense-experience which its truth would make.

The motivation for reductive analyses is based on a contrast. The commitments expressed in some original vocabulary (the

A-vocabulary, or A-commitments) must be felt to introduce some apparent puzzle, either of meaning, or of epistemology, or of metaphysics, not introduced by statements made in the analysing, B-vocabulary. An analysis represents a piece of imperialism on behalf of the concepts expressed in B-terms, and will be motivated if the A-statements are in some particular way puzzling, or if there is a background view that everything which it is possible to say truly can be said in B-terms. If only we did not have the additional A-commitments, the puzzles would go: the solution is to propose that in the relevant sense we do not have them – they are not additional, because their true content can be revealed entirely in B-terms. Examples on a local scale, suggesting the kind of relief which reductive analysis can bring, are quite persuasive. Suppose I tell you that Henry's prestige is enormous. Suppose that you are attached to an ontological doctrine – roughly that everything which exists has a place in space and time, and has scientifically measurable properties of weight, charge, velocity, etc. Then Henry's prestige seems an odd kind of object: you cannot put it into a bucket or weigh it or measure it – what kind of *thing* is it? Your problem is removed by analysing the original A-remark so as to remove reference to this mysterious thing: it means nothing different from this B-remark: other people admire Henry enormously. If your world-view allows for this kind of fact, then there is nothing further to jib at in talking of prestige. Notice of course that other problems might still remain – problems with the kind of statement to which the original was reduced. Your world-view might make it difficult to accommodate people admiring one another; in which case you have to continue the analysis until you find statements which you can put up with. B-statements might need reduction to C . . . W which is respectable.

In itself the claim that one statement has the same content as another is quite symmetrical: this suggests that the problems affecting the first must also affect the second. But, as the example about prestige shows, this is not inevitable. The problem might arise only because of a feature of the original which is not shared by the analysing statement. In this example the feature was the *apparent* reference to a non-physical thing. Once it is accepted that this feature is not essential, since the same content can be expressed without it, the problem resolves itself. Usually, however, it is not so obvious whether the analysis does more than draw other statements into the problematic class. For instance, a *counterfactual* analysis of causal remarks is quite attractive: to say that X causes Y is, perhaps, to say something like 'if X had not happened, and other things had been the same, Y would not have happened'. But even if this equation works, its significance is debatable. What is the contrast which motivates such a reduction? What problem of meaning, epistemology, or metaphysics, does the initial statement have, which is removed if we can see its content as the same as that of the second? Or does the counterfactual come to seem just as problematic, in terms of what makes it true or what shows it to be true, as the original causal statement? A prominent example of this difficulty is the equation of arithmetical with set-theoretical remarks. Propositions about numbers may be reduced to propositions about sets in various ways. But even if one of these is taken to really give us the meaning of the original arithmetical statements, the question is whether sets then take on a good deal of the mystery of numbers, posing substantially the same problems of existence, mind-independence, and of knowledge and logic, which originally make arithmetical statements into desirable objects of analysis.

So for a successful reduction we need an A-discourse which poses some problem, a B-vocabulary used to say things which do not pose this problem, and an equation between any propositions expressed in the first and some set of judgements expressed in the second. Now, however, we can see that there can be considerable tension between the disappearance of the problem, and the equation of meaning. If the original problem is a substantive or persistent one, then the fact that A-statements are subject to it *by itself* suggests that we take them to mean something different from the B-statements, so that the equation fails. This is a kind of Catch 22: if the reduction is really well motivated, then it cannot be true. For example, we have given our moral vocabulary a meaning which results in moral statements posing characteristic problems of proof or verification, of truth and objectivity. For this very reason, we might urge, they cannot be identical in meaning with other statements which do not pose these problems. Moralizing is a specific activity, so how could these other statements give us a non-moral way of doing it? The reply has to be that the problems prompting the reductions are in some sense only apparent – in other words, they arise only because we misapprehend the true content of A-statements. When these are seen for what they are – in B-terms – the temptation to puzzle over the problems disappears (as with prestige). However, this reply in turn raises a query: what right has anyone to separate out the reduced content as the only true content of the original, if our practices, including our doubts, problems of verification and proof, and so on, all suggest that we take those statements to have a further or different content?

A sharp formulation of this problem comes with the classical "paradox of analysis". Consider as an example the proposal that 'X ought to be done' means the same as 'X would bring about more happiness than any alternative'. Now it is quite intelligible to describe someone as wondering, or doubting, or thinking, whether all and only things which ought to be done would bring about more happiness than any alternative. Indeed, faced with the proposal the first thing to do is exactly to try the thought-experiment of finding a counterexample – a thing which satisfies the one concept, but not the other. But how is this possible, if the analysis is correct? If the two notions just mean the same, then it would seem that the doubt or wonderment can have no content – it would be the same as doubting whether all and only things which ought to be done ought to be done, or whether all and only things which bring about more happiness than any alternative bring about more happiness than any alternative. The paradox (which has other forms) gives rise to quite difficult technical problems, some of which I discuss under the general heading of difficulties over substitution of synonyms for one another, in 9.5. Here it illustrates the general point, that frequently one set of terms is *given* a sufficiently different role by us, as witnessed by our beliefs, doubts, queries, etc., for the claim that it has the same role as some reducing set of terms to seem implausible from the beginning. A common aspect of this is an asymmetry in the way we regard A-truths and B-truths, in respect of explanation and evidence. Frequently the B-truths (e.g. about sense experience, or behaviour, or non-moral states of affairs) are regarded as evidence for the A's but not vice versa. This asymmetry is incompatible with the view that the content of the A-statements is identical with that of some suitable set of B-statements. Now reductionism often has just this kind of asymmetry as its target: it is sceptical whether there is a legitimate inference from B-truths to a *different* set of A-truths. This is why it prefers to reduce the A's down, meaning that the inference is no longer vulnerable. It leads nowhere different, outside the B-range. But since this *revises* the natural belief, it hardly gives the meaning of the original concepts, but suggests substitutes.

Because of this problem, there is a tendency for reductionist programmes to take on a revisionist air. It becomes tempting to shelve the question of whether the reductions mean the same as the original statements. Suppose our doubts, puzzles, or other practices illustrate a way in which we take A-statements as having more content than B-statements. Still, perhaps the B-statements exhaust the legitimate content of the A's. In that case the extra can be dismissed as the product of muddle, of "prehistoric metaphysics" and failure to see the A-vocabulary's only legitimate role. The extra that we add is to be pruned away, in a programme of reconstruction. Reductionists from Berkeley right to Russell have tended to uncertainty over the relation of their analyses to the original discourse. One part of them wants to *accept* the original discourse – the A-statements – because, of course, they have identical content with quite legitimate B-statements. But another part wants to voice *suspicion* of the A-statements, because along with the pure content, there is the intruding illegitimate element which disguises it. Thus Berkeley presents himself as siding in all things with the mob: his analysis of the world as a community of spirits and ideas allows us to think that there exist tables, chairs etc. However, in another mood he will insist that it is a vulgar *error* to suppose, for example that anything is ever both touched and seen (since the ideas of touch and those of sight are quite different from each other, and his idealism disallows any common object). Yet chairs and tables are ordinarily thought to be both seen and touched. So Berkeley havers over whether the reduced, legitimate content exhausts the actual meaning we can give to statements, or whether in the actual meaning there is additional, false material, arising because of our misunderstanding of the idealist truth, and resulting in statements which ought to be rejected. Russell too presents an uncertain attitude towards statements of the A-kind: a phenomenalist analysis means, on his view, that chairs and tables become 'logical fictions', but whether this allows us to say that there really are tables and chairs (surely something the mob, the vulgar, want to say) is not certain.[3] The one line would be that we can say this (meaning by it something susceptible of expression in terms of actual or possible sense-experience), the other line would be that we cannot, because it involves views which are themselves impugned by the phenomenalist reduction.

Not that it is too discreditable to sit on this particular fence. From the reductionist point of view the legitimate content is given by the B-statements. Whether the A-statements have a meaning which supplies them with more, but illegitimate, content, may be left relatively indeterminate. Suppose, for example, that false views about the relation between A-sayings and B-states of affairs have prevailed – prehistoric metaphysics which supply us with images and metaphors, ways of taking A-statements which serve to separate them from B's. Then it may be indeterminate to what extent we accept these particular views when we accept A-statements. If we do, then the B-statements should be seen as replacements. If we do not, they may be analyses revealing the real content. A phenomenalist may happily admit that ordinary people are so infected by false views about the independence of objects from our sense-experience, that there is something of a shock in his analyses. And, according to me, given that the shock is one of realizing that some of our thoughts about objects and ourselves were wrong; he need not try to settle whether these thoughts were part of the content of our ordinary remarks, so that the proposal is to replace these, or whether on the other hand these thoughts were mere accidental sideshows, not part of what we ever said, so that the full content of this is revealed in the reducing B-statements.

A nice example comes from moral theory. Suppose people are naturally drawn to the realist options when they think about moral remarks. Then the realist thoughts might become so

[3] e.g. Russell, 'The Philosophy of Logical Atomism', in *Logic and Knowledge*, pp. 272–3. Berkeley, *Principles of Human Knowledge*, §§ 38–51.

associated with the vocabulary that anti-realist theory is no longer perceived as giving an analysis or reduction of the original content (or as treating it in some other anti-realist way) but as proposing to replace that content by some purged substitute. An anti-realist who accepts that realist views were 'part of the meaning' of the original saying will have an 'error view' of these, and urge replacement not reduction: someone who denies this may regard himself as merely revealing the meaning. As we have already seen, if we grow up to use a given vocabulary *and* have various views about the subject matter, there is no likelihood of definite conventions determining how many of those views are properly part of the content of statements made in the vocabulary. This does not take the interest out of reductionist claims. The interest remains in whether sufficient approximations to A-statements can be made in the B-vocabulary, for us to regard any differences as in effect detachable – the product of erroneous ways of thinking of the area. Serious questions can still remain about the adequacy of a B-vocabulary, as either a reconstruction or substitute for an A-vocabulary, even if we remain agnostic about which of these it is best taken to be.

4. *The Holistic Objection*

The most pressing motive for reductive analysis will be given from one of the perspectives already introduced – from where moral, mathematical, mental, or whatever facts become impossible, since the world is perceived as capable of providing nothing but some one kind of states. So the A-states of affairs have to be brought down to the B-earth, and the natural way to set about this is to equate A-statements with particular B-statements. But is it the only way? To put it the other way round, if we find that we cannot equate the content of some particular A-statement with anything claimed in purely B-terms, does this show that in committing ourselves to A-statements we are claiming there to be other realms of fact than B-facts?

Most twentieth-century philosophy, and ways of writing the history of philosophy, suppose that the answer is obviously that we are. The option is either to attempt a reduction, or to admit more facts, more and different objects of knowledge, into our ontology and epistemology. So philosophers such as Hume, who have ambitions to diminish our epistemological and meta-physical commitments, must be seen as proposing, in a primitive and unsophisticated way, reductive analyses: attempting to say, in acceptable terms, exactly what we say when we talk about morals, or about causal connections, or numbers, or whatever. But there is another option. What philosophers certainly want is a way of *explaining* our propensity to use and understand the problematic vocabulary given only that we live in a world in which we are sensitive to no more than the *underlying* truths. The problem they set themselves is to explain the thoughts without invoking the enlarged reality, with moral facts or numbers, or with causal powers between particular events to which we are responding. But must any such explana-tion proceed by reducing the content of the original vocabulary, showing that exactly the same can be said in the underlying B-terms? We can appreciate that it need not do so, by consider-ing some of the reasons why reductions are rarely obtainable. For the objections may themselves leave it open whether the metaphysics is as the reductionist thought, even if meanings do not drop down in the way he hoped.

Currently reductions are mostly attacked on "holistic" grounds. These argue that the individual statement is the wrong unit of analysis. Any individual statement in a given area will be given its meaning partly by its connections with a multitude of other statements and concepts. These multifarious connections, these interanimations in a web of belief, mean that no one individual statement, considered in isolation, will be wholly identified through any purely downward anchoring in a different (B) vocabulary. It is a body of belief, a network of doctrines, which arises as a whole when we start to appreciate the world in any given terms – be they moral, or causal, or involving independent objects in space and time, or numbers, or whatever. As Wittgenstein put it: "When we first begin to *believe* anything, what we believe is not a single proposition, it is a whole system of propositions. (Light dawns gradually over the whole.)"[4]

This image has a destructive impact on reductionist hopes. We can illustrate it by considering the positivist ideal of a

[4] *On Certainty*, *141.

language of pure sense-experience. Suppose an individual could make a complete record of how he experienced things at each moment, having at his disposal an extremely untheoretical, inactive medium for recording this – a sense-datum language; the "fancifully fanciless medium of unvarnished news", as Quine puts it.[5] Suppose now that the individual conceptualizes things further, beginning to regard his experience as experience of objects in space and time, which continue independently of his experience, and which have aspects which at given times he does not experience, and further which have their own causal powers and laws of behaviour. How do these new thoughts relate to the descriptions in the old language? The verificationist ideal was that they should each have a determinate *footing* in the language of experience: each should correspond to some large but definite bunch of theses expressed in the bare reportage of sense experience. The interanimation of sentences destroys this ideal: no single statement using the new, theoretical, concepts, will have a "fund of implications to call its own".[6] To put the point the other way round: if things go wrong, so that experience does not fall out as expected, there will be no one theoretical statement which *must* alone be regarded as falsified, as if just its footings have been knocked away. There is the possibility of spreading the blame across different theses of any theory, creating saving hypotheses, adjusting the web of belief in different ways.

The holistic objection to reductionism was impressed on philosophers by Quine.[7] But Quine maintained an odd penchant for putting these sophisticated thoughts about theoretical interanimations alongside primitive verificationist views about meaning – in particular the idea expressed by C. S. Peirce, that the meaning of a statement actually consists in *the difference its truth would make to possible experience*.[8] The result is explosive. If this is what you say about meaning, and you then prove that no individual statement has such a footing in experience, you have a proof that no individual statement means anything! But the

---

[5] *Word and Object*, p. 2.

[6] W. V. Quine, 'Epistemology Naturalized'.

[7] Initially in 'Two Dogmas of Empiricism'. See also the discussion of the British Idealists in 7.5 below.

[8] W. V. Quine, 'Epistemology Naturalized', p. 68.

dramatic result comes from marrying the sophisticated view of verification with a definition of meaning which presupposes the crude view. It is exactly as though you have only seen Stonehenge, and so define the function of a piece of architecture as *that bit of the roof which it supports*. You then find Sydney Opera House, and realize that it is so structured that you can never attribute to any one part of the structure one definite bit of roof which it supports. The webs of engineering interanimate each other. Perhaps any one part could be taken out without any of the roof falling down. If we cling to the Stonehenge definition, this would mean that no bit of the structure *has any function*. But this is not the best reaction. The path of wisdom is to revise the crude definition to cope with the sophisticated reality. The function of an element in the structure is not a matter purely of its "vertical" connection with a part of the roof, but also of its "horizontal" connections of support with other members of the structure. Quine's reluctance to modify Peirce's definition is a striking example of the power of verificationist ideas. The idea that a proper belief should have just one determinate footing in experience here survives realization that it cannot, to deliver the odd result that there is no such thing as a single belief, or the meaning of any single sentence.

If there were a B-vocabulary which stuck especially closely to the stream of sensations, it would be plausible to suggest that an ordinarily theoretical A-vocabulary would fit over it holistically. The tribunal of experience would deliver, in the first instance, B-verdicts, and the A-theory would face this tribunal en bloc. But it is not as though there actually *is* such a B-vocabulary. In Chapter 7 we see what difference this makes to the way we must think of experience controlling belief. But the holistic point remains valid in a conditional form: if there is a B-scheme devoid of certain concepts, and a richer more theoretical A-scheme, the judgements of the latter will have their own horizontal connections, meaning that they fit only loosely over the former. And this destroys the enterprise of isolating distinct footings for the richer beliefs, identifying their content in the poorer way.

How is it then that in spite of their general acceptance of these thoughts, philosophers still pursue relatively local attempts at analysis: semantics to psychology, actions to events, rights to

duties, causes to regularities, and so on? Perhaps they are not
yet comfortable with other ways of explaining an A-vocabulary
in terms of our reactions to a B-describable world. But the
better defence is that it is often impossible to tell in advance
whether the prestige/admiration model is the right one. In
other words, only after attempting the reduction can we tell
whether it is right to talk of a different scheme of concepts, or
whether instead we just have different ways of putting the
B-thoughts. It is only with hindsight that we can say that
the conceptual scheme of meanings, or causes, or whatever,
is different, and could only relate holistically, to the related
descriptions couched in weaker terms.

Suppose that in a particular area we become convinced that a
reduction will not be found, because the A-vocabulary fits only
holistically over the B-terms. How does this affect the original
impulse to attempt a reduction – the metaphysical, or epistemological, or logical motivations? Remember that the key concept
is that of *explanation*. If we can explain why it should come about
that we have the A-concepts, with their horizontal connections,
loosely fitting the B-descriptions, and in this explanation rely
only upon our exposure to a B-describable world, then at least
the metaphysical and epistemological motivations will be
answered. We will be able to do away with a distinct area of
A-facts, which troubled the metaphysician. And we will be able
to explain the reliability of our A-beliefs without demanding a
queer mechanism enabling us to know about them, which
troubled the epistemologist. Let me give an example. Consider
a system of arithmetic, with its mysterious reference to abstract
objects. One attitude might be that we should do away with it,
reject the vocabulary, and try to do "science without numbers".
Another is that we should reduce the problematic sayings: 'To
say that $2 + 2 = 4$ is to say that . . .', where the paraphrase
avoids the abstract reference. The third attitude is to see the
whole arithmetical system (the thing over which light dawns as
a whole) as an explicable and legitimate instrument for pursuing
our concerns in the world – a world which does not contain any
abstract objects. The hope would be that we can explain why
we should think as if there are numbers, taking arithmetical
sayings quite literally and seriously. But this would be done
without postulating that there are numbers and that we can

fortunately intuit them and their properties, and without pretending that thinking as if there were numbers is really just thinking in another, reduced, way.

It is as though nature permits portraits in richer or more austere styles. The portraits are different, but it does not follow that we have to imagine a different sitter for each of them.

To work out these thoughts will require different detail in different areas. It is not likely that the explanation of why we think arithmetically could share much with an explanation of why we think morally or causally or in terms of space and time; nor is it evident that there will always be a legitimate project of attempting such an explanation on the thinner base. For example, if we can have no conception of a non-spatial or non-temporal world, nor of our exposure to it, we cannot really mount an explanation of the spatial and temporal aspects of our thinking by mentioning it (see further on Kant and this, in 6.5). But the problem to which I now turn is not this, but is the puzzling question of the status of reductions, and whether, when we reflect upon their status, we can always accept the benefits they appear to bring.

5. *The Status Problem*

There is not much problem about the equation between having high prestige and being much admired. The fact that the one concept is identical with the other is not, as it were, a mysterious fact about a realm of concepts and thoughts which exists independently of our understandings and our words. We would rather say that there is just one concept, and we have slightly different ways of expressing it. This indeed raises serious questions – most pressingly, the question of how a person can understand each term in an equation such as this, yet fail to realize that the equation is true. This is a version of the paradox of analysis, and I discuss it briefly later (9.5 and notes). But there are other reductions, or attempted reductions, where the problem of status becomes very pressing indeed. I shall illustrate this with reference to the problem of personal identity.

In 2.1 I described how the best philosophical problems arise because we have a metaphysic, a view of the kinds of fact which make up the world, and discover that some particular kind of judgement does not seem to be made true by those facts. We are at a loss to see what makes it true. And reduction is a hopeful way of answering this problem. One such judgement is that of personal identity through time. We might have a metaphysic of physical and psychological atoms: physical atoms are the self-subsistent basic building blocks of physical stuff, and psychological atoms are the particular mental states whose succession makes up the conscious life of any person. These atoms have relations to one another: through time they group together, enter into causal relations, and these groupings can come and go; through long enough time, they will all go. We draw a line around some groups: they make up the life of one person. But what kind of fact is it, that some previous mental state, say, and some present one, both belong to one person, to *me*? Which relation do they bear to each other for this to be so?

There are many possible answers. We can select, for instance, the causal facts, and look for personal identity when the earlier stage of the person is causally in some favoured relation to the later one. We can ask for identity of underlying physical stuff. We can ask for sufficient mental continuity, and we can ask for an amalgam of any of these. The literature is full of thought experiments, or puzzle cases, which tell stories of rearrangements of the physical and mental atoms, and ask whether various proposed criteria give the right answers in these bizarre possibilities: could a person survive teletransportation, in which a physical replica is created elsewhere; does a person survive gross amnesia and personality changes; does he survive replacement of enough cells by others; does he survive fusion with another, in some massive graft, or fission into separate people in some massive break-up?

Suppose that after considering these examples, we hit upon one solution. We would say: given a history of physical and psychological atoms, in such-and-such groupings, we should group them into persons by principle X. (X might allow for borderlines and questions of degree, of course.) This would allow a reductionist claim: there are no facts in the world beyond the onward flow of physical and psychological atoms in different groupings, and the fact that some such groupings are united under principle X; those that are we call persons. The question of status is then this: what kind of truth is it that if two mental states belong to one X group they belong to the same person, and if they do not, then they do not belong to the same person? There seem to be three possibilities:

(1) Such a claim is justified by *convention*. It reflects the way *we* have chosen to group atoms into persons: it represents our solution to a problem which could equally well have been solved in other ways. The trouble with this is that it is hard to believe. If two experiences are both mine, it is hard to believe that an alternative linguistic arrangement could have led a group to say with equal propriety that one was mine and one was not.

(2) Such a claim is contingently true. In the actual world, X groupings make up persons, but God could have chosen to sort things so that some other groupings did. The trouble with this is that it is the end of reductionism. For it admits that there is this further fact of the matter – the one which actually obtains or which, as it were, God selected – and it offers by itself no account of what kind of fact that is. The fact of personal identity through time remains unexplained.

(3) Such a claim is necessarily true and represents a deep truth about the way we *have* to think of persons. It is not a question of choice, but neither is it a question of a contingent actual truth. This is rather like the status that Kant sought for truths about time and arithmetic – the *synthetic a priori*. But then it is one thing to say that we do think of X groupings as making up persons; it is quite another thing to say why we have to do so; to say what kinds of (conceptual? logical? moral?) mess would arise if we did not choose just X, but some other unifying relation X^*.

The problem of status was insufficiently remarked by twentieth-century reductionists, because they were happy with a rough concept of synonymy which had one foot in (1) and the other in (3). In other words, reductionist claims would be logically true, representing the right way to think about the problematic judgements and their relation to the underlying facts, but also, like other logical truths, somehow protected only by convention. But this fudges the issue. The problem of status is quite crucial whenever we start out by believing that there is a serious issue, an issue to be got *right*, when we are selecting a favoured class of underlying B-truths to represent an A-truth. It thus arises when naturalistic analyses are proposed in ethics (what is the status of the claim that just these features are good?) when possible worlds analyses are proposed for counterfactuals (what is the status of the claim that just *this* relation between possible worlds makes it true that if he had jumped off the cliff he would have fallen?), when set-theoretical reductions are proposed for numbers (what makes it true that just this set is the number 7?), and indeed whenever serious metaphysical doubts prompt the reductive search.

I think the problem of status raises profound difficulties for the enterprise of doing metaphysics by searching for reductions. I do not think it is an insurmountable problem: we would expect the doings of nations to be reducible to the inter-related doings of people in them; the identity of bicycles to reduce to the identities of groups of bicycle parts; and we would expect it to be at least *possible* for categories of A-fact to evaporate into B-facts. But this can only be claimed to have happened when we have both selected a plausible bunch of B-facts, and solved the status problem.

I now return to other ways of pursuing the debate between realism and anti-realism. I shall illustrate this by following out the detail in one case, that of evaluations and of ethical or broadly moral language. Apart from its intrinsic interest this also gives us some leverage against quietism. For always in the wings there is the doubt that we cannot finally make any of these explanatory attempts stick. The quietist will argue that there is no independent access to the true face of nature, to show us which portraits have added the least realistic stylistic flourishes. We only have our own descriptions, our own collection of portraits to rely upon. Quietism argues that this blocks anti-realist explanations of any commitments. But it does not: we can get further insights into the sitter by walking around the collection of portraits, and thereby determining which are adding gay-coloured vesture, and which are nearer the undraped figure of nature herself.

6. *Expressive Theories: Contrasts with Truth*

This brings us to the third point of departure for anti-realism: the attempt to explain the practice of judging in a certain way, by regarding the commitments as *expressive* rather than *descriptive*. The commitments in question are contrasted with others – call them judgements, beliefs, assertions, or propositions – which have genuine truth-conditions.

Two classic examples of such theories are instrumentalism, as a philosophy of science, and emotivism in ethics. According to this latter, the commitment that a thing is good or bad, right or wrong, permissible or impermissible, is not a judgement with truth-conditions of its own (probably irreducible to other terms, by the argument of the last section, and therefore highly mysterious). It is a commitment of a different sort, maintained not by *believing* something but by having an *attitude towards* it. The theory was expressed with characteristic vigour by A. J. Ayer:

The presence of an ethical symbol in a proposition adds nothing to its factual content. Thus if I say to someone, "You acted wrongly in stealing that money", I am not stating anything more than if I had simply said, "You stole that money". In adding that this action is wrong I am not making any further statement about it. I am simply evincing my moral disapproval of it. It is as if I had said "You stole that money," in a peculiar tone of horror, or written it with the addition of some special exclamation marks.[9]

Emotivism is sometimes dubbed the "boo-hooray" theory of ethics. Ayer here presents it by a contrast between what is *stated* and what it *evinced*. The same contrast can be put in terms of what it is to accept a moral remark; it is to concur in an attitude to its subject, rather than in a belief. Alternatively we might say that the speech-act of putting forward a moral opinion is not one of asserting that some state of affairs obtains, but one of evincing or expressing an attitude, or perhaps of exhorting or encouraging others to share an attitude.

In the heyday of linguistic philosophy similar suggestions were applied to a wide range of commitments:

[9] A. J. Ayer, *Language, Truth and Logic*, ch. 6, p. 107.

Saying that X causes Y	=	Offering X as an instrument or recipe for obtaining Y
Saying that action X is voluntary	=	Expressing willingness to blame or commend the agent
Saying that you know X	=	Allowing other people to take your word for it
Saying that a statement is true	=	Endorsing it
Saying that a statement is probable	=	Expressing guarded assent to it
Saying that a statement is possible	=	Refusing to endorse ruling it out of consideration.

Expressive theories contrast with reductions. On an expressive account there is a considerable difference between saying, for instance, that X causes Y, and saying anything which might be a plausible candidate for a reductive analysis – e.g. that events similar to X are always followed by events similar to Y. You might only offer the recipe if you believed this latter thing. You might be open to criticism if you offered it when this latter thing was false. In other words, the regularity might provide a *standard* for endorsing the recipe. Nevertheless the standard might, in principle, be variable or displaced by something more subtle, but this would not be a change in the meaning of the causal saying. This is particularly important in the moral case. Naturalism finds it impossible to say how disputants with different standards mean the same by moral remarks. On the account according to which the meaning of such a remark is given by the standard for saying it which the speaker has, people with different standards mean different things. But that makes it impossible to see how they are expressing conflicting opinions. If a utilitarian says that contraception is an excellent thing, he would mean that it promotes happiness; if a priest says that it is an awful thing, he might mean that it is against the wishes of the creator of the universe. But in that case each remark could be true, and there would be no contradiction between them. The expressive theory avoids this undesirable consequence. It locates the disagreement where it should be, in the clash of attitudes towards contraception.

Expressive theories must be sharply distinguished from more naïve kinds of subjectivism. An expressive theory does not give a moral utterance a truth-condition which concerns the speaker. A man saying 'Hitler was a good thing' is expressing or evincing an appalling attitude. But he is not *saying that* he has got this attitude. If he were, what he said would be true, provided that he is sincere. But we do not regard his remark as true; we allow that he is sincere, if he is, without accepting his remark (which, on the expressive theory, would mean endorsing the attitude it expresses).

The point of expressive theories is to avoid the metaphysical and epistemological problems which realist theories of ethics, and of the other commitments in the list, are supposed to bring with them. Again it is important to remember the overall motivation. This is to explain the practice of moralizing, using causal language, and so on, in terms only of our exposure to a thinner reality – a world which contains only some lesser states of affairs, to which we respond and in which we have to conduct our lives. Unless this is borne in mind, it is easy to charge expressive theories with irrelevant mistakes. For instance, it is frequently pointed out that a term may occur in an utterance which *both* is a description of how things are, *and* expresses an attitude. If I say that there is a bull in the next field I may be threatening you, or warning you, or expressing timidity, or challenging you to cross, or doing any of a range of other things, and expressing any of a range of subtle attitudes and emotions. But none of these doings has any bearing on the meaning or content of my remark, which is true or false in a determinate range of circumstances, and is a paradigm of a saying with a truth-condition. If I say that someone is a Kraut, or blotto, I may express an attitude of contempt towards Germans, or of wry amusement at drunkenness, but I also say something true or false about their nationality or sobriety. In the bull example the attitudes expressed are incidental to the conventional meaning of the remark. In these other examples they attach to the vocabulary as a matter of convention. You should not use those terms unless you sympathize with those attitudes. But in each case it would be wrong to infer that *no* description is given from the fact that an attitude is *also* expressed. Similarly, critics have pointed out, it is wrong to infer that there is no strict and literal content, capable of truth and falsity, in the remark that X causes Y, or X knows the truth about Y, or X ought to be done, from the fact that when these things are said, attitudes are expressed. This "speech-act fallacy" has been widely accepted as the root mistake of expressive theories.[10]

However, the fallacy need not be committed (and I rather doubt if it ever was). There are two reasons why not. First of all, an expressive theory should not infer that the attitude gives the role of the saying, simply from the fact that it is expressed when the saying is made. So long as the attitude *may* give the role, the argument for saying that it does is the superior explanation of the commitments which we then arrive at. There is no inference of the form 'this attitude is expressed, *so* these remarks have no truth-conditions', but only 'this attitude is expressed; if we see the remark as having no truth-conditions the philosophy improves; so let us see the remark as expressive rather than descriptive'. There is no fallacy there. And there is a second point. Remembering the anti-realist motivation, we can see that it does not matter at all if an utterance is descriptive as well as expressive, provided that its *distinctive* meaning – the aspect which separates it from any underlying B-descriptions – is expressive. It is obviously a useless argument against anti-realism about values to point out that the word 'Kraut' has a descriptive element. That is quite acceptable. It is the *extra import* making the term evaluative as well as descriptive, which must be given an expressive role. It is only if that involves an extra truth-condition that expressive anti-realism about values is impugned. But perhaps there is no good reason for supposing that it does: the natural thing to say about such terms is that the extra ingredient is emotive, expressive.

There are, however, much more respectable arguments surrounding expressive theories. These concern the extent to which they can explain the appearance that we are making judgements with genuine truth-conditions. Ultimately it is the attempt to explain this which introduces the need for a wider theory of truth, and enables us to appreciate the point of the different contenders. We should realize that expressive theories, like reductive theories, may be uncertain about how much they need to explain. Suppose that we say we *project* an attitude or

[10] J. Searle, *Speech Acts*, p. 139. H. Putnam, *Reason, Truth and History*, pp. 208–10.

habit or other commitment which is not descriptive onto the world, when we speak and think as though there were a property of things which our sayings describe, which we can reason about, know about, be wrong about, and so on. Projecting is what Hume referred to when he talks of "gilding and staining all natural objects with the colours borrowed from internal sentiment", or of the mind "spreading itself on the world". Then expressive theorists often tend to the view that this projection is a *mistake* – that itself it involves flirting with a false realism. (Ayer entitled his chapter from which I quoted, "A *Critique* of Ethics and Theology".) John Mackie believed that our ordinary use of moral predicates involved an *error*, because the underlying reality was as the expressive view claims, whilst in using those concepts we claim more.[11] For this reason he denied that emotivism gives the actual *meaning* of moral terms, and this claim is frequently put forward as almost self-evident. But it is not. The issue is whether the projection is only explicable if we mistake the origins of our evaluative practices. The idea would be that were we aware of these origins we would give up some or all of our tendency to practice as if evaluative commitments had truth-conditions, and were not expressive in origin and in their essential nature. But perhaps there is no mistake. I call the enterprise of showing that there is none – that even on anti-realist grounds there is nothing improper, nothing "diseased" in projected predicates – the enterprise of *quasi-realism*. The point is that it tries to earn, on the slender basis, the features of moral language (or of the other commitments to which a projective theory might apply) which tempt people to realism. The issues are complicated enough to deserve a chapter to themselves. It is only when we have understood them that we can properly assess the final divisions between realists and their opponents, over mind-dependence and over truth.

7. *Metaphor and Truth*

There is one other overtly expressive phenomenon of interest to the philosophy of language: metaphor. Metaphor has not commanded the respect of many mainstream theorists of meaning: it can appear to be merely a poor relation of proper judgement,

[11] J. Mackie, *Ethics: Inventing Right and Wrong*, pp. 30–5.

arising only when language is on holiday, and the appropriate attitude is that voiced by Hobbes:

In Demonstration, in Councell, and all rigorous search of Truth, Judgement does all; except sometimes the understanding have need to be opened by some apt similitude; and then there is so much use of Fancy. But for Metaphors, they are in this case utterly excluded. For seeing they openly professe deceipt; to admit them into Councell, or Reasoning, were manifest folly.[12]

By contrast with this stark hostility we can mention Nietzsche's attitude that truth itself is merely good dead metaphor.[13] Those who appreciate a good metaphor certainly seem to acquire a gain of *some* sort. So we should at least ask how this gain compares with that of acquiring a true belief. I can best organize this issue by comparing four different positions, in ascending order of the importance they attach to metaphor.

(1) The prosaic end of things. Some metaphors scarcely deserve the name: they are close to being dead metaphors, or idioms. If I tell you not to cross the path of someone who is prickly, steaming, or up in arms, you understand my language, for all its figurative nature, as immediately and certainly as if I had chosen more literal ways of expressing myself. The words I use are customarily associated with features of things which I could have expressed directly. Let us say that the figurative language *yields* an interpretation if the interpretation is customarily given, and customarily expected. If the custom has hardened into a convention we have a case of an *idiom*, and it will be right to say that we have a new or extended literal meaning. Perhaps 'prickly' in this context means 'easily aggravated'. In that case a dictionary ought to report the fact, and a learner ought to be taught it. And someone could fully understand sentences in which people are described as prickly, without knowing that the word has a use in which it applies to cacti and hedgehogs. But a term may yield an interpretation reliably enough without this having happened: the yield is given firstly by the literal meanings of the terms, and secondly because some feature of the original thing meant is 'salient', or an associated commonplace. In other words it is a feature

---

[12] Hobbes, *Leviathan*, p. 44.
[13] See start of chapter 6 below.

people think of when they think of the original, and which in the context is a likely feature to apply to the subject-matter. 'Bert is a real gorilla' yields that Bert is strong, rough, and fierce. It does this because the word 'gorilla' has its normal meaning, and because people (wrongly) associate these features with gorillas.[14] Any hearer aware of this can follow the metaphor to its intended interpretation.

In these first-level cases the metaphor has an intended interpretation which is reliably given. But the mechanism goes via the ordinary meaning of the terms, to the suggested meaning: we have only an indirect way of suggesting some definite truth by saying some definite falsehood (for Bert is not really a gorilla). There can be some debate about how we fit these facts into other theoretical categories. Is it right to describe the speaker as having asserted falsely that Bert is a gorilla? Is it right to describe him as having asserted truly the yielded propositions, that Bert is strong and rough and fierce? Because of our analysis of convention and tone we need not find these questions too hard. The speaker said that Bert is a gorilla, but did not assert it: he did not intend anyone to believe that this was the truth, and would not normally be taken to have displayed that it is. He did, on the other hand, intend people to believe that Bert is strong, rough, and fierce, and chose a reliable method of transmitting this belief, and of being taken to do so. But the method was one of reliable suggestion, and we do not allow that people assert everything that they reliably suggest, and are known to be reliably suggesting.[15] However, the responsibility the speaker bears is much the same as if he had said straight out what he transmits only indirectly. He has chosen a customary and certain way of representing to his audience that Bert is strong, rough, and fierce: if he is not, Bert has an equal right to feel aggrieved (if he is really like a gorilla, perhaps he will not do much about it).

---

[14] People may think of these features although they do not believe gorillas to have them. But in a population which comes to realize this, the metaphor will begin to die out, or degenerate into an idiom. For consider children learning. They will only realize the intended yield by learning that it is a distinct custom to use 'gorilla' as if fierceness were a feature of the animal, when natural history has told them it is not. This is not readily distinguishable from learning a distinct convention, or meaning.

[15] See also 9.1.

(2) The next cases differ from the previous ones in that they maintain an open-ended or creative element. The range of features indicated remains indefinite: both speaker and listener are able to explore the comparison or image suggested, and find new features of the subject matter as a result. The critic I. A. Richards talked of poetic language as a "movement among meanings": there is no single literal truth which the figure or metaphor yields, and no single class of such truths. Thus when Romeo says that Juliet is the sun we can profit from the metaphor indefinitely: we can move among respects in which someone's lover is like the sun: warm, sustaining, comforting, perhaps awesome, something on which we are utterly dependent . . . This process is quite open-ended. Shakespeare need have had no definite range of comparisons which he intended, and it is quite wrong to substitute some definite list and suppose that the exploration is complete. The metaphor is in effect an invitation to explore comparisons. But it is not associated with any belief or intention, let alone any set of rules, determining when the exploration is finished.

This is the first sense in which metaphor is both valuable and ineliminable. It is valuable because it directs our attention towards aspects of things which we might not otherwise have thought of. It is ineliminable because there is no single list of literal thoughts which cashes it in. In this respect the metaphor may work like a picture (we talk in the same breath of metaphorical and figurative uses of language, or uses of imagery). Possessing a picture I may think of the subject pictured, and the picture may lead me to think of all kinds of things. But no list of these things substitutes for the picture, just because the picture has an unlimited potential for directing me to further aspects of the subject, whereas the list does not. As Davidson puts it, "Joke or dream or metaphor can, like a picture or a bump on the head, make us appreciate some fact – but not by standing for, or expressing, the fact."[15]

(3) The preceding level is enough to defend and in a way to explain the value of metaphor. It gets us beyond the crass thought that using metaphor is always an indirect and inferior way of putting what would best be put directly (although it can

<hr />

[16] 'What Metaphors Mean', in Platts (1980), p. 253.

be this, and at the first level often is). Still, at the second level
the value of a metaphor is essentially that of a means to an end.
The end product is appreciation of a literal truth or several
literal truths. The metaphor suggests how to go about finding
some such truth or truths. Its success is dependent upon their
value to us, and perhaps too upon providing us pleasure in the
exploration. (There is pleasure in exploring the metaphor of the
Church as a hippopotamus even if we do not believe anything
about the Church at the end that we did not believe at the
beginning.) So far, however, the only way that a metaphor can
provide a gain in understanding is by provoking a quest which
may end up in our grasping some new strict and literal truths.
The third level of description queries this. It alleges that there is
a distinct, intrinsically metaphorical, way of understanding.
The appreciation of the metaphor constitutes a different, distinctive success of its own: the success of seeing one thing *as*
another. Seeing history as a tidal wave, or architecture as frozen
music, is doing something different from believing, and different from accepting an invitation to search for a range of beliefs.
But it is a gain in understanding, a success, of its own kind.

It is absolutely vital to see that this kind of description is not
forced on us by level (2) facts. And it is a defect of some of the
best literature on the subject that it does not clearly separate the
two ideas. Some even explain the ineliminability of metaphor
via its alleged level (3) powers. Davidson, at the end of his highly
illuminating paper on the subject, says: "Since in most cases
what the metaphor prompts or inspires is not entirely, or even
at all, recognition of some truth or fact, the attempt to give
literal expression to the content of the metaphor is simply
misguided." But the attempt to give literal expression would be
misguided even if we accepted only the *second* level of description, where the metaphor *does* prompt or inspire a search for
literal truths or facts. It is quite another question whether it can
prompt or inspire a mode of insight all of its own, so that the
appreciation of one thing *as* another or *in the light of* another is a
distinctive metaphorical way of understanding. It is this idea
which Hobbes was opposing.

The sheer psychology of coming to appreciate a good
metaphor, like seeing a joke or seeing the point of a comparison,
may suggest this way of describing things. If I suddenly see

architecture as frozen music, or history as a tidal wave, it feels
like a gain which is quite akin to acquiring a new piece of
knowledge. It seems like possession of a self-sufficient *thought*. It
doesn't seem just like accepting an invitation to explore the
comparison, because I may relish the metaphor and yet have no
sense at all that anything remains to be done, which is the
distinctive aspect according to (2) descriptions. In support of
this we can notice how often we assent to a remark without
realizing that there is metaphor buried in it. A large amount of
philosophy consists in unravelling how much is metaphorical,
and how much literal, when we talk of: the *foundations* of
knowledge; bodies *acting* upon one another; the *flow* of time;
propositions *corresponding* to facts; the mental *realm*, and so on.
Suppose we decide that there is a large amount of metaphor
involved when we talk, say, of the foundations of knowledge.
What then do we say of someone who passionately believes that
knowledge has foundations, and in no sense realizes the degree
of metaphor? He does not realize how much exploration needs
to be done to arrive at some literal truth about knowledge, so he
does not see himself as someone who has just accepted an
invitation to look for such truths. And he is not someone who
has come to a literal belief about knowledge, because he may
have no non-metaphorical way of expressing himself. Are we to
credit him with a metaphorical piece of understanding (or
misunderstanding, if knowledge needs no foundations)?

The opposing view would be that there is no distinctive
understanding here. The man says the words supposing that
they mean something true, and that he knows what it is. More
thought would disillusion him. So he simply believes he has a
belief, when in fact he has none. He thinks he is rich when he has
a cheque which he cannot actually cash. But he has not therefore come into possession of a different kind of currency. Consider too the exercises of imagination involved in seeing history
as a tidal wave, or architecture as frozen music. We present
ourselves with images; we put a sense of the inexorable sweep of
a tidal wave alongside our thoughts of the progress of historical
events, or our sense of the structure of a cathedral alongside a
sense of the structure of a piece of music, suddenly stopped in
time. Such exercises are pleasurable, even marvellous. But the
ability to conduct them is not itself the exercise of a distinctive

piece of understanding. A historian who performs the exercise every so often may enjoy the idea; he may even find that in some way it guides his writings or his attitudes to events. But it is what he then says which means that he understands history well or badly. In short, it is not necessary to postulate a distinctive success which the metaphor provides. Its virtue lies in prompting insights, but the insights themselves are strict and literal truths.

(4) This rebuttal of level (3) descriptions of metaphor may leave some dissatisfaction. I would express it like this: the rebuttal takes for granted the kind of success involved in acquiring a (strict and literal) *belief*. But what right have we got to contrast this with seeing one thing *as* another? We have seen how ordinary belief involves the transference of a term from one set of things to another, and it was the business of chapter 3 to search for some conception of the rules and intentions which govern this process. In that chapter we met the idea that only natural propensities to find things similar underlie any kind of description of things. Why shouldn't a natural propensity to see one thing as another or in the light of another, which yet falls short of applying the same predicate to them in the same meaning, not serve to found a self-standing piece of metaphorical insight? I take it that this is why Nietzsche describes literal truth as worn-out metaphor (see the start of chapter 6). Is belief perhaps just one end of a spectrum of attitudes which can go with the new application of a term: at this end, pure prose, and at the other end, pure metaphor?

To think of this, compare two populations. Each of them is taught a certain term initially in connection with a certain range of cases or range of procedures. In one population they find it natural to describe some new cases by the same term. In the other they find it natural to see the new cases in the light of the old, or see them *as* possessing the feature, but they view this as irreducibly a case of 'seeing as'. These think of the extension as metaphorical, whereas the ohers think of it as a simple case of belief. What is the difference?

A plausible example might help. Consider the way in which we use terms which also describe physical affairs to describe psychological affairs. We talk of matches in boxes, and thoughts in the head; of being pulled by ropes, or being pulled by desires; of jumping to attention, or jumping to a conclusion. Metaphorical, of course. Or is it? We most probably cannot cash the metaphors, either by giving a single literal way of saying something which they yield or even by indicating a range of comparisons which they suggest. On the other hand we should not be happy with just postulating two different senses of the terms: it is not pure accident that we talk of thoughts in the heads, for example. If it were simply a case of the word 'in' being ambiguous we might just as well have planted the ambiguity on some other term, and talked of thoughts being *on* the head, for instance. Yet we should also be unhappy with the idea that there is a smooth or natural extension of the terms from the physical to the mental. Someone who understands what it is for one thing to be in another physically has a definite range of capacities: he can find things, obey instructions, perform a range of tasks which exhibit or exercise that understanding. These tasks are not the same as any (whichever they might be!) which exercise an understanding of thoughts being in the head.

It is profitable here to recall the bent learners of chapter 3. Imagine a bent learner who responds perfectly well to some range of cases, but whose capacity to exercise his concept involves odd bends and blind spots. From our point of view his capacity is flawed or partial. From the point of view of the population which finds it natural to spread a term over a larger range, people who do not find it natural, but who regard the extension in the spirit of a metaphor, would similarly be flawed or partial. Now if we sympathize with either conventionalist or even naturalist responses to the bent learner it will seem that such reactions are all that there is to go on: it is then a matter merely of our reactions which determine whether an affirmation expresses a belief or only a metaphor. But if the opposition to nominalism which I tried to force in 3.2 is roughly right, we do not get this result. According to me there is a distinctive fact whether the extension over new cases is, or is not, an exercise of the same capacities that are involved in applying the term to the original kind of case. This ought to give determinancy to the issue of whether a new kind of application is metaphorical or not.

But even if the issue is determinate, it is often not easy.

Remember the examples of philosophical descriptions/metaphors, and the difficulty of disentangling the literal from the metaphorical which they illustrate. I suggested that the man affirming that knowledge has foundations may only think he is expressing a literal belief, but not be doing so; similarly for someone saying that thoughts are in the head, or that we are often pulled by desire. If such a person recognizes no obligation to find a better way of putting it and insists on resting content with his way, what can we urge? We show the way the *practice* differs: what verifies whether a building has foundations, whether one thing is inside another, whether one thing is pulling another. We show how in the ordinary cases these truths influence things which, for example, we want; beliefs in them therefore couple with our desires to have consequences for action. Since the practice is different in the disputed case, however much we sympathize with the passive acceptance of the same terminology, the obligation to look for the points of similarity and difference remains.

Sadly, then, I incline to Hobbes's view that understanding things metaphorically is not understanding them at all, although it may often immediately yield understanding, and guide it and increase it. On this account a good metaphor at the open-ended level is expressed by an utterance which does not say that such-and-such is the case, but rather expresses an invitation or suggestion that a certain comparison be followed up. In this respect such an utterance is like the other speech-acts listed in the last section. It does not have truth conditions, but is successful or not in a different dimension. In the next chapter I explore this contrast a little more, and consider objections which such accounts tend to meet.

Notes to Chapter 5

5.3   Reductionism in the Philosophy of Science deserves much more discussion than I have been able to give it here. A good literature would include:

A. J. Ayer, *The Foundations of Empirical Knowledge*.
I. Scheffler, *The Anatomy of Inquiry*, Pt. II.
R. Carnap, 'The Methodological Status of Theoretical Concepts', *Minnesota Studies in the Philosophy of Science*, vol. i (1956).
B. van Fraassen, *The Scientific Image*, ch. 2.

5.4   The status problem is not well highlighted in most of the literature. This is probably because undue optimism about the conventional status of logic, and the logical status of reductions, made it seem enough to find a good correlation between A-facts and B-facts, without worrying too much about the status of the correlation.

5.5   It is important to be clear about the distinction between projectivism and quasi-realism. Projectivism is the philosophy of evaluation which says that evaluative properties are projections of our own sentiments (emotions, reactions, attitudes, commendations). Quasi-realism is the enterprise of explaining why our discourse has the shape it does, in particular by way of treating evaluative predicates like others, if projectivism is true. It thus seeks to explain, and justify, the realistic-seeming nature of our talk of evaluations – the way we think we can be wrong about them, that there is a truth to be found, and so on. One might believe that quasi-realism is successful, yet still dislike projectivism, and one might like projectivism, but still believe that ordinary features of our thought are not explicable, quasi-realistically, but indeed involve error. This was the position John Mackie took in his influential book *Ethics: Inventing Right and Wrong*. But quasi-realism at least removes the most important range of objections to projectivism – namely, that it cannot account for the phenomena of ordinary moral thinking. However, a full defence of projectivism would need to discuss moral motivation more than I have done.

5.6   The most comprehensive recent collection on metaphor is

A. Ortony (ed.), *Metaphor and Thought*.

However, I think nobody would claim that the study of metaphor has been one of analytical philosophy's brighter achievements. In particular, a number of discussions seem to presuppose that the problem is one of how we "compute", according to rules and principles, a non-literal meaning from a literal one. I hope that the stress in the text on the dynamic and open-ended exploration of metaphor removes the idea that we do any such thing.

CHAPTER 6

Evaluations, Projections, and Quasi-Realism

What then is truth? A movable host of metaphors, metonymies, anthropomorphisms: in short, a sum of human relations which have been poetically and rhetorically tempered by, transferred, and embellished, and which, after long usage, seem to be fixed, canonical and binding. Truths are illusions which we have forgotten are illusions; they are metaphors that have become worn out and have been drained of sensuous force, coins which have lost their embossings, and are now considered as metal and no longer as coins.

Nietzsche, 'On Truth and Lies in a Normal Sense'.

1. *More Detailed Motivations*

A projective account of some commitments puts them at the top of the following picture:.

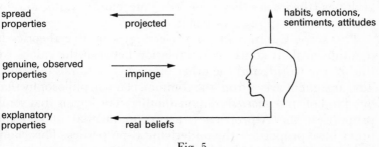

Fig. 5

This is contrasted with the two other places for them. In the middle one, the features talked about (e.g. the possession of value by things, or the existence of rights, duties, and so on) are themselves part of the genesis of our beliefs. It would be *because* values, etc. are distributed in some way around the world, and because we are capable of reacting to them, of knowing them by some acquaintance or intuition, that we moralize as we do. In the other lower place there would be no cognizance of these features, nothing to be compared with a more ordinary mode of perception. All the information about the world which we take in would be describable in natural terms. But just as we can use that information to construct theories involving higher-order concepts, such as those of physics, so we can use it to construct the moral concepts. But when we have done so, we have a further description of the world, and are regarding it as containing further, moral, states of affairs.

To ensure that a projective theory starts at reasonable odds, I shall briefly mention three motives for preferring it to either of its rivals. The first of these is economy. The projective theory intends to ask no more from the world than what we know is there – the ordinary features of things on the basis of which we make decisions about them, like or dislike them, fear them and avoid them, desire them and seek them out. It asks no more than this: a natural world, and patterns of reaction to it. By contrast a theory assimilating moral understanding to perception demands more of the world. Perception is a causal process: we perceive those features of things which are responsible for our experiences. It is uneconomical to postulate both a feature of things (the values they have) *and* a mechanism (intuition) by which we are happily aware of it.

The second argument for preferring projective theories is metaphysical. It concerns the relation between the values we find in the world, and the other properties of things of value.[1] The argument arises from the common claim in philosophy that one kind of state *supervenes* upon another. The idea is that some properties, the A-properties, are consequential upon some other base properties, the underlying B-properties. This claim is supposed to mean that in some sense of *necessary*, it is necessary that if an A-truth changes, some B-truth changes; or if two situations are identical in their B-properties they are identical

---

[1] The argument of the next few pages is quite hard, and self-contained. It can quite easily be skipped, especially if the reader already sympathizes with projectivism. The main thread is resumed in 6.2.

in their A-properties. A-properties *cannot* (in this same sense) vary regardless of B-properties. Now there are very different strengths of 'necessity' and of 'cannot'. Most people would say that colour properties cannot vary independently of underlying physical properties, such as those of surfaces, the kind of wavelength of light reflected, and so on. This is a physical, empirical, claim. It is easy to *imagine* finding that the colours of things have started to vary independently of their physical properties, so that two things which are reflecting the same wavelengths nevertheless have different colours. No doubt scientists would either disbelieve this, or start to search for other, more obscure physical differences which cause this variation. But there is no conceptual inevitability that they succeed: the supervenience of colour on other (primary) properties is a matter of physical rather than conceptual necessity. By contrast moral properties seem to have to supervene upon natural ones in some much stronger sense. It seems conceptually impossible to suppose that if two things are identical in every other respect, one is better than the other. Such a difference *could* only arise if there were other differences between them. So suppose that we have a complete, base description of a thing, B*, telling us everything that *could* be relevant to determining its A-state. The supervenience claim is that necessarily *if* there is a thing which is B* and A, then anything else which is like it in being B* is like it in being A as well. There is no possible world in which one thing is B* and A, but other things are B* and not A (in this it is important to remember that B* is some complete specification of the B-states of a thing, whereas A is some particular A-property – being good to a certain degree, being of a certain colour, or whatever). Call this *B*/A supervenience*.

This property now needs contrasting with a stronger property, that necessarily, if a thing is B*, it is A. This links B* to A *rigidly* – in all possible worlds, if a thing is B*, it is A. It is a stronger property, for B*/A supervenience does not rule out possible worlds in which there are things which are B* but not A. It merely rules out any in which there are both things which are B* and A, and things which are B* and not A. Thus even if the supervenience claim holds, it does not enable you to infer that a thing is A from the fact that it is B*. It just means that once you know of something which is A and has this underlying state, you can be sure that anything else just like it is A as well. Call the stronger property B^*/A *necessity*.[2]

The point of introducing these two properties is that philosophers sometimes find it plausible to claim B^*/A supervenience without going so far as B^*/A necessity. In particular in the moral case it seems conceptually or logically necessary that if two things share a total basis of natural properties, then they have the same moral qualities. But it does not seem a matter of conceptual or logical necessity that any given total natural state of a thing gives it some particular moral quality. For to tell which moral quality results from a given natural state means using standards whose correctness cannot be shown by conceptual means alone. It means moralizing, and bad people moralize badly, but need not be confused.

How does the argument proceed that this point favours projectivism? The argument is best thought of by imagining possible worlds – complete states of affairs corresponding to the various possibilities involved. If a truth is necessary, then it obtains in all possible worlds. Otherwise there is one in which it does not. A contingent proposition, which merely happens to be so, is true in some possible worlds and not in others. Then the structure is that possible worlds divide into *two* sorts. There are those in which *something* B^* is A, and in those everything else B^* is A also. But there are those in which things are B^* *without* being A. Now this distribution of possible worlds needs explanation. For at first sight there should be a further mixed kind allowed – in which some things are B^* and A; but in which some things are like those whose possibility is already allowed – B^* and not A. So we need to explain the *ban on mixed worlds*, and the argument goes that anti-realism does this better than realism.

Consider a different example from the moral one. It has been influentially argued that there can be no 'psychophysical laws', meaning no necessity that a given physical state B^* produces a given mental state, A'. The reason why there cannot be such laws is, in Davidson's view, that mental predicates, expressing

---

[2] The contrast is neatly expressed formally:

$N((\exists x) (B^*x \& A'x) \to (\forall y) (B^*y \to A'y))$, as opposed to:

$N(\forall y)(B^*y \to A'y)$,

the latter being the necessitation of the consequent, when the former only necessitates the conditional.

as they do a different set of concepts from the physical, answer
to different constraints, so that we would never be in a position
to insist upon the existence of a given mental state, on the basis
of a given physical state.[3] We can leave on one side whether this
argument is forceful (at first sight the same thought rules out
e.g. laws connecting wave length of light and colour, or forces
and motions, or indeed any interesting laws). But Davidson
also believes in the supervenience of the mental upon the physical. So we have the same structure: we should allow the possibility of B* which might be, for instance, a given pattern of
neurones or brain stuff without A', but given that *one* B* thing is
A', the others in any particular world *must* also be. It is as
though God had it in his power to make a given physical state
underlie one mental state – e.g. thinking of my aunt – or
underlie another – e.g. thinking of my dog. But once he had
decided to let it underlie the one state in *me*, say, then he has to
do the same for *you*. Whereas at first sight if we allow that he
could associate the states as he likes, we would expect him to be
able to associate the one state with B* in me, and the other one
in you, breaking supervenience. So why is God thus constrained? The whole point of talking of possible worlds is to
allow as many as we can conceive of. Equally, if it could be true,
as far as conceptual constraints go, that Fred has some set of
dispositions and is vicious, but also that he has the very same
set, and differs in no other way except that he is not vicious, then
why could it not also be true that Fred has the set, and is vicious,
whereas Bill has the set and is not? The matter is especially
obvious with physical necessity. If there is no necessity that a
given wavelength underlies a given colour, how could there be a
necessity that if it does in one case, then it does in all the others?
Why the ban on mixed possible worlds?

These questions are especially hard for a realist. For he has
the conception of an actual A-state of affairs, which might or
might not distribute in a particular way across the B-states.
Supervenience then becomes a mysterious fact, and one which
he will have no explanation of (or no right to rely upon). It
would be as though some people are B* and thinking of dogs,
and others are B* and thinking of their aunts, but there is a

[3] Davidson, 'Mental Events'.

ban on them travelling to inhabit the same place: completely inexplicable. From the anti-realist point of view things are a little easier. When we announce the A-commitments we are projecting, we are neither reacting to a given distribution of A-properties, nor speculating about one. So the supervenience can be explained in terms of the constraints upon proper projection. Our purpose in projecting value predicates may demand that we respect supervenience. If we allowed ourselves a system (shmoralizing) which was like ordinary evaluative practice, but subject to no such constraint, then it would allow us to treat naturally identical cases in morally different ways. This could be good shmoralizing. But that would unfit shmoralizing from being any kind of guide to practical decision-making (a thing could be properly deemed shbetter than another although it shared with it all the features relevant to choice or desirability).

Supervenience claims are very popular in philosophy, because they promise some of the advantages of reduction without the cost of defending B*/A necessity claims. But the promise is slightly hollow: supervenience is usually quite uninteresting by itself. What is interesting is the reason why it holds. Thus in the philosophy of mind, although many writers claim the supervenience of the mental upon the physical, not so many are clear about why we ought to accept it, nor about the strength of the necessity involved. From a Cartesian perspective, according to which mental properties are logically quite distinct from any physical ones, and as it were are only accidentally found in conjunction with any given physical set-up (brains rather than wood fibres) there would be no right to rely upon supervenience. So when we rely upon it we are in effect promising an alternative to the Cartesian picture of mind and body. But the supervenience claim does not by itself fulfil that promise, and the pair of properties, supervenience and lack of necessity are awkward bedfellows in the theory of mind just as they are in moral theory. If there is no necessity that a given physical set-up generates a particular mental property, it is hard to force the ban on mixed worlds, in which it sometimes does and sometimes does not. And it is not nearly so plausible to take the anti-realist way out, thinking of our attribution of mental states to one another in other terms than descriptions (although Wittgenstein was tempted to an expressive theory, at some points in the later philosophy).[4] All in all, then, philosophers of mind who want to oppose Cartesianism are better off trying to defend the stronger necessity claims. Merely relying upon supervenience, and disowning the stronger thesis, seems likely to leave an unstable position.

It should also be noticed that the relation between theoretical facts in a science, and the empirical facts which afford evidence for them, is not like that in the moral case. Suppose we imagine a total phenomenal description of a world, giving an answer to every possible question about what is observed or would be observed under any circumstances. Suppose that this B* description does not as a matter of conceptual necessity entail the truth of any particular scientific theory, A: it merely affords evidence for it, whilst leaving open the possibility of other and perhaps conflicting theoretical truths, A'. Just because of this there is no conceptual pressure to suppose that wherever we have B* we must have the same truth A. Nor is there any reason to suppose that if one part of a world is phenomenally just like another, there must be the same underlying A-truths. At least for a scientific realist, the real underlying A-facts, the theoretical states of affairs which explain the appearances, might be different in one case from another. It would be only considerations of simplicity and economy which would make it natural to *hope* that they are the same from case to case. Whereas in the moral case it is not just simpler and more economical to believe that naturally identical states of affairs compel the same moral description. It is absurd, contradictory, a failure to understand the nature of evaluation, to believe otherwise. This damages the approach to moral language according to which we infer the existence of moral states of affairs in the same kind of way that we infer the nature of scientific truths.

This argument for a projective moral theory is in effect a development of the simple thought that moral properties must be given an intelligible connection to the natural ones upon which they somehow depend. It generates a metaphysical motive for projectivism. The third and last motive I shall mention comes from the philosophy of action. Evaluative commitments are being contrasted with other, truth-conditional judgements or beliefs. This contrast means that to have a commitment of

[4] *Philosophical Investigations*, p. 178.

this sort is to hold an attitude, not a belief, and that in turn should have implications for the explanation of people's behaviour. The standard model of explanation of why someone does something attributes both a belief and a desire to the agent. The belief that a bottle contains poison does not by itself explain why someone avoids it; the belief coupled with the normal desire to avoid harm does. So if moral commitments express *attitudes*, they should function to supplement *beliefs* in the explanation of action. If they express *beliefs*, they should themselves need supplementing by mention of *desires* in a fully displayed explanation of action (fully displayed because, of course, we often do not bother to mention obvious desires and beliefs, which people will presume each other to have). It can then be urged that moral commitments fall in the right way of the active, desire, side of this fence. If someone feels moral distaste or indignation at cruelty to animals, he only needs to believe that he is faced with a case of it to act or be pulled towards acting. It seems to be a conceptual truth that to regard something as good is to feel a pull towards promoting or choosing it, or towards wanting other people to feel the pull towards promoting or choosing it. Whereas if moral commitments express beliefs that certain truth-conditions are met, then they could apparently co-exist with any kind of attitude to things meeting the truth-conditions. Someone might be indifferent to things which he regards as good, or actively hostile to them. Being moral would need two stages: firstly discerning whether the truth-conditions are met, and secondly forming desires to which those truth-conditions matter. But if that were the right account, morality could be short-circuited. You could hope to obtain the *same* actual dispositions, the same choices for or against things possessing given natural properties, the same behaviour, the same indignations and passions, by reacting to the natural features of things. It is an unnecessary loop to use those *natural* features to determine a belief in further *moral* features, and then to hope for a particular attitude to the revealed moral features.

Unfortunately this argument is not quite as compelling as it looks. The relationship between evaluative commitment and action is subtle. For there is undoubtedly an attitude of "not caring about morality". As Philippa Foot has persistently argued, there is no straight inference from moral commitment to desire. People often care more about etiquette, or reputations, or selfish advantage, than they do about morality. So the moral attitude, if it is an attitude, cannot be distinguished from belief through an inevitable connection with choice and action. Its influence on these things is indirect. But in turn this does not completely block this third argument. For other attitudes also have indirect and variable influences on action. If I find it wryly amusing that a colleague is drunk I may channel my sentiment into a variety of actions or inaction. But finding it amusing is surely a matter of having an attitude rather than a further belief, true or false, about my colleague.

To establish projectivism would need a close exploration of the nature of the attitude which is spread on the world. This involves locating what it is about an attitude which makes it a moral one, whether we would be better off without having such attitudes, what their best replacement might be, and so on. It would involve discussing whether moralizing is a relatively parochial habit of people with particular cultural and theological traditions, or whether any society whatsoever can be regarded as holding distinctively moral attitudes. But the philosophy of language can remain relatively quiet about these juicy issues. Our concern is whether one range of argument, starting from the theory of the meaning of moral remarks, blocks projectivism. The issue is whether quasi-realism (see 5.6 above) is successful in explaining why we can permit ourselves the linguistic expressions, and the thoughts they enable us to express, if projectivism is true. For my part I would say that the success of quasi-realism, as I shall try to present it, leaves a projective account of morality far the most attractive, on grounds of economy, of metaphysics, and of the theory of desire and action. It is, in fact, the only progressive research programme in moral philosophy. But why does the philosophy of language provide any kind of obstacle to it?

2. *Frege's Argument*

In a very influential article, P. T. Geach used a point of Frege's to block expressive theories.[5] The "Frege point" is very simple.

[5] 'Assertion', *Philosophical Review* (1964).

Sentences containing given predicates may occur in utterances by which we are claiming the predicates to apply, as when I call something good, true, probable, a cause of something else, and so on. But such sentences may also occur unasserted, inside the context provided by other words, making up larger sentences. I may assert: 'It is wrong to tell lies.' But I may also assert: 'If *it is wrong to tell lies*, then it is wrong to get your little brother to tell lies.' In this latter occurrence the italicized sentence is not asserted. It is the antecedent of a conditional – in other words, it is put forward to introduce an hypothesis or supposition. The Frege point is that nevertheless the sentence *means the same* on each occurrence. The proof of this is simple and decisive. The two sentences mate together to make up the premises of a valid argument:

> It is wrong to tell lies.
> If it is wrong to tell lies, it is wrong to get your little
> brother to tell lies.
>
> *So*   It is wrong to get your little brother to tell lies.

This is a valid argument, illustrating the general form: *P*; if *P* then *Q*; *so Q*. But the argument is only of this form because the sentence 'It is wrong to tell lies' means the same on each occurrence. If it did not there would be a fallacy of equivocation, as in: 'He is working at the bank; if he is working at the bank he must have his feet in the river; *so* he must have his feet in the river.' Here the second premise is true only if 'bank' is taken in a different sense from that in which, we might imagine, it makes the first premise true, and if so the argument does not illustrate the valid form. The question now is: how does an expressive theory explain the identity of meaning? For anyone asserting the second, hypothetical premise is *not* expressing an attitude of condemnation towards telling lies. He commits himself to no attitude towards it at all. He just says: 'If telling lies is wrong . . .' without offering any indication of whether he thinks it is. Let is call contexts in which a sentence occurs like this, an *unasserted* context. Then the question is whether expressive theories can cope with unasserted contexts in such a way as to allow sentences the same meaning within them, as they have when they are asserted.

It is a nice sharp problem. It might seem to provide a swift refutation of expressive theories. In unasserted contexts no attitude, etc. is evinced when the sentence is uttered; the meaning is the same as in direct contexts when such an attitude is evinced; therefore this (variable) feature does not give the (constant) meaning. But before quasi-realism surrenders it needs to see whether expressive theories can give any account at all of these contexts.

There are in fact two distinct aspects to this problem. Firstly, can we explain what we are up to when we make these remarks? Unasserted contexts show us treating moral predicates like others, *as though* by their means we can introduce objects of doubt, belief, knowledge, things which can be supposed, queried, pondered. Can the projectivist say why we do this?

Here he faces two questions. Consider the fact that we can conjoin evaluations and ordinary expressions of belief: 'It is wrong to tell lies and your mother is going to be annoyed'. Now it is surely not surprising that we might link together two commitments, even if one expresses an attitude, and the other a belief. The one sentence conjoins the two disparate commitments, and since we often want to communicate that we have both, it is hardly surprising that we have a way of doing it. That gives us an idea of *what we are up to* in offering the conjunction. But it does not fully answer the second question: why do we have this *particular* sentence to serve that purpose. For we might want to say other things about 'and', which make it difficult to see why it is serving this function. For instance, we might explain the semantic function of 'and' like this: it stands between two sentences to make one large sentence out of them; the large sentence is true if and only if each smaller one is true. Otherwise it is false. Now this little semantic theory fits badly, initially at any rate, with the occurrence of the evaluation as a conjunct. For suppose, according to the expressive theory, the evaluation is not susceptible of truth or falsity. Then it should not mingle with an operator which needs truths and falsities to work on. But there are ways of easing around this obstacle. One is to expand the way we think of 'and'. We have to do this anyway, for it can link utterances when they certainly do not express beliefs which are genuinely susceptible of truth-value e.g. commands: 'hump that barge and tote that bale.' We would instead say something like this: 'and' links commitments to give

an overall commitment which is accepted only if each component is accepted. The notion of a commitment is then capacious
enough to include both ordinary beliefs, and these other attitudes, habits, and prescriptions.

So to tackle Frege's problem the first thing we need is a view
of what we are up to in putting commitments into conditionals.
Working out their implications, naturally. But how can attitudes
as opposed to beliefs have implications? At this point we must
turn again to the projective picture. A moral *sensibility*, on that
picture, is defined by a function from *input* of belief to *output* of
attitude.[6] Now not all such sensibilities are admirable. Some are
coarse, insensitive, some are plain horrendous, some are conservative and inflexible, others fickle and unreliable; some are
too quick to form strict and passionately held attitudes, some
too sluggish to care about anything. But it is extremely
important to us to rank sensibilities, and to endorse some and to
reject others. For one of the main features affecting the desirability of the world we live in is the way other people behave, and
the way other people behave is largely a function of their
sensibility. So much is obvious enough. And amongst the features of sensibilities which matter are, of course, not only the
actual attitudes which are the output, but the interactions
between them. For instance, a sensibility which *pairs* an attitude
of disapproval towards telling lies, and an attitude of calm or
approval towards getting your little brother to tell lies, would
not meet my endorsement. I can only admire people who would
reject the second action as strongly as they reject the first. It
matters to me that people should have only this pairing because
its absence opens a dangerous weakness in a sensibility. Its
owner would have the wrong attitude to indirect ways of getting
lies told (and for that matter the wrong attitude to his little
brother).

The conditional form shows me expressing this endorsement.
Of course, it is an endorsement which is itself the expression of a
moral point of view. Some casuistry might lead people to the
other commitment, that there is a great difference between
telling lies and getting your little brother to do so (am I my

---

[6] Or, more generally, an input of *awareness* rather than belief. A man may respond to
perceived features without realizing that they are the ones responsible for his reactions.
For example, we often do not know what we find funny in a situation.

brother's keeper?).[7] Such people would reject the conditional. But it is quite satisfactory that the conditional expresses a moral point of view. The task was not to show that it does not, but to explain what it does at all. Other conditionals have the same general role:

If lying makes you feel good, then it's all right.
If you ought to give him £10, then you ought to give him something.

The latter is held on logical grounds. I can only endorse a sensibility which, in the presence of the antecedent attitude, also has the consequent one, because it is logically impossible that the action specified in the antecedent can be done without giving the man something. I could not endorse at all an illogical sensibility, which itself paired approval of an action with disapproval of a logical implication of the performance of the action. The former conditional is the expression of a repulsive *standard*: it endorses a function from an input of knowledge that a lie has made you feel good to an output of satisfaction with it. Finding better descriptions of admirable input/output functions is the task of moral philosophy.

This account of what we are up to when we use the conditional form with evaluative components now needs supplementing by a semantic theory. We can put the need this way. Imagine a language unlike English in containing no evaluative predicates. It wears the expressive nature of value-judgements on its sleeve. Call it E_{ex}. It might contain a 'hooray!' operator and a 'boo!' operator (H!, B!) which attach to descriptions of things to result in expressions of attitude. H!(the playing of Tottenham Hotspur) would express the attitude towards the playing. B!(lying) would express the contrary attitude towards lying, and so on. For the reasons I have developed, we would expect the speakers of E_{ex} to want another device, enabling them to express views on the structure of sensibilities. They would need a notation with which to endorse or reject various couplings of attitudes, or couplings of beliefs and attitudes. Suppose

---

[7] Examples of genuinely controversial commitments of the form may help: 'if something ought to be done, any means to it ought to be allowed'; 'if a group has been discriminated against, it is now right to give it better treatment.'

we talk *about* an attitude or belief by putting its expression inside bars: |H! (X)| refers to approval of (X). And suppose we use the semi-colon to denote the view that one attitude or belief involves or is coupled with another. Then the speakers of E_{ex} will need to express themselves thus:

H! (|H! (Tottenham)|;|H! (Arsenal)|)
H! (|B! (lying)|;|B! (getting little brother to lie)|)

The first endorses only sensibilities which, if they endorse Tottenham, also endorse Arsenal, and this is what we express by saying that if Arsenal is a good team, so is Tottenham. The second is our old friend.

E_{ex} will naturally want further constructions. We want to say things like 'X used to be a good thing, but now it is not', in which evaluations connect with tenses. Notice that this does not mean the same as 'I used to approve of X but now I do not': it implies that X has changed, not that I have. The favourable evaluation attaches to X as it was, so E_{ex} will need a device to express this: perhaps an index indicating that the past state is the object of evaluation. Again, consider our different attitudes to our own attitudes. Since I have the concept of improvement and deterioration in a sensibility, I know that I am vulnerable to argument that in forming a particular attitude I am myself falling victim to a flawed input/output function. I may be exhibiting dispositions which I do not endorse, or committing myself to pairings of attitude and attitude, or attitude and belief, which I also cannot endorse. So in some cases I can be uncertain not only of the facts of the case, but of how to react to them. I will need to explore the other aspects of my moral commitments, and see whether, when they are brought to bear, one attitude or another begins to settle itself. And when I have taken up an attitude, I might be uncomfortably aware that it may turn out to be vulnerable to criticism. So E_{ex} will need a way of signalling different degrees of robustness in our attitudes: different ways in which they can be regarded as likely or unlikely to succumb to an improved perspective. H!(X) can co-exist with something like ? H! (|H! (X)|): uncertainty that one's own attitude of approval can itself be endorsed.

E_{ex} will be spoken by people who need to signal and respect consistencies and inconsistencies. Consider:

B! (lying)
H! (|B! (lying)|;|B! (getting little brother to lie)|)

Disapproval of lying, and approval of making (disapproval of getting little brother to lie), follow upon (disapproval of lying). Anyone holding this pair must hold the consequential disapproval: he is committed to disapproving of getting little brother to lie, for if he does not his attitudes clash. He has a fractured sensibility which cannot itself be an object of approval. The 'cannot' here follows not (as a realist explanation would have it) because such a sensibility must be out of line with the moral facts it is trying to describe, but because such a sensibility cannot fulfil the practical purposes for which we evaluate things. E_{ex} will want to signal this. It will want a way of expressing the thought that it is a logical mistake that is made, if someone holds the first two commitments, and not the commitment to disapproval of getting your little brother to lie.

In short, E_{ex} needs to become an instrument of serious, reflective, evaluative practice, able to express concern for improvements, clashes, implications, and coherence of attitudes. Now one way of doing this is to become like ordinary English. That is, it would invent a predicate answering to the attitude, and treat commitments as if they were judgements, and then use all the natural devices for debating truth. If this is right, then our use of indirect contexts does not prove that an expressive theory of morality is wrong; it merely proves us to have adopted a form of expression adequate to our needs. *This is what is meant by 'projecting' attitudes onto the world.*

What I have done here is to explain how conditionals can be regarded as ways of following out implications, although it is not imperative that the commitments whose implications they trace have 'truth-conditions'. Now you might say: even if this can be done, hasn't the quasi-realist a very dreary task in front of him? For remember that the Frege point was entirely general: it could cite any unasserted context. So mightn't others arise which require separate and ingenious explanations, and is the quasi-realist faced with an endless task? Isn't he like Ptolemaic astronomers, having to bolster his theory with ever more complex or *ad hoc* epicycles, whereas by comparison there is a simple, common-sense view that moral predicates are just the same as more ordinary ones, so that there is nothing to explain about the way they function in unasserted contexts?[8]

Questions of what does or does not require explanation involve delicate matters of philosophical judgement, but the objection here is surely overdrawn. For what plays the role of Copernicus to the allegedly Ptolemaic complexities? What was wrong with Ptolemaic astronomy (by the end of its reign) was that there was a better way of explaining the same things. But this better way did not just take those things for granted. It was not the stultifying position that everything is just in order without our bothering to explain it. We have seen enough of why projectivism is a plausible moral philosophy. And this being so it is extremely important to tell whether it is blocked by arguments from the philosophy of language. Nobody denies that the surface phenomena of language – the fact that we use moral predicates, and apply truth or falsity to the judgements we make when we use them – pose a problem for projectivism. This is why they tempt people into realism. But by overcoming the problem projectivism also steals a march on its rivals. For it removes the temptation to think that our surface forms of expression embody a mistake, that they are "fraudulent" or "diseased": it *protects* our ordinary thinking, in a way that mere reminders of the way we do actually proceed cannot do. It solves Kant's question of the *right* to our concepts, as well as the question of what they are actually like.

But now a new and rather surprising vista is opened. For if this is right, might 'it is true that . . .' also be given this quasi-realist explanation? Initially, an expressive theory stands in stark contrast to one giving moral remarks truth-conditions. But if we sympathize with the pressures I have described, we come to appreciate why it should be natural to treat expressions of attitude as if they were similar to ordinary judgements. We come to need a predicate, whose behaviour is like that of others. Why not regard ourselves as having *constructed* a notion of moral truth? If we have done so, then we can happily say that moral judgements are true or false, only not think that we have sold out to realism when we do so.

---

[8] This response was made to me by Professor Geach.

3. *Constructing Truth*

The arguments of the last section may give us a right to a notion of an *improved* set of attitudes; they give us some right to a notion of the *coherence* and *consistency* of such a set. But do they suffice to build all that we need from a conception of truth, applicable to moral judgements?

The root disquiet here runs very deep. In effect, quasi-realism is trying to earn our right to talk of moral truth, while recognizing fully the subjective sources of our judgements, inside our own attitudes, needs, desires, and natures. The sense of subjectivity triggers all kinds of wild reactions. Can the projectivist take such things as obligations, duties, the "stern daughter of the voice of God", seriously? How can he if he denies that these represent external, independent, authoritative requirements? Mustn't he in some sense have a schizoid attitude to his own moral commitments – holding them, but also holding that they are ungrounded? And when the tension comes out, shouldn't he become frivolous, amoral? A recent influential book even believes that an emotivist should approve of manipulating people, bullying and lying and brainwashing as we please, rather than respecting their independence.[9] Words like 'relativism' and 'subjective' focus these fears; books and sermons alike pronounce that the projectivist should, if consistent, end up with the morals of a French gangster.

Fortunately, all this is ridiculously beside the point. Just as the senses constrain what we can believe about the empirical world, so our natures and desires, needs and pleasures, constrain much of what we can admire and commend, tolerate and work for. There are not so many livable, unfragmented, developed, consistent, and coherent systems of attitude. A projectivist, like anyone else, may be sensitive to the features which make our lives go well or badly; to the need for order, contracts, sources of stability. If his reflection on these things leads him to endorse a high Victorian love of promises, rectitude, contracts, conventional sexual behaviour, well and good: there is nothing in his meta-ethic to suggest otherwise. For instance, a proper respect for promises, the kind of respect which sees them as

---

[9] A. MacIntyre, *After Virtue*, p. 22, and throughout.

making requirements, as bounds on conduct, is certainly a good attitude to foster. But it may, for all that, be just that: an attitude.

The problem is not with a subjective source for value in itself, but with people's inability to come to terms with it, and their consequent need for a picture in which values imprint themselves on a pure passive, receptive witness, who has no responsibility in the matter. To show that these fears have no intellectual justification means developing a concept of moral truth out of the materials to hand: seeing how, given attitudes, given constraints upon them, given a notion of improvement and of possible fault in any sensibility including our own, we can construct a notion of truth. The exercise is important. For one moral of the brush with Goodman's paradox and the rule-following considerations (chapter 3) is that judgement never involves quite the pure passivity which is supposed to be an untainted source of objectivity and truth. We have to see our concepts as the product of our own intellectual stances: how then are they suitable means for framing objectively correct, true, judgement, describing the mind-independent world as it in fact is? It is not only moral truth which starts to quake. But we can learn how to approach the general problems of truth by starting with it.

The simplest suggestion is that we define a 'best possible set of attitudes', thought of as the limiting set which would result from taking all possible opportunities for improvement of atti-tude. Saying that an evaluative remark is true would be saying that it is a member of such a set, or is implied by such a set.[10] Call the set M^*. Then if m is a particular commitment, express-ing an attitude m:

$$m \text{ is true} = m \text{ is a member of } M^*$$

To test this suggestion we must find conditions which truth obeys, and see whether they square with it. In particular, does the definition justify the constraint of *consistency* (m cannot be true and false)? The first hurdle is to define the idea of a unique best possible sensibility. Certainly there is improvement and deterioration. But why should not improving sensibilities

[10] Although this is the simplest projectivist account of truth, and is one used by many anti-realists, I do not myself think it is the best. It is only a first approximation, but serves to make the immediate points. See below (7.7).

diverge in various ways? An imperfect sensibility might take any of several different trajectories as it evolves into something better. We might imagine a tree (see Fig. 6). Here each node (point at which there is branching) marks a place where equally admirable but diverging opinion is possible. And there is no unique M^* on which the progress of opinion is sighted. So there is no truth, since the definition lapses. More precisely, truth would shrink to only those commitments which are shared by all the diverging systems: truth belongs to the trunk.

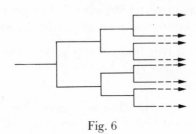

Fig. 6

This is the deep problem of *relativism*. It is not the vague and unfounded disquiet that I have no right to judge unfavourably people with any other opinion – those who practice human sacrifice, or murder Jews, for instance. Of course I have. My attitudes, and those involved in any system I could conceive of which might be superior to mine, alike condemn them. The deep problem is the suspicion that other, equally admirable sensibilities, over which I can claim no superiority of my own, lead to divergent judgements. This does take away my right to think of mine as true, which is equivalent to unsettling my commitments.

The classic introduction of the problem is Hume's superb and neglected essay 'Of the Standard of Taste'. He introduces "such diversity in the internal frame or external situation as is entirely blameless on both sides". He illustrates it with the difference between "a young man, whose passions are warm" and "a man more advanced in years, who takes pleasure in wise, philosophical reflections concerning the conduct of life and the moderation of the passions". The former prefers the amorous and tender images of Ovid, the latter the wisdom of

Tacitus; in the twentieth century no doubt the one reads *Playboy*
and the other *The Economist*. Now we imagine the young man's
literary sensibility improved and refined into a system M^*_o and
the old man's into a system M^*_t, and one containing the commitment that Ovid is a better writer than Tacitus, whilst the
other contains the reverse. How can we recover a notion of truth
for either judgement? Hume's answer is subtle: it consists in
expanding the difference between a (mere) matter of predilec-
tion, and a fit object of literary comparison: "it is plainly an
error in a critic, to confine his approbation to one species or style
of writing, and condemn all the rest." The point of this emerges
if we ask the question: who is to adopt the following three views:

(1) $M^*_o \rightarrow$ it is true that Ovid is better than Tacitus
(2) $M^*_t \rightarrow$ it is true that Tacitus is better than Ovid
(3) There is no possible improvement on either M^*_o or M^*_t

(where '$M^* \rightarrow$ it is true that m' means that M^* contains an
attitude which is expressed by the sentence m).

How can you have each of these? Think of the detail. Is
someone who has either of the two sensibilities aware of the
other? If not, it would surely be an improvement if he were. But
if so, then quite what is the combination of attitudes required?
It surely begins to seem wrong to hold, straight out, that Ovid
is better than Tacitus, or vice versa. If we admit a really
developed rival way of looking at it, are we not required to
soften the opposition – to say, for instance, that Ovid and
Tacitus are of equal merit, although each has features which
appeal to different people? In short, as soon as *I* hold that a case
begins to look as though the tree structure applies, *I* also hold
that there is a truth about the subject on which the divergent
attitudes are held, and, holding that, *I* would also judge that
one or both of the rival sensibilities is capable of improvement,
until it yields my own attitude. Hume's case depends upon the
audience accepting that Ovid and Tacitus actually are of equal
merit – otherwise it would not be just the different tastes of
different ages which result in the different rankings. But if we
think this, then each of the two systems is flawed. The young
but able literary critic is insensitive to the virtues which appear
to the older man, and which in truth result in the two writers
coming out equally; similarly for the older literary critic.

What does this mean? It means that an evaluative system should contain the resources to *transcend the tree structure*: evidence that there is a node *itself* implies that it is wrong to maintain either of the conflicting commitments. It is itself a signal that the right attitude – the truth about the relative merits of Ovid and Tacitus – is not that expressed by either of these partial perspectives. The better perspective may judge the merits equal, or it may award the prize to just one view, or it may regret and change the terms of the discussion, by losing interest in the simplistic question of whether Ovid is a better writer than Tacitus, and concentrating upon different merits of each, with no intention of finding a summary comparison. In that case the system of *each* of these literary critics is defective, by containing too many crude comparisons. So in practice evidence that there is a node is just treated as a signal that the truth is not yet finally argued, and it goes into discussions as part of the evidence. We are constrained to argue and practise as though the truth is single, and this constraint is defensible in spite of the apparent possibility of the tree-structure.

It is as though the trunk – the core of opinion to which there is no admirable alternative – contains the power to grow through any of the choices of opinion which lead to branching: the choices become themselves part of the knowledge which the progress of attitude must use to form its course.[11] In so far as acquaintance with another value-system makes me respect it, then it properly makes me rethink both systems, transcending the tree-structure.

One common element of "relativism" is the thought that if we can conceive of different, equally admirable systems, then that must weaken our own in favour of *toleration*. It seems to be particularly the attitudes associated with *obligation* which are vulnerable to worries about rival systems. The explanation of this is quite pleasant, although perhaps slightly peripheral to language.

Suppose we symbolize 'it is obligatory to do A' by OA, and 'it is permissible to avoid A' by 'P$\neg A$'. P$\neg A$ contradicts OA. Now imagine:

---

[11] Readers may be reminded of the Hegelian three-step (look left, look right, and then cross over) of thesis, antithesis, synthesis, by which we lurch towards the Absolute.

(1) $M^*_1 \to OA$

(2) $M^*_2 \to P\neg A$

(3) There is no possible improvement on either M^*_1 or M^*_2.

This is the tree structure. One way of transcending it goes:

(4) (3) implies that it is permissible to hold M^*_2; this implies that it is permissible to hold that $\neg A$ is permissible, which in turn implies that $\neg A$ is permissible;

(5) So any view, such as M^*_1 which implies the reverse, is wrong, and *ipso facto* capable of improvement.

This transcends the tree by showing that if we suppose that the choice leading to M^*_2 is permissible, then we must dislike the other. We cannot maintain the even-handed, Olympian stance which finds them each blameless. But now notice that if we have a *prima facie* case of (1), (2), and (3), it is *likely to be the obligation* which is the more threatened. Suppose we try to transcend the tree by the reverse argument:

(4') (3) implies that it is permissible to hold M^*_1; this implies that it is permissible to hold that A is obligatory, which in turn implies that A is obligatory;

we need the different reduction principle that if it is permissible to hold that A is obligatory, then A *is* obligatory, and that is not nearly so intuitive.[12] Evidence of a permissible system which permits $\neg A$ is evidence that $\neg A$ is permissible; evidence of a permissible system which obligates A is not so plausibly thought of as evidence that A is obligatory. So here, once we have an initial inclination to each of the three propositions, we are more likely to escape the inconsistency by seeing M^*_1 as capable of improvement. This is why travel broadens the mind.

So on this account it is correct, as well as natural, to find faith in particular obligations shaken, if what seem to be admirable sensibilities do not recognize them.

---

[12] Formally the reduction principles differ in a way analogous to the difference between the modal system S4 and the stronger system S5. If 'it is permitted to permit A' implies 'A is permitted', we have $PPx \to Px$, which corresponds to S4. This does not demand that 'it is permitted to obligate x' implies 'x is obligatory', for which S5 is needed. The comparison is suggestive, and indicates a respectable side of worries about relativism.

4. *Interlude: Bivalence, Fiction, Law*

Because of the writings of Michael Dummett it has become common for people to think that an anti-realist will not accept that every commitment in the relevant area is either true, or false. The idea is that only a realist can adopt such a logical principle. For the construction of truth suggested might evidently leave it that M^* neither implies that m, nor that m is false, in which case on the definition m *is* neither true, nor false. It is worth exploring this connection a little. Dummett associates his views about the justification of bivalence with a quite different problem which he believes he has discovered for realism – the problem of what it is to 'manifest a grasp of' sentences whose truth-conditions in some sense outrun our capacity to verify whether they obtain. I mentioned this in chapter 2: it all depends on the manifestee. But the connection of bivalence and realism is independently interesting. In particular it introduces an intriguing possibility – that a conception of truth underlies logical principles, so that if it is abandoned, they must be so too; conversely, adopting the logic is in itself a commitment to the conception.

We must first distinguish two possible views about falsity:

m is weakly false = it's not the case that m is a member of M^*

m is strongly false = the attitude expressed by 'not m' is a member of M^*

To see the difference between these, remember the remarks about the ways in which improved theories may relate to their predecessors, not by containing direct denials of theses previously held, but by transcending those terms of discussion. For example, suppose then that m is a proposition that there is a right to strike. And suppose that we believe M^* to be likely to have abandoned the concept of a right altogether – perhaps for Marxist reasons, it sees the concept as part of a way of thought about human affairs which is itself defective and due to be transcended. Under the first definition it is then *false* that there is a right to strike: this commitment is no part of a true system. But under the second definition it is *not* false that there is a right to strike. The true system does not contain 'there is no right to strike' either. It simply does not speak in those terms. This is actually quite a common reaction, on a small scale, in the face of some kinds of evaluation. It's not that we take up the attitude expressed by directly contradicting someone's commitment, but we reject the terms of the discussion. If someone asserts that Beethoven is a better composer than Brahms I might not respond by asserting that Brahms is a better or equal composer, but by regretting these simplistic comparisons. Certain kinds of tendency to see everything in moral terms are best met by de-moralizing issues, rather than taking up opposing moral attitudes (although one of the subtleties here is that a wish not to discuss a choice in moral terms is itself describable as a moral attitude, and as argued above, usually one in favour of tolerance and permissions).

A useful example to distinguish the first and second definitions of falsity is that of fiction. We can assert that Hamlet had this or that feature: he had a murdered father, a difficult family life. He did not have a peg-leg or a harem. What do we mean by regarding the first two remarks as correct, and the last as incorrect? They are *grounded* in Shakespeare's text in some such way as this: we imagine a character conforming to the way Shakespeare describes or shows Hamlet, and if we are compelled to regard him as φ, then it is true that Hamlet is φ; if we are compelled to regard him as not φ, then it is wrong to say that he is φ, and false, under each definition, that he is φ. The notion of compulsion here is not purely mechanical or formal: it can be a matter of sensibility to realize that the texts compel a particular reading of Hamlet's character, meaning that seeing him in accord with that reading best fits or explains the course of the drama. If we call the grounding text G, and the relevant notion of compulsion $\rightarrow$, then we can have

$$G \rightarrow p \; = \; \text{It is true that } p$$
$$G \rightarrow \neg p \; = \; \text{It is false that } p \text{ (on each definition)}$$

But we also expect cases where neither obtains. The texts do not compel us to regard Hamlet as having a nice light baritone, nor as not having one: neither proposition appears in any admirable list of truths about Hamlet. So is it false that Hamlet had a nice light baritone? It is weakly false. But it is not strongly false: the proposition that Hamlet had some other kind of voice appears in no such list either. The distinction between weak and strong falsity matters whenever the grounding, in virtue of which propositions are true or false, is potentially incomplete, failing to yield just one verdict on every question.

Consider now truth in law. A contract is valid if the law makes it so. But law is a matter of human arrangements, actions, and decisions. The contract is valid if these – the grounding – compel the judgement that it is. Jurisprudence is weighed down by wrangles over quite how much may be added to the grounding, and quite how much can be read into the notion of compulsion. But this does not matter, for in any event we have the same structure as in fiction. If p = 'this contract is valid', and $\neg p$ = 'this contract is not valid':

(1) $\mathrm{T}p \ = G\,(p) \text{ compels } p$
(2) $\mathrm{T}\neg p = G\,(p) \text{ compels } \neg p$

where $G(p)$ represents the sum total of circumstances, precedents, statutes, pertinent to the issue, and compulsion is interpreted according to the best view of how those things should be used. But it now seems possible that neither p nor $\neg p$ is compelled by the grounding. Perhaps the arrangements of a society have simply not "got up to" a certain issue, either by providing directly for it, or providing indirectly, by laying down what is to be decided when direct provision fails. Is a defamatory naval signal libel (written) or slander (spoken)? Is an ice-cream van a place of sale? Is a prisoner-of-war a resident in an alien country? We might well suppose that even if these examples are determinate, there will be others where grounding fails, and the verdict is, as we should say, a matter of discretion. In the terms so far suggested, if p is in this way a matter of discretion, each of p and $\neg p$ is weakly false. But one might just as well call each of them weakly true. Weak truth would correspond to the idea that judgement in favour of p is at least not *in*correct:

$$\mathrm{F}_w p = \mathrm{T}_w p = \neg(G(p) \text{ compels } p) \ \& \ \neg(G(p) \text{ compels } \neg p)$$

In these circumstances $\neg p$ is weakly true as well; and each is weakly, but not strongly false. The natural way of symbolizing this state would be Dp – discretionary whether p – meaning that the issue is one to be settled by a decision of a court which could, so far as the proper use of the grounding goes, fall either way. The question now asked is: if all this is right, why is any legal system *bivalent* or *polar*, admitting just two verdicts (it is true that the contract was valid, it is false that the contract was valid)? Why don't we characteristically find three sides in each dispute: one arguing for the judgement Tp; one arguing for Fp; one arguing that Dp? If this question has no answer, then the fact that systems are polar should be surprising. Why, then, do we find so little flicker in the smooth determination of lawyers to regard every contract as either valid or not valid? Literary critics put up with incompleteness and the absence of strong truth or falsity about Hamlet's voice. And if two of them mounted a Mad-Hatter debate about it, the most respectable view would be a third advocating that the matter is ungrounded. Why not at law?

Professor Dworkin supposes that these questions force us to review the view that law is grounded in human arrangements in such a way as to invite incompleteness.[13] The ingredients which Dworkin brings to plug the gaps are twofold. Firstly, as well as "black letter" statute and precedent, we must consider the political theory which best justifies settled law. If that theory suggests an answer one way, then even when hard legal facts give out, then that answer is correct. The other ingredient is determinate moral truth. If on each issue just one side is morally in the right, the verdict should go to him. Neither ingredient escapes the problem. The shape which M^* is likely to take will leave it quite silent on many issues at law (do Right and Truth attach only to the cause which sees an arrangement of flags as libellous?). The problem is that there is often no such thing as *the* political theory best justifying settled law. In many jurisdictions the political theories of people starting the patchwork would be virtually unintelligible to us, as ours would be to them. And the particular conceptions of the values, rights, etc. enshrined in any theory, even when it is explicitly part of a constitution, shift and bend and change: the tree-structure threatens again. But if we cannot regain completeness, how do we answer the questions?

[13]   R. Dworkin, 'No Right Answer', in *Law, Morality, and Society*, ed. Hacker and Raz.

We arrange things so that the law is to deliver one of two verdicts: p or $\neg p$. Why do we not allow a judge to shelter behind incompleteness, able to deliver the answer 'Dp'? Because Dp answers nothing: we *need* to know (for instance) whether the contract is valid, and one party to pay the other, or invalid, and vice versa. For this pragmatic reason a judge must *think and argue as though* there is one proper verdict, even if the overall theory of grounding licenses no such optimism. So some constitutions *explicitly* rule Dp out; the Swiss legal code, for example, dictates that a judge shall not shelter behind insufficiencies of the law.[14]

Disallowing Dp as a verdict is therefore explicable. We wouldn't expect this crack in bivalent practice. We might expect others. A system could make place for a third answer (the contract was middling: neither party wins or loses quite as much as if the case had gone a definite way). But having three answers, or five, or indeed any number, is not the same as allowing Dp to stand as a verdict. Consider a case hinging on whether a man was of sound mind when he made his will, in which case I benefit, or of unsound mind, in which case the Royal Corgi Society does. A court may have only two verdicts at its disposal. Given the spectrum of soundnesses of mind, it might be better if it had many, and was empowered to apportion the money according to the degree of lunacy. But things would not be at all better, under either system, if it was entitled to announce that the issue is discretionary, and then walk off the site.

It is then explicable that a court should need to practise as though there is one truth, one correct verdict, out of *however many* it is empowered to give. It is therefore no argument against the equations (1) and (2) that it so practises. We have here a pragmatic argument for practising as though there is a legal truth. But shouldn't this induce schizophrenia in a judge, if he has to practise as though this is so, although his background philosophy allows failure of grounding? Perhaps if he was operating a really incomplete, poor system, it should. But two features, also relevant to the moral case, apply to diminish the difficulty. The first is that legal and moral reasoning are sufficiently open-ended for it never to be a matter of certainty

[14] I owe this information to H. L. A. Hart.

that we are at a node in the tree – that a proper decision could go either way (this is why I have talked only in terms of *evidence* that we are at a node). So it seldom becomes rational to stop arguing as though there were just one right answer, which progressively more generous and engaged views would embrace. The second is that we often stack things so failure of grounding cannot apply. We can do this by putting the "burden of proof" on one side. If that side fails to get a grounding, then the negation automatically does, and completeness is restored. This is parallel to the moral structure about obligation and permissions. If M^* does not oblige us to refrain from A, then it permits A. There is no way in which it can remain silent on whether A is permitted.

These two points are merely suggestive. There will doubtless remain cases where a judge will regard his verdict as discretionary, as one on which reasonable men may have differed, and where the controlling idea of one legal truth is a fiction. It may be that if he so regards a verdict, he ought to feel self-conscious about delivering it, as though he is claiming there to be one right answer, when there is none or are several. But this degree of discomfort is one that judges manage to tolerate. Notice that moralists do not: in this situation, like Hume's literary critics, they have the option of ceasing to regard the issue as a moral one.

We have been dealing with cases where one type of proposition has its truth grounded in other facts. Legal and fictional judgements are good examples; on the projective theory, truth grounded in membership of M^* is another. If there can arise incompleteness in grounding, there will be propositions which are not true, and not strongly false either. There are other subjects where the same structure suggests itself. Arithmetical truths gain their status as something more than mere formalisms because numbers matter: they are what we count and measure with, and because of this we are not free to invent propositions about them as we wish. But it is quite unclear how far this constraint goes. It seems to compel just one ordinary arithmetic. But mathematicians can devise systems which contain conflicting accounts of how many infinite numbers there are, and how they are packed. Is one of these true, and the other not? Perhaps the correct account of how mathematical truth is grounded in practice shows that the grounding does not extend so far, and that we have here only a matter for choice. Or perhaps it does not. Again counterfactuals are types of proposition, about what would have been the case if things had been otherwise, which seem to have their truth grounded in facts about the real world (for more on this see the next section). But this grounding too might fail: there may be no fact of the matter whether if I had thrown this coin yesterday, it would have landed heads, or would have landed tails. Perhaps many such assertions are only weakly false (or weakly true). But again we may need to practise as though there is one genuine truth to be had, if we can find how to argue it.

It is tempting, because of these structures, to say that only a realist can commit himself to strong bivalence (every proposition is strongly true or strongly false). He imagines (and perhaps it really is just an image) a determinate legal, moral, arithmetical, counterfactual, etc. *fact* existing quite independently of any incompleteness in grounding, filling up the gaps. But the matter is more subtle than that, on two counts. First, we have seen how a system can be organized so as to transcend the tree-structure by putting the onus on one side: unless there is a proof of p, the proof of an absence of one *counts* as a proof of $\neg p$. This is the likely structure with obligations and permissions, as I have argued. If M^* spoke only about obligations and permissions, we could presume it to obey strong bivalence, in spite of a projective or anti-realist account of what we mean when we so talk. However, this point by itself will not force strong bivalence. For (as with Hamlet's voice) p and $\neg p$ are often symmetrical, so that there is no reason to describe the fact that the ground does not compel one, as *itself* a compulsion of the other. The second point is the pragmatic need to practise as though there is just one truth, as in the case of law. A judge should regulate his practice like this: in every case that comes up he must *proceed as though* the grounding compels p, or the grounding compels $\neg p$. This bivalent practice is earned on an anti-realist basis, and itself no sign that legal reality is any more complete than the nature of the grounding suggests. This means that it is wrong simply to *identify* bivalent logical practice with acceptance of realism, for it can be explained and justified on a more economical basis. When we judge, with the aim of giving assent to *p* or assent to its negation, we will practice under the umbrella that *p* is true, or *p* is false, just as a court must do. But this practice is quite consistent with realizing that each might be a half-truth, or that perhaps no facts exist to ground just one option.

5. *Other Anti-Realisms: Causes, Counterfactuals, Idealism*

Let us get back to projectivism.

Apart from its own interest as an account of moralizing, there is one supremely important point about a projective theory. Suppose the quasi-realist earns us the right to put our commitments in the terms we do. It is just that the explanation of this right starts from the subjective source, in attitude and sentiment. It follows that the issue of whether projectivism is correct is *not readily decidable*. That is, you cannot rely upon first thoughts, or immediate armchair reactions, or your unprocessed knowledge of what you mean by some commitments, to determine whether the theory is true. This alters the terms in which anti-realism needs discussing: in particular it alters it from those in which the analytic tradition has usually tried to discuss it. That tradition has persistently tried to make the anti-realist a reductionist, bent upon giving an account of all we mean by various commitments; from the armchair we can announce that we really mean more (and this can be supplemented by arguments that we do), and then this is seen as a victory for realism. Whereas now there need be no attempt to deny the distinctive nature of the commitments, and the unique meaning of the various vocabularies, and this still leaves open a projective theory of what is true of us when we use them. This implies that the pure philosophy of language has less to offer to such problems than most recent discussions assume. Nevertheless such a return to an *explanatory* mode, away from an *analytic* mode, is essential, especially if we are to understand the history of philosophy rightly.

Consider for instance Hume's treatment of causal necessity, perhaps the classic projective theory in philosophy. The central thought is that dignifying a relationship between events as casual is spreading or projecting a reaction which we have to something else we are aware of about the events – Hume thought of this input in terms of the regular succession of similar such events, one upon the other. Exposed to such regularity, our minds (cannot help but) form habits of expectation, which they then project by describing the one event as causing the other. We are more subtle than Hume suggests: we take more into account than regular succession of similar events.[15] But this does not matter to the overall nature of the theory. The essential anti-realist core is quite missed by counterexamples where we think that A causes B, although B's do not regularly follow A's (e.g. because of countervailing circumstances), or where B's do but we do not think that A's cause them (e.g. because some third thing causes them both). We may both be subtle and active in choosing to dignify various relations as causal: it is still possible than when we do we give expression to a habit of reliance, a habit which we depend upon in inference and in other practice, and which we project when we insist upon the existence of causal connection. Again, since we have a purpose in so projecting we will have standards by which to assess the evidence we use for the existence of causal connections, and the quasi-realist can again earn a right to the notion of truth, and a notion of the true causal structure of things.

Since this is the basic structure of Hume's theory, it follows that he has been shamefully abused by many commentators and their victims. He is not denying that there exist causes; he is not inconsistent when he says that there are unknown causes of things; he is not concerned to say that causal propositions can be analysed into ones about the regular successions of events, which then capture their entire content. He is merely explaining our normal sayings, our normal operations with the concept, in terms of the reactions we have, after exposure to a reality which exhibits no such feature. The explanation may be defective; even in principle it may not work, but at least it needs tackling for what it is. We fail to do this if we insist on seeing it as a meaning equation (consider again my strictures against naturalism in ethics). We also fail to do it if we merely insist, as many thinkers do, that we properly describe the *perceived* states of affairs in causal terms – *see* bricks splashing in water, balls

---

[15] Although Hume is more careful than often realized: *Treatise*, Bk. I, pt. III, sect. XV.

breaking windows, things pushing and pulling. Certainly we do: but what is the best explanation of our so seeing them?

Amongst the questions which genuinely arise the most prominent will be the kind of conception of a non-causal reality whose features explain our reactions. Hume thought in terms of a regular succession of events, describable in purely phenomenal terms. But is this even a possible conception of the world? Perhaps we have to use the concept of a causal connection to describe the world at all (ordinary descriptions involve *things* with all their *powers*). In that case there is no way to explain our causal sayings as projections generated by something else, for there will be no stripped, B-vocabulary in which to identify the something else.

These questions loom still larger when we get to Kant, and the whole description of the world as spatially extended and temporally ordered is seen as the work of the mind, whose only exposure is to a noumenal, inaccessible reality of things-we-know-not-what. For the picture at the beginning of this chapter defines one of the central problems of philosophy. How far does the projected reality extend: what is our creation and what is given? When the spread world drips down entirely over the real world, whose nature is blotted out and left completely "noumenal", we have idealism. Before rushing to embrace it, there are two points to remember. One is that respectable projectivism is an explanatory theory. But in so far as we lack a conception of the noumenal reality on which our reactions depend, we also fail to explain how its features are responsible for our reactions. A particularly gross instance of this general problem is Kant's removal of the noumenal reality from space and time. For there is no prospect at all of an explanatory account of how our reactions depend on the features (events? changes?) of such a reality: *depends* is a causal notion, and at home only within the familiar world.[16] Secondly, in my development, projectivism needs a sense of the role of a saying contrasted with simple expression of belief – in the case of evaluations, a role of expressions of attitude, or in the case of cause, a role as dignifying a regularity for some theoretical or practical purpose – and this is the foundation for the belief-

---

[16] Kant is well aware that this is only a form of explanation and that we can, on his own grounds, do nothing to fill it out: *Critique of Pure Reason*, B146, B166, footnote.

expressing appearance. But describing a world in spatial and temporal terms is just that – describing. These two points suggest that each class of commitments faces the decision on its own: quasi-realism needs detail, not pictures.

Amongst commitments which seem particularly likely to benefit from such treatment are those involving modal idioms – possibility and necessity. As already noticed, these come in different strengths. We talk of physical possibility and neces- sity; metaphysical possibility (is it metaphysically possible that there should be minds without body, experience without time, etc.?); logical possibility (the bare possibility that persons should fly or horses talk is not ruled out by logical considera- tions); sometimes epistemic possibility – situations left open by some body of knowledge. How are we to understand claims of necessity and possibility? Naturally, the sources of these judge- ments, in our connections of logic, or of metaphysics, or of natural laws, attract detailed philosophical treatment, and have their own problems. But as far as the realist/anti-realist debate goes, there are some general points to be made. Consider this famous passage from the chapter on 'Foundations', in David Lewis's book, *Counterfactuals*:

I believe that there are possible worlds other than the one we happen to inhabit. If an argument is wanted, it is this. It is uncontroversially true that things might be otherwise than they are. I believe, and so do you, that things could have been different in countless ways. But what does this mean? Ordinary language permits the paraphrase: there are many ways things could have been besides the way they actually are. On the face of it, this sentence is an existential quantification. It says that there exist many entities of a certain description, to wit 'ways things could have been'. I believe that things could have been diffe- rent in countless ways; I believe permissible paraphrases of what I believe; taking the paraphrase at its face value I therefore believe in the existence of entities that might be called 'ways things could have been'. I prefer to call them 'possible worlds'. (p. 84)

Lewis goes on to make two further comments: that talking about possible worlds leads to no decisive problems, and that the modal idioms are irreducible. You cannot express things that we say using 'necessary', 'possible', and closely connected notions, such as 'ways things might have been', in other terms. Given this, he wants to take the idioms "at face value", which means, in his view, having a realistic theory of possible worlds. There really are such things, and we really describe them, and can know what they contain and what they do not. Now it will be evident that this ignores the resources of anti-realism, and in particular the possibility of a projective view. For does the fact that we have commitments expressed in modal terms, and that those commitments are irreducible, support realism? Only if rejecting an idiom or reducing it are the only anti-realist options, and they are not. (Of course, an identical mistake is made by those who dislike realism about possible worlds, and conclude that we *must* either reject or reduce the idiom.)

Thinking about necessities and possibilities in terms of related possible worlds is helpful for many purposes. It provides a picture or image which aids thinking; it enables logicians to approach modal arguments by mapping them onto more familiar arguments. For instance, the inference from 'necessarily p' to 'p', is mapped into 'in all possible worlds p' to 'in this possible world p', and becomes just the instantiation of a generalization. This is a familiar inference form of basic 'first order' logic. But *realism*? In present terms the issue must be one about how we explain our making of modal commitments. We certainly do not explain it by thinking that we are made sensitive to possibilities because of some quasi-sensory capacity which responds to the presence or absence of possible worlds. Firstly, since the only possible world that is actual is the actual world, others cannot *actually* influence us: we cannot receive information about them, because there is nothing to actually influence any receptors. Ways things might have been cannot be seen or heard. Secondly, the position that we are simply describing different aspects of reality needs a supplementation which it finds hard to give. If the possible worlds, like moral properties, represent a new realm of fact, why should we be interested in it? Talking of possibilities would be as optional to us, interested in the actual world, as talk of neighbouring countries or different times would be to us, if we are interested in the here and now. But it is not. We want to know whether to *allow* possibilities or *insist upon* necessities because we want to know how to conduct our thinking about the actual world. The possibilities we allow or which we rule out, determine how we conduct our inferences, and eventually our practices in the actual world. It is quite inexplicable how they should do that, if we relied upon the image of different spheres of real facts or states of affairs. Why should it interest me if in such spheres something holds, or in some it does not, or if in ones quite similar to the actual world things do or do not hold, if I want to discover and use truths about the ways things actually are?

Thus consider the claim that if you had fallen off the edge of some cliff, you would have hurt yourself. Think of this as Lewis wishes: it means that in any possible world as closely similar to ours as may be, but in which you have fallen off the cliff, you have hurt yourself.[17] But then there is debate over what makes for *similarity*. After all, a world just like ours, except that your fall off the cliff was followed by a minor miracle restoring you to the top (perhaps with amnesia), continues just like our world – isn't that similarity for you? There has been considerable debate over how to select the *right* similarity ranking, for otherwise we would endorse the wrong counterfactuals (on this occasion: if you had fallen over the cliff, you would have been quite unharmed). There is then a question over whether rightness can be defined without circularity.[18] But suppose it can be. There is still something crucial to explain. Why are we interested in just that "right" kind of similarity? If our interest lay exclusively in possible worlds, it would seem legitimate to roam around describing the various dimensions of similarity and difference with equal concern and respect. We only select one kind of similarity as the "right" one because we *use* counterfactuals in the real world – for the purpose of arguing, modifying practice, avoiding falling over cliffs, and so on. In other words, the person who thinks that if you had fallen over the cliff you would have been unharmed is not just someone who describes possible worlds with idiosyncratic standards of similarity. He is not just like a tourist who makes odd judgements of similarity between two places bcause he is more concerned with the botany than with the food. He is a menace. Lewis's realism leaves this use unexplained. It would need supplementing by a theory of why

[17] I abstract here from the complications of counterpart theory, which do not affect the present point.

[18] The kind of circularity which threatens is this. Perhaps a minor miracle makes a world *very* dissimilar from ours because it involves breaking a law of nature, but perhaps laws of nature are identified by thinking of which counterfactuals we hold true. Myself, I doubt whether this problem is decisive against Lewis.

one kind of similarity between possible worlds should be the one which *matters*. But then the whole package becomes extravagent, like the moral theory which sees us as responding to a real world of duties, obligations, and so forth, and *then* has to add an explanation of why we bother about these things, as well as the pains, pleasures, harms, and desires which make up the actual world.

By contrast the quasi-realist will start by seeing the remark (whether formulated in terms of possible worlds or not) as expressing a commitment – one which endorses the structuring of our beliefs about the world in a certain way. Notably, it endorses an inference from supposing that someone has fallen off a cliff, to supposing that they have got hurt. It dignifies this connection, allowing it to be a reliable guide to the conduct of affairs. The quasi-realist must then pursue the way we can come to treat such a commitment as if it represented a judgement with genuine truth-conditions. Similar problems arise as in the moral case. Consider a simple example. We can regard even our most reasonable counterfactual commitments as potentially false. We know Henry's habits: we know that the best bet is that if he had come to the party he would have got drunk. But for all that it may be true if he had come he would have stayed sober. Once again, this contrast must be explained, essentially with the same materials as in the case of evaluations. We have a sense of the potential for improvement in any argument: our reliable estimate of Henry's behaviour might be supplemented by information unknown to us (he had a cold, has just got a girl-friend in the Salvation Army, etc.). We need a proper notion of the *improvement or deterioration in the bases* for argument and proceed to construct a notion of truth. The eventual theory (counterfactuals are intricate, and this is not the place to pursue all the detail) would be one which maintains the benefits of possible-world imagery, but disallows the metaphysical extravagance.[19]

Projectivism is also a promising option in the theory of logical necessity. We not only believe it to be true that $7 + 5 = 12$, but we also find the truth inexorable: it could not have been

---

[19] The treatment of counterfactuals as condensed arguments was begun by John Mackie, 'Counterfactuals and Causal Law', in Butler, ed., *Analytical Philosophy, 1st Series*.

otherwise. We cannot imagine it otherwise; we could make nothing of a way of thought which denied it. But this may be just a fact about us and the limitations of our present imaginations, and it is natural to complain that this fact cannot justify us in saying that the proposition *has* to be true, or is true in all logically possible worlds. One reaction would be to avoid saying this, and eschew the category of logically necessary truth: this is Quine's position. But another is to face the fact that such truths do occupy a special category, for we can easily imagine otherwise many of our most cherished beliefs, and to say that when we dignify a truth as necessary we are expressing our own mental attitude – in this case our own inability to make anything of a possible way of thinking which denies it. It is this blank unimaginability which we voice when we use the modal vocabulary. It is then natural to fear that this has nothing to do with the *real* modal status of propositions. (Compare: what have our sentiments to do with the *real* moral truths about things?) But the quasi-realist will fight this contrast: he will deny that anything more can be meant by the real modal status of a proposition, than can be understood by seeing it as a projection of our (best) attitude of comprehension or imagination towards it. Once again, the advantage of such a theory is that it avoids the mystery of a necessity-detecting faculty and it avoids the strained scepticism which tries to avoid admitting that any truths are necessary at all.

6. *Mind-Dependence*

There is one more aspect of such theories I need to mention. It is tempting to think that a projective theory must leave the truth of commitments on which it works "mind-dependent". And this prompts hostility. It is not because of the way we think that if kangaroos had no tails they would topple over. We discover such facts, we do not invent them. It is not because of the way we form sentiments that kicking dogs is wrong. It would be wrong whatever we thought about it. Fluctuations in our sentiments only make us better or worse able to appreciate how wrong it is. It is not because of the way we conduct our arguments that trees cause shade. The "mind-independence" of such facts is part of our ordinary way of looking at things. Must a projectivist deny it? On his construction is truth mind-dependent?

Fortunately the quasi-realist treatment of indirect contexts shows that it is not. Suppose someone said 'if we had different sentiments, it would be right to kick dogs', what could he be up to? Apparently, he endorses a certain sensibility: one which lets information about what people feel dictate its attitude to kicking dogs. But nice people do not endorse such a sensibility. What makes it wrong to kick dogs is the cruelty or pain to the animal. *That* input should yield disapproval and indignation as the output. Similarly, if someone so organizes his beliefs and the way he makes inferences that he cannot let the presence of a tree in suitable sunshine suffice to give him confidence that there is a shadow, but needs information about whether people think one way or another, he is in a mess. He will fail to be confident in truths about the actual world when he should be.

Of course there *are* moral truths and counterfactuals which are "mind-dependent". Behaviour which we call rude is often wrong only because people think that it is wrong; sermons cause people to switch off because people have those kinds of minds. The point is that when a commitment is unlike these in being independent of our minds and their properties, the projectivist can conform to ordinary claims that it is. He does not need to deny any of the common-sense commitments or views about the way in which their truth arises. This is extremely important. Idealists always face the problem of finding an acceptable way of putting what they want to say about the involvement of the mind in the world. Some fudge it: it is quite common to find people writing that 'objects' do not exist outside our conceptual schemes, or that we 'create' objects (values, numbers) rather than discover them.[20] This is not a good way to put anything. With the inverted commas off, such remarks are false. (We do not create trees and galaxies, nor the wrongness of cruelty, nor the evenness of the number 2. Nor can we destroy them either, except perhaps for the trees.) But what can they mean otherwise: what is meant by saying that 'trees' are mind-dependent, if trees are not? Perhaps just the platitude that if we did not have minds of a certain kind, we could not possess the concept of a tree. The problem for the idealist, or the anti-realist

[20] e.g. Putnam, *Reason, Truth and History*, p. 52.

in general, is to steer a course between the platitude and the paradox.

The quasi-realist way of approaching indirect contexts offers a better approach. The utterance 'whatever I or we or anyone else ever thought about it, there would still have been (causes, counterfactual truths, numbers, duties)' can be endorsed even if we accept the projective picture, and work in terms of an explanation of the sayings which gives them a subjective source. The correct opinion about these things is not necessarily the one we happen to have, nor is our having an opinion or not the kind of thing which makes for correctness. The standards governing projection make it irrelevant, in the way that opinion is irrelevant to the wrongness of kicking dogs. The temptation to think otherwise arises only if a projective theory is mistaken for a reductionist one, giving the propositions involved a content, but one which makes them about us or our minds. They are not – they have a quite different role, and one which gives them no such truth-condition. When I say that Hitler was evil or that trees cause shade I am not talking about myself.[21]

It may now appear that a projective approach is too good to be true. Initially, the contrast between expressive theories and ones giving the same commitments genuine truth-conditions seemed reliable enough. But the subtleties, the earning power of quasi-realist devices, have tended to blur it. We can hear the philosopher who gives a projective explanation say highly realistic-sounding things. Why not regard him as giving the

---

[21] Wittgenstein may have come close to the kind of theory here explained. He certainly seems to want an anti-realist theory of arithmetical necessity without in any way regarding truths of arithmetic as truths about *us* or as truths of natural history. And my projective way with mind-dependence offers a model for doing this.

It should be noticed tht because of the twist in construing these counterfactuals this way, it comes out *false* that if we had thought or felt otherwise, it would have been permissible to kick dogs. This means that the metaphor of 'projection' needs a little care. Values are the children of our sentiments in the sense that the full explanation of what we do when we moralize cites only the natural properties of things and natural reactions to them. But they are not the children of our sentiments in the sense that were our sentiments to vanish, moral truths would alter as well. The *way* in which we gild or stain the world with the colours borrowed from internal sentiment gives our creation its own life, and its own dependence on facts. So we should not say or think that were our sentiments to alter or disappear, moral facts would do so as well. This would be endorsing the defective counterfactuals, i.e. endorsing the wrong kinds of sensibility, and it will be part of good moralizing not to do that. Similarly, it would have been true that $7 + 5 = 12$, whatever we had thought about it.

commitments in question genuine (mind-independent) truth-conditions? He practises soberly and responsibly, as though there were one truth which it is his business to find. So perhaps the right thing to say is that the commitments are true or false, in a straightforward way, after all. Perhaps expressive theories, properly developed, pull themselves into truth-conditional ones by their own resources. It is just that by disavowing the direction of explanation associated with the idea of a truth-condition, they do this without entering troubles of metaphysics and epistemology, and the resulting scepticism which plagues other approaches. To assess whether this is right, we need to turn to more general considerations about truth.

Notes to Chapter 6

6.1 Supervenience, in the sense of this section, should not be confused with the stronger requirement often called 'universalizability', following the usage of R. M. Hare. There are actually three importantly different notions:

> Consistency: the requirement that you do not contradict yourself, both judging that something is the case and that it is not.
> Supervenience: the requirement that moral judgements supervene, or are consequential upon natural facts.
> Universalizability: the requirement that moral judgements are somehow dependent only upon universal facts; facts specified without reference to particular individuals or groups.

The last of these is an attempt to build into the very definition of morality a requirement of impartiality, or of treating like cases alike, or of abstracting from any personal position or interest in achieving a moral point of view. Little is gained by building this into the definition of morality, or into the "logic" of the term moral and its dependent vocabulary: this just invites the question: why be moral? why not be "shmoral" – something a degree or two less strenuous than being moral, allowing one to pay some attention to other people's interests, but discounting for their distance from oneself? A clearer approach is to admit that it is a substantive question whether we conduct our practical reasoning by abstracting away from particular interests, and to stress the advantages (to themselves or to the community) of bringing up people to do so. This would be a variety of what is called 'motive utilitarianism': universalizing is defended as being a good thing to do, because if we can get people to respect the results of doing so, things go better. The relevant literature is, in my view, rather muddy on this. It includes:

R. M. Hare, *Moral Thinking*, esp. ch. 6.
J. Mackie, *Ethics: Inventing Right and Wrong*.

and specifically on supervenience:

J. Kim, 'Supervenience and Nomological Incommensurables', *American Philosophical Quarterly* (1978).
J. Dancy, 'On Moral Properties', *Mind* (1981).

The argument from the modal relations between moral and natural judgements, to anti-realism, can be challenged. If we pay careful attention to the different possible ways of taking the necessity involved, there is a possible counter. This would involve distinguishing metaphysical necessity from logical or conceptual necessity. The realist might say that if we are talking of metaphysical necessity, then once a total natural grounding for a moral judgement is located, it will be metaphysically necessary, i.e. true in all possible worlds, that when that grounding is present, the relevant judgement is also true. In short, he would accept B*/A necessity. If we are talking of conceptual or logical necessity, then he does better to deny this, although he must still accept the conceptual necessity of supervenience. But then he could try accepting the conclusion: saying that it is a conceptual or logical constraint on the moral vocabulary that it supervenes on the natural, whereas no particular B*/A connection is logically forced upon us. The request for explanation still arises, however. Where does the logical constraint come from if realism is true? Logic is interested in what can be true, and as far as realism can show us, it could be true that the moral floats quite free of the natural.

6.2   The theory of conditionals with evaluative components, which I develop in this section, is just part of the larger programme of quasi-realism, the attempt to show how an economical, anti-realist, and expressive theory of such things as ethics can account for the phenomena which lead people to realism. Papers in which I pursue the same theme include:

'Truth, Realism and The Regulation of Theory', in French *et al.* (1980).
'Opinions and Chances' in Mellor (1980).
'Rule Following and Moral Realism', in Holtzman and Leich (1981).

6.3 '. . . a schizoid attitude to his own moral commitments . . .'
Why is it that people want more than the projectivist gives them?
Thomas Nagel talks (*The Possibility of Altruism*) of philosophers such as
Kant, "driven by the demand for an ethical system whose motivational grip is not dependent on desires which must simply be taken for
granted" (p. 11). This is the permanent chimaera, the holy grail of
moral philosophy, the knock-down argument that people who are
nasty and unpleasant and motivated by the wrong things are above
all *unreasonable*: then they can be proved to be wrong by the pure sword
of reason. They aren't just selfish or thoughtless or malignant or
imprudent, but are reasoning badly, or out of touch with the facts. It
must be an occupational hazard of professional thinkers to want to
reduce all the vices to this one. In reality the motivational grip of
moral considerations is bound to depend upon desires which must
simply be taken for granted, although they can also be encouraged
and fostered. Notice that this is consistent with saying that there are
values which we come to recognize or discover, just as there are
rewards and satisfactions which we come to recognize and discover.

'. . . we are constrained to argue and practise as though the truth is
    single . . .'
This needs some care. People may be wrongly tempted to relativism
by this thought. There are obligations which we feel although we are
also aware that other equally admirable systems do not recognize
them. The best examples are those of ceremonies and rituals which
arise, we suppose, because there is some deep need in us which they
serve, although how this need is served can then be highly variable.
For example, I might feel the strictest obligation to dispose of the
body of a relative in some prescribed way, even when I know that
other societies would do it differently. In this case I do not assent to
'all human beings ought to bury (say) their dead'; I do assent to 'I
ought to bury my dead'. But this is not relativism in the sense of the
text, for I would also regard each judgement (that I ought to bury my
dead, that not everyone ought to bury their dead) as true, and there is
no equally admirable conflicting alternative to either of them. It is
just that what creates such obligations are parochial facts about
people and their societies and their customs.

6.4 A basic reading on bivalence would include:

M. Dummett, Preface to *Truth and Other Enigmas*, and the papers
'Truth', and 'The Philosophical Basis of Intuitionistic Logic',
collected therein.

C. Wright, *Wittgenstein's Remarks on the Foundations of Mathematics*, pt. II, especially ch. 7.

D. Prawitz, 'Meaning and Proofs', *Theoria* (1977).

D. Edgington, 'Meaning, Bivalence and Realism', *Proceedings of the Aristotelian Society* (1980).

6.5 '. . . Hume's treatment . . .'
The two classic places are:

Treatise of Human Nature, Bk. 1, Pt. III, sect. XIV.
Enquiry Concerning Human Understanding, sect. VII.

For possible worlds, and some of the disputes over their standing, see:

A. Plantinga, *The Nature of Necessity*, chs. VI–VIII.
S. Kripke, *Naming and Necessity, passim.*

6.6 The relationship between post-Wittgensteinian attempts to avoid realism and the actual work of Wittgenstein is hard to unravel. Two modern metaphysicians tempted towards recognizably idealist positions include Hilary Putnam and Richard Rorty (see Rorty, *Philosophy and the Mirror of Nature* and more recently, *The Consequences of Pragmatism*). I discuss some of these things further in the next chapter. An excellent paper is 'Wittgenstein and Idealism' by Bernard Williams, reprinted in his collection *Moral Luck*.

In this chapter I have not discussed directly the 'anti-realism' about science which allows theoretical sentences to have an intelligible truth-condition, and allows us to accept them and to use them when they are empirically adequate, but counsels us not to *believe* them. This is the position of van Fraassen, and perhaps Popper. It needs faith in some distinction between accepting a statement with a truth-condition, and believing it, and I see no such distinction. I would urge that the right path for instrumentalism is to deny that the commitments have a truth-condition, at least until the quasi-realist does his work.

CHAPTER 7

Correspondence, Coherence, and Pragmatism

Her terrible tale you can't assail
With Truth it quite agrees;
Her taste exact for faultless fact
Amounts to a disease.
W. S. Gilbert, *The Mikado*.

1. *Vacuity and the Quietist Regress*

We have come to the theory of truth through trying to understand a contrast. Some commitments do not have truth-conditions, do not mark genuine judgements, but are somehow expressive. This allowed the quasi-realist supplement, which in turn gave us the right to treat the commitments *as if* they had truth-conditions, and justified our common practice. But is this anything other than the real thing? Our conception of truth, as the point of judgement, or as success in judgement, must tell us whether truth is ever more than these hopefuls earn. So what is there to say about truth in general?

The first things are platitudes. A true judgement gets things right, says that things stand in a certain way when they do so stand, tells it like it is. The classic expresson is Aristotle's: "To say of what is that it is, or of what is not that it is not, is true."[1] The trouble is that these platitudes are only a prelude to serious attempts to understand what truth is. If we worry about the nature and point of the division between judgements which are true and those which are not, or between utterances which express judgements and those which express other commitments, these truisms about truth are no help.

The first suggestion which looks as if it might be more substantial is that a judgement is true if and only if it corresponds to the facts. A taste exact for faultless fact is just the same thing as a

[1] *Metaphysics*, Γ 7.27.

taste for truth. And it is, presumably, a suspicion that on the theories of the last chapter there is no such thing as moral, counterfactual, arithmetical, etc. *fact* which still prompts disquiet about genuine truth in those areas.

The platitudes are harmless. And we do not seem to raise the theoretical temperature very far if we substitute 'corresponds to the facts' for 'says of what is that it is' and the like. So it must surprise students to find how hostile most writers are to what they call 'the correspondence theory of truth'. Some think it vacuous; others false. First of all it is necessary to state the theory. There is nothing objectionable in introducing 'corresponds-to-the-facts' as a grammatical predicate having just the same use as 'is true'. Someone trained in the Pentagon might introduce any number of such paraphrases: 'is-currently-operative', 'is-operationally-valid', and the like. It is not predictable from the normal meaning of the words in such predicates that the phrase is to be a synonym for 'is true'. But people manage to learn them. Suppose, then, that 'corresponds-to-the-facts' is in fact synonymous with 'is true'. It does not follow that it provides a "theory" of truth, any more than the Pentagon's imaginative synonyms make it a theorist of truth. It just provides one more way of saying that things are true. So to deserve the title a correspondence *theorist* must say more than that a judgement is true if and only if it corresponds to the facts. He must say that this is not a mere rephrasing, but sets afoot a genuine elucidation of the idea. He must say that we have some genuine conception of what facts are, and what correspondence is, so that thinking in terms of correspondence with the facts will help us to answer the kind of question left at the end of the last chapter. I define a correspondence theory as any theory holding that there is this content, enabling correspondence and facts to play some role in elucidating truth. This means that there is not *one* such theory. There is room for different conceptions of correspondence and of fact. All we have is an invitation to explore in a certain direction. Should we accept it?

The first objection is that 'corresponds with' and 'facts' have no independent substance. They trade entirely with each other. Neither has an identity outside the other's company, and in that company they gain a use *only* by being allowed as a substitute for 'is true'. The charge is that the equation is vacuous. It is harmless, only so long as we do not think of it as providing any key to the nature of truth.

To meet this kind of criticism means showing that there is a kind of content to 'corresponds with the facts', which is predictable from a prior understanding of its component notions, and not wholly derivative from its synonymy with truth. 'Corresponds', after all, is a word with other subject matter. Pictures correspond with scenes, music corresponds with moods, memories with events, outcomes with intentions. Doesn't this suggest a general conception of correspondence, carrying a content from other contexts to this one? Perhaps facts too live their own lives: facts cause things, they can be witnessed, they matter. So can't we have two conceptions locking together to provide us with our understanding of truth? Of course, it is possible that particular philosophers have held conceptions of fact and of correspondence which are inadequate. Debates supposedly on the correspondence theory often rush to introduce, say, Wittgenstein's early picture theory of language (as though picturing it were the only kind of way one thing could correspond to another). Or, they point to unappealing things people have said about our acquaintance with facts (see below, 7.4). But it is much harder to pin the weaknesses of particular developments onto the invitation itself. Indeed, how could it be proved that there can be *no* such conceptions as the invitation demands?

2. *Transparency: Dummett and Frege*

Surprisingly there exists argument that there cannot be any. Consider what is sometimes called the "equivalence thesis": a judgement p is true iff p.[2] It is true that there is a cat on the mat iff there is a cat on the mat; it is true that $2 + 2 = 4$ iff $2 + 2 = 4$; and so on. We can take this equivalence to be as strong as possible: to judge that p is nothing different from judging that it is true that p. In fact let us suppose that, for any judgement and any relation we may hold to it, it makes no difference whatever if we preface the judgement by 'it is true that'. To ask, prove, enquire, deny, wonder, imply . . . that p is always the very same

---

[2] Dummett, *Frege*, ch. 13. 'Iff' means 'if and only if'.

thing as asking, proving, etc. that it is true that p. This is the strong equivalence thesis. It might be helpful to call the property of 'it is true that . . .' which it illustrates, the 'transparency property'. It is as though you can always look through 'it is true that' to identify the content judged, inquired after, and so on if the reference to truth was not there. Now the transparency property is a peculiar one. In particular it puts a dilemma in the way of any analysis of 'it is true that'. Either the proposed synonym is no real analysis, but a vacuous, Pentagon-type paraphrase; or it is a genuine analysis. But in the latter case there is a content to the notions it introduces. And in that case 'it is true that p' contains that content, whereas mere 'p' does not (does not for instance mention correspondence and facts). And in that case the two propositions are different. Adding 'it is true that' alters things, and in that case the transparency property is lost. There will be no general presumption that wondering, doubting, proving, etc. that p is the same as wondering, etc. that it is true that p.

To make this problem vivid, imagine that on some theory there is always a difference of content between 'p' and 'it is true that p'. Then call this latter judgement 'q'. We can then make a yet different judgement, that it is true that q: call this 'r'. We are off on an ascending hierarchy of different judgements, each claiming that its predecessor is true. But it is impossible to believe in the distinctness of each member of this series. We can get a kind of visual sense of the awkwardness, if we imagine the correspondence theory developed by some genuine understanding of what a fact might be, as a kind of entity of good standing, fit to be corresponded with. Then starting with a judgement that p, proceed to the judgement that p corresponds (C) to some fact, say W: $p \, C \, W$. The judgement that $p \, C \, W$ is itself capable of truth: perhaps it corresponds to W^*: $p C W \, C \, W^*$. For this to be true it must correspond to W^{**}, and so on. If you imagine a judgement at one point, and above it a fact to which it corresponds, then the *fact* that it so corresponds seems to be somewhere else – out at a tangent – and the fact that the judgement that the original judgement corresponds to a fact, corresponds to this fact, is out at another tangent, and so on.

The image is worrying, but does the argument actually work?

We can lay it out like this. Consider some proposed analysis of truth, in terms of some concept φ. Then consider the two series:

p Tp TTp $TTTp$ . . .
p φp $\varphi\varphi p$ $\varphi\varphi\varphi p$ . . .

then:

(1) In the first series, each member has the same content as any other; none says anything more than or different from the first. (Transparency property.)

(2) If φ is an elucidation, analysis, or definition of truth, then it must share the transparency property.

(3) Either φ is a genuine predicate, containing concepts of its own, or a manufactured synonym of T.

(4) If the latter, then it offers no elucidation, etc.

(5) If the former, then it cannot share the transparency property, and again (by (2)) is no elucidation, etc.

(6) So there is no possible elucidation of truth.

The argument is accepted in this strong form by Frege, who regarded it as refuting not only the correspondence theory, but any other attempt to define truth as well. Dummett does not allow it this much power; he thinks that it refutes the kind of definition embodied in the correspondence theory, but leaves the possibility of others.[3] But he does not say how it might be evaded – what it is about some proposals for φ and not others which would make them targets. Apparently any φ unaffected by the argument would have to be a genuine elucidation, but one which shares the transparency property. But if that is a possible combination, it must be something peculiar about 'corresponds to the facts' which disqualifies it from being so regarded. Perhaps it too can slip between importing more than the transparency thesis tolerates, being taken as a manufactured synonym.

In parenthesis I should mention that the issue is particularly delicate for Frege. He held the curious doctrine that a sentence is true if it refers to a particular abstract object – the truth-value

[3] Frege, 'The Thought: A Logical Inquiry' in Strawson, ed. (1967) p. 19. Dummett, *Frege*, pp. 443 ff.

'True'. This will be so only if the thought the sentence expresses relates in some suitable way to this object – say 'determines' it. Now this doctrine may not have been intended as an elucidation or analysis of the concept of truth. But it is still pertinent to ask how it fares in face of the transparency property. The issue whether p, generates the issue whether *the thought that p determines True*; this in turn leads to the issue whether the thought that (*the thought that p determines True*) itself determines True, and so on. If 'determines True' does not have the transparency property, then these issues may be different from each other. If it does have the transparency property, in spite of being intended to have a definite content, describing the relation of a judgement to an abstract object, then why cannot 'corresponds to the facts' have the same combination?

3. *Redundancy: Ramsey and Wittgenstein*

The issue would be clearer if we knew why truth has the transparency property in the first place. At first sight the property robs the word of any content at all, making it vacuous or *redundant*. Some writers, notably Ramsey and Wittgenstein, have so concluded. They are often described as holding a 'redundancy theory of truth'. This is the view that truth is not a contentful notion, and not a fit object of analysis. The role of the word is not one of introducing property which some utterances or judgements have and others lack. I prefer to call this view 'quietism', for it is not really the view that the word is redundant on all occurrences. It is the view that it never marks a property of judgements. But does the regress really suggest that we have no general conception of success in judgement, or of what correctness is, and how it might relate to other concepts, such as those of rationality, evidence, proof? Someone who lacks any notion of assessing sayings for truth or falsity lacks the idea that they express judgements at all – words remain wooden to him in the sense of chapter 3. How can the concept be redundant if it plays such a central role in our reaction to utterances? Is there to be no way at all of describing something that all true judgements share, and all false judgements lack? In the view of a redundancy theorist there is no such property. But what then of issues such as those of the last chapter, which result in the query whether different classes of judgement are true in the same sense as others? It seems ill-judged to abandon any such discussion merely because of the transparency property.

The best way for the student to appreciate the attractions of a redundancy theory is this. We can say equally that judgements (statements, thoughts, beliefs, propositions) are true, and that sentences (or sentences in contexts, or utterances) are true. (There are differences between these, as 1.4 described, but for the moment they do not matter.) Now compare 'is true', as a predicate of either judgements or of sentences, with a genuine target of philosophical analysis: 'is conscious', or 'has rights', for example. We investigate these by looking for the principles which determine whether something is conscious, or has rights. These principles are intended to govern any such judgement, so that we get a unified class: the class of conscious things, or things that have rights. Each item in such a class is there because it satisfies the same condition, which the analysis has uncovered. Or, if this is slightly idealized, we find only a "family" of related conditions or "criteria" for application of the terms. Still there is then a family relationship between the members of the class. But now contrast 'is true'. We know *individually* what makes this predicate applicable to the judgements or sentences of an understood language. 'Penguins waddle' is a sentence true, in English, if and only if penguins waddle. It is true that snow is white if and only if snow is white. The reason the first sentence deserves the predicate is that penguins waddle, and the reason why the judgement that snow is white deserves the predicate is that snow *is* white. But these reasons are entirely different. There is no single account, or even little family of accounts, in virtue of which each deserves the predicate, for deciding whether penguins waddle has nothing much in common with deciding whether snow is white. There are *as* many different things to do, to decide whether the predicate applies, as there are judgements to make. So how *can* there be a unified, common account of the "property" which these quite different decision procedures supposedly determine? We might say: give us any sentence about whose truth you are interested, and simple by "disquoting" and removing the reference to truth, we can tell you what you have to judge in order to determine its truth. Since we can do this without any analysis or understanding of a common property of truth, the idea that there is such a thing is an illusion.

Perhaps the conjuring trick was pulled before we were looking. Truth is *internal* to judgement in the sense that to make or accept a judgement is to have it as an aim. So how could there be a difference between making a judgement on the one hand, and describing the judgement as meeting the aim, on the other? Consider some parallels. In a game there is an equivalence between making a move and judging that the move is a good one. Or, there is an equivalence between choosing a key and supposing that the key fits. Discounting cases of fraud, acting, and so on, a normal choice of move, or choice of key, is governed by these aims. It would therefore be redundant to add, when moving or choosing, that the move is one which promotes winning, or the key is one which fits. This is already implicit in the choice. But this redundancy does not suggest that we have no conception of what it is to win or what it is for a key to fit. Even more closely, consider commands. Since the internal point of command is to get something done, it is redundant to add to a command a 'do this' indicator. 'Shut the door' and 'Do this: shut the door' come to the same thing. But this transparency does not stop there from being a contentful notion of obeying an order. The analogy is that since truth counts as success in judgement, making a judgement and describing it as true are evidently equivalent. But for all that we may have a substantive conception of what that success is. Discussing, proving, querying, etc. whether p is of course the same as discussing, etc. whether p is true. But that is not, on this account, because 'is true' is somehow vacuous. It is because its content has already gone into the bag: if we are discussing, etc. a *judgement* then we are already governed by a conception of success in judgement, and one which philosophers should try to explain. Judgements are those amongst our commitments which admit of truth or falsity.

A theory would deprive the equivalence thesis of justification if it appeared to show that one might correctly judge that p without judging that it is true that p, or vice versa. A view will not do this provided its favoured conception of truth *allows* for truth being the point of judgement, the goal which we suppose a judgement to have achieved when we assent to it. This point is to be internal or essential to judgement, in the sense that nothing could count as judging unless it had this aim. So the question boils down to whether a correspondence, or other, theory fails because it is impossible to reconcile it with the demand that truth be this internal point of judgement. And at first sight, a correspondence theory should do well at just that point. The reason we make judgements is that we want the facts.

It seems then that an elucidation of truth can have content, and not only permit the transparency property, but in a sense explain it. Which step in the above argument should be denied if this is right? There is room for some choice. The most direct line would be to deny (5). Provided the concepts involved *do* define the internal point of judgement, they should themselves have the transparency property. A more subtle line would expand our notion of an elucidation. So long as we are confined to seeking a synonym, we need a substitute with the same capacity for vacuous repetition as 'it is true that . . .'. But suppose our elucidation took a different form. Consider again the difference between crude naturalism in moral theory, and the more subtle approach to moral language suggested in the last chapter. In such developments we seek to understand a concept not by reduction, but by explaining its properties; the explanation is not aimed at providing a substitute (a non-moral way of moralizing, as it were) but at making the phenomenon of moralizing unproblematic. There is no principled reason why a conception of what truth is might not play the same role, although it provides no analysing phrase which shares just the same repetitive powers as 'it is true that . . .'. It would explain what we are doing when we make judgements, display a conception of success or correctness which governs judgement, and make it unsurprising that we have a notion of truth, and the consequent behaviour of predicates announcing it. On such an account we escape the Frege argument by denying (2).

For good measure we might notice that (1), the strong equivalence thesis itself, is not entirely unproblematic. Remember that we may use a vocabulary in some area where we are uncomfortably aware that there might be an improved way of looking at things – one of those descendant theories from whose standpoint our classifications and judgements appear not actually false, but best avoided (see 6.3 above). But we may have no sense of how to improve ourselves, and therefore go on judging in the best terms we have. So I may assent to the opinion that Schubert was a romantic, that Macbeth was ambitious, or that America is democratic, whilst being at the same time aware that superior opinion might make qualifications, distinctions, turn things in a different light, and perhaps end up avoiding these terms altogether, leaving my present commitments at best half-truths. In that case I accept the opinion more readily than I accept its truth. The natural similes and metaphors for such worries chime in well with the correspondence image: it is as though we paint an approximate or distorted picture, or an inferior picture, or a partial sketch.

The blockbuster argument against searching for an elucidation of truth fails, then. Is correspondence to the facts an answer to that search? There are other, more traditional obstacles.

4. *Facts and Judgement: Kant*

When people first start to sympathize with the correspondence theory, they are apt to seize upon some homely, immediate, truth, a truth which "leaps to the eye". I consider, say, the fact that my typewriter is on the table, and say 'well, *that*'s a fact, *that* is what my judgement that the typewriter is on the table is made true by'. This seems as pure a case of sheer acquaintance with a fact as can be got (nobody with this kind of experience is going to deny that my typewriter is on the table). The instinct behind such a choice of case is sound. The critic is pressing for a conception of 'the facts' which is not wholly derivative from an antecedent conception of true judgement. So it is right to turn to a good case where we might talk of acquaintance with the facts, where the facts leap to the eye. For then that acquaintance might give us an understanding of one end of the relationship (the facts), and then we could look forward to building correspondence in the light of that.

This is why the correspondence invitation to truth has often seemed tied to a view which emphasizes an element of 'the given': some bare unvarnished presentation of fact to a purely receptive mind. Philosophers are virtually unanimous in condemning any such notion, and its ill-fame (coupled, perhaps, with the thought that nothing else even looks like a candidate for elucidating truth) is the main cause of quietism. The critics of "the given" have a simple, and strong, case. Experience cannot be regarded as an independent source of a conception of a fact – independent, that is, of the operation of judgement – for two reasons. The first is obvious: to see a situation as one containing or illustrating or displaying a fact is *just* to judge and interpret. Even such a low-grade judgement as that my typewriter is on the table involves recognizing that the elements of the situation are spatially external to me, that they are objects with a temporal history, that they have various physical properties such as solidity, and so on. Judgement just *is* the isolation of facts. Now, faced with only this point, we could retain an intuitive distinction between experience – the "raw" uninterpreted presentation – and the judgements we make in the light of it. But the second point is that our conceptual powers themselves infuse and condition the experience. Interpretation goes into the making of the experience. And since that is so, experience can no more be a judgement-independent source of acquaintance with facts than dough can be a flour-independent source of bread.

This interweaving of the categories of thought with experience is a central element in Kant.

> Without sensibility no object would be given to use, without understanding no object would be thought. Thoughts without content are empty, intuitions without concepts are blind.[4]

Kant carefully goes on to say that this is no excuse for confusing the two contributions. But the point is that their separation is not given to us. When we see the typewriter on the table, we see the situation *as* involving extended and independent objects. Kant, like Hume before him, and Wittgenstein after him, understands this "seeing as" as a product of imagination; it is essentially a matter of *linking* the present impressions to actual and possible perceptions of similar things. By imagination we fill in the continuities and stabilities which turn our experience from that of a disconnected sequence of independent

---

[4] Kant, *Critique of Pure Reason*, A 51–2; B 75–6. The content of thought is here its connection with the sensible world; intuitions are what we receive; they are the materials delivered by the senses.

events, into that of a stable world of spatially extended objects with enduring histories. Our experience would not be what it is if it were not infused with this interpretation. This general fact is most apparent when we consider cases of "gestalt switch" or double-aspect figures. With these, when we change from one interpretation to another (seeing a figure as a black shape on a white background or vice versa; seeing the ambiguous figure as a duck or as a rabbit), we start to have a quite different visual experience. But these cases just illustrate a universal interdependence of experience and judgement.

The theme is commonplace in writers on perception. What is not so well agreed is the implications for our conception of a fact and of the control of beliefs by facts. Clearly an initial burst of seeing something as a duck, or a smile, or a circle, may be followed by painful realization that it is actually a rabbit, or a snarl, or an ellipse. As more experience comes in, initial judgements may have to give way. But if no judgement or experience has a pure footing in the way things are, uncontaminated by our powers of thought and imagination, how are we to think of this control? Is it even possible to think of our beliefs as *responding* to facts, let alone corresponding to them? Or are we left with a kind of majority tyranny in which any odd judgement, formed on an occasion, but surrounded by occasions which prompt conflicting judgements, is deemed false, whilst the majority are deemed true (and said to correspond to the facts)? It is this problem that leads to the coherence theory of truth.

5. *Coherence: Russell, Bradley, and Peirce*

If the innocent student thinks that nothing much can be wrong with the idea that truth consists in correspondence with the facts, he probably also thinks that nothing much can be right with the idea that it consists in some kind of coherence between a judgement and other judgements. And the idiom of the philosophers usually credited with this direction of theory is scarcely calculated to overcome this initial scepticism. Bradley, Joachim, Bosanquet, and other "British Idealists" of the late nineteenth and early twentieth centuries now get a poor press, or no press at all. Yet it is easy to present their views in a favourable light.

The first attractive doctrine of the Idealists was the "holistic" nature of meaning (see 5.4). No belief is an island; to understand it entails being able to use its concepts in other contexts, to make other related judgements: it involves mastery of a web or system. In chapter 5 I mentioned this doctrine in connection with Wittgenstein and Quine, but they were not the first. Here is Joachim, writing in 1906:

No universal judgement of science, then expresses in and by itself a determinate meaning. For every such judgement is really the abbreviated statement of a meaning which would require a whole system of knowledge for its adequate expression. It is this larger meaning, embodied more or less fully in such a system, which, so to say, animates the single judgements and gives them determinate significance.[5]

The second point of contact with modern work is the same disbelief in passive acquaintance with facts. Bradley writes that "the merely given facts are the imaginary creatures of false theory" and that the given facts "show already in their nature the work of truth-making". He emphasizes that even if there ever existed a datum of sensation or feeling wholly unmodified by thinking and judgement, then we would not know of it, for in order to become an object of *knowledge* it would need description and interpretation, and this reintroduces the work of judgement. This is the Kantian theme of the last section. It means that there is no way in which any mind can step back from its own system of belief, survey without its benefit a reality the system attempts to depict, and discover whether it is doing well or badly. Any such survey produces only more beliefs to blend in with the original system. If we think in terms of the ship of knowledge controlled by tides of experience, it is as though all the tide does is cast up more planks – more elements to take into the system.

At this point we are liable to suffer a sharp sense of loss. If the senses are "impregnated with the work of truth-making" what is their title to control the way in which we form systems of belief? Bradley, like everyone else, believes that they should do so:

[5] H. H. Joachim, *The Nature of Truth*, p. 96.

I do not believe in any knowledge which is independent of feeling and
sensation . . . our intelligence cannot construct the world of perceptions and feelings, and it depends on what is given – to so much I
assent.[6]

The difficulty is that the assimilation of observation to judgement makes it seem as though our faculties are simply ready,
cheap, and fertile sources of belief. When we open our eyes
experience floods in, but so far as truth goes, we might just as
well say that judgements do.[7] The tribunal of sense experience
delivers only further beliefs. So it seems that it offers no independent test of truth. To test the truth of a belief, to find its
truth, must be to try to fit it to others (no doubt gained from the
senses). So we arrive at the suggestion that perhaps this coherence is, in effect, what truth is. To develop the suggestion means
exploring the virtues which systems of belief might have, and
trying to erect a concept of truth on their basis. This copies the
procedure the quasi-realist adopted in the case of morals, where
a notion of the virtues in different sensibilities produced enough
to justify a workable concept of moral truth. *The root idea is that
the virtue of truth is constructed from the virtues of method.*

Examples of the attractions of this idea offset its initial
strangeness. Consider the common marks of merit in scientific
theories: simplicity, responsiveness to experiment, utility,
theoretical elegance and strength, fertility, association with
familiar models rendering processes intelligible, and so on.
There is an inclination to think: but what have all these virtues
got to do with *truth*? A coherence theorist cuts this knot, most
simply by proposing that scientific truth *is* membership of some
system which, like M* (see 6.3), would be the ideal possessor of
all these virtues. For example, consider the "holistic" attribution of beliefs and desires to people, as ways of rationalizing
their sayings and doings. There are better and worse ways of
doing this. If we can define the virtues of some ideal method of

---

[6] F. H. Bradley, 'On Truth and Copying', *Essays on Truth and Reality*, p. 108.

[7] I am not here assenting to the view that having an experience just *is* being disposed
to make a judgement. I do not believe that it is. There are experiences, such as hearing
indescribable sequences of sound, whose nature is not identifiable by any judgement
the subject could make about them. We can see this must be so, because the experience
could change, although the subject cannot judge how it has changed, nor say anything
about how the new experience differs from the old one. And any experience will have
aspects of which this is true. The point in the text is only that judgements have to be
distilled from experience before questions of truth arise.

doing it, someone might still ask why we suppose that this method gives the truth about what people believe and desire: the coherence answer is that this is what psychological truth is. It is true that someone believes that p or desires that p if and only if the use of this method would rationalize his sayings and doings in such a way that this comes out true. Evidently the advantage of this approach to the theory of knowledge is that it ensures that our preferred methods of forming theories are adequate to the truth. It ensures it by so defining truth. This is why the early British Idealists thought of themselves as *good* empiricists with a sane appreciation of what observation is, of the way theory is grounded in experience, and of the way to answer scepticism. This too is why the Logical Positivists also come to favour a coherence theory of truth, in the 1930s (see notes).

The Idealists were led to the doctrine mainly by reflection upon method in history, but later on, reflection on method in science performed the same office. Bosanquet, for instance wrote:

The facts, in history, at any rate, are not simply there, so that they can act as a given standard correspondence to which is truth. The primary working standard is critical system, or, what is the same thing, scientific investigation.[8]

But the passage is misleading in presenting the virtues of systems of well-judged belief as mere *standards* of truth. A coherence theory does not simply describe the common-sense virtues which good methods of conducting enquiry must exhibit. What is distinctive is that it sees truth not as an independent property, which these virtues are hopefully signalling, but as a construct out of them.

To assess the idea, we must start with the classic objection. This is that we can make up coherent stories ad lib entirely without regard to the way the world is. By following our fancies, and paying attention only to consistency, we can generate comprehensive descriptions of possible but non-actual worlds. For any such description to be true of the actual world requires more than its mere presence in any such set. Russell made this objection both to the early coherence theorists, and to their

---

[8] B. Bosanquet, *Logic*, vol. ii, p. 287.

positivist successors.[9] His argument can be put like this. Suppose we have a coherent and reasonably comprehensive description of some historical period. Call the system, S. Then we might maintain or increase coherence, and increase comprehensiveness, by adding the proposition that some late prelate died on the gallows ($S + E$). But for all its membership of the system, E might be false. So the ideals of comprehension and coherence give us no reason to control admission to the system in sane accepted ways. As a consequence they not only admit falsehood, but also allow increasingly divergent systems, each of which meets the ideals.

Bradley's response to this devastating objection is interesting. Reminding us of the requirement that a system be made as comprehensive as possible, he says:

But imagine my world made on the principle of in such a case accepting mere fancy as fact. Could such a world be more comprehensive and coherent than the world as now arranged? Would it be coherent at all? . . . The idea of system demands the inclusion of all possible material. Not only must you include everything to be gained from immediate experience and perception, but you must also be ready to act on the same principle with regard to fancy . . .[10]

He then points out that this requires the admission of contradictory fancies, and so is ruled out by the requirement of coherence.

At first sight this is an evasion. Russell's charge is that if S is comprehensive and coherent – I abbreviate this to CC – or approaches being so to some degree, then so is $S + E$, to a greater degree, in spite of the falsity of E. Bradley's retort is that a different set is not CC. This different set includes what I shall call a pedigree, telling how E got into the first set. So the set he is considering is $S + E + F$, where F tells us that E is the product of fancy. In fact Bradley argues that this set is only CC if the *principle* on which E is allowed in is accepted – in other words, only if $S + E + F + G$ is CC, where G generalizes the principle that you can add E on the basis of F, i.e. it endorses the admission of any old fancy. And this set is not CC, because the principle enjoins the admission of inconsistencies. But Russell wanted to consider only $S + E$. So Bradley missed his point.

[9] B. Russell, *An Inquiry into Meaning and Truth*, ch. 10.
[10] F. H. Bradley, 'On Truth and Coherence', *Essays on Truth and Reality*, p. 213.

Or perhaps Russell missed Bradley's. A coherence theorist is quite within his rights to describe the virtues of his system of beliefs how he likes, provided that he avoids smuggling in an independent reference to the truth of any of the members. So Bradley may insist that his preferred system is, as far as possible, what we can call *controlled*: it should not contain elements without also containing a pedigree for them, and once it contains an element on the basis of a pedigree, it should allow any others with equally good pedigrees. So whenever an addition to a system is proposed, the test may be run on the element and the principle on which it is proposed. And then Russell's counter-example fails, because as Bradley points out, a fanciful pedigree could be given to any belief at all. Bradley seems to regard the ideal that a system be controlled as implicit in the idea that it be comprehensive. But it is worth separating it out. The proposal then refines into regarding truth as membership of a CCC – controlled, comprehensive, coherent system. The essence of the defence is that the wrong type of control, applied comprehensively, lets in inconsistent pairs of belief (you might just as well believe anything you first think of, as that the prelate died on the gallows), destroying coherence.

The defence is subtle. But does it work? From a common-sense standpoint the trouble with fanciful origins for a judgement is precisely that fancy might just as well have issued the opposite judgement, regardless of which is *true*. That is the point of Russell's challenge. Bradley retorts that he can discriminate against fancy, and in favour of observation, memory, induction, and sober practices of enquiry and judgement, just as much as Russell. The ground of *his* discrimination is that a comprehensive use of fancy destroys coherence. A CCC system must not use a method of control with this property. Well, suppose we followed a policy of admitting fancies-tailored-for-consistency? I might inflate my belief system by adding fancies, only paying judicious attention to their coherence with anything else also believed, like any good story-teller. What is wrong with that? From the common-sense standpoint it is uncontrolled in the sense that it has an even chance of delivering a judgement or its negation *regardless* of which is true. But Bradley has to earn this concept of truth. He has to describe the virtues of proper control, comprehension, and coherence, *without smuggling in the idea that they are midwives to truth.* Story-telling is a poor policy for delivering the truth. But it might be a good policy for delivering CCC systems of judgements.[11] If Bradley then claims that it is not, because it involves the wrong sort of control, we need to know where he gets this standard from.

It will help to remember here the relationship between moral truth and progressively more admirable systems of attitude. The development of the last chapter was possible just because we have, in our own normal attitudes, the basis for comparing and preferring one system to another. This gives a content to the judgement that one system is "nearer the truth" than the other. In the ordinary case it is harder to say what is wrong about belief systems controlled in bizarre ways, *except* that they are likely to contain falsehood. And if this is so, there is no prospect of a genuine elucidation of truth in this direction.

The same result affects philosophies which, out of admiration for scientific method, construct a notion of truth as membership of an ideal scientific theory. There are many difficulties with this view, including that of saying what counts as progress, and, as in the moral case, saying how we avoid the threat of the tree structure. But the present problem is that of saying what is so good about progress, except that it leads to the truth. Consider this analogy. It would be no merit in a house to be one on which all modern architectural design would eventually converge, because there is nothing particularly superior about later houses as against earlier ones. A limit definition of truth is only possible if there is a firm sense of the virtues of the processes leading to the limit. Bradley or Peirce can *select* features, like a given kind of control and coherence and comprehensiveness. But they need to say what is *good* about systems with those features, without mentioning the idea that they deliver the truth.

Pragmatism offers the utility of beliefs as the virtue needed at this point. An improved system will be more useful than its ancestor: the virtue of scientific progress, from which truth can be constructed, is that of achieving ever more useful systems. This need not be the crude idea that all and only beliefs which it is useful to have are true. That is open to familiar counter-

---

[11] And if only we could believe in stories, it would be a good policy for removing the anxieties of doubt, which Peirce regarded as one of the main incentives to inquiry.

examples. There are many things useful to believe, although false, and vice versa. A little credulity here and a little ignorance there makes for success in life. No, the virtue should be attached to the *kinds* of control admitted: the judicious use of the senses, for instance, as opposed to fancy and invention. It is hard to see how it could be generally useful to form beliefs without respecting the judgements delivered by the senses, by memory, or by sober processes of enquiry. Beliefs direct our actions, and systems of belief direct habits and courses of action which may or may not be useful. Surely there is a virtue in those controls which make for useful systems?

There is, of course, but it seems a doubtful place to build truth upon. The difficulty is that so much of what we normally think about utility presupposes a notion of truth. The reason why it is useful to believe that there is a typewriter here, in the face of this morning's experience, is that there is one. My utility is increased by my capacity to move around in, control, and react with a world which my senses and my judgement tell me about. That they tell me about it truly seems to explain their utility, rather than be in any sense a construct *out of* their utility. Epistemologically we have the same direction. Knowing how well my ends are being served is just an aspect of knowing about the world. It needs the 'proper' use of the senses, memory, etc.

A different, and in some ways appealing, suggestion is that nature has solved Bradley's problem for him. Bradley is talking about systems of belief, not of propositions in the abstract. Now there is nothing difficult about manufacturing oddly controlled systems of propositions, but they will not be systems of belief if nature commands us not to believe them. And she often does. If we open our eyes we have little or no control over what we see and believe as a result. Conversely we cannot believe what we know ourselves to have just invented. (Thus one thing amiss with Russell's example is that we cannot add the belief to our historical system while we know ourselves to have just invented it. We would have to go through some process of attaining conviction.) Perhaps nature has built us to be knowers: truth might attach to members of *naturally* controlled, coherent, and comprehensive systems of *beliefs*. When we alert our senses nature forces us to the beliefs which then flood in. The most we can do is to use those, and our best ways of forming CCC systems. If truth is anything *more* than this, how could we possibly regard ourselves as knowing anything about it? And how would it matter, if it were so remote from the human world we find ourselves in?

6. *What is Right about Correspondence?*

I hope that at this point a coherence theory begins to look attractive. But it tends to keep bad company, particularly in contemporary developments. In particular is it just accidental that a coherence theory of truth associates with Idealism – a view of the ordinary world as in some sense a mental construction? The loss of the "barely given" fact, and the difficulty of describing the control of a system of beliefs by experience, seems to leave an image of such a system as entirely self-absorbed. Beliefs are fitted with other beliefs, everything adjusted to make for a CCC system, but the image is of a system disconnected from the world. Neurath's famous picture of the system of science as a boat – a structure with no foundations, but with a strength given by the mutual support of members – left us searching for the control of the shape of the boat. If the tides of experience just throw up further planks then they are merely our most fertile source of boat-building material: so what can we do but walk around inside the boat, testing and adjusting for coherence? At this point we go back to starting at the typewriter – *that*'s a fact, *that*'s what makes true the belief that there is a typewriter on the table. Surely it is just common sense, not the higher reaches of theory, which sees us as responsive to mind-independent facts? In the *Mikado* (see chapter epigraph) Pitti-Sing's tale might have been unassailable, but it certainly wasn't *true*.

What makes true the belief that there is a cat in the garden, is there being a cat in the garden. There being a cat in the garden is, on the face of it, a very different kind of thing from there being a system of beliefs, controlled in whatever way we like, which would have this belief as a member. It is the *cat* which we respond to, not anything mental. We are good instruments for detecting cats, and that is why, if we are careful, our beliefs about them tend to be true. Suppose, then, we have, as part of this common sense, a rough notion of what counts as a sane, sober practice of enquiry, enabling us to find out whether there is a cat in the garden. We can now formulate what I shall call a *correspondence conditional*:

(1) If I form only beliefs with a proper pedigree, and end up believing that there is a cat in the garden, then there is a cat in the garden; if the same is true and I believe there is no cat, then there is no cat.

In other words, I am a good signaller of the presence or absence of cats. My belief responds to the cat. If I am to assert this, then such correspondence conditionals as (1) need to be assertible. If they are not, then our conception of the pedigree, the certificate given by the sane sober practices of enquiry, leaves it disconnected from truth. Of course, we know we may be deceived on occasion. The conditionals represent a general truth, not an unbreakable one. It is the task of epistemology to make sure we can believe such conditionals, and to explain why.

Now the reason why we are good at cats is nothing like the reason why we are good signallers of duties, numbers, possible worlds, and the like. We are good at cats because our senses make us *causally* receptive to their presence or absence. This may not be the whole story about why we can assert (1), but it is certainly part of it. It is part of our conception of the world – part of our system of beliefs – that it is only because we are in this way responsive that we have any right to the correspondence conditional.

However, if a coherence theorist is unwise enough to present membership of a CCC system as just the same thing as truth, his grip on these correspondence conditionals becomes very strange. Consider by the side of (1):

(1*) If I form only beliefs with a proper pedigree, and end up believing that there is a cat in the garden, then it is true that there is a cat in the garden; . . .

This differs only in adding 'it is true that' to the consequent of the conditional, which is legitimate because of the transparency property. Now substitute a coherence conception of truth:

(1**) If I form only beliefs with a proper pedigree, and end up believing that there is a cat in the garden, then the belief that there is a cat in the garden is a member of some best CCC system of beliefs; . . .

(1**) seems quite different from (1). It threatens to be a tautology, because the notion of proper pedigree and of the best
CCC system are simply *interdefinable*: *any* notion of proper
pedigree can yield a corresponding notion of the maximal
system of beliefs with such pedigrees! But common sense does
not regard us as good signallers of cats because of any such
tautology. It demands that we look to the cat and our causal
responses to it. It does not want to see us as good signallers of
whether our beliefs would enter into a maximal coherent and
comprehensive set of beliefs controlled in the ways we find
natural.

The point is obvious if we imagine two different views of the
virtues of systems of belief. A hardline empiricist ("Carnap")
may choose one kind of pedigree as the only worthwhile one
(V_c), whereas a hardline Catholic ("Newman"), say, may
choose a somewhat different set, (V_n). Suppose that each set of
virtues allows us to define a maximal set of beliefs possessing
them: V^*_c and V^*_n, respectively. Then consider:

If a belief has V_c then it belongs to V^*_c
If a belief was V_n then it belongs to V^*_n

Each of these is harmless – an uncontroversial tautology. Each
of Carnap and Newman can believe each of them. But this just
shows that they fail to capture the real point of difference, which
is that Carnap thinks that if a belief has V_c and not any other
kinds of feature, then *it* is true, whereas Newman disbelieves
this, but believes that if a belief has V_n, and not any other kind of
feature, then *it* is true. As in the case of ethical disagreement,
where there is divergence over the right standards, we cannot
see the disputants as each with his own, standard-given notion
of truth. For that makes the dispute disappear.

In sum, there is a distortion in any definition of truth in terms
of membership of a system of belief, where the members need
some correct pedigree to enter. The distortion is rather like that
which assailed the "democratic harmony" theory of universals
(3.3). Our judgement that a cat is in the garden is made true, if
it is true, by the cat being in the garden. The issue of how other
people would judge it is no part of this truth-condition. Nor is
the question of whether the belief that it is would enter into any
proposed system of belief. We don't, as it were, look sideways,

either to other people or to systems of belief. We look at the cat and look round the garden.[12]

It is a general maxim in science that a good new theory should be able to explain what was attractive about a superseded old theory. In view of the rooted and stubborn place that correspondence with the facts has in normal thinking about truth, it would be surprising if there was nothing right about it. This is now becoming apparent. The notion of correspondence at least registers a half-truth: whether or not true beliefs *correspond with* the facts, true believers must certainly *respond to* the facts. The world has cats in gardens, and it has believers: the believers must be able to see themselves as properly responsive to the facts they take to obtain. Our causal theory of the world insists that the fact that there is a cat in the garden (or the state of affairs of there being a cat in the garden) can bring about many things: the shadow on the parsley, the absence of the birds, or my realization that it is there.[13] If my belief does not respond to the fact then I am a poor register of cats being in gardens, and my confidences in these matters are disconnected from their truth. Neurath's boat, the ship of our interlocking confidences, may need no foundations. But it does need to be built in response to the states of affairs which obtain in the world in which it sails. In the next section I show how this demand makes room for a proper theory of knowledge. Meanwhile the question is whether these virtues in the concept of correspondence undermine the coherence theory entirely. Does any such theory founder on the distinction between (1**) and (1)? Must it misrepresent the ways in which we are forced to

[12] This is not the objection (see Hartry Field, 'Realism and Relativism', *Journal of Philosophy* (1982) p. 556) that some propositions are true but not members of any CCC system – e.g. a proposition of the form 'there have been exactly n dinosaurs', which nobody could ever know or even reasonably believe. There are such propositions but it is a mistake to urge them against a proper coherence theory, which will reply that our conception of the world permits truths which *would* enter an idealized set of beliefs, created in accordance with *our* virtues – in this case the virtues attending proper use of observation, memory, and counting, in situations to which we don't actually have access. The objection in the text is not that a coherence theory delivers the wrong class of truths, but that it delivers the wrong conception of truth.

[13] It is common to find contemporary philosophers speaking as though only *events*, not states of affairs, enter into causal relations. This is just wrong. It makes nonsense of the notion of a stable *equilibrium* in which a thing's being at a place or being thus-and-so causes nothing to change. Events are changes in states of affairs, and lack of change can need causal explanation just as much as change.

think of beliefs being sensitive to facts? We must remember here the subtle route whereby an elucidation of truth might generally escape from Frege's regress. This meant giving up ambitions to provide a synonym for truth, but insisting that a substantive conception of success in judgement is nevertheless possible. Now our causal theory of the world is undoubtedly a central component of our system of beliefs. Surely a coherence theorist should not *deny* these elements of common sense. His role must be to incorporate them (to speak with the vulgar but think with the learned, again). In other words, he must try to respect the real content of conditionals like (1). He must recognize the causal element underlying them. He must avoid the mistaken equation giving (1**). But he must still maintain that he has a distinct conception of success in judgement, and that it sees success in terms of membership of a CCC system.

Is this combination of attitudes possible? The idea would have to be that *internally*, we talk of states of affairs, or of correspondence, and of the causal theory allowing (1); but that this permits an *external* reflection that all this is part of our own system of beliefs, and that truth accrues to any such system in virtue of its coherence, comprehensiveness, and control. The model would be the quasi-realist's approach to the mind-independence of moral truth. He faced the similar obstacle that we think as though the wrongness of doing something were quite different from any question of the sentiments we happen to feel about it. He respected this claim, seeing it as in effect internal to any admirable system of attitude, but not seeing it as settling the issue of the construction of moral truth. The parallel coherence theorist respects the claim that as believers we are sensitive to the presence of the cat, the very state of affairs which makes our judgement true, if it obtains, and false if it does not, but rolls this into the overall CCC system, whose virtues he hopes to describe, and out of which he supposes himself to construct a notion of truth.

These are deep waters, and nobody, as far as I know, has ever swum very far in them. It is as though the CCC conception of truth is, like Idealism, a kind of optional gestalt-switch: you can see things, wilfully and in the study, as if the virtues of systems of beliefs are all that we have to build a notion of truth out of, just as you can think as though the world is a mental construction. But out of the study the vision goes; objects, facts, re-emerge and demand their independence of us and our believings.

7. *Epistemology Regained*

There are writers who associate epistemology, as the systematic account of ourselves as knowers of the world, with the correspondence theory of truth. Since they regard that as refuted, they regard epistemology as misdirected as well. It is important to understand that this is not so.

As I have tried to stress, there is not really a correspondence "theory" of truth: there is rather an invitation to think of the relation between true belief and whatever it is in the world which makes it true. This invitation may lead to bad developments: to the idea of the mind's awareness of fact as something which, favourably, is uncontaminated by judgement, and purely passive; or to the idea of thoughts as pictures in the mind copying the world, or to the idea that each individual judgement has its own identity regardless of its associations with any others in a body of belief, and is in turn made true by one isolated, self-subsistent state of affairs. Any of the bad developments could prompt a bad epistemological tradition. For example, the idea of *vision* as the paradigm of knowledge, and yet itself different from judgement, undoubtedly dominated the theory of knowledge throughout the seventeenth and eighteenth centuries. (God just has to *look* to know.)[14] The goal of the theory of knowledge was to show how our ideas represented reality – a correspondence which forever seemed fugitive, because we only had our ideas to go on. It is then tempting to jump to the view that if this concept of correspondence, this accent on copying and re-presentation, is jettisoned, all the problems of knowledge disappear with it. If we substitute a pragmatic or coherence conception of success in judgement, that success seems more assured, and scepticism easier to avoid.

The truth in this is that epistemology may become easier. It may no longer be possible to mount a wholesale contrast between our total CCC system of belief, and The Truth. We may have no concept of truth, on the coherence development,

[14] I owe this point to Edward Craig.

which entitles us to make any sense of the idea that all of our
best, most careful, refined, useful, simple, virtuous ways of
building belief are leading to falsity. There would then be
no problem of answering wholesale scepticism. Descartes's
demon, who allegedly systematically feeds us misinformation to
delude us into believing that we are in a world which does not
exist, would fail in his plan: he would put us in a world which is
truly as we take it to be (so would Berkeley's God). Nor, of
course, does the ship with which a system of belief is compared
need foundations – the bare, incorrigible, passive reception of
fact, imprinted without the intervention of judgement. But the
ship does need constant inspection. As we walk around it, we
may find it hard to preserve coherence, and may also find that
doing so demands giving a good deal of time to traditional
epistemological problems. Otherwise a system breaks down
from the inside.

I have cautiously said that if we sympathize with the coherence theory wholesale worries of a sceptical nature *may* disappear, not that they *must* do so. This is because I mistrust one
more proposal for marking the realist off from the anti-realist
(here represented by a coherence theory). This proposal is that
the realist, for better or worse, can make sense of the idea that
even an idealized successor of our own system of belief might be
false, whereas the anti-realist can make no sense of this possibility. If the anti-realist adopts the Peircean equation of 'Tp' with
'p is a member of M^*' then, of course, he cannot understand the
suggestion that the members of M^* might be false: membership
of M^* is defining truth. Hence, if this equation is accepted, there
is no space for wholesale scepticism. But looking at it the other
way round, we can ask why it should be a *virtue* in a system that
this space should disappear? What is so good about a system
which does not permit its adherents to formulate a contentful
doubt about its own overall adequacy? The undergraduate
student who is impressed by the possibility of Cartesian
demons, hypotheses that we are all brains in a vat, and so on,
may be using legitimate aspects of our own conceptual scheme –
ones which would be present in any idealized successor as well.

If this is right, the coherence theorist or anti-realist would
allow sayings like 'perhaps all our experience is a dream;
perhaps our best procedures still fail to give us the truth'. He

would see the concept of truth (explained, remember, in terms of other virtues) as elastic enough to allow this, because amongst the virtues he ranks highly expressions of fallibility and consequent attempts to secure the boat. Although many writers, most notably in recent years Hilary Putnam, believe the contrary, it would not be true that only a crude "God's eye view" or "copy" theory of truth permits wholesale worry. The coherence theorist could share it. So he would avoid any definition such as Peirce's, for it closes the space which I want the coherence theorist to keep open. Naturally, it does not trouble me that this leaves no precise definition of truth. For we have already seen good reason why the investigation into truth should be more oblique than this. Already in the last section we found a difference between (1) and (1**) which is itself sufficient to force the coherence theorist to avoid direct analysis. In effect I am allowing him to do this, and then to exploit the possibility of incorporating into his idealized or imaginary set of virtues the virtue of insisting upon the fallibility of all judgement.

However, I am fully aware that this is a delicate and surprising position. In what follows I shall not rely upon it. I return instead to the relatively local and internal problems of epistemology which arise as we walk around our boat, attempting to secure its internal coherence.

Thus, consider the incoherence from which a belief-system will suffer if its account of the correspondence conditionals leaves them unassertible. These conditionals allow us to see a favoured method of forming opinion as a signal of its truth. If we find we cannot assert this, then the system fractures: we will have confidence in some element, but no confidence that this confidence is placed in a way which leads to the truth. Our naturalized epistemology – our best description of ourselves as knowers of the world – must avoid this *extended incoherence*: extended because there is no actual contradiction in both believing that p, and believing that the belief that p is formed in a way disconnected from the truth of p. I take it as obvious that extended incoherence is a defect. It would be like trusting the readings of an instrument whilst supposing it to be disconnected from whatever it is allegedly registering. And inconsistency can quickly develop. For if the system is rich enough to speak about chances, we can express our confidence by saying that there is a good chance that there is a cat in the garden, and the sceptical disconnection by saying that the observation leaves no better chance that there is a cat in the garden than there would have been had it not been made.

Now it is very easy to say things in epistemology which introduce failure of extended coherence – in other words, which leave the correspondence conditionals unassertible. The thrust of traditional sceptical problems in philosophy is to challenge our conceptions of ourselves as good signallers of various kinds of truth. So a coherence theorist must pay as much attention to those problems as anyone else: it is a mistake, and unfortunately a common one, to suppose that they affect only some crude foundationalism or crude conception of correspondence with the facts. On the contrary, since virtues falling short of extended coherence will certainly not serve to define truth in a system, a coherence theorist needs to make sure he can retain it. I shall illustrate this point, and the difficulty of meeting it, with reference to the bent-predicates, Goodman's curious dimensions of similarity and dissimilarity, introduced in 3.2.

The traditional problem of induction is that of showing why it is reasonable to put belief in the straight continuation of some regularity: reasonable to expect future blood samples to be red rather than red^{BR}, to use the example of that section. We can define a "space" of alternative things which could happen to the colour of blood throughout a certain period. Staying red is just one of many conceivable happenings. Goodman's predicates take some alternative – changing yellow at some particular time, for instance – and define a property so that retention of it means following that alternative. A thing remains red ^{BR} if it turns yellow at the end of 1985. We expect presently red things to remain red; a red^{BR} user is supposed to expect them to stay red^{BR} – i.e. to turn yellow. Our prediction that blood will remain red means that we expect him to be wrong. He expects us to be wrong. Why have we any reason to trust our opinion against his?

The answer which introduces extended incoherence sees nothing but convention or accidental linguistic arrangement to which to point. We speak and have always spoken a language which classifies and predicts in terms of redness. We could have spoken one, on this account, which classified and predicted in terms of red[BR]ness. Had we done so we would now be sitting in equal confidence that blood will turn yellow at the end of 1985. But the fact that we use English and not this rival, English[BR], is as conventional, and as much subject to our habits and arrangements, as any other aspect of vocabulary and syntax.

This account of the pedigree of our belief that blood will be red after 1985 will simply not cohere with the confidence we have in that modest prediction. Mention of convention is relevant only if our needs, natures, or causal interactions with colours and other features of things, might *equally well* have left us holding the inconsistent prediction. Convention fills the gap between such things and our actual arrangements (see chapter 4). But then it is an explanation of why we hit upon one arrangement and one prediction, which is quite disconnected from anything which affects the likelihood that the belief is true. In this it is like conceding a fanciful origin for a belief; indeed fancy, or the toss of a coin, or any random or accidental happening, is just the kind of thing to determine which convention to adopt out of a space of competing, equally serviceable ones. But you cannot coherently regard yourself as a good signaller of the future colour of blood, if you also think that what determines the colour you predict is itself quite disconnected from anything affecting or affected by that colour. The correspondence conditional becomes unassertible, and extended coherence fails. The general point is that unless there can be a causal story connecting the likely future colour with the factors making us select one commitment, it will be incoherent to maintain the commitment. But if there can be such a story, showing us why it is natural or inevitable for us to speak the one language and not the other, the point of mentioning linguistic arrangements and conventions is lost. Our predicting that the blood will be red and not red[BR] will be explained not by our linguistic conventions, but by whichever story best explains why we must make our actual classifications, and not others.

Fortunately, if the arguments of 3.2 are right, it is wrong in any case to see our preference for redness rather than red[BR]ness as in any sense arbitrary or conventional. For we can form no real understanding of how these other dimensions can really be perceived as free from change. Using this point to found a better theory of ourselves as good signallers of the future needs a head-on attack on the classical problem of induction – of why the future or the unobserved is reliably indicated by the present or the observed – and this is therefore a traditional problem of epistemology which a coherence theory of truth must face. The extended incoherence which must be avoided is not imposed only by some exalted conception of truth. Nor is it the product of a delusive desire for certainty or proof where none can be had, nor of a desire for "foundations" of systems of belief, when all that can be had is the mutual support of elements of such systems. It is just that when a perfectly natural account of ourselves as judgers and signallers involves a conventional explanation of our commitments, it imposes a definite chance of there having been other commitments, and it is this chance which produces the incoherence. It emerges from something presented as a piece of straightforward human psychology.

It has been extremely common in epistemology this century for philosophers to think they reach bedrock in mention of our ways, our conventions, arrangements, or "linguistically imposed" practices (the "linguistic turn" again). The idea that a particular claim to knowledge can be justified if it is part of a "language game" permitting us to assert it, has become extremely widespread since Wittgenstein introduced the term. But what status can this give to any belief? That depends on the way we regard alternative arrangements. If it is just a matter of convention that we have the one game and not another, then extended incoherence threatens, and we do nothing to certify the claim as likely to be true.[15] The conventionalist *geist* blows philosophers who are quite different in spirit from Wittgenstein close to this peril.

Consider, for instance, Quine's attempt to describe the way in which experience controls systems of belief. Quine is acutely sensitive to the problems of the holistic nature of systems and of the difficulties with "the given". But he wants some conception of an observation sentence, or verdict properly prompted by experience, and with genuine authority over what beliefs can be truly held. He describes it like this: "a sentence is observational

---

[15] Wittgenstein himself, in spite of careless use of notions like 'game', seems largely to think that nature rather than convention forces aspects of our intellectual lives onto us.

insofar as its truth value, on any occasion, would be agreed to by just about any member of the speech community witnessing the occasion."[16] The laudable intention behind this definition is to exclude highly theoretical remarks, dependent upon specific background knowledge, from being regarded as observational. But Quine also intended his definition to "accord perfectly with the traditional role of the observation sentence as the court of appeal of scientific theories".[17] It is not clear that his definition does that. For what is the authority which resides in the speech community and what is its source? Just about any English speaker, looking out of the window, would agree that the grass is green. But is it the fact that they would so agree which *gives* this belief its authority as an observation? Surely that depends upon our account of why the agreement arises, or, in other words, of what is so good about this feature of the English-speaking community. Then if at *this* point we simply cite conventions, or what our speech community has us do or say, implying that there could equally well be other arrangements leading to verdicts inconsistent with ours, then we lose any grip on the authority of the report. Once we suppose that equally meritorious languages could lead their users to look out of the window and dispute whether the grass is green, we have lost any right to see ourselves as good signallers of colour. The correspondence conditionals become unassertible. and extended incoherence sets in. Quine did not intend his definition in this conventionalist way, but others, notably Richard Rorty, have so construed it.[18] The difficulty is that if the speech community is mentioned at all, then unless we have some story about why the community's reaction to experience is reliable or authoritative, the road to conventionalism is wide open. Rorty takes Quine to imply that it is the consent of the people which makes it true that in saying any particular thing we are making an observation. But then, unless we can hope for some theory according to which that consent is *itself* a reliable sign of the fact reported, we have incoherence, and conventional origins of the consent block any such theory. They do this because convention explains a

---

[16] W. V. Quine, *The Roots of Reference*, p. 39.

[17] W. V. Quine, 'Epistemology Naturalized', in *Ontological Relativity and Other Essays*, p. 87.

[18] Richard Rorty, *Philosophy and the Mirror of Nature*, esp. pp. 174 ff.

feature only if any of a space of other different features would have *served us equally well*.

The theory of knowledge has always struggled to form some conception of the control of belief by experience and observation. It is not my purpose to enter that struggle here. The point is that the conventionalist stance, either towards Goodman's problem or towards the definition of observation sentences, is incoherent. The search for something better is a quite proper part of naturalized epistemology, *even if a coherence theory of truth is favoured*. For the incoherence of a false step at these points is an internal, structured fault in any system of belief, noticeable as we inspect our boat. It is not a fault, or alleged fault, which only exists on a correspondence vision, whereby we can, as it were, detach ourselves entirely from any of our actual beliefs, and adopting a "God's eye view", or standing on an "Archimedean point" outside the whole system, discuss whether it depicts Reality well or badly, draped or undraped. We can attempt to understand ourselves as good signallers of the truth without worrying about any such idealized perspective. The conventionalist turn represents a false step in any such attempt. And reference to our ways, our customs (games, conventions, languages, consensuses), cannot be bedrock when we make the attempt, for, as I have tried to stress, unless such reference is supplemented by an account of why these arrangements lead us to opinion which is well connected with how things are, it is no better than mentioning fancy or any other random pedigree for a belief, and leaves the correspondence conditionals quite unprotected.

It is only when we believe that the correspondence conditionals are properly assertible that we can be happy with ourselves as registering the truth, or happy that our procedures for forming belief are reliable, or scientific. It is because the proponents, say, of some wilder psychoanalytic theories, or of some dogmatic versions of Marxism or other social theories, do not appear to form beliefs in a way which enables the belief formed to vary with the truth about the issue, that they are deemed unscientific: as soon as we can say that someone would have believed what he does regardless of what the facts are, we remove any respect for his opinion. I think it was this demand which was approached, but not quite accurately, by Sir Karl

Popper's famous demarcation criterion, according to which to behave scientifically is to be open to falsification, whereas to behave unscientifically is to hold beliefs as immune to falsification. The difficulty with this, as Lakatos showed,[19] was that the most respectable, paradigm scientists often hold theories in ways which the criterion would condemn. An adherent of Newton in the nineteenth century might have been quite unable to conceive of circumstances which would lead him to declare the general principles of mechanics false; any disturbing results would be deemed to be mere anomalies, and met with relatively *ad hoc* adjustments to the overall theory. And why should we demand higher standards from psychoanalysts or social theorists than from physicists? According to the view I give the real difference is that the physicist has a coherent story, showing why his belief in Newton's laws depends on the facts in the way that beliefs ought to; if he is genuinely unscientific the psychoanalyst or social scientist will have no parallel story to offer. Closing one's mind to falsification is not at all the primary criterion of demarcation. It would serve, at best, as a secondary symptom, that the theorist is not concerned about the need to protect the correspondence conditionals, and it is here that his unscientific vice lies.

8. *Truth Again*

We are now armed with some sense of what is right about a correspondence theory, and of what is distinctive and attractive about a coherence theory. But we have also learned to be wary of attempts at direct analysis, for such attempts tend to distort the simple platitudes, such as that what makes it true that there is a cat in the garden, is there being a cat in the garden. The exploration so far conducted does, however, cast some light on the question hanging at the end of the last chapter. A system of attitude, admirably controlled, is in many ways like a system of belief. It permits argument, inference, improvement, deterioration, assessments of acceptability, and a quasi-realist construction of truth. Is it then right to say that a moral commitment is true or false in just the same sense in which any other belief is?

---

[19] 'Falsification and the Methodology of Scientific Research Programmes', *Philosophical Papers*, vol. i.

The difference will come, of course, in the theory of the correspondence conditionals. There is no causal story, parallel to that which must be given to justify ourselves as good signallers of cats, to justify ourselves as good signallers of virtues, duties, obligations, and goods. Just because values and the rest are the children, and not the parents, of our sentiments, there is no need for any such theory, and its absence is no obstacle to the regulative use of truth in moral contexts. Does this make moral commitments true in the same sense as others, or only in a different sense? I do not greatly commend the question. What is important is our right to practise, think, worry, assert, and argue as though they are. The extent to which we see this as a valuable fiction will depend in the end on how much we sympathize with the coherence gestalt-switch which permits us to see all truth as constructed out of membership of virtuous systems. If we sympathize with this in general, then moral truth will be just a kind of real truth; if not, then we will regard it is a legitimate, but imaginary, focus, upon which the progress of opinion is sighted. But at present I know of no way of forcing the issue.

There has been one notable absentee from this discussion of truth. Many philosophers believe that the work of Tarski either augmented or even superseded more traditional problems, such as the debates I have related. The so-called "semantic conception of truth" might seem a promising, modern, approach to the area. To see whether this is so, and what Tarski's achievement actually was, demands a separate chapter.

Notes to Chapter 7

7.1　The most useful single collection on truth is still *Truth*, edited by George Pitcher. But substantive theories of truth have not been in philosophical fashion recently. Partly this is because of the arguments of the next section, partly because of a vague feeling that Tarski and Wittgenstein showed that there could be nothing to say about truth itself, but only about the way truth-conditions are attached to particular sentences in particular languages. And a great deal of the literature is involved with technical problems, arising from paradoxes of the liar family, or arising from the attempt to avoid admitting a general concept of truth (see below, under notes to 7.3).

7.2   There is a careful discussion of the transparency argument in Peter Carruthers, 'Frege's Regress', *Proceedings of the Aristotelian Society* (1981).

7.3   The redundancy theory is initially found in Frege. In 'My Basic Logical Insights' (1915) Frege says: "If I assert 'It is true that sea-water is salt', I assert the same thing as if I assert 'sea-water is salt' . . . This may lead us to think that the word 'true' has no sense at all. But in that case a sentence in which 'true' occurred as a predicate would have no sense either. All one can say is: the word 'true' has a sense which contributes nothing to the sense of the whole sentence in which it occurs as a predicate." (*Posthumous Writings*, p. 251.) Similarly F. P. Ramsey: "there is really no separate problem of truth, but merely a linguistic muddle" (*The Foundations of Mathematics*, p. 142). Like Frege, Ramsey saw that the transparency property enabled us to paraphrase away direct ascriptions of truth to judgements: it is true that p reduces down to straightforward: p. But he realized that this does not by itself cope with less direct contexts, such as: 'everything he says is true'. The natural suggestion would be: $(\forall p)$ if he says that p, then p. But this is not uncontroversially well-formed, and philosophical logicians have disputed the matter ever since. The problem is whether the variable 'p' is functioning as a variable normally does, in which case '. . . then p' is not well-formed, since the terms needs completion by a predicate: $(\forall p)$ if he says that p, then p is . . .; and the only way of filling in the dots would be to reintroduce 'true'. The literature on this knotty point includes:

C. J. F. Williams, *What is Truth?*
J. Mackie, 'Simple Truth', *Philosophical Quarterly* (1970).
D. Grover *et al.*, 'A Prosentential Theory of Truth', *Philosophical Studies* (1974).
P. Geach, *Reference and Generality*, *69 ff.

But as the discussion in my chapter shows, I do not believe that the central issue over the redundancy theory is its formal ability to do away with mention of truth from all contexts. The real question is the possibility of a substantial theory of what success in judgement amounts to.

7.4   "The critics of the given have a simple and strong case . . ." I hope it is clear from this section that this is only so when they are attacking a particular conception of the footing that judgements have in experience – the conception that fails to realize the way in which judgement conditions experience. It should not be inferred from this that there is no sense in which things are "simply given" to us. There is no avoiding that: if you are run over by a bus it is simply given that you are. There is no control for you, no exercise of judgement or choice or interpretation of facts. Perhaps one thing which makes it hard for students in this area is that so obviously many facts are simply borne in on us whether we like them or not. In this sense the world *presents* us with so much, and what it presents *is* given. This is true, but it does not affect the point that to take what it presents in any given way is to exercise our understanding.

7.5   I have taken the British Idealists as the best source for the ideas leading to a coherence theory of truth. There is a fascinating further history in the way the logical positivists became embroiled in such a theory: the theory is a permanent temptation for rigorous empiricists. See:

C. Hempel, 'On the Logical Positivists' Theory of Truth', *Analysis* (1935).
O. Neurath, 'Protocol Sentences', in Hanfling (1981).
I. Scheffler, *Science and Subjectivity* (1967).
J. A. Coffa, 'Carnap's Sprachanschauung Circa 1932', *Philosophy of Science Association* (1976).
B. Russell, *An Inquiry into Meaning and Truth*.

In the last of these (ch. 10) Russell repeats the arguments he used against Joachim and Bradley, but against the positivists' version of the coherence theory, represented by Neurath and Carnap. (Russell explicitly recognizes that the new, positivist doctrine is a repeat of the Idealist doctrine, and formed in answer to the same pressures – see e.g. p. 133). As in the earlier work, Russell refuses to allow a form of coherence theory in which language still maintains a relation to non-linguistic occurrences. He insists on seeing the coherence theory as making the world of words a self-enclosed world, and this makes it easy for him to ridicule it.

". . . pragmatism offers the utility . . ."
It may seem strange that I present pragmatism here as a version of a coherence theory, whose distinctive stress is on utility as the virtue of a system. It is more common to find it presented as though a pragmatic theory of truth is a quite different animal altogether. But I do not accept that it can be. (At present the title seems to be conferred on almost anything from a vague sympathy with empiricism, to a redundancy theory or disbelief in the prospects for any serious theory of truth at all. See R. Rorty, Introduction to *Consequences of Pragmatism*:

Rorty sees the *rejection* of questions as the distinctive theme of what he calls pragmatism.)

7.6   It is not common to find writers with anything at all good to say about a correspondence theory of truth. So the introduction of the correspondence conditionals represents a concession to common sense rather than to any specific philosophical position of which I am aware. But Putnam notices the need for such a theory (*Reason, Truth and History*, p. 132) although generally hostile to the kind of epistemology I want to protect. The line I try to sketch at the end of this section is supposed to be reminiscent of Hume's famous division between the attitude to the external world which we find forced upon us when we think about it, and that which is forced upon us by nature. There is a tantalizing amount of philosophy which consists in balancing such images or visions of how things are against one another.

7.7   This attack on conventionalism can be followed up by consulting 3.2 and the notes to that section.

CHAPTER 8

Truth and Semantics

GENERAL. I don't think we quite understand one another. I ask you, have you ever known what it is to be an orphan, and you say 'orphan'. As I understand you, you are merely repeating the word 'orphan' to show that you understand me.
KING. I didn't repeat the word often
GENERAL. Pardon me, you did indeed

W. S. Gilbert, *The Pirates of Penzance*.

For what does a proposition's *'being true'* mean? 'p' is true = p. (That is the answer.)

Wittgenstein, *Remarks on the Foundations of Mathematics*, I,
Appendix I, §6, p. 50.

1. *Truth Theories: Tarski's Suggestion*

In view of the struggles with predication, rule-following, and judgement in the later work, it might be surprising that Wittgenstein expresses such a dismissive attitude to truth. We would expect him to be well aware of the difference between offering a remark as a metaphor, invitation, prescription, expression of attitude, or rule, and offering it as a judgement; to isolate judgements it also requires some account of their dimensions of success – truth and falsity. But we also found, in the last chapter, some faint reason to respect this quietism. The transparency property of truth provides an obstacle to head-on attempts to analyse what truth is. And we found no sharp way of developing either the coherence or the correspondence suggestions into plausible definitions of truth. In fact, the only equations which seem cast-iron are those of the equivalence thesis – it is true that snow is white if, and only if, snow is white; true that penguins waddle if and only if penguins waddle. Turning to sentences we can say that the English sentence 'snow is white' is true if and only if snow is white; 'penguins waddle' is true, in English, if and only if penguins waddle.

It was the suggestion of Alfred Tarski that these equations enable us to propound what he variously called a definition of truth, or a "materially adequate and formally correct definition of the term 'true sentence' ", or a semantic conception of truth which makes precise and improves upon preceding notions. Tarski's work inspired virtually all subsequent formal and logical approaches to language. But from the beginning it provoked the most divergent reactions. To some philosophers it finally solved the problem of the nature of truth. To others it was quite irrelevant. Attempting to explain its real significance is treading on sacred ground. I shall therefore give rather more textual backing to my discussion than I have tended to do. The three papers of Tarski which are important to the philosophy are the classic first paper, 'The Concept of Truth in Formalized Languages' (CTFL); 'The Establishment of Scientific Semantics' (ESS); and 'The Semantic Conception of Truth' (SCT).[1]

CTFL begins: "The present article is almost wholly devoted to a single problem – *the definition of truth*. The task is to construct – with reference to a given language – a *materially adequate and formally correct definition of the term 'true sentence'*." (Tarski's italics.) Tarski's papers make constant use of the ideas of set theory, and even elementary modern expositions presuppose an understanding of quantification theory which, at this stage, I do not want to rely on. So the nature of the enterprise is hidden from all except advanced students. I shall introduce it by reference to an exceedingly simple language – so simple that the difficulties Tarski faced and which required his masterly technical achievements do not arise. To logicians this will seem like discussing Hamlet without the Prince, but it is the other characters who claim philosophical princedom.

Imagine, then, an abstract language like that of 1.3 which has a few names and a few predicates, enabling it to make altogether a small number of sentences. The syntax of language tells us that if 'a' is one of the names, and 'P' is one of the predicates, the result of putting a next to P (Pa) is a well-formed sentence; nothing else is a sentence. How are such sentences to be understood? What is needed is a way of saying what the

---

[1] Page references for the first two are to the volume *Logic, Semantics, Metamathematics*; to the third, to *Readings in Philosophical Analysis*, eds. Feigl and Sellars. CTFL was first made public in Polish in 1931.

different categories of component do – in this case, what names do and what predicates do. This semantic role or semantic value is that they contribute to the overall meaning. The obvious choice is that names refer, and predicates introduce properties, or rules or principles of grouping things. Any sentence is interpreted as saying, of the thing named, that it satisfies the property, or satisfies the rule or principle of grouping introduced by the predicate. This is what has to obtain for the sentence to be true. It can be put as a "compositional axiom" saying what makes the sentence true in terms of the semantic roles of its constituents:

(D$_1$) Any sentence Pa in any language of this sort will be true if, and only if, the predicate applies to or is satisfied by whatever it is that the name refers to.

What we have here is a *framework* with which to describe any of a whole family of abstract languages – those containing only names, which *refer*, and predicates, which we can say *apply*, to things or *are satisfied by* things. D$_1$ reveals the issue of whether any such sentence is true as a twofold issue – one of the reference of the name and the other of the satisfaction of a predicate. This reassuring thought does not touch, of course, any of the philosophical issues we have been involved in. By itself it does not tell us when a sign in a community is being used as a name; what determines the particular thing it does name if it is; when a sign is being used as a predicate; what determines the 'application' of the predicate (remember the difficulty with rules) if it is. Thus when in chapter 6 we struggled with truth of evaluations, it would hardly help to be told D$_1$: puzzling whether evaluations are true can be thought of as puzzling whether evaluative predicates apply to their subjects (or do so in the same way as other predicates do), but it doesn't advance the philosophy to put it that way.

Because D$_1$ yields only a framework of description, to describe semantically any particular abstract language within the framework, we must specify what the names refer to and what the predicates apply to. To illustrate this stage I shall run two abstract languages in parallel. Each has two names (a, b) and two predicates (P, P').

a in L_1 refers to Lenin	a in L_2 refers to Paris
b in L_1 refers to Marx	b in L_2 refers to Rome
P in L_1 applies to bald things	P in L_2 applies to French things
P' in L_1 applies to pink things	P' in L_2 applies to warm things.

Each language can express a modest four sentences. Let us call the framework (D_1) and these interpretations, the *applied framework*. Then using the applied framework we can work out, for instance that the sentence 'Pa' is true in L_1 if and only if (hereafter 'iff') Lenin is bald, and in L_2 iff Paris is French.

It is now important to consider the status of the clauses. What is meant by saying that 'a' in L_1 refers to Lenin? We must distinguish between taking such a proposition as (to use Carnap's terms) a piece of *descriptive* semantics and a piece of *pure* or abstract semantics. As a piece of descriptive semantics we imagine a term 'a' used in the mouths of some people, whose language we call L_1; it is an empirical fact, established by observation or experiment, due to their behaviour, thoughts, or conventions, that this sign refers to Lenin. As a piece of pure semantics we are not interested in any actual people. We are merely specifying what I called an abstract language – a possible, but not necessarily spoken, language. Since that is all that we are doing, nothing empirical or contingent enters into it. That will all arise when we fit the abstract language we have specified to any particular people, for it is then that the question arises whether they actually use any signs in the ways stipulated. Pure semantics, in this sense, is entirely stipulative – merely a matter of armchair invention. So the clauses saying what the terms of L_1 and L_2 do are definitional – part of the stipulation of which abstract language, or semantical system, we are considering. Since such a system is created by *fiat* nothing yet touches the question of what would make it true that a sign functions in any of these various ways, or of how we could discover it.

2. *Truth-in-L and Convention T*

We can think of the applied framework as a manual. Using it, and supplied with a sentence of the object language (L_1 or L_2) we can compute what has to obtain for the sentence to be true. 'Pa' is true in L_1 iff Lenin is bald, and so on for each of the four sentences. The manual is complete, for no sentence that can be formed in either of these languages escapes it. It would be natural to say that such a manual characterizes the abstract languages. However Tarski favoured the slightly surprising description that it characterizes truth, or reference, or satisfaction for those languages. What lies behind this shift of emphasis? At first sight, all that the manual tells us about truth for these languages is what was contained in D_1, that it arises out of the reference of names and the application of predicates. But Tarski describes himself as having constructed, for the language he treats, definitions of the semantic concepts, which include reference, and the satisfaction of predicates by things, as well as truth (e.g. CTFL, p. 252; ESS, p. 406; SCT, p. 63). He thought of the definitions as establishing semantics on a scientific footing, by showing how to replace semantic terms altogether, for suitably simple languages. What is going on?

The essential change in perspective has been well described in a classic paper by Hartry Field.[2] The key is that Tarski means what he says when he describes the clauses in the applied framework – the clauses stating that 'a' in L_1 refers to Lenin, and so on, as *partial definitions* of the semantic concepts, whose *full* definitions are given by the total set of these partial definitions, and their consequences, (e.g. CTFL, p. 192; ESS, p. 404; SCT, p. 55). How can such things as the clauses for L_1 and L_2 be regarded as "partial definitions" of any semantic concepts?

Initially they seemed best regarded as partial definitions of the abstract languages L_1 and L_2. But suppose we decided to view them as partial definitions of six hyphenated concepts: reference-in-L_1; satisfaction-in-L_1; truth-in-L_1; and similarly for L_2. What are these hyphenated concepts? Here is the answer:

X refers-in-L_1 to Y iff: X is a and Y is Lenin, or X is b and Y is Marx

Y satisfies-in-L_1 X iff: X is P and Y is bald, or X is P' and Y is pink

S is true-in-L_1 iff: S is Pa, and Lenin is bald; S is $P'a$, and Lenin is pink; S is Pb and Marx is bald; S is $P'b$ and Marx is pink.

[2] H. Field, 'Tarski's Theory of Truth', *Journal of Philosophy* (1972).

The reader can construct the corresponding clauses for L_2. It is important now to try to think of these lists as full and final accounts, *definitions*, of the hyphenated terms. They are not mere lists; they are definitions, and each item on the list is part of the definition. So we have been given a definition of truth-in-L_1; furthermore, a definition which *makes no mention* of any semantic terms. Using these definitions you can tell whether any sentence in true-in-L_1 without making any semantic judgements at all. You only have to be able to tell which sentence you are faced with, and such things as whether Lenin is pink.[3] I shall call these definitions *list-accounts* of the hyphenated concepts.

The little languages L_1 and L_2 are unusual in that a list-account of true-in- . . . can be provided. This can only be done because there is a finite number of sentences (CTFL, p. 188). If the devices of the language enabled us to construct sentences ad lib, we would need a recursive clause, that is, one which shows how to add to the true-in-L list an arbitrarily complicated sentence of L, in terms of the semantic properties of its parts. This would be like the complex rule governing ANN.[4] It is easy to see how such clauses go. For instance, supposing we enriched L_1 to L^+ by adding a connective '&', meaning conjunction. At a stroke we can create an infinite number of sentences, for any pair of sentences can be conjoined, the result conjoined with any other, or with itself again, and so on. But we can also see how the truth-in-L^+ of any such sentences is constructed: 'P & Q' will be true-in-L^+ if and only if P is true-in-L^+ and Q is true-in-L^+. By using this rule on any conjunction you will eventually reduce the question of its truth-in-L^+ down to a sequence of questions of the truth-in-L^+ of some of the four original sentences. Tarski's great technical achievement was to see how to give a recursive clause for truth-in-L for languages containing quantifiers: I describe this in the notes to 9.1. (List-accounts with rules like this added are called 'recursive accounts' of the hyphenated concepts.) But the philosophical question is most easily appreciated by returning to L_1 and L_2.

Can the lists really be taken as definitions of anything? Notice

---

[3] "To tell which sentence you are faced with": if the semantics is fully formalized, a sentence is identified by a structural description, representing it as a sequence of letters. This does not affect the philosophy.

[4] 1.3 above.

that if they are, then 'refers-in-L_1' and 'refers-in-L_2' are *entirely distinct* relations. In fact, the appearance of a common relation (reference) is misleading. For X refers-in-L_1 to Y iff X is 'a' and Y is Lenin, or X is 'b' and Y is Marx. But X refers-in-L_2 to Y iff X is 'a' and Y is Paris, or X is 'b' and Y is Rome. These are utterly different notions, for they are *defined by* totally distinct lists. Consider some analogies. Suppose I am again troubled by jurisprudence, and wonder what it is for a legal verdict to be properly grounded at some time. Someone advances a proposal. Seeing which verdicts are properly grounded on Wednesday (say, a, b, and c), and which verdicts are so on Thursday (x, y, and z), he urges the following definition:

A verdict is properly-grounded-on-Wednesday
 iff it is one of a, b, or c;
A verdict is properly-grounded-on-Thursday
 iff it is one of x, y, or z.

What is the point of this manoeuvre? Its most immediate point is to stop the hyphenated concepts from having anything to do with one another. In fact, we would do better to drop the hyphens, and regard the lists as defining two new terms – properlygroundedonWednesday, and properlygroundedon-Thursday. But these new terms no more contain the concept of proper legal grounding than the word 'concatenation' contains the notion of a cat. That is, in each case the term can be used in entire ignorance of any meaning attaching, in other contexts, to the embedded strings of letters. 'Cat' is not a semantic contributor to 'concatenation', and 'properly grounded' is not a contributor to 'properlygroundedonWednesday'; the proof in each case is that to tell if the term applies nobody need know anything connected with the (apparently) embedded terms. To tell if a word is a concatenation of letters (how it is spelled) you need know nothing about cats; the ultimate proof whether a verdict is properlygroundedonWednesday is whether it is one of a, b, or c. This has nothing to do with jurisprudence (jurisprudential judgements might have gone into making up the list).

Or take this parallel. I am interested in reference to numbers. I define my systems ANN and ANN* (1.3), and give the base clauses and the recursive rule determining the reference or arbitrarily long numerals. I have done something, certainly, but what I have done and left undone needs careful identification. Suppose I describe myself as having defined numerical reference for those languages. That sounds good: what is the definition? Well, a numeral refers-in-ANN-to-*n* iff the numeral is *1* and the number is 1, or the numeral is *2* and the number is 2. . . Because of the recursive rule I can know whether any numeral/number pairing is on this list. On the other hand, a numeral refers-in-ANN*-to-*n* iff – and then follows the different list; so on for any system I care to invent. To know whether a numeral '*n*' refers-in-ANN-to-*n* you need know nothing of reference to numbers – you just look at the list. Does this put the semantic relations between numerals and numbers onto a sound scientific footing? Is it a definition of reference to number, or a theory of it?

Suppose firstly that we consider it as a piece of pure semantics. Then I am just inventing systems. I am not concerned with the question of *what it would be* for a population to actually use one of these systems; or what kind of truth it would be, and how it would be known, that a population uses *7* to refer to 7. Since I offer nothing to that question my account does not put reference to numbers on a scientific footing, or indeed on any footing at all. For instance as far as it tells us, numbers may be objects in the mind of God and reference to them a kind of telepathy. The issue is simply not addressed.

Suppose on the other hand that we regard one of the systems as a piece of descriptive semantics. Then I pass to you a piece of paper saying that in the system, ANN of some population, *1* refers-in-ANN to 1 . . .; since I give you the rule, you have a complete manual for reference-in-ANN. You ask what use that is; I tell you that it enables you to determine reference-in-ANN. You ask me what that is, and I repeat that reference-in-ANN is defined by the list. This gets us nowhere. To connect with something you might want to know – such as which number someone in the population was referring to by some sign – I have to tell you that the reference-in-ANN of a sign is *also* the number they use it to refer to. That is fine for you: you can now interpret them. But it's only fine for you because I myself could detect which numbers they referred to by which signs! And once again we are given no further understanding of what it was that I discovered; how I could discover it, or what makes it true. I had to *apply the contentious* notion in drawing up the list. Compare my telling you that *a, b, c* are properlygroundedonWednesday; you say 'What is that?'; if I say it is defined as applying to one of *a, b,* or *c* I have got nowhere; if I tell you that when something is properlygroundedonWednesday it is also a properly grounded legal verdict in the system of some population I do tell you something, but I don't advance any understanding of what would make that true, or of what I did to discover it, or how you might detect proper legal grounding in any new system.

The obvious moral is that the idea that the lists (or lists plus recursive rules) *define* any semantic property is completely misguided. How was this disguised? Two large fig-leaves hide the enormity. The first is that a common proposal for ensuring that we know what we are talking about suggests that the word 'semantic' is reserved for the notions used in the construction of abstract semantic systems, and the title 'pragmatics' is used for any science or art of interpreting a population as using any one such system. As a terminological proposal this would not matter, except that it suggests that you can, for instance, tell what people refer to without raising any semantic problems unsettled by list-accounts. It sounds an advance to say that I have a complete account of numerical reference, because I have a recursive definition of reference-in-ANN, so the only problem left with reference to numbers is one of pragmatics, of fitting an abstract language to a population. But since the pragmatic problem is just that of telling whether a group uses '*n*' to refer to *k*, there is a genuinely *semantic* concept left to use, and whose problems are still untouched.

The second fig-leaf is the ambiguity of such phrases as "relativizing truth to a language". It is common to find Tarski's definitions defended on the ground that this is all that he is doing, and a good thing it is too, since the truth of a sentence is indeed relative to the language in which it is used. This is because the same sentence may be used in different languages to say different things. Tarski himself stresses this point (e.g. SCT, p. 53) and Quine uses it to introduce the hyphenated concepts, in the course of approving of Tarski's method.[5] But it is quite insufficient to motivate list-accounts. Of course a horse

[5] W. V. Quine, 'Notes on the Theory of Reference', in *From a Logical Point of View*, p. 134.

may win one race and not another, or a verdict be well-grounded in one system of law and not another; '2' may refer to 2 in ANN and 5 in ANN*. But it does not follow that there is *nothing in common* to winning different races, or being well-grounded in French law and well-grounded in English, or referring to a number in one numerical system and in another, or for that matter to truth as expressed in English sentences, and as expressed in those of any other language whatsoever. Reflection upon the application of an abstract semantic system to any actual population shows that there must be.

The lists may not themselves serve as definitions of semantic concepts, but it might still be suggested that they have a philosophical role. The line would be to turn Tarski to the service of a redundancy theory of truth. This was the approach considered above (7.3). This points out the fact that application of the predicate to a sentence is determined, for each sentence, by a different matter (which the truth-theory identifies for us). This is then used to block attempts to find a unified concept or property of either sentences or judgements, which the predicate expresses. I rejected that line on the grounds that it fails to put out of court the search for a (correspondence, coherence, etc.) conception of success in judgement. Tarski's way of connecting truth, reference, and predication in the semantic description of complex languages does not actually affect this. It leaves quite open the dazzling but elusive prospect of a substantive theory of truth.

Let us call the connection of truth, reference, and satisfaction the 'neutral core' of Tarski's work. For the simple languages we are considering, and for the more complex ones which Tarski succeeded in describing semantically, the neutral core connects together truth, reference, and satisfaction. But it gives us no theory of how to break into this circle; that is, of how to describe what it is about a population which makes it true that any of their words or sentences deserve such semantic descriptions. As far as the neutral core goes, we might prefer a "bottom-up" approach, thinking of the semantic properties of words first, and believing that sentences are secondary to them. This would run contrary to the ideas of chapter 4; influenced by them we might prefer the other "top-down" direction, in which the semantic properties of names and predicates are thought of as abstracted out from the features of whole sentences in which they occur, rather as the fact that a few dots in a newspaper photograph represent Sophia Loren's ear is secondary to the fact that the whole photograph represents her face. But before considering the ideas philosophers have added to this neutral core, I want to introduce the famous 'Convention T' and the semantic conception of truth which Tarski endorsed.

A semantic account of ANN is complete if it enables us to determine the reference of any numeral of the system. If we can do this, we can write something of the form '*n* in ANN refers to *k*' for any numeral *n*. Tarski laid down a similar desideratum for languages. Corresponding to the sentences we want for ANN he took the form: '*s' is true in L iff p*. He called these, equivalences of the form T, and they are referred to as T sentences. (SCT, p. 55. Tarski does not explicitly put in the reference to L, but it is clear that this is simply for ease of exposition.) A semantic description of a language might be thought of as incomplete if it cannot deliver an equivalence of the form T for each sentence of the language. Putting the matter in the way criticized, a definition of truth-in-L is incomplete unless it enables us to do this. That is apparent, given that each particular T-sentence is a partial definition of the notion, and their totality is the whole definition. Naturally, just as '*n' in ANN refers to k* will only be true, for a given fixed notation ANN, if the sign '*k*' refers to the same number as the numeral '*n*' does, so '*s' is true in L iff p* will only be true, for a fixed language L, if '*p*' expresses something bearing the right relation to whatever '*s*' means; Tarski requires that it is the same sentence as '*s*' if the metalanguage includes the object language, or is a translation of it into the metalanguage if it is not.[6] (Don't be surprised that it can be the very same sentence. Remember that the merit of the rule for ANN is that it enables you to see *why* '219' refers to 219.) Therefore, a definition of truth-in-L requires a complete list, or way of showing how to calculate a T-sentence for each sentence of the language considered. Such a definition meets Tarski's *material adequacy condition* for a definition of truth-in-L; the notorious convention T.

For the reasons brought forward in this section we ought to be reluctant to see a definition of any semantic concept at all in

---

[6] If we are just stipulating then we *make* '*p*' the interpretation of '*s*' in the metalanguage, and it is wrong to describe this as a requirement.

any such list or rule for producing one for a language. If I produce Convention N, requiring a semantics for a numeral system to enable a referent to be determined for any numeral the system can form, I *could* describe it as a 'material adequacy condition' on a definition of reference to a number, or (better) of reference-in-S to a number, where S is an arbitrary system. But that suggests, misleadingly, that when we have a list, or list and recursive rules, meeting the material adequacy condition, we have thereby achieved an advance in understanding reference to numbers, and we have seen that this is not true.

Tarski did not see it like this. He is insistent that there is a distinct and genuine conception of truth somehow implicit in his work – a semantic conception of truth. He regards it as just a proper, modern, way of "grasping the intentions which are contained in the so-called *classical* conception of truth (truth – corresponding with reality)" (CTFL, p. 153; the same claim is made in SCT, pp. 54–6). He himself cheerfully admitted that his conception of truth might be merely one amongst others, "including pragmatic conceptions, coherence theory, etc." But he goes on to doubt whether these have been put in an intelligible and unequivocal form. And in true positivist spirit he allows himself considerable scorn for "the philosophical problem of truth";

I have heard it remarked that the formal definition of truth has nothing to do with 'the philosophical problem of truth'. However nobody has ever pointed out to me in an intelligible way what this problem is. (SCT, p. 66.)

But as we have seen, list-accounts, or recursive definitions, of truth-in-L or reference-in-L or satisfaction-in-L, *involve no particular conceptions* of semantic relations. To repeat, this is because they address no question of what it would be for a sign to be used to refer, or for a sentence to be used to say something true; they address no question of what it would be for a population to use a language L for which the adequate truth-definitions are given – in other words to refer, apply predicates, or assert the things paired with their signs in the clauses governing L. A 'recursive definition of reference-in-ANN' is simply *silent* over what numbers are and what it is to refer to one; it can be accepted by people who believe that they are sets, who believe that they are not, who think that they are mental, who think they are ideas in God's mind, even who think that they are nothing. And silence is not the same as introducing a distinct conception of reference. The same is true of truth. To get rid of any temptation to think otherwise, ask which part of a semantic description, such as that given of L_1, or that governing ANN, is *unacceptable* to people with distinct and differing conceptions of truth – non-classical ones, if Tarski is elaborating a distinct classical viewpoint. Take pragmatists, coherence theorists, or correspondence theorists (Tarski is sometimes taken to have superseded a correspondence theory, rather than as he himself thought, merely laid it out properly). Do they *deny* that a subject–predicate sentence is true as the framework principle D_1 says? Do they deny any of the clauses in the lists and recursions – for instance, that 'London' refers in English to London, that 'red' applies to things that are red, and 'good' to things that are good? Of course not. Their contributions and differences relate to what it is for these things to be so, not to whether they are so.

3. *Top-Down and Bottom-Up*

It is not now very controversial that the neutral core of Tarski's work leaves us with reference, satisfaction, and truth in a tight little circle, nor that it would be acceptable to philosophers of any bent: realist, anti-realist, correspondence, coherence, dismissive neutralist, or whatever. The question is how to add to that core to generate philosophical body. One possibility is that more is added when we come to more complex languages. Tarski's technical achievement lay in describing the structure of languages with expressions of generality. To do this he regarded sentences as having a relationship to things analogous to that which a predicate bears to the things which satisfy it. Truth of a sentence becomes the "satisfaction" of a sentence by everything. It is possible to suggest that it is just here that the work gains philosophical importance. But the suggestion is not attractive, for two reasons. The first is that when we understand why Tarski was led to this move, we can see that it should not be a move which offends any kind of anti-realist, coherence theorist etc. The second is that the move in fact represents a kind of trick. It is made in answer to a technical problem, and the technical problem can be solved in other ways. In those other ways, sentences are not regarded as kinds of predicate, but rather predicates are thought of as in effect kinds of sentence. But the compositional insights remain the same. The reader can follow up these allusive comments in the notes to 9.1. For present purposes I am going to put this way of adding to the neutral core aside. The other way would be to find a separate range of ideas which can be added to it.

I described a "top-down" direction of explanation as one which takes the functioning of sentences as primary, and believes it can abstract out reference and satisfaction. A "bottom-up" direction works the other way round. Because in a truth-theory the thing we end up saying about a sentence (that it is T iff . . .) is deduced from what we say about its components, it is natural at first blush to associate truth-theories with the bottom-up direction.

Thus in 1969 Donald Davidson wrote:

Statements are true or false because of the words used in making them, and it is words that have interesting, detailed, conventional connections with the world. Any serious theory of truth must there-fore deal with these connections, and it is here if anywhere that the notion of correspondence can find some purchase.[7]

The idea appears to be that the truth of a sentence is explained in the bottom-up direction, from the self-standing, "detailed, conventional" semantic properties of its constituents, notably the satisfaction conditions of predicates. But do predicates have these self-standing, detailed or conventional connections with the world? Is it not from understanding what is judged, when it is judged that a thing is yellow, that we come to understand the idea that the predicate stands for a certain property, or is satisfied by various things (yellow things)? In chapter 4 we learned to think of a word as a recurring feature of sentences which share some similarity of content. One persuasive reason for that direction was the way in which radical interpretation seems to be based upon attributing a content firstly to whole messages, and only derivatively to features of them. Another

---

[7] 'True to the Facts', *Journal of Philosophy* (1969), p. 754.

reason would be the impossibility of imagining a society which has succeeded in giving detailed conventional semantic properties to words, but without ever putting them together in sentences. The incoherence of this is rapidly apparent. Even if they say 'rabbit' just when there are rabbits about, or 'Napoleon' just when they have a mental image of a little man in a cocked hat, there can be no reason to allow the words to refer (to the rabbit? to the image?) unless something is then *done* with it. Something might indeed be done: for instance, the group might take someone uttering the word as a signal of the presence of rabbits or whatever. But then it is treated in effect as a sentence meaning that there is a rabbit or are rabbits present. There is simply no way in which a word can be given a detailed conventional role as referring or applying to things, in the absence of a habit of conveying information by using it.

In the paper cited Davidson was not only defending a bottom-up direction, but also claiming that the particular thing Tarski would have us say about predicates – that they are satisfied by things – gives us a legitimate sense in which truth is explained as correspondence: "the notion of truth can be explained by appeal to a relation between language and the world." But even if the notion of truth is regarded as explained via a prior understanding of what it is for a predicate to be satisfied, it is not at all clear that Tarski weds us to a correspondence theory of this. The clause for a predicate can take a variety of forms, compatibly with working in a smooth recursive theory of a language: 'banana' in English is satisfied by a thing iff: it is a banana/is a member of the set of bananas/has the feature of being a banana/is one of $x, y, z, \ldots$ where these are all the bananas that there are/is a yellow curved fruit of the banana tree . . . Some of these appear more concerned with a relation between the predicate and the world than others – for instance, the ones which mention things $x, y, z,$ or the ones which mention features and sets. But once again it is difficult to believe that this appearance is reliable. Nobody is going to deny that the predicate will apply to a thing x iff x is a banana; people may dispute over the kind of thing this judgement is, and the way coherence and pragmatic virtues form it.

Davidson took a very different view in later work. The whole idea that the semantic properties of sentences depend upon interior relations such as reference of words and application of predicates is swept aside:

Having explained directly the semantic features of proper names and simple predicates, we could go on to explain the reference of complex singular terms and complex predicates, we could characterize satisfaction (as a derivative concept), and finally truth. This picture of how to do semantics is (aside from details) an old one and a natural one. It is often called the building-block theory. It has often been tried. And it is hopeless.[8]

The switch he advocates is to a top-down theory, but it remains to be seen how such a theory looks.

Top-down theories seem unnatural because of two things. Firstly the semantic description of a language will have a bottom-up appearance: the properties of sentences are deduced from the properties of their parts. Secondly we have a feeling that this is psychologically right: it is because I know which words come in a sentence, and what they do, that I can understand it. But we can avoid worries on the first score by distinguishing the abstract description of the language from the question of what makes it true that a population is speaking that described language. The description may move from small words to large sentences. But it may be in their use of the large sentences that we get the basic fact that makes it true that the group is using the language. Davidson makes the same distinction in terms of explanation (of the semantic properties of bigger units of speech) *within* the theory and explanation *of* the theory – showing why it is not a mere abstraction but connected with actual human populations, their ends and interests.[9] It is when we interpret a population, by seeing how they use their language to express their beliefs, needs, and wishes, that the primacy of the sentence is apparent. The second point, that psychologically there is something to the bottom-up direction, need not be denied. An explanation of how I understand a new sentence as I do ought indeed to cite the familiar words in their familiar roles. But this does not at all work against the idea that those roles are essentially sentential, so that the word has no detailed or conventional function of its own, isolated indepen-

---

[8] 'Reality without Reference', in Platts (1980), pp. 134–5.
[9] Ibid., p. 137.

dently of what it does in whole sentences. Consider that a chess-player can appreciate a new position in a game because he knows the power of the pieces; but the powers of pieces in chess are entirely given by how they affect the game.

4. Radical Interpretation Again

So far I have talked airily about abstracting the semantic properties of words from those of whole sentences. But what kind of detail should we add to this idea? This can be focused by considering again the familiar figure of the radical interpreter. I want to contrast two ways in which he can be added to the picture: a *bleak* way and a *homely* way; each label may cover a spectrum of real procedures, but it is the families which are interesting.

A homely radical interpreter starts with hypotheses about what members of the group are likely to be interested in, saying, and communicating. His initial hypotheses are therefore highly specific: he wonders whether by S said on such-and-such an occasion they mean that it is raining; whether by S^* they mean that it has not been a good year for water-melons, and so on. He guesses at the determinate intentions and meanings lying behind utterances. What controls him in these guesses? Mainly a desire to see the natives as intelligible – as having certain intelligible aims, and performing actions, such as saying things, as sensible means of furthering those ends. Another desire will be to see their language as systematic: for reasons mentioned at the end of chapter 4 this is not too far distant from seeing them as having a language at all. In any case, it will certainly be necessary if their language is elastic enough to allow them to comprehend new sentences. The desire to see the natives as intelligible may include quite specific constraints on how to interpret them – for instance, if they all appear to have their attention focused on one place or thing, whose changes are exciting them, not to regard them as talking about a different thing which they cannot see. I suppose that most of us, faced with the radical interpreter's predicament, would be homely.

A bleak radical interpreter, by contrast, dislikes this armchair psychologizing. He likes his evidence cut and dried, which in this case might mean a bare description of what was said, and of what purely *natural, non-psychological* features of the native's situation surrounded the saying of it. His evidence is to be presented in non-psychological terms, and of course, in non-semantic terms, for it is evidence which he is going to use to construct a scientific semantics of the native language. What controls the way he does this? Mainly a principle of charity, or desire to see as many of the native utterances as true as he possibly can (by contrast, I will call the principle of intelligibility used by the homely interpreter a principle of *humanity*). The bleak interpreter is to be regarded as embodying the scientific or physicalistic truth about the natives. The homely interpreter enters straight away into their psychology.

The interesting thing is that the *position of the bleak interpreter is hopeless*. There are a variety of results which show this. For workers in formal semantics have long known that sentences can be "interpreted" in very different ways. That is, a given result at the macro-level (what to say about the whole sentence) may be compatible with very different properties of words at the micro-level (different interpretations of individual words). The grandfather of these results is the Lowenheim–Skolem theorem. They show that any theory of a standard form, and considered purely as a set of affirmed sentences, if it is interpretable as speaking truly about some set of things, is equally interpretable as speaking truly about any other set of things of equal or greater number. In other words, if your relationship with me is confined to knowing which sentences I hold true, then as far as that goes I could be talking about cows or cabbages or numbers or sets or stars. You could, in principle, provide an interpretation of my words which has me saying just as many true things about any of these domains. This should not be surprising. It is as though you have a list of sentences I hold to be true, and several lists, each of many propositions, but about entirely different things. You then play the game of mapping my sentences onto theses first from one list and then from another. It is no wonder that different solutions are possible. Now of course we only get this wild indeterminacy by putting the macro-knowledge so sparsely. (By contrast, the homely interpreter will control his interpretations by the principles of common-sense psychology. It will not be sensible, for instance, to interpret football fans evidently intent upon a game as talking about transcendental set theory.) The sparseness here is taking as data *only* the list of sentences to which assent is given. Can the bleak interpreter do more?

He can look at any natural (physical, or causal, for example) relations speakers have with things. For instance, if the football game seems to be causing the comments, he may take that as a reason for supposing the comments to refer to the game. But we have a multiplicity of causal relationships to things. When I refer to Napoleon, I may be prompted to do so by a text containing words; the words were written via a printing system, via an author himself relying on other authors, and so on. But it is Napoleon I am referring to, not any of the intermediate elements of the causal chain. Two questions arise. First of all, is there any prospect of a purely natural description of just the relations to things I have when I refer to them? Secondly, even if there is, what is it that makes just *that* causal or natural relationship the relationship of *reference*? (A similar question to that asking what makes just one particular similarity ranking across possible worlds the *right* one for counterfactuals – 6.5).

If we think in terms of the homely radical interpreter, we are asking how *we* determine the facts about meaning, reference, and satisfaction conditions of predicates. If we think in terms of the bleak radical interpreter, we are asking, as David Lewis puts it, how *the facts* determine the facts – how semantic interpretations sit on top of physical facts about things. And the trouble seems to be that there is no unique way in which the physical facts seem to determine the semantic ones. Two supernatural beings, each acquainted with all the physical facts about us and our world, each aware therefore of all our causal relationships with things and their features, might yet choose different ways of co-ordinating these facts with semantic descriptions, and end up regarding us as saying different things, referring to different things, and selecting different features of them for comment. At least, so many philosophers have argued.

If we accept this line of thought, then it can suggest a number of different conclusions. The most radical, but also the most partisan, would be to confine truth to physical truth (the perspective from which meaning becomes impossible, again). Then there is no literal truth in interpretations of people, saying what they said and what they referred to. Reports saying these things are not, as Quine put it "limning the true and ultimate structure of reality", but are indulging a second-rate "essentially dramatic idiom"; useful in the market-place, but no good in the study. This is partisan because of the high-handed confinement of truth to physical truth: anyone who has sympathized with the general difficulties we have had with truth, and in particular anyone who has seen the resources of other anti-realist attempts to earn the notion, will hardly be confident that physical descriptions are the only kinds of saying that merit truth. And apart from general considerations, there is the point often made against Quine that the parallel move can deprive even physical descriptions of truth. Two omniscient beings each acquainted, for instance, with the whole story of all the experiences of sentient beings in our world, might construct very different physical theories on that basis.

The state of play, then, is that the bleak radical interpreter will not arrive at a determinate reference or satisfaction condition for the names and predicates in sentences, nor at a determinate interpretation of overall sentences. The homely radical interpreter, by exercising a principle of humanity and entering into the likely needs, desires, thoughts, and beliefs of his subjects, may well do so. Is it right to see his method as exclusively top-down? The principle of humanity, enjoining him to make them reasonable and intelligible, certainly suggests that he first consider the likely intentions behind their whole utterances, and perform the abstraction of subsentential elements on that. But it may enjoin other things as well. In particular it may offer general constraints at a subsentential level. Two principles of common-sense interpretation would plausibly be: don't interpret people as referring to a thing if there is no means by which they could have been brought to be aware of it; don't see them as ascribing a feature to a thing if the feature is undetectable by their sensory modalities (don't interpret blind men as talking about shades of colour). And, as the football match example shows, there will be a natural inclination to see reference as often determined by attention: the first thing that may come to mind on hearing utterances made in the crowd is that the likely reference is the match, and only secondarily do we think of what might be being said about it.

Let us call the preferred method of interpretation of the homely radical interpreter, W^*_h, and that of the bleak one, W^*_b. Then, provisionally, it would seem that neither justifies an exclusively top-down direction. W^*_b indeed excludes it, in that what it allows us to say about sentences is quite insufficient to enable anyone to abstract out determinate semantics, either for subsentential elements, or for whole sentences. By contrast W^*_h may enable us to do this, but also may incorporate direct constraints on what we are allowed to say about reference and predication.

It would be nice if the indeterminacy which afflicts W^*_b did not exist. For then we would have a proper sense of how the physical universe makes room for meaning – how the referential, intentional powers of our minds and words arise in the order of nature. But if we accept the indeterminacy, then even if we do not allow the high-handed confinement of truth to physical truth, still unease remains. Are we to conclude, with the philosopher Brentano, that the semantic properties of our words and sentences refute physicalism – that they prove the existence of a realm of fact which is quite additional to and separate from the physical universe? Or are we to conclude, with Quine, that there are no such determinate semantic facts to warrant such a conclusion? But after all, I know what I mean when I say that rabbits are good to eat – I know what I refer to and what I say. Indeterminacy may afflict the bleak physicalistic outsider looking at me, but to me and to my fellow-speakers there is no shadow of indeterminacy to be seen. Again the brute problem of incorporating meaning into a physicalist's universe lies heavily across the landscape.

5. *Truth and Extensionality*

The observant reader will have noticed an asymmetry between the semantic description of ANN, and the truth-theoretical way of characterizing the sentences of a language. In the case of ANN we want to know what complex numerals refer to, and this is what we are told. In the case of language, we want to know what complex sentences mean, but this is not what we are told. We are not told that sentence S means that . . ., but only that sentence S is T iff . . . And this is a very different thing. For

as logicians use it, 'iff' is an extremely weak relation. Any
sentence of the form 'p iff q' holds provided p and q have the
same truth-value – i.e. provided both are true or both are false.
If you take any two true propositions, p_1 and q_1, you are allowed
p_1 iff q_1, and similarly if both are false. The moon is a star iff
penguins fly; rivers flow downhill iff money circulates. Similarly
rivers flow downhill is true-in-English iff money circulates. But
this does not tell us what it means. Why then put it at the centre
of an attempt to construct a semantics? Why not obey the
natural course, and go directly for an explanation of how it is
that s in L means that p? On the formal approach, this would be
a formal proof of s in L meaning that p.

It is important to understand the size of the gap. 's' is true iff p
is as weak as this: 'you would be as right or wrong if you said
that 's' is true, as if you said that p.' This allows for any true
sentence to be paired with 's', if 's' is true, and any false one to be
paired with it, if it is false. The subject-matter can be different,
the structure, the concepts, anything. You would be as right to
say that *men have landed on the moon* is true-in-English, as if you
said that bees make honey, or as if you said that penguins
waddle. Some authors misleadingly suggest that the use of the
T-form is justified because it incorporates the insight that giving the meaning of a sentence is doing something called 'giving
its truth-condition'.[10] This is not so: there is no legitimate sense
of 'truth-condition' in which the sentence *men have landed on the
moon* has the truth-condition that penguins waddle. If there
were, then all true sentences would have the same truth-
condition, and all false ones too.

The advance due to Davidson, which hopes to extract more
from the T sentences, comes as follows. Imagine an abstract
language, English* characterized by a truth theory. Suppose a
T-sentence for English* yields a clause stating that 'penguins
waddle' is true in English* iff men have landed on the moon. As
far as that goes English* is like English. But now ask: How does
it get this clause? There are two cases. It might treat the
sentence as unstructured – i.e. just give a one-off axiom coupl-
ing this interpretation to it. But then there is good evidence that

---

[10] Mark Platts, *Ways of Meaning*, ch. 1, cites many writers who seemed to think this.
Platts himself approves of the idea partly because he supposes that the lists or recursions *do* define reference and truth.

we do not speak English*. For we are sensitive to the presence of words in understanding the sentence: we understand it as we do on the basis of the systematic effect the words 'penguin' and 'waddle' have on the content of what is said. So a decent W^{*11} should not attribute English* to us. Suppose on the other hand that the theorem is derived from some clauses governing the components. Perhaps in English* *penguins* refers to men, and *waddles* is satisfied by things which land on the moon. But then things are liable to go wrong elsewhere. Suppose the predicate *covered in black and white feathers* is satisfied in English* (as it is in English) by things which are covered in black and white feathers. Then consider further sentences. *Penguins are covered in black and white feathers* is true in English* iff men are so covered. And now W* comes in. Most of us disbelieve that men are so covered, but believe that the sentence is true in the language we actually speak – English. If W* is sensitive to this (for instance, it finds that people hold the sentence to be true, but behave in no way which suggests that they believe that men are covered in black and white feathers), then it is likely to disqualify English* from being thought of as the language we actually speak.

So the idea is that the fine-grained difference between sentences – differences of meaning – can be constructed on the basis of a coarse-grained relation – sameness of truth-value – if we put enough constraints, in the form of W^*, on the *way* the coarse-grained truth is certified. To take another example, consider the two predicates *has physical shape* and *has physical size*. They apply to exactly the same things. So it might appear that we could write, indifferently, that *has physical shape* is satisfied in English by things which have physical shape, or *has physical shape* is satisfied in English by things which have physical size. Yet intuitively they mean something different. Can an approach which deals only in such clauses salvage this intuition? The idea is that it can, if the right description of the predicate – the meaning-giving one – is the only one that can occur as part of an overall compositional account of English which ends up truly describing each sentence. Thus *x has physical shape* is true in English iff *x* has physical size. But now take, for instance, the English predicate modifier 'nice'. A compositional semantics

---

[11] In either a homely or a bleak form.

will want to write down a clause saying how the meaning of 'is a nice φ' relates to that of 'is a φ'. However this is done, it has to avoid the result that if we apply the rule to compute the meaning of 'x has a nice physical shape' we get the result: 'x has a nice physical shape' is true in English iff x has a nice physical size. For this last remark is *false*: there are things and people with nice shapes but not nice sizes, and vice versa. If we fed in the wrong 'intuitive' meaning at one point, we get false T-sentences at another.

It would thus appear that the discipline of finding a true T-sentence for *every* sentence of a population's language rules out false entries. If the wrong role is assigned to a meaning-giving feature, then, although in an isolated case (*penguins waddle*/men have landed on the moon) a true T-sentence can arise, over the whole spectrum of T-sentences which the feature helps to compute, there will be false ones. The interpreter adopting this discipline then forms hypotheses about what a population is likely to believe and say to one another (seeing them as reasonable, by our lights); he observes which sentences they use to communicate, and which they assent to and dissent from, and he works his way into identifying the fine-grained meaning of each sentence. If, for instance, he finds Englishmen assenting to 'penguins have black and white feathers', and his manual tells him that this sentence is true iff men are so covered, then since we are unlikely to believe this, he should suspect that he has gone wrong.

Of course, at any stage he may make a wrong turn, but the beauty of the idea is that error eventually reveals itself. A good illustration of this comes from an example of Quine's. In chapter II of *Word and Object* Quine pointed out the size of the step from observing when a speaker assents to or dissents from an announcement, to assigning any precise semantic role to the terms of the announcement. The example he took was native assent to 'gavagai!', supposed to be made when and only when rabbits are about. Quine pointed out that although it might come naturally to us to interpret the word as meaning 'rabbits!', other hypotheses are possible. In particular the natives might carve up the world differently; they might be more interested in parts of rabbits, or perhaps by not thinking in terms of continuing objects as we do, think in terms of rabbitform appearances,

or time-slices of rabbits. Nevertheless, as interpretation continues, these possibilities can be ruled out. For example, if the
people are sensitive to number, and we incline to interpret some
signs as numerals, we may enter the hypothesis that 'zonk'
refers to 2; if they then assent to 'zonk gavagai' just when there
are two rabbits around this confirms that they are thinking in
terms of rabbits and not, for instance, undetached rabbit parts,
since two rabbits presumably involve more than two undetached parts. Or a black and white rabbit may have black
rabbit parts and white rabbit parts, so if the word 'gavagai'
referred to undetached parts, we should expect the natives to
infer from 'black and white gavagai' both 'black gavagai' and
'white gavagai', whereas given a black and white rabbit we
would not allow that we have both a black rabbit and a white
rabbit.[12] So we can test an entry by matching it up with other
conjectures until we get a theory which best fits their inferential
and descriptive behaviour.

Quine inclined to the alternative view that a wrong entry at a
first stage could be compensated by other wrong entries (e.g.
over numerals, or which words function as conjunction, or the
syntax of adjectives) together conspiring to give a different
manual of interpretation. It would be wrong to infer this possibility from the example, for on the face of it the discipline of
system *enforces* the right interpretation, just as the discipline of
the crossword puzzle can enforce one solution, even if on any
one clue or on the initial clue various answers seemed possible.
Much depends on whether we are surreptitiously imagining the
procedure of the bleak or the homely interpreter. The homely
procedure will undoubtedly use such methods to enforce
unique interpretation. The bleak procedure will have a whole
universe of bizarre, irrational, and indeed unintelligible
interpretations to select from, and indeterminacy will remain.

The advantage of concentrating upon T-sentences is that the
fine-grained property of meaning emerges from the discipline of
finding a coarse-grained property: a good way of putting it is
that the truth theory, if it characterizes a language which can
properly be attributed to a population (by W*), *serves as* a
theory of meaning for the sentences of the language. Yet in spite

[12] Evans, 'Identity and Predication', *Journal of Philosophy* (1975).

of the attraction of the idea, it brings difficulties which ultimately demand modifications. These arise if we contrast the
intensionality of our own language, with the extensionality of
the theory. I now turn to introducing these notions.

The root idea of the extension of a term is that it is the thing to
which the term applies. The extension of a name is thus its
reference; the extension of a predicate the set of things which
satisfy it. A highly doubtful argument of Frege's extends the
notion to sentences, and leads theorists to say that two sentences have the same extension if they are each true, or each
false. For present purposes we do not need to worry about the
argument: the notion of extensionality relevant to this discussion is one which accepts it. Because of it, two sentences s and s'
have the same extension just when it is also true that s iff s'. Two
predicates may have the same extension, but, intuitively,
determine it in quite different ways and mean quite different
things. ('x has a heart' versus 'x has a liver' is the classic pair.
They apply to just the same creatures, but apparently say
different things about them.) Still more, any two true sentences
or any two false ones have the same extension although obviously there are differences of meaning between them.

Now we can think of a language as a way of putting names,
predicates, and sentences into *contexts*. A context might, for
instance, be 'the father of . . .', which filled by a name makes up
a term referring to the father of the person named. Of course a
language provides for the embedding of names, predicates,
sentences, and any other components within progressively
more complex contexts, making up larger sentences. For
instance, in English, the name 'Napoleon' might occur in the
sentence 'Napoleon is squat', or in the sentence 'Because of his
genes, Napoleon is squat'. The predicate 'is squat' also occurs
embedded in each sentence, and the first sentence is embedded
in the second. Any sentence can therefore be thought of as
providing a context upon its component predicates, names, or
embedded sentences.

A context is *extensional* if and only if the extension of the whole
which it makes up, is a function of the extension of the parts.
Thus the context 'the father of . . .' is extensional, because its
reference is determined by the reference of any name introduced. The context 'there are seventeen . . .'s' is extensional,

because when it is completed by a predicate to make a sentence (e.g. there are seventeen people in this room who have hearts) the extension (truth or falsity) of the whole sentence is dependent upon the extension of the predicate. Because of this, if any other predicate with the same extension were substituted, the truth or falsity (truth-value) of the whole sentence will be unaffected: if there are seventeen people who have hearts, and all and only people who have hearts have livers, then it follows that there are seventeen who have livers. If we consider only contexts which make up whole sentences, then the result is, respectively for names, predicates, and sentences, that:

$C(a)$ is extensional iff $C(a)$ & $a = b$ together entail $C(b)$
$C(F)$ is extensional iff $C(F)$ & all and only F's are G's together entail $C(G)$
$C(s)$ is extensional iff $C(s)$ & s iff s' together entail $C(s')$

A language is extensional if all its contexts are – in other words, if the extension of large parts is determined by the extension of small parts. The language of, say, elementary arithmetic is extensional, for the reference of an expression such as $(5 \times (3 + \ldots))$ depends purely on what is referred to by any expression substituted. The way the expression refers to the number is immaterial – for instance, the value is the same if you put in '7', or if you put in $(1/3 \times 21)$.

English, however, is not on the face of it extensional. The sentence 'penguins waddle' has the same extension as the sentence 'men have landed on the moon', but the referring expressions 'a description of how . . .', or 'an explanation of why . . .' is wildly different depending on which is substituted. The extension of these expressions is therefore not a function of the extension of components. Similarly 'John believes that . . .' may be true if one sentence is substituted, and false if the other is. Quite simple contexts are not extensional. Suppose Fred dived into the pool, and also that John did. The two sentences 'Fred dived into the pool' and 'John dived into the pool' are both true. But the sentence 'Fred dived into the pool and then John dived into the pool' may be true, while the sentence 'John dived into the pool and then Fred dived into the pool' is false. In other words, whether you get a truth by saying '. . . and then . . .' depends not merely on the truth-value of sentences you feed in, but on something else as well – the order of the events they relate.

The best understood logics are extensional. That is, they consider the inferential relations amongst sentences, where the sentences are built up by extensional constructions. Because of this it seemed formally sensible to require that the language in which the truth theory is couched, and in which the deduction of T-sentences from base clauses is done, be extensional – in other words, that it should be sensitive to no more than the extensions of elements of the inferences. Hence the need to operate in terms of the T sentence, which has an extensional form. By contrast 's' *means that p* is heavily intensional, for it can obviously change its own truth-value when different sentences are substituted for p, even if those sentences have the same truth-value themselves.

There now arises tremendous tension between the evident fact that natural languages permit intensional constructions, and the avowed aim of describing them in an extensional way. If a language permits intensional constructions, this is because, as speakers and hearers, we are sensitive to *more* than the extensions of the terms or sentences which are the input in those contexts. Consider for example that the two sentences 'Bert came' and 'Fred came' may have the same truth-value. But 'Ethel was glad that Bert came' and 'Ethel was glad that Fred came' may differ: the first could be true and the second false. So the embedded sentences are not merely contributing their extensions (truth-values) as their part in the overall process of arriving at a truth-value for the total sentence. In turn this means that there can be no truth-theoretic description of 'Ethel was glad that s' which contents itself with an extensional description of s. That is, it is futile to search for a rule which goes:

If s is T iff p then 'Ethel was glad that s' is T iff φp.

In the first occurrence you can substitute any two sentences with the same truth-value. But if 'φp' gives the sense of 'Ethel was glad that p', then in the second you cannot. The only rules of this form that you could get would need to use a much stronger S/p relationship:

If S means that p, then 'Ethel was glad that S' is T iff φp,

for example.

This does not immediately destroy the prospect of giving an extensional semantics for such a construction. The escape would come by redescribing the 'logical form' of the sentence. If 'Ethel was glad that . . .' and '. . . and then . . .' are sentential operators, we have the need for intensional descriptions. But suppose we parse them differently. Perhaps for example, there is concealed reference to *events* in them. 'Ethel was glad that Fred came' relates Ethel to an event – Fred's coming. Provided that this is a different event from Bert's coming (which it is) Ethel may be glad at one and not the other, just as she can kick one chair and not another. So the project of giving an extensional construction brings with it a heavy commitment to concealed logical forms: sentences are reparsed so that their real ("logical") form enables the inferences they permit to be laid out in an extensional form. But the need for other theoretical categories rapidly arises: 'Ethel was glad that she owned Broadacres' does not relate Ethel to an event, but at best to a state of affairs (and Ethel is not ambiguously glad).

There are many excellent and ingenious suggestions for forcing recalcitrant contexts into an underlying extensional form. But is the motivation so very convincing? I suggest that it is not. For remember that the promise is to build the fine grain of meaning upon the coarse grain of purely extensional description. And then there is a kind of schizophrenia in the requirement that semantic structure be exhibited in a purely extensional way. For this dissociates the radical interpreter, operating W^* (in one version or another), from the ordinary user of the language. The promise is that by using W^*, the radical interpreter can sift out which among the enormous number of true T-sentences is the interpretational, meaning-giving one: the one that serves as a theory of sense. This gives him a *stronger* s/p relation, empirically and properly discovered, than merely that s is T iff p. But if *he* can do such a thing, then so can *users* of the language. And if they can do it then they can also build constructions which are sensitive to the difference – in other words, which do not get their interpretation on the basis of the extensions of the inputs, but on the basis of the stronger properties. For instance, it can matter to the truth of what we say that an embedded sentence means one thing or another, not just whether it is true or false. It can matter to the truth of what we say whether a predicate picks out a set of things by one feature or by others, and not just (or even not at all) what the actual extension of the predicate is.

Let me put the point this way. Suppose a population is one of what we can call Hopeless Extensionalists. They just cannot make themselves aware of anything except the extension of terms: the reference of names, the set of things satisfying predicates, and the truth-value of sentences. Then *they* cannot build contexts like '. . . and then . . .', or 'is a nice . . .', whose extension is a function of anything finer grained than the extension of components. Since they cannot do this, W^* will have nothing to do: any extensionally correct description of their sentences will do as well as any other. There will be no advanced contexts where a wrong input lower down, by finer-grained standards, gives a wrong extension to a term or sentence higher up. So conversely if this is to happen, it is because the population is not one of Hopeless Extensionalists in which case it is absurd to treat their language as though they are.

The classical intensional contexts are those which tell what someone thinks, believes, desires, etc. A sentence starting 'x thinks (etc) that . . .' and completed by an embedded sentence identifying what x thinks, naturally puts the embedded sentence into an intensional context, for it is its content and not merely its truth-value which determines whether the report of x is true. Obviously a person may think that s and not think that s^* although s and s^* share the same truth-value. So the kind of clause which gives the semantic form of 'x thinks that s' cannot start off 'if s is true iff p then 'x thinks that s' is true . . .' because the information the antecedent gives us about s is too thin to provide an input (intuitively: even if s is true iff p, there is no way of connecting the truth of the saying that x believes that s to p, just because of that). Why not avoid schizophrenia, and use the fact that a good 'interpretational' truth theory contains a clause stating that s is true iff p? The clause would be of the form 'if a good, interpretational truth theory contains a clause saying that s is true iff p, then 'x believes that s' is true iff x believes that p'. This uses an intensional input – a stronger s/p connection than merely that s is T iff p. But it is an input which Davidson's programme need not eschew as unscientific. Its respectable status comes from the background theory, telling us of the virtues which a truth-theory would have and which would make it fit to serve as an identification of the sense of sentences.[13]

The detailed semantics of belief contexts is complex, and there are many suggestions in the field. Many try to sidestep the problem, by in effect denying that the sentence 'x believes that s' has semantic value which is a function of any feature (such as the sense or content, or even truth-value) of the embedded sentence s. The crudest version of such a theory would equate 'x believes that s' with a direct quotation: 'x believes this: "s".' The embedded sentence is mentioned, not used, and since this is so the semantic value of the overall sentence is no function at all of the meaning of the embedded one – just as the sentence 'x spelled this word: "dog" ' means what it does regardless of what the word 'dog' means. You could understand it and tell that it is true without knowing what the English word means. Unfortunately exactly this separates it from 'x believes that s'. To evaluate whether 'Galileo believed that Venus is a planet' is true you need to understand (at least) what 'Venus' refers to, and what is meant by being a planet. Someone, for example, who does not possess enough astronomy to understand the concept of a planet cannot understand the report of Galileo's belief either. Since this is so, a semantics of these contexts (called 'propositional attitude contexts') cannot escape the problem of showing how we use our understanding of the embedded sentence to arrive at an understanding of the whole. And this requires finding some property of it beyond its extension, and properties of embedded predicates beyond their extensions (since Tom may believe that if a thing is a mammal it has a heart, but not believe that if a thing is a mammal it has a liver).

There are two broad motives for suspicion of anything stronger than extensional semantics. One is that if we allow that the truth value of 'x believes (etc.) that s' if a function of some stronger property of the embedded sentence (its sense), we

[13] I have been encouraged to urge this by finding the point well developed in T. Baldwin, 'Prior and Davidson on Indirect Speech', *Philosophical Studies* (1982).

must ask when we allow two sentences to have the same sense. The difficulty arises that we are fairly unprincipled, in practice at any rate, about the substitutions we allow and disallow in propositional attitude contexts. The very ideal of sameness of sense (defined as the property which permits this substitution) has seemed spurious to many. For instance, consider the two predicates '. . . is a widow' and '. . . had a husband, who died while still married to her, and has not since remarried'. These are surely excellent candidates for sameness of sense. They not only apply to the same objects, but do so in virtue of the same feature: they represent the same principle of classification. They are synonyms. And yet there are sentences which appear to change in truth-value depending upon which we substitute: we may incline to describe someone as realizing that Sheila is a widow, but not realizing that she had a husband, etc. (because, for instance, we fail to draw one of the obvious consequences). We may certainly describe someone as puzzling whether all and only widows are people who, etc., yet it seems wrong to describe such people as wondering whether all and only widows are widows. Everyone knows *that*. The intuitive idea we want is that although two predicates may have the same sense they may somehow display that sense in a different way. The difficulty for the theory of understanding is that of trying to make sense of this idea. The difficulty for semantics is to connect any such feature of predicates to their lack of substitutivity in propositional attitude contexts. Why isn't the pure fact that the predicates represent the same principle of classification, and are understood in the same way, enough to show that anyone whose thoughts, beliefs, doubts, etc. are truly described using one of them, is equally truly described using the other?

By themselves problems of substitutivity could not show that there is no coherent ideal of sameness of sense. They only show the need for a theory connecting sense and substitutivity. (*Every* kind of term suffers from substitutivity problems – names, demonstratives, predicates, adverbs, etc. See 9.5.) To show that the ideal of sameness of sense is itself delusive another range of argument is needed. One I have already touched upon in 5.4: the Quinean move of insisting both that the sense of a sentence must be identified by its method of verification, or its correct anchoring in experience, and that sentences (and predicates) do not have such individual anchorings. But the bias towards extensional semantics is fed from another source.

This is the idea that the cautious or scientific radical interpreter takes only evidence of the extensions of terms, and makes only conjectures about them. The image is that of the scientific observer noting *when* something is said, but not indulging speculation about *why* it is said or the principles which make it correct in the group to say it. However, if we are speaking of W^*_b it is not as though the interpreter even gets as far as determinate attributions of extensional properties (attributing references to names, or attributing sets of objects satisfying them to predicates). So talk of extensional properties of terms is as unscientific as anything else. On the other hand if we are speaking of W^*_h then the whole bias towards extensional descriptions is quite unrealistic. It is not as though the human infant or the sensible foreigner actually take in data or make hypotheses about extensions in the complete absence of evidence and hypotheses about how those extensions are determined. It is not as though nature builds us with a preference for the form of hypothesis: 'someone saying *s is true* in this language is as right or wrong as he would be if he said that *p*' *in advance of* restricting *p* to give a plausible meaning to *s*. Initial conjectures concern objects of attention, the determinate needs and wishes and beliefs and projects of those with whom we communicate, and the determinate features of things and responses they cause. It is in fact conjectures about the meaning of parts and of wholes which solidify into views about the meaning of wholes and of parts.

6. *Composition, Logic, Translation*

There is one pay-off which would arise if we translated a construction into an extensional language: we would come to know its logical capacities – why inferences involving it are valid, if they are, and invalid, if they are not. For extensional languages are logically beautifully understood. But it is not at all likely that explanations sufficient to remove the miracle of understanding all the new sentences which a connective, say, can form, is also by the same token sufficient to provide a logic for it. To illustrate the difference, consider the English conditional: the form of sentence arrived at when two component sentences are embedded in 'if . . then . . .'. This has a systematic effect. For any sentence 'if s then s^*' we can say that if the small sentence s means that p, and the small sentence s^* means that p^*, then the sentence 'if s then s^*' means that if p then p^*. This is of course hardly news, any more than it was news that '219' refers to 219. But anyone who can appreciate that point of the inductive description of ANN can also appreciate that this description of 'if . . . then . . .' might perfectly well take part in an inductive description of the build-up of meaning of English sentences which meets a similar need. The need it meets is to exhibit system. If we had to think of each sentence of the form 'if . . . then . . .' as learned afresh, so that its meaning bore no systematic relationship to the meaning of its components, then it would be a miracle how speakers could use the connective outside cases in which they learned it. But they can do this, just as we can interpret new numerals, and the informal rule I gave describes the meaning which they arrive at.

But 'if . . . then . . .' is logically extremely puzzling. Principles of inference involving it are notoriously unreliable. For example, one might expect this to be a valid form of argument: 'if p then q, if q then r, so if p then r'. This is the property of transitivity, and we rely on it quite happily: 'if he comes then she'll come; if she comes things will hot up. So if he comes things will hot up.' Encouraged by such examples we might write transitivity into our logic for the connective. But then suppose Smith and Jones are two candidates for an election. We might happily suppose that if Jones wins Smith will be envious of Jones. And obviously if Smith dies, Jones will win. But by transitivity the two together yield that if Smith dies, Smith will be extremely envious of Jones. This isn't true, or at least doesn't follow, or we would have a quick proof of a particular kind of afterlife.[14] A logician needs a theory of the connective which explains these conflicting appearances. Obviously the description given above does not explain them, because it simply uses the connective itself to describe its semantic place in English. Logical puzzles about that use are simply not addressed, any more than puzzles about the whole notion of referring to numbers were addressed by the structural account of ANN.

[14] Ernest Adams, *The Logic of Conditionals*.

Fairly obviously, we could describe 'if . . . then . . .' in this logically unhelpful way because we are allowed English, which itself contains the connective in all its obscurity, as our metalanguage. But if we had some logically perspicuous language, containing only connectives of which we do have a logical theory, then describing what 'if . . . then . . .' does in this logically favoured language would reveal its logic at the same time as describing what it does. For example, if we have a full logical theory of 's and s^*' '$it is not the case that s$', '$s$ or s^*' we can try to describe the role of 'if . . . then . . .' using only these devices. If we succeed, we reveal its logical powers at the same time. Thus we might try saying that if s means that p, and s^* means that p^*, then 'if s then s^*' means that *either* it is *not* the case that p, *or* is the case that p and p^*. This interpretation uses only the logically perspicuous connectives.

In fact, these connectives are extensional, or 'truth-functional'. From *not p* and *p iff q* you can deduce *not q*. If you know that *either p or q* is true, or that r has the same truth-value as p, you can validly infer that *either r or q* is true. These extensional operators are studied in the propositional calculus: it would be nice for logic if the English conditional could be expressed in their terms. But in fact it cannot be: the evidence is overwhelming that conditionals are intensional; that is, it makes a difference to the truth of a conditional whether the components mean one thing or another, and substitution of differently meaning but extensionally equivalent sentences, turns an acceptable conditional into an unacceptable one. For instance, it is likely false that nuclear war will break out in the next ten minutes, and also false that the whole humen race will become marvellously wise and happy in the next ten minutes. But the conditional 'if . . . then we shall all enjoy ourselves more' is false or unacceptable if one of these is substituted, but true and acceptable if the other is. Once again we face the fact that it is the fine-grained fact about the input sentences, not the fact certified by any T-sentence, which is needed to determine whether the overall sentence is true or false. Meaning matters. Of course, the logic of conditionals is studied successfully by non-extensional means. But it remains that we can meet the *compositional* aim of removing the miracle from our systematic understanding of conditional sentences, before we have a satisfactory logic. The compositional aim is one thing; logical understanding is quite another. Notice, then, that we can say that we 'give the semantics of' a connective or other part of speech in two quite different circumstances. One would be when we had a clause sufficient to remove the "miracle" of our indefinitely elastic use of the construction, to build any of an indefinite number of sentences. The very bland description of 'if . . . then . . .' does that. The other would be when we had a logic of the connective: when we knew how to describe the inputs and outputs that matter, so that we could determine which inferences were valid and which were not. One reason why formal theorists dislike the use of meaning in describing the function of a connective like 'if . . . then . . .' is that it provides no help at all with this latter task. But this just means that we must separate the two tasks.

Our modes of composition need not be miraculous or unsystematic just because they do not operate in a way which makes the T-form an adequate characterization of sentences, fit to feed into theories of how they contribute to the meaning of bigger parts of speech. But there is another feature of the T-form which raises at least some doubt about the role it is to play in a theory of composition. This can be illustrated with the example of demonstrative expressions, such as 'this' or 'now', which have the trick of having different references on different occasions of use. Similar problems arise with ambiguous names.

We can see the problem these raise by contrasting L_1 with a minutely enriched language L_1^+, just like it except that there is one further name, 'Jones'. This name is however ambiguous: on some occasions it is used by speakers to refer to Jim Jones, and on others to refer to John Jones, in the same way as ordinary English proper names are apt to be. Now there was a list "defining" true-in-L_1, and which itself contained no semantic terms. But for L_1^+ we can give no such list. Consider the sentence *P Jones*. We might try any of:

P Jones is T iff:　　Jim Jones is bald
　　　　　　　　　　　John Jones is bald
　　　　　　　　　　　Jim Jones is bald and John Jones is bald
　　　　　　　　　　　Jim Jones is bald or John Jones is bald

But none is these is right. An ambiguous name may occur in a true sentence provided the intended reference or the reference on that occasion possesses the relevant property, and none of these clauses captures that. Neither of the first two allows for the opposite reference; the third does not allow the sentence to be true regardless of what the other Jones (the one not talked about) is like; the fourth allows it to be true because of what the other Jones is like.

The kind of clause really wanted is something like:

P Jones is true on an occasion of use iff whichever Jones is referred to on that occasion of use is bald.

Similar considerations lead to similar clauses for sentences involving demonstrative expressions:

This is bald said by a speaker s in a context C is true iff the thing which s indicates (demonstrates, refers to) in the context C is bald.

I am pink said by speaker s is true iff s is pink.

There is nothing at all wrong with these clauses. But they have two noticeable properties. They use undefined semantic terms – notions of something being referred to on an occasion or in a context. And they do not provide *translations* of the input sentence: the clauses describe when the input sentences are true, but not by giving interpretations with the same content. Let us consider each point in turn.

Tarski writes that "in particular we desire semantic terms 'referring to the object language' to be introduced into the meta-language only by definition". He says that if this is so the definitions will fulfil what we intuitively expect of them, and if not, then presumably they are at fault through describing truth-in-L only by using some undefined notion of reference. Now the clauses given for the ambiguous name and the demonstrative do just that. For there is no list definition of reference-on-an-occasion in $L_1{}^+$. So if he uses such a clause, Tarski fails to provide a list definition of truth in $L_1{}^+$. To put it another way, the manual for L_1 could be used by someone who is quite incapable of making semantic judgements. But the corresponding manual for $L_1{}^+$ can only be used by someone who can tell what is referred to or demonstrated on an occasion. Tarski himself was well aware that his method could not define truth in L, in non-semantic terms, for languages containing demonstratives and ambiguous terms. And if the aim is to give a non-semantic, list account of truth he is quite right. On the other hand, if the aim is simply to exhibit the structure of a language, it is not at all crippled by the presence of these clauses. For there is no sense in which L_1^+ is semantically less well understood than L_1. There is nothing peculiarly difficult to the philosopher of language in the phenomenon of ambiguity: if we have any idea at all of what it is to use a sign as a name referring to a thing, we will *ipso facto* understand what it is to use it sometimes to refer to one thing and sometimes to refer to others. If we know at all what would make L_1 the actual language of a population, we would also know what would make L_1^+ their actual language. (This is not an argument that we should not study the phenomenon of ambiguity. It is a good source of problems – in other words, a good way of discovering that we do *not* understand as much as we would like to about reference or meaning. All I am asserting is that the mere presence of clauses using the semantic terms does not make the language structurally less well understood.)

Now, however, we face the problem that because of the form they take, these clauses do not provide translations of the object language sentences. A speaker using a demonstrative or an ambiguous name does not refer to himself and say that he is referring to something. He just does it. Thus suppose I say to you that this is pink, indicating as I do so a scarf in my hand, and you understand me, and agree with me. I am a particular person, Simon Blackburn, talking, say, at 10.47 on 13 April 1983, in my rooms at Pembroke College. Nevertheless, I have not said that the object referred to by Simon Blackburn at 10.47 on 13 April 1983 in his rooms at Pembroke College is pink, and this is not what you understand or agree to. You might not have the least idea whether this latter proposition is true: you might not know the time, nor the place, nor for that matter who is talking to you. So the description of the utterance given by such clauses does not proceed by producing an interpretation which means the same, or serves to give the real sense of the original.

This point is a familiar one. Davidson, for example, wrote in

1969 that "when there are indexical terms (demonstrative, tenses), what goes for 'p' cannot be in general what s names or a translation of it . . ." What is not so clear is how it affects the enterprise of revealing the semantic structure of a language by providing formal derivations of T-sentences for each sentence. If the T-sentence can claim to pair s with its translation into the metalanguage, then we can see why we can fairly suppose ourselves to have given the semantics of s. But if s is *not* paired with a translation the achievement seems slightly different. It seems that we have given a perfectly satisfactory discursive account of when the ambiguous utterance, or the demonstrative-containing sentence, will be true – it is not as though there is any mystery of structure or meaning lurking in the sentences – but not by providing anything which identifies the sense of the original. So we need to look sceptically both at the idea that a satisfactory truth theory provides a theorem which gives the sense of the original sentence (or serves as a theory of sense), and at the idea that a discursive description of what words do is somehow inferior to the formal provision of an interpretation into a metalanguage.

The purpose of finding semantic structure is to remove the miracle from the elasticity of language. To do this we need a description of how terms function which explain how we come to understand new occurrences in unfamiliar sentences. This explanation would *have* to take the form of a formal derivation delivering the content we give to the new sentence only if the fresh understanding *were itself* an instance of a translation of the new sentence into an antecedently understood medium. But that is the mistake of chapter 2: it imposes a regressive theory of understanding.

This section has not been much concerned with truth, but rather with the problems and issues which arise when formal truth theories are used to elicit the structure of natural language. None of these problems suggests that the enterprise of formal semantics is in any way misguided; that would be absurd. They only show that we must be very careful of arbitrary impositions of form on such theories, and of supposing that the connection between the theories and meaning is closer than it actually needs to be. But the chapter started with the aim of relating Tarski and his successors to the problems of realism and of rival classical theories of truth. And the upshot of that is that the relation is highly indirect. I have argued that not only is there no distinct rival conception of truth implicit in Tarski's work, but also that to use it at all in connection with issues of truth and reference means adding to the neutral core. The additions can be controversial and subtle, as the top-down/bottom-up division is; they can suggest various conclusions if the persona of the radical interpreter is presented in different ways. But overall the impression is one of philosophical neutrality, of investigations which stand to the philosophy of language as the description of ANN stands to philosophy of arithmetic, or as good book-keeping does to the theory of the economy.

Notes to Chapter 8

8.1   Other elementary expositions of Tarski's work include

M. Platts, *The Way of Meaning*, chs. 1 and 2.
S. Haack, *Philosophy of Logics*, ch. 7.

As may be clear, I believe that Platts mislocates the real significance of Tarski's work, both for the philosophy of truth and for the philosophy of meaning. Haack is a useful guide to modern theorizing about truth. Carnap was the first writer to be really clear about the difference between taking a semantics as a stipulative characterization of an abstract language, and as a description of the way we actually use a language: see his *Introduction to Semantics*.

8.4   Homely and bleak radical interpreters, principles of charity etc. As well as the literature cited under 2.4, readers might like to consult:

D. Lewis, 'Radical Interpretation', *Synthese* (1974).
M. Friedman, 'Physicalism and the Indeterminacy of Translation', *Noûs* (1975).
C. McGinn, 'Charity, Interpretation and Belief', *Journal of Philosophy* (1977).

Hilary Putnam stresses the lack of a backward road from certain macro facts about sentences to determinacy of reference and meaning in their components, in his recent book, *Reason, Truth and History*, ch. 2. He shows that even if we knew the truth-value of a sentence a speaker uses, and knew the truth-value it would have in any possible world, still we could assign references to terms, and meanings to predicates, in non-standard, highly divergent ways. If such truth-values had to be *the* facts determining references and meanings, then this would show that they are not up to the job. But this is a highly implausible version of the 'top-down' route. It certainly distorts the position of any actual interpreter of the speech of another, to see him first acquiring this highly esoteric knowledge of truth-values, and their distribution under different possibilities, and *then* using that to find subsentential interpretations. Consider, for instance, how this simply ignores evidence of causal influences – of the effect upon utterances of what a speaker is looking at or evidently responding to, of the place of the utterance in a whole psychology. Putnam goes on to use his indeterminacy result to argue for an 'internal' view of interpretation, which somehow puts up with the idea that there are no objective external facts, discernible from a 'God's eye point of view', about what terms refer to and what predicates mean. It is hard to be sure that this helps: the problem Putnam finds arises within a perfectly ordinary view of the world – one which sees it as containing words and things, and a multiplicity of possible relationships between them. It is more plausible to suggest that the facts which do determine the interpretation of subsentential components do not lie where Putnam looked for them. They lie in the psychology of the speakers and the history of their terms (see also 3.1 and 9.7). See also the interchange between Field and Putnam, in *Journal of Philosophy* (1982).

8.5 A difficult paper using compositional arguments against Quine's argument 'from below' is

G. Evans, 'Identity and Predication', *Journal of Philosophy* (1975).

8.6 The problem of why the disquotational axioms and theorems of a compositional theory should have an extensional form, rather than going straight for meaning, is addressed by Barry Taylor in:

'On the Need for a Meaning Theory in a Theory of Meaning', *Mind* (1982).

A famous paper urging caution about supposing that semantic theory must take one particular form, such as Tarski's, and in particular urging that the philosophy of meaning should not be bludgeoned by obscurely motivated formal constraints (such as ones leading to the dismissal of intensional contexts) is Saul Kripke's:

'Is There a Problem about Substitutional Quantification', in Evans and McDowell (1976).

CHAPTER 9

Reference

It was Gatsby's mansion. Or, rather, as I didn't know Mr Gatsby, it was a mansion inhabited by a gentleman of that name.

F. Scott Fitzgerald, *The Great Gatsby*.

1. *Reference versus Description*

Two preoccupations have constantly surfaced in previous chapters. First we need to make our theory of our understanding cohere with our views of the reality which surrounds us. Secondly, we need to improve our conception of the way our thoughts relate to the things they concern. Both preoccupations get full expression in the philosophy of reference. Referential expressions ('that man over there'; 'this chair'; 'Napoleon'; 'today'; 'I' . . .) identify the things about which we think and talk, and we understand them to do so. The philosopher's task is to improve our grasp of each of these facts.

Some of the topics of previous chapters have been relatively neglected in recent philosophy of language, although others are hotly debated. The philosophy of reference is the very reverse of neglected. Indeed if analytical philosophy has one great glory to its name, it must be the tradition which goes from Frege through Russell, to modern writers such as Saul Kripke and the late Gareth Evans, and which wrestles with the problems of classifying and understanding the various ways we have of referring to the world around us. The story is a long and satisfying one, and in this work I can only indicate what seem to me to be the most interesting aspects of contemporary positions. Like many writers I locate the interest in a certain tension, which arises because we can easily come to feel both that our understanding of referential expressions must be intimately connected with the object referred to, and also that it cannot be. This tension threads its way through the tradition I have mentioned. Also the different strategies for resolving the tension illustrate the delicate balance of power between mind and language, foreshadowed in chapter 1. It is no easy matter to discover whether we are to understand reference first, and thought second, or to approach it the other way around.

To set the scene we need some terminology. We begin by considering reference to the familiar spatially located and bounded things which surround us, and which we can perceive by the unaided senses – houses, animals, people, tables and chairs. We think of particular things, and utter our thoughts. Such utterances characteristically contain a term whose function is to identify the object thought of – the *singular term*. Prime examples include demonstratives (this cup; that cat; . . .) and ordinary proper names (Napoleon; Regan; . . .). A demonstrative needs a *context* to give it a reference: it can refer to different things on different occasions, and a competent user of the language will know this. The rule for recovering the reference of a demonstrative from the context gives its *character*. For example, the term 'I' refers to whoever uses it: this rule is known by competent users, who can use that feature of an utterance (who produced it) to yield its reference in that utterance. 'That cat . . .' would normally require some accompanying indication which would direct the audience's attention.

Now consider the position of someone who understands all this, but on an occasion does not know which is the relevant feature of the context. For example he hears someone in the next room say 'This one is a real diamond', but cannot see the accompanying indication of which thing is referred to. It is natural to say that he knows the meaning of the sentence, but does not know *which particular* truth or falsity it is used to communicate. He may assume that something is being said to be a real diamond. But not knowing which thing it is he does not know which information is expressed. This can be put by saying that although he knows the character of the utterance, he does not on this occasion know its *content*. But 'content' is a tricky word, and has been used for other things. So I shall say that someone not knowing the identity of the thing referred to does not know the particular information expressed by the utterance. I shall say that in such a case the information is *identity-dependent*. An utterance may be described as identity-dependent if the information it expresses is so. Knowing the information or misinformation given requires knowing which thing was referred to.

An utterance may be identity-dependent with respect to some thing, but not with respect to others. For instance, consider the sentence 'the richest man in Germany is hardworking'. This can be understood by someone who does not know who the richest man in Germany is (in case that seems odd, I explain it below). But it cannot be understood by someone who does not know which country Germany is. Similarly 'the man who murdered this poor girl must be a maniac' can be said, understood, and believed when we do not know who the murderer is; but it would be necessary to know which poor girl is being referred to.

Russell discovered the crucial importance of the fact that many sentences which appear to be identity-dependent in some respects are not really so. To understand this we have to consider various ways of "deconstructing" and reconstructing sentences. Start with a simple sentence with one singular term, and a predicate: 'that cat is mangy'. Deleting the singular term leaves an incomplete expression – a predicate expression or 'open sentence': '— is mangy'. A singular term is a device for turning such an expression into a full sentence expressing identity-dependent information. But there are other ways of reconstructing a full (closed) sentence. Suppose that we are restricting attention to some range or domain of things (the animals in some zoo, perhaps). I might then say 'some tiger is mangy'. This is information, but it is not identity-dependent. It can be understood and believed without knowing which tiger is mangy, and even when it is not true that any tiger is mangy, or indeed when it is not true that there is any tiger in the zoo. The expression 'some tiger' is therefore not functioning as a singular term. So how does the sentence work? Its truth depends upon whether a certain procedure yields a certain result. The procedure is that of taking the predicate around the domain, and asking of each animal in turn 'is *this* mangy?' The sentence reports that if you do that, then at some point, when the question is asked of a tiger, the answer is affirmative. This does not inform us which tiger is mangy, and the information may be perfectly apprehended although no tiger is in fact mangy. This information is *identity-independent*.[1]

---

[1] In respect of tigers. It can only be understood, as I have presented it, by someone who knows which *domain* (which zoo) is in question.

These ideas are put slightly more formally like this. Starting with a closed sentence with a singular term, we may delete the term. Its position may be marked by a letter: usually x, y, z (with indices if more are needed). The letter may be treated as a *variable*, meaning that the open sentence may be taken into a given domain, and the letter can be treated as an 'instant name' of items of the domain in turn. We can then construct the information that if you do this then at no point do you get a truth, or at some point you do, or always you do, or mostly you do, or on exactly n occasions you do . . . Such reports of the *quantity* of instances on which the predicate is satisfied are made using *quantifiers*. The two most familiar are $(\exists x)$ Fx, saying that there is at least one instance of F, and $(\forall x)$ Fx, saying that there is no instance which is not-F, or that everything is F. You can obviously understand such a report about a domain without having the first idea *which* things are in it.

The power of quantificational analyses arises when we consider step-by-step constructions. Consider a particular domain: say, a philosophy class. Perhaps Tom loves Amanda. Perhaps someone loves everyone, or everyone loves someone. We can represent the way these last two differ by a different order of construction. Deleting both names from 'Tom loves Amanda' and putting in different letters gives the open sentence 'x loves y'. Notice then that putting one quantifier in – e.g. '$(\exists x)$ x loves y' still leaves an open sentence. It can be hawked around the domain, and various people may satisfy it as the variable y serves as an instant name for them. They will do so if someone loves them. I can tell you the quantity of times this is true. If it is always true I can say '$(\forall y)$ $(\exists x)$ x loves y', meaning that of everyone it is true that someone loves them. Notice how different other sequences of reconstructing full (closed) sentences would be. From 'x loves y' I could quantify over the y position – e.g. '$(\forall y)$ x loves y'. I can take that predicate into the domain, now letting the x variable light on individuals in turn. Perhaps there is an example which satisfies the predicate: $(\exists x)$ $(\forall y)$ x loves y. Someone loves everyone. In a really jolly class, $(\forall x)$ $(\forall y)$ x loves y.[2]

Quantification theory is the heart of modern logic. For our

[2] Or, perhaps not. It might be better if $(\forall x)$ $(\exists_1 y)$ (x loves y & y loves x) where $(\exists_1 y)$ . . . means that there is exactly one y . . .

philosophical purposes, it depends on two essential ideas. Firstly, the information conveyed by a whole sentence may be reconstructed in a sequence of operations on an open sentence or predicate expression, itself understood as the result of deleting actual names from a full sentence. Secondly, the information so reconstructed may be identity-independent: understanding it need involve no knowledge of which items, if any, satisfy the predicate of the sentence. Perhaps this last point is at its most visible when the sentence has the explicit form: 'not $(\exists x)$ Fx', saying that nothing is F.

I mentioned in chapter 8 that Tarski's achievement was to produce a truth-theory for quantificational languages. This involved turning the informal introduction of the role of quantifiers into something more precise. In particular it meant unifying the role they have in turning open sentences with some number of free variables into open sentences with one less (the change from 'x loves y' to '$(\exists x)$ x loves y') and the role they have in turning an open sentence, such as this last one, which is still a predicate, into a full sentence saying something true or false, when the last free variable is mopped up. The same duality is seen with other simpler terms, notably connectives. 'And' can connect sentences ('Tom was ill and Harry was ill as well'), and predicates ('someone was drunk and ill' – which does *not* mean 'someone was drunk and someone was ill'). A good semantic theory should provide a unified account of what the word does when it conjoins predicates, and when it conjoins sentences. In the case of conjunction it is not hard to see the underlying explanation: from conjoined sentences with the same subject we can delete the singular term, and get 'x was drunk and x was ill' where repetition of the variable corresponds to the cross-reference. Something satisfies this if *it* was drunk and *it* was ill, or, as we put it, it was *drunk and ill*. The predicate forming role of 'and' is *explained* as a natural extension of its operation on sentences. I sketch further in the notes how the same thing is to be tackled for quantifiers.

A particularly important kind of identity-independent information tells us that just one thing has a property. 'x is a much-loved philosopher who writes poetry' may be true of just one person. When I suppose this is so I can introduce a *definite description* – and talk of *the* much-loved philosopher who writes poetry. It was Russell who first realized that sentences involving definite descriptions may be taken to express identity-independent information. They can be understood without knowing who satisfies the description, and indeed when nothing does. This is because the information expressed can be represented quantificationally. This can be done in several ways. 'The much-loved philosopher who writes poetry was here last night' may be represented:

$(\exists x)$ (x is a MLPWWP)   *and*
not $(\exists x)$ $(\exists y)$ (x is a MLPWWP and y is a MLPWWP and $x \neq y$)   *and*
$(\forall x)$ (if x is a MLPWWP then x was here last night).

The second conjunct is the uniqueness clause. It says that there are not two separate MLPWWPs. Intuitively, the second clause says that a certain question is always answered no: the question 'is *this* a MLPWWP and separate from another MLPWWP?' Since there is no value for the x variable of which this is true, we get the second clause. Another quantificational representation of the original is:

$(\exists x)$ (x is a MLPWWP and $(\forall y)$ (if y is a MLPWWP then $y = x$) and x was here last night).

Here the quantifier tells of the satisfaction of a complex condition: being a MLPWWP, and uniquely so, and being here last night. This is logically equivalent to the tripartite conjunction above. Russell's famous theory of definite descriptions is the assertion that the information expressed by many English sentences using definite descriptions may be represented in one of these ways. This has the consequence that the information is identity-independent. From this in turn it follows that such sentences can be understood although nothing actually satisfies the description. There may be no much-loved philosopher who writes poetry, but we can understand the assertion that there is one, since we understand the predicates involved; understanding that, we can appreciate the assertion that there is exactly one, and that he was here last night.

It can be seen that Russell's is an *empirical* theory about the kind of information actually expressed by many English sentences. As such, it has been hotly debated. Some moves in the debate are peripheral to the main topic of thought and things, which is the heart of Russell's contribution, but I shall mention them here, since they throw up other points of general interest. The main value of this part of the debate has been that it has taught philosophers to respect a number of needed distinctions – for instance, between semantics and pragmatics, and between literal meaning and speaker's intention.

Keith Donnellan produced a famous counterexample to Russell along these lines.[3] At a party I point out to you a man, with the words 'the man in the corner with the Martini is a lord'. According to Russell, I have said that there is at least and at most one man in the corner with a Martini, and he is a lord. This would be false if, for instance, nobody had a Martini. Perhaps the man whom I am trying to indicate is holding a glass of white wine. But, *he* might be a lord, and this is what I intended to communicate. My purpose would be to tell you that this particular man is a lord, and mentioning the Martini is just a means to that end: my purpose is identity-dependent. Yet the sentence I choose is a perfectly natural way of trying to fulfil it. So how can it be right to analyse the sentence as if it merely talked of the satisfaction of a complex predicate, and bore no essential reference to the actual object of my interest?

This attack pays too little attention to the distinction between what is strictly and literally *said* by an utterance on an occasion, and what is *conveyed*, and intended to be conveyed, by it. Compare this case: we are sitting together, and a vain young man walks by. I say 'some people from Australia are too big for their boots'. My saying this on such an occasion strongly conveys that I think that *that* particular man is an example of what I have in mind. And this may be what I primarily wish to communicate. But I do not actually say it. What I say – that some people from Australia are too big for their boots – may be false, since they are all modest and shy, although that young man, not being Australian, is indeed appalling; conversely what I say may be true, although that young man is modest and shy, so that what I convey is false. This is an example of the distinction between saying and conveying, or between an implication of the *content* of an utterance on the one hand, and on the other hand, what is often called an 'implicature', or conclusion which

[3] 'Reference and Definite Descriptions', *Philosophical Review* (1966).

the hearer will naturally draw from the fact that the utterance was made, or made in just that way, or with just that intonation, or instead of something else. (In some situations, just remaining silent can have such implicatures.) If an implication arises out of the content of what was said, it is part of the *semantics* of the utterance; if it arises in one of these other ways, it is a *pragmatic* implication. 'I see that the Professor is sober today' implies semantically that the Professor is not drunk today, for it cannot be true unless this is true. But it implies pragmatically, or has as a "conversational implicature" that he is normally drunk. It is the difference between:

It cannot be true that p unless it is true that q,　　*and*

'He wouldn't have said that 'p' (in just that way, in those words, etc.) unless he believed that q'

Russell may use this distinction to deal with Donnellan's case. What is strictly and literally said is identity-independent, and analysed quantificationally. What is conveyed because of the surrounding context, and manifest intention of the speaker, will be that some particular man is a lord. But that is no more reason for complicating the semantics or descriptions than the parallel case is for complicating the semantics of 'some Australians . . .'.

Another attack which founders on this distinction is one which points out that sometimes, faced with a definite description which we know to be empty, we refuse to categorize the overall utterance as *false*, when Russell says that it is. If someone tells me 'the divorce between the Queen and the Duke of Edinburgh was great fun' I am not likely to reply 'that's false', but rather I am likely to boggle or ask what he means or deny that there has been any such event. If I just say that it's false I seem to imply that there has been such a divorce, but that it wasn't fun. Russell's reply here is that we often avoid saying things, or *just* saying things, which may be perfectly true and correct to say, but may generate unfavourable implicatures. Suppose that *mostly* a certain kind of remark is false for one reason, but that on occasion it is false for a different kind of reason altogether. Then just saying that it is false is likely to be highly misleading – to leave the audience supposing that we have a normal case. The classic here is the lawyer's question: 'have you stopped beating your wife?' The hapless witness does not want to answer either 'yes', or 'no'. But in fact 'no' is the correct answer for an innocent witness to give. Stopping doing something entails having at some time done it, and at a later time to not be doing it. If you never beat your wife, then you never stopped doing so. Normally, however, we only discuss the question of whether someone has stopped doing something when we know they once did it: this is why the answer 'no' by itself is likely to mislead the jury. It needs signalling that the case is the unusual one, and in the absence of such a signal ('no – because I never started') the wrong information may be conveyed to the jury. Russell can make exactly the same point. We normally talk of objects and events whose existence is not in question. If someone makes a mistake about existence, such as supposing that there was such an event as the Queen's divorce, which he goes on to say something about, we naturally want to signal that the remark is false in an unusual way.

The strategy is to keep the semantics of definite descriptions as simple as possible, which means regarding them as Russell did, and to use ordinary pragmatic principles, governing what it is natural or unnatural, or helpful or misleading to say, in order to explain apparent surface divergences from the account. Looking at it the other way round, we can stipulate that a population should be speaking an abstract language in which descriptions are Russellian, and inquire whether we would expect just the same reactions to utterances as we show. My own belief is that we would, so that there is nothing in our linguistic behaviour which shows that we take descriptions in any way other than Russell's.

2. *Putnam's Strategy: Spinning the Possible Worlds*

I have been defending Russell's theory as an empirical theory of English descriptions. But its impact does not depend upon that. Its importance is that it raises a possibility. For it gives us an account of how utterances using definite descriptions *can* be identity-independent in respect of whichever item satisfies the description. That is, we can see how 'the richest man in Germany is hard-working' can be understood, and believed,

and express information, even amongst people who do not
know who the richest man in Germany is. The information is
composed from understood operations on understood predicates. It is general or quantificational in form. Now let us return
to the contrasting, genuinely singular proposition.

Suppose I met someone, or hear a musical instrument, or see
a planet, and on a later occasion talk of *that* person, instrument,
planet. Following Evans[4] I shall call the original occasion the
informational episode; the later thought is based on the original
episode. The intention is to refer to the person, instrument, or
planet involved in the original informational episode. Of
course, talk of one episode is an idealization: it is important that
most of the things we commonly talk about have been seen or
heard by us on numerous occasions. But concentrating upon
one informational episode and one subsequent saying simplifies
the exposition. The information expressed in the saying is
identity-independent. The utterance is understood only if it is
known which person, instrument, or planet was involved, and,
as already said, it is this which the speaker intends to talk of.

The tensions which dominate modern problems with reference can now be seen like this. In the original episode the
speaker was affected by the object. He was put into a state of
seeing or hearing something, and as a result he talks *of* the
object which affected him. But now we ask a familiar
philosophical question. What might have been the same, about
the subject, even had it been a different object causing the very
same difference to him? The question is of a familiar form,
because it dominates the philosophy of perception. Any exploration of the relations between our experience and the objects of
the world which we experience, must consider the way in which
our experiences might have been the same, even had other
objects caused them. Some philosophers might like to deny that
different objects could have caused the very same experiences.
They fear the split between experience and object, and consequent epistemological worries which this might usher in. But
since, apparently, other things might have presented the same
appearances, by having the same features, and impinging on us
in the same way, this cannot be an attractive way to exorcise the
fear.

[4] *The Varieties of Reference*, pp. 121 ff.

The importance of this kind of question in the theory of meaning was first stressed by Hilary Putnam, notably in his paper, 'The Meaning of Meaning'. Putnam invites us to imagine different worlds: earth and twin-earth. On twin-earth the substance that plays the part of water is not chemically water, but is something else, XYZ rather than H_2O. However we are to imagine that XYZ has just the same phenomenological properties – the same appearance – as water. It looks the same, tastes and gurgles and splashes and washes the same way. It is called 'water' in the language of twin-earth, which indeed is like earth in every single other aspect, so that if one were transported instantaneously from one to the other, one would notice nothing different at all. Now most philosophers accept that the natural kind term 'water' is a singular term referring to the particular chemical kind of stuff, H_2O. From this it follows that we ought to describe twin-earth by saying that they don't have water there, although they have this perfect substitute. It is not true of twin-earth, for instance, that the seas contain salty water. They contain this other stuff, no doubt with salt in it. The problem which now causes tension is what to say about the thoughts and meanings of terms in the language of twin-earth. What is the same, and what is different? Is it right, for instance, to say that a person similar to me on twin-earth – my *doppelganger* – has the same thoughts that I do, when I reflect on the wonderful properties of water, or attaches the same meanings to his words? Or are we to say that because the reference is different, everything else is too?

Before starting to answer the question, it might help if we have some other examples in mind. As in the case of earth and twin-earth, we "spin the possible worlds", or try to keep things as much as possible the same from the subject's point of view, while imagining different external causes of his being in the state he is in. I shall imagine a couple of episodes staying the same from the subjects' points of view, although caused in three different ways. Firstly, suppose you and I are musicians, and we hear the most magnificent violin playing. We think: 'we must purchase that instrument', and set about tracking it down, amassing money to buy it, and so on. In the first possible world (w_a) the violin was one particular instrument, Stradivarius number 1. In the next or *substitute* possible world (w_s) it was a different instrument we heard – Stradivarius number 2. Finally in the third situation there was no instrument and nothing resembling one. There was a computer simulation of the sound of an early Stradivarius which was good enough (as computer simulations now are) to completely deceive us. I call this the *empty* possibility (w_e). Again, consider two astronomers looking through their instrument, and suddenly seeing a new planet where there should be no planet. In w_a they have indeed spotted a particular planet, in w_s they have spotted a different heavenly body (a star perhaps), and in w_e they are victims of a defect in the optics of their telescope which made it look as though there was a planet. But in each story we are imagining the situations to be the same from the standpoint of the subjects. And in each case there is a subsequent intention to refer, voiced by some utterance such as 'we must buy that violin' or 'let's get the radio telescope onto that planet – it'll make our fame and fortune'.

Since these demonstratives are functioning as singular terms, in w_a there is reference to some particular planet or violin, and in w_s to a different one. In w_e the speakers do not succeed in referring to anything at all. But we have said that in each case the situation is the same from the subjects' point of view, and so it is natural to say that *their* understanding of what they have said is the same in each situation. If we say that, then we need another ingredient than reference to locate their understanding. There is need for a notion, traditionally called that of *sense* as opposed to reference, which can remain constant across these differences of reference, and whose identity gives the thought, or object of understanding. This sense would be identified by the way in which the objects appeared, or the "mode of presentation", in Frege's phrase. And it is this which determines what the speakers manage to understand by their use of the singular term. This way in which the objects appeared, or mode of presentation, is *universal* in just this sense: it can remain constant across changes of possibility which result in different objects having been presented in the same way. In our cases it remains constant across earth and twin-earth, or between the three possible situations w_a, w_s, and w_e. I shall call the view that *all* thoughts are essentially identified or individuated by these universal features, the universalist view of thoughts.

This view of thoughts would accept the following argument:

(1) In each possible world, the subject's experience or mental states, and the features of the environment to which he is responding, are all the same;

(2) Ascribing thoughts is identifying the subject's psychology: it is ascribing mental states;

(3) So in each possible world all the thoughts are the same, i.e. thoughts are universal.

But there is an apparently inconsistent argument. This one goes:

(1') In the different possible worlds the subject apprehends different *truths* or facts (in w_a the truth that Stradivarius number 1 is mellow; in w_s the truth that number 2 is, and in w_e there is no such truth);

(2') A thought should be individuated by its truth-conditions;

(3') So some at least of the thoughts differ from world to world, and are not universal.

These thoughts, individuated by *reference*, could be called singular thoughts. One possible reaction to a pair of arguments pulling in different directions is to postulate ambiguity. Perhaps in one sense thoughts are psychologically real, and then universal, and in another sense they are tied to a common notion of a truth or a fact, and then, since there are some different truths or facts in each possible world (that is how we draw them up, after all) in this second sense thoughts are singular. The prospects for saying that just one of these is the right way to classify thoughts might seem to be fairly bleak. But before adjudicating this, I wish to explore the idea of the essentially universal character of thoughts a little more.

On the universalist view, thoughts are identity-independent even in favoured cases like the ones I have described, where the thought directly answers to an informational episode. The thought is identity-independent, or universal, just because thinkers could think the same even were they in the presence of a different cause of their thinking. It might then seem that we should represent the psychology of the thinker best by referring directly only to the mode of presentation itself, rather than to the object which it latches onto. In other words, the subject's thought would be that the object determined by *this* mode of presentation should be bought however much it costs (or will make our fame and fortune). Let us symbolize such thoughts as 'the determinant of this mode of presentation is φ' by '(D(MP) is φ)'. As a definite description 'D(MP)' is identity-independent, and can be understood in the same way in any of the possible worlds described. This development is motivated by the idea that when I think of a thing I do so because it has features which have impinged upon me. Objects are the sources of sounds, visual effects, or stories and descriptions, in the light of which we are aware of them. But the looks, sounds, and so forth which we have to go on are themselves universal – in principle other things could have been responsible for them. Russell was the pioneer of reference who was most acutely aware of this line of thought. Because of it he made one move which is now generally regarded as mistaken. He thought that ordinary names and demonstratives functioned to introduce the universal features, or in other words that they are equivalent to the definite descriptions 'D(MP)'. But this is not so, for the very reason that it is true, for instance, in both of our possible worlds w_a and w_s that D(MP) is making a beautiful sound (the violin example) or is visible through the telescope (astronomical example). The very same thought or proposition is true in each situation. But it is only true in w_a that Stradivarius number 1 is making a beautiful sound, or that some particular planet is visible. This is not a truth about w_s or w_e. This is because when we use the singular term we go into a different semantic register, as it were. We intend to refer to a particular definite and individual thing or substance, and nothing we say could have been true had that not existed, but had been substituted for by other things. This is why the second argument $(1')-(3')$ was able to insist that the different possible worlds contained different *truths*. But even if Russell was mistaken about the semantics of singular terms, and the way in which they function differently from definite descriptions, his instincts about thoughts may remain plausible.

Russell believed that only items which did not allow for substitute and empty possibilities could be referred to directly. Only names referring to such a privileged class would function, for him, as genuinely singular terms. For only when we refer to such an item will it be true that we *couldn't* have been thinking as we are had *that* thing not existed, and Russell thought that this condition on thinking was the hallmark of an understood use of a singular term. Other candidates for singular terms would be demoted to identity-independence – that is, seen as definite descriptions. Which things do not allow the possibilities? Evidently only ones which could not be replacéd by *doppelgangers* or could not be absent altogether whilst leaving our thinking the same. Russell shrank the field down to thoughts about my own self, to the present time and place, to my own experiences and properties of things (which themselves define modes of presentation). Nothing else, in his view, could have the right essential connection with the very identity of my thoughts. For others we must peel reference away from sense: in other words, other singular terms are understood by their connection with a sense or mode of presentation, rather than directly by their connection with an object.

One consideration which might seem to count against Russell can be ignored. Notice that there should be no requirement that a subject should be able to put words to all the features which made up the way an object presented itself to him. Characteristic qualities of appearances – shades of colour, shapes, qualities of sounds – are just the kinds of thing we find it impossible to describe adequately. So a subject will often be unable to put words to the features or qualities making up a mode of presentation: they will form an indescribable element of his thinking. Now it might be argued that it is wrong to ascribe to a subject thoughts which are individuated in ways which the subject cannot himself put words to. But this is unattractive. For we shall see that every theorist, not just the universalist, is going to have to admit some universal thoughts, regardless of whether the subject is good at articulating them. Otherwise we deny too many obvious facts – such as the fact that the subject in the empty world is actually thinking, when he expresses himself on the apparent object of his experience. This will become apparent later.

3. *Singular Thought Theories*

Many modern writers suppose that Russell's conclusion should

be avoided. It makes modes of presentation too much like intermediaries, getting between us and the things we directly think
about. Once again there is a direct parallel with the philosophy
of perception, where nobody likes the idea that our experiences
act as intermediary, direct objects of perception, forming a veil
between us and the real world.

Consider again the universalist argument of the last section.
It required us to say that the subjects' thoughts are constant:
the same in w_a, w_s, and w_e, or the same across earth and
twin-earth. Why should we accept this? Certainly, if thoughts
are directly expressed using descriptions, as when I say 'the
richest man in Germany is hard-working', I will be thinking the
same regardless of who this fortunate person is. But if after an
informational episode I think 'that violin sounds lovely', why
can't we tie the identity of my thought to whichever violin it in
fact is, thence denying outright that in w_s I think the same, or
even that in w_e I express any thought at all? Why not *only* accept
argument $(1')–(3')$?

Everyone is going to admit that the reports of thoughts must
be different according to whichever possible worlds we
describe. Just as on twin-earth people enjoy bathing in XYZ,
whereas we enjoy bathing in water, so in w_a our musicians
thought that Stradivarius number 1 sounded lovely, whereas in
w_s they thought that number 2 did. Since we here have names or
singular terms occurring inside the 'that'- clauses, which report
thoughts, we can only properly name items which are being
thought about, and this means one violin in one situation, and
another in the other. The question is whether this difference of
report marks a difference of thought reported, or whether it just
marks the difference of an external property of the thinking,
that in one case it is about one thing, and in the other case about
a different thing. In other words, the universalist will claim that
the thinking is essentially or intrinsically the same, in spite of
having a different object. But the opponent – whom I shall call
the singular thought theorist – claims that the thoughts are
themselves different, and that their identity is given by the
object referred to.

It is now necessary to define the opposition to the universalist
more closely. Does he say that there are no universal thoughts,
constant across the different possibilities? Or does he admit that

there are, but also insist that there is a legitimate, self-standing category of singular thoughts, individuated by reference? And does he *merely* stand on the possibility of using argument (1')–(3'), perhaps admitting that the term 'thought' may be ambiguous, and that we can classify thoughts differently, according to whether our interest is in psychology or in facts and truths? And in any case, are we talking about thoughts which a subject *has*, or rather of the thoughts he manages to *express* by his utterances? There are at least two different versions of two different theories:

(SSTT) Strong singular thought theories. The subject characteristically has/expresses by his utterance no thoughts which are constant from world to world. He only has/expresses genuinely singular thoughts.

(WSTT) Weak singular thought theories. The subject has/expresses by his utterance universal thoughts. But in addition he has/expresses by his utterance genuinely singular thoughts.

Clearly a particular problem for SSTT arises with the empty world. If the identity of the thought is given by reference, what of the case where there is apparently good, rational, thinking going on, although through bad luck or bad management, there is actually no object being referred to? Recently there has been a renewed tendency for theorists to grasp the nettle.[5] They claim that the kind of singular thought which can be had, about a violin or a heavenly body, in w_a or w_s is simply "not available" in w_e. When the experience was caused by nothing like a violin or planet, then the subjects only purport to be expressing thoughts, when they subsequently say things like 'we must plot the orbit of that planet' or 'we must buy that violin however much it costs'. The most forceful arguments in favour of this surprising option are given by Gareth Evans. He offers two direct considerations, and a number of indirect ones.

Evans tries to show that when there is no object nothing can count as understanding utterances which contain singular terms purporting to refer to an object of the relevant kind. Since nothing counts as understanding them, no thought is voiced by

---

[5] Gareth Evans, *The Varieties of Reference*, esp. chs. 5.1, 9.4, and 9.5, and the appendices to ch. 6. Also John McDowell, 'On the Sense and Reference of a Proper Name', *Mind* (1977).

them either (understanding just is grasping the thought voiced). The first argument is in two parts. To begin with it is argued that only someone who *believes* that a singular term refers can understand sentences in which it is embedded. Then it is argued that this belief, standing as it does as a necessary condition of understanding something, cannot itself be false. For understanding is a success – it is telling which thought was expressed, and that is apprehending a truth about the utterance – and it can never be a condition on a success that it require a belief in a falsehood: "truth is seamless; there can be no truth which it requires acceptance of a falsehood to appreciate" (p. 331). Myself, I suspect that this attractive principle nevertheless fails when we come to appreciations of psychological truths. For example, there is a truth about what it is really like to enjoy neo-classical art, or the music of Wagner, but it may require the acceptance of falsehood, or at least the indulgence of various cognitive and emotional defects, to come to understand what it is like to do so. Fortunately I do not want to adjudicate this, for the first part of the argument fails. Consider the astronomical case. Suppose one astronomer voices 'I will compute the orbit of the planet, and plot its reappearance'. Suppose he is heard by a colleague who has himself observed the matter, and knows perfectly well why it is thought that there is a new planet there, but is himself bewildered or agnostic. He cannot bring himself to believe that they have really seen a new planet, but has no other explanation of what is going on. Is it really true that such a person cannot *understand* his more credulous colleague's utterance? He himself might naturally fall into using the singular term: 'Well, it's highly unlikely that there is a planet there – still, you get the radio onto it and I'll do the sums.' It is not belief which is necessary for understanding but – well, understanding: knowing why the speaker is making that remark, and why he is right to choose those words to do so. (Notice that the agnostic astronomer does not *pretend* that there is a planet there when he talks about plotting it: he merely supposes that there is one, for the sake of planning what to do.)

Evans's second argument raises the problem for the conditions for communication, when an empty singular term is used. A problem which is left unresolved by the train of thought of the last section, and by any simple talk of thought being identified by modes of presentation, is to settle what is necessary and sufficient for mutual understanding. Communication, or understanding the thoughts voiced by someone, would apparently require knowing the mode of presentation under which they think about or came across or recognize or remember whatever thing they talk about. It would apparently not suffice for understanding that we just know *which* object they talk of, because for the universalist it is not reference which identifies thought. Now Evans believes that in the normal case, when there is successful reference, it is quite sufficient for mutual understanding that the hearer know which object was involved in the original information episode, and hence which the speaker intends to refer to. There is no requirement that the ways in which speaker and hearer think of the object be the same, or even approximately the same. This will occupy us later. But it clearly opens the way for a challenge. If shared reference is the requirement permitting understanding in the normal case, what corresponds to it in the empty case?

So the challenge, to whose who wish to argue that information-invoking referential communication can take place in the absence of an object, is to state a communication-inducing relation between the origin of the speaker's information and the origin of the hearer's information which does not presuppose that the information originates in episodes involving the same object, but which, when the information *is* from an object, holds in just those cases when it is from the same object. (p. 337.)

But there is an easy answer to this challenge. Our two astronomers are so related that *had* their information been veridical, they would have been thinking of the same object. In general, if the same illusion, or fiction, or cause of hallucination, explains why you and I take ourselves to be talking of the same thing, then we communicate. The condition is that there should be an identity (or at least a sufficient overlap) in the explanation of why we are each saying what we are. This is just the condition which is met by ordinary communication when there is an object. For then the same object figures in the informational episodes which prompt our thinking, and itself provides the same explanation of the thinking. (There will be a question of borderline cases, when the way the object figures in the explanation becomes violently different. On this, more in 9.5.) If the condition is not met, then there is a lack of communication. This explanatory criterion for communication is used when we ask whether two people or two cultures think of the same imaginary or mythical entities. The Greeks have a god Hermes, and the Romans a god Mercury. Is it the same god? Their roles are similar, in the Heavens of Greece and Rome; if we press the question of identity, we are asking whether whatever explains one cult also figures in explaining the other. Obviously direct links (the Romans having picked up the cult from the Greeks, for example) suffice; or a common causal origin (in the doings of some god in an ancestral cult, responsible for each of the later developments), or perhaps simply response to some shared psychological impulse to which talk of this god gives.[6]

Is this criterion arbitrary, or is it clear why we operate it when we think of the detail? Suppose our two astronomers, or two violin seekers, are victims of the same illusion, causing each of them to suppose that they are on the track of a definite violin or planet. Then this criterion allows them to be communicating, when they eack talk of *it*. But suppose that just at the time that one receives the visual illusion, the other is victim of a faulty radio receiver. These coincidental mistakes might lead them to talk together of 'that planet . . .'. On this account, they would not be rightly understanding one another. For although they suppose that their episodes are explained by a common source, they are not. So it might have turned out that only one of them was really talking of a planet, and the other was the victim of a delusion. Had it turned out that way, there would certainly have been no one single truth or falsehood which they would each have expressed by the utterance 'that planet is . . .'. For one might have been right – in touch with the truth – and the other not. So although they would have taken themselves to express the same thought, they would be mistaken. Communication requires a correspondence between whatever it is which explains my saying what I do, and whatever it is which the hearer takes to explain those sayings. In the normal case the object presented in the informational episodes provides the

---

[6] G. E. Moore, ' "Real" and "Imaginary" ', *Lectures in Philosophy*, ed. Casimir Lewy. Evans quotes Moore's view with approval, and gives the same answer to problems of communication about an avowedly fictional character or object. But, curiously, he does not realize how this answers his own challenge (p. 338).

common explanation which cements our thinking together. And, again, if one object explains one person's thinking, and another explains another person's, then although they might utter the same words and take themselves to be communicating, they will not be. For example, you may see a person and describe him to me; I identify him with someone I too have seen, and we go on to talk at cross-purposes, mistakenly supposing that our thoughts have the same relationship to reality; the same truth-condition.

I distinguished above four different singular thought theories. In the light of what we have said, the stronger versions (SSTT) become either unattractive or unmotivated. For there is no reason at all to deny that there is thinking going on in the empty world, and that some of that thinking is just what is going on in the other worlds. And there is no good reason, in my view, for insisting that none of the universal thoughts are expressed by the utterances the subjects make, and which enable them to be understood: no good reason for saying that even if they have universal thoughts, nevertheless they do not voice them, when they go into the singular register. In these cases, understanding their utterances is no different from understanding *them*. At least, if this is denied it must be because of some semantic thesis concerning *expression*: it may hinge upon our precise attitudes to people who use empty terms. It is open to a society to regard them as having failed to fulfil the conditions for assertion. But this will be a boring issue, depending upon fine discriminations in our attitudes to the deluded subjects. However, the weaker versions (WSTT) may still justify a fight. So what is in play, when we admit different *truths* across these worlds, if we yet worry whether there are different *thoughts*?

4. *Singular Thoughts and Method*

I have urged that Evans's direct arguments in favour of the singular thought theory, and against the universalist, are not convincing. But what exactly is at stake if we ask whether there is a *sui generis* singular thought, which changes its identity from world to world, and vanishes altogether in the empty world, w_e? Let us be sure of common ground, before making quick decisions. First of all, we have already acknowledged what we can call the weak semantic thesis, that the thoughts we ascribe to our subjects will be described differently, depending on the real state of affairs surrounding them. This is because they will be described by putting singular terms into the descriptions of the thought; and hence although in one world subjects may be thinking that Stradivarius number 1 is lovely to hear, if the situation is different those same thinkers would be correctly described as thinking that Stradivarius number 2 is lovely to hear. The issue, remember, is not over the difference of description of thought. This is uncontroversial. The issue is whether this difference of description is accidental, marking only an external property of the thinking, or whether there is a thought had by subjects in one world which is simply not to be had in the others. Secondly, since the strong versions of the thesis are implausible, any realistic defence of the singular thought theory must allow the subjects to have some universal, quantification-ally expressed, thoughts. For instance, once the illusion was operating, the subjects who formed plans and projects because of it certainly had *some* thoughts. They wanted to track down the violin responsible for the sound, or to track whichever heavenly body caused the observation. There is no problem about these: they are universal, and capable of being entertained or apprehended in any of the possible worlds. This is why any weak thesis (WSTT) cannot use the fact that a subject may be unable to put words to his general thoughts to oppose Russell, for he himself must countenance an inexpressible element in the subject's thinking.

The universalist analysis will be this. Someone is thinking that *a* is *φ*, where *a* is any singular term, if *a* is rightly related to his thoughts. But for that to be so, his thoughts need not be intrinsically connected with *a* (so that under substitute or empty possibilities, the thoughts themselves are different). It is just that the same thinking may or may not have a different external relation, to one object, or another, or to no object, and will be describable accordingly. For the universalist, there are two different styles of *description* of thoughts (sometimes called *de re*, where the thinker is related to a thing, and *de dicto*, when he is described in universal terms), but there is only one kind of thought, which may be describable in different ways.

One natural idea here is that we know enough of what

thoughts are from our own consciousness of them, just to see straight away that thoughts might be the same in each different possible world. This line urges that we know what it would be like, from the inside, to be in the position of my subjects in the various possible cases. And when we think what it would be like, we can see that the thoughts we would have under substitute and empty possibilities would be just the same, regardless of how they were caused. This after all is how the possibilities are drawn up (so that everything shall appear the same to the subjects). Hence, it is urged, the intrinsic nature of thought is indeed universal. Modern singular thought theorists tend to condemn this approach as "Cartesian": implying a spurious authority in the subject, whose knowledge of the contents of his own mind is made into something certain and incorrigible.

But this charge is in turn groundless. The *doppelganger* and empty possibilities are drawn, as I have remarked, so that everything is the same from the subject's point of view. This is a legitimate thought-experiment. Hence there is a legitimate category of things that are the same in these cases; notably experience and awareness. Since this category is legitimate, it is also legitimate to ask whether thoughts all belong to it. In fact the matter is even worse for the charge of Cartesianism than this implies. For the different possible worlds w_a and w_s are not only the same from the subject's point of view, but also in respect of the features (sounds, light waves) of the world which impinge on the subject. So one might even hold that psychology, and the theory of thoughts in a psychological sense, is concerned not only with what happens "in the head", but also with certain relations between the subject and his environment, yet still oppose WSTT. There is a recent tendency in philosophy to see the facts about a subject's thoughts as facts about his relation to his environment. This line opposes the idea that possession of thought might be just, for instance, a matter of the right inner representations, and indeed we sympathized with suspicion of this in chapter 2. Perhaps the question of what a subject is thinking is at least partly a question of his place in an environment and his reactions to it. Even if this were so, it would not establish a WSTT. For it remains quite open that the relevant features of an environment are themselves universal. The thinker in w_s and even the thinker in w_e is impinged upon by the same sounds, etc. as his counterparts: indeed the only case which differs in this is that of the pure hallucinator. He is not impinged upon by the same features. He only has the same inner experience as if he was. An environmental theory of thought can try to deny that this suffices to make it true that he thinks the same: I do not say that this is plausible, but only that even if it is plausible, it still does not establish a WSTT. Another way of putting the point is this. Some theorists suppose that if we had a molecule-by-molecule replica of a subject's brain, then the replica would be possessed of the same thoughts (the psychological supervenes upon *this* part of physical reality). Others might deny this, but say that the psychological only supervenes upon facts about the brain *and* its relationship to the environment. The present point is that even if this latter view were correct, thoughts could still deserve to be individuated universally, in terms of features of the environment, which could in principle be duplicated by different things.

This will not convince the singular thought theorist. He can reply that 'thought' is after all a theoretical term; if other considerations of theory suggest that we ought to classify thoughts as identical only when reference is constant, un-tutored responses which suggest otherwise will scarcely count. So we need to turn to theory, and primarily to the purpose of ascribing thoughts to each other, to see whether that suggests an answer. Since what is at issue is the existence of a distinctive kind of thought – the singular thought, whose identity is tied to that of the object figuring in any actual informational episode which prompted the thinking – we should ask what we know about thoughts and the purpose of ascribing them to one another. If all our purposes are served by theorizing in terms of thoughts whose identity persists across the substitute and empty possibilities, then the singular thought is an unnecessary abstraction.

Here is an analogy which might suggest this. Suppose I design a computer program for classifying candidates taking some large examination. The program takes in names and marks, and classifies according to some decision procedure. Suppose one year I run it on Abbott to Zylkovich, and next year on Acland to Zorowski. Did it function the same way or diffe-rently each year? The first year it classified one lot of candidates, and the next year a different lot. So we could say that it functioned differently. But this is not what we would say. We would say that it did the same each year, provided that the program it followed was unchanged. The decision procedure is independent of whichever candidates are actually input. If I call my program ClassStar and sell it, it always does the same. Perhaps you have a rival, ClassMate. ClassStar and ClassMate do different things, but only in a sense in which each of them separately does the same thing, year after year. Now consider earth and twin-earth. On twin-earth there are people who love XYZ, who bathe a lot, fish and own yachts, and wake up looking forward to a day on the XYZ, or giving themselves kinaesthetic pleasures imagining the soft cool XYZ trickling over their bodies. Such a twin-earther is just like a water-loving earthman: in fact, if he were suddenly transported here he would not notice the difference, and would continue to enjoy the wetter aspects of life just as before. But he and water-loving earthmen function differently from other kinds of people. Those are people who on twin-earth fear and mistrust XYZ, don't bathe or fish or like yachting, and who on earth fear and mistrust water similarly. They function differently. But this sameness and difference of functioning cuts clean across the question of whether they are actually faced with XYZ or H_2O. Now, the story continues, it is the similarity which cuts across worlds – the one which groups together water- and XYZ-lovers, and groups together water- and XYZ-haters, which determines psychological classifications. People who are similar in that sense are the ones who think the same, just as programs can be working the same although in one year they are working on one set of candidates and in the next year on another. Our psychologies are determined by the way we react to what we are aware of. Since the features whereby we are aware of things are universal (water, or violins, or planets can look or sound or taste or appear the same as other things of the same kind or even different kinds), so are psychologies.

This argument certainly makes the case for the category of universal, identity- or reference-independent thoughts. But does it succeed in ruling out the other kind – genuinely singular thoughts? A reply might be that we ought to consider another aspect of the reason we ascribe thoughts to one another. This time it is the explanation of behaviour. People do things because of what they think and believe and desire. Hence the objects of thought must be identified in a way which matches the ways we identify doings. Now often what we want to explain is why someone relates in some way to things: why did he kick *that* table, tread on *that* snake, study *this* historical figure? If our interest is in someone's doings in relation to a particular thing, then he is best interpreted or explained by ascribing thoughts which themselves concern that particular thing: he wanted that table out of the way, he thought that snake was dangerous, he wanted to emulate that historical figure. Once again, however (and by now perhaps predictably) the reply invites a counter. The universalist, remember, allows that it is quite legitimate to ascribe thoughts in the *de re* style. This decomposes into saying that some universal thinking is going on, and that some particular object relates in the right way to that thinking. It is when these are both true that people act upon particular things, and it is the joint truth which explains why they do so. In other words, I explain why someone attacked *that* snake by seeing him as in the grip of snake-hating thoughts which will, on this occasion, be caused by, and, like the subject's attention, be focused on that snake. Had another identical snake been the one to cross his path, the thoughts would have been the same, but their cause, and the subsequent action, would have been directed against the substitute. Once again, constancy of universal thought, in spite of difference of object.

By now it should be becoming doubtful whether the kinds of argument in play are going to determine the issue between singular thought theorists and universalists. Certainly there are no easy victories: properly protected, each side can do justice to the phenomena which the other side urges against it. Is there any prospect for a new kind of argument, settling the matter? A bold line would be to search for a "transcendental" consideration, showing that thought of one kind is only possible because thought of the other kind exists. So at least we would achieve a ranking of importance. And here there is one gleam of hope for the singular thought theorist. Remember how the notion of the identity-independent, universal or quantified way of presenting information was introduced. It was introduced by imagining a transformation on an original atomic sentence, containing a singular term and a predicate. Does this suggest that it is an essentially secondary matter, only understood via an understanding of genuinely singular information? It is a tempting line. To pursue it would, I believe, demand looking at issues beyond this book: issues of the relation between discourse about individual, identified things, and discourse which is only "feature-placing" (like 'it is raining'). The issue over thought and things which we have been discussing, and which seems in some ways to peter out in indeterminate arguments, really gets its steam from this old clash: the opposition between theories taking the notion of a thing as somehow fundamental to our way of conceptualizing the world, and those which believe we can think best in terms of manifestation of properties, with the world of enduring and reidentifiable things a secondary, conceptual construction on top.

5. *Modes of Presentation and Substitutivity Problems*

We have been tackling the issue between singular thought theorists, and universalists, strictly in terms of the conception of thought which we need, and which might buttress either position. And, in default of the highly ambitious argument suggested at the end, we found the considerations indeterminate. We might now go back to more detailed *semantic* phenomena to see if they make a difference. That is, do the phenomena of language, of the way we actually ascribe thoughts using singular terms, suggest one line rather than another?

This is the primary source of argument for the universalist position. For singular terms inside 'that'-clauses often seem to be doing more than just telling us *of what* someone is thinking. They seem to suggest not only the object of thought but the way it is thought about. The classic discussion of this is Frege's 'On Sense and Reference'. Frege considered cases where someone comes across the same object by different ways, so that the appearances do not make it obvious that it is the same object. For example, a tourist might take the train up the highest mountain in Wales one day. He steams up a rather bare and not very steep hillside, which he knows to be Snowdon, and doesn't enjoy himself much. Next day he moves to better things, buys the Ordnance Survey map, and takes the scramble up Yr

Wyddfa across Crib Goch. He goes back after a great day, saying things like: 'Snowdon was lousy, but Yr Wyddfa is magnificent'; 'Today's mountain was a good deal better than yesterday's'; and generally he compares Snowdon unfavourably with the great Yr Wyddfa. Unfortunately they are the same mountain. Then, it is urged, we have to be careful which name of the mountain we put into reports of what he thinks, or we can turn true reports into false ones:

He thinks that Snowdon is duller than Yr Wyddfa.   (true)
He thinks that Snowdon is duller than Snowdon.   (false)

There are now, in the enormous literature on substitutivity problems, many variants of these cases. They affect all singular terms equally, and can arise although there is no difference of singular term (no two separate names or demonstratives). For example, a conjuror might explain a trick, which depended upon showing the same object in two different lights or under different aspects, without the audience realizing that it was the same: 'they didn't realize that this [he shows it one way] is identical with *this* [he shows it the other way].' So it is not just a problem for names, and hence is not to be approached by considering anything peculiar to names, as opposed to demonstratives or other expressions. An important class of cases concerns personal pronouns. Consider someone seeing himself in a mirror, without realizing that it is himself he is seeing. Suppose his trousers are on fire, and he sees that the person in the mirror – whom he calls *that* person – has his trousers on fire:

He thinks that that person has his trousers on fire.   (true)
He thinks that he has his trousers on fire.   (false)

Or, in the first example, the subject might not have expressed himself using names, but just demonstratives: this mountain is a good deal nicer than that other one.

Why does it matter to semantic theory that we cannot substitute co-referential singular terms inside these reports, and preserve truth? After all, we can all see in these cases what is going on. The subject is deceived by the two separate appearances of the mountain, or by the fact that he doesn't recognize it to be himself whose image is in the mirror. What's the problem? The problem is to describe how singular terms function, so that we can see *why* they don't substitute in these reports of thought. For it is tempting to say that the two terms have exactly the same semantic role: each occurrence of 'Snowdon' and 'Yr Wyddfa' refers to the same mountain: 'that person' and the pronoun 'he' refer to the same person. If reference exhausts their contribution to the meaning of the sentences in which they occur, then how can substitution of a different term with exactly the same role change the truth-value of the report?

A theorist attracted to modes of presentation can now suggest a semantic role for them, and one which ties in very nicely to the universalist position on thought. He can say that modes of presentation determine thought, by the considerations of the last two sentences, and that what happens in these cases is that there are different modes of presentation of the same thing. If we shift the reference of the singular terms so that in these reports they function to refer to modes of presentation, then the problem is solved. Using the terminology of 9.3, the subject is aware of the mountain as Snowdon in one way (MP_s), and as Yr Wyddfa in another way (MP_y); the reports now say:

He thinks that $D(MP_s)$ is duller than $D(MP_y)$.   (true)
He thinks that $D(MP_s)$ is duller than $D(MP_s)$.   (false)

Unfortunately this elegant solution cannot be quite right. For consider that this is a valid argument:

Snowdon is a popular mountain;
X thinks that Snowdon is a popular mountain,   *so*
X thinks something true.

Whereas this is not:

Snowdon is a popular mountain;
X thinks that $D(MP_s)$ is a popular mountain.   *so*
X thinks something true.

This is not a valid argument, because X might be in the very state reported in the second premise, although he is not thinking of Snowdon. This would be so if he had been presented with just the same (universal) features which Snowdon in fact presented, but not because he was on Snowdon. He might have been on some unpopular *doppelganger* mountain, in which case he would believe only falsely that it was popular. In other words, this solution (Frege's own) does not preserve the fact that when a singular term occurs inside a report of thought, the subject must be related in some favourable way to the item the singular term normally refers to.[7]

Obviously we want to preserve the instinct that it is the difference of modes of presentation which causes the apparent lack of substitutivity. But the argument just presented seems to block the direct way of doing this, which is to shift the reference of singular terms, in reports of thought, to those very modes of presentation. No logic of the issue can afford to shift the references of terms from occasion to occasion of use, or quite ordinary arguments become invalid.

To avoid this problem a theorist using modes of presentation must bring in the right relation (RR) which a subject must have to a particular thing in order to count as thinking about it. The argument can then become:

Snowdon is a popular mountain;
X thinks that $D(MP_s)$ is a popular mountain;
Snowdon is RR to this thinking of X;   *so*
X thinks something true.

This can be valid. X is now thinking of Snowdon, that it is popular, and anybody thinking that is thinking truly. But protecting the argument this way, we open the way to this:

X thinks that $D(MP_y)$ is not a dull mountain;
Snowdon is RR to this thinking of X;
X thinks that $D(MP_s)$ is a dull mountain;
Snowdon is RR to this thinking of X;   *so*
X thinks of Snowdon that it is dull, and that it is not dull

The same form of argument will show that X thinks of Snowdon that it is duller than Snowdon. But this can be tolerated. The deluded climber does think, of Snowdon, that it is a duller mountain than Snowdon. But he wouldn't recognize this as a correct way of putting anything that he thinks. The idea will be that there will be true reports of people, in the *de re* style, which seem to impute actual contradiction to them. But that is just because someone might believe *of* the one mountain that it is

---

[7] This argument is one which Russell used against Frege. I give more references to literature on this difficult point in the notes.

dull and that it is not; if he gets into this state after the episodes we described, he makes no logical mistake. His "notional" world (described in the universal, D(MP) style) is perfectly consistent. Once again an analogy may help. Imagine a computer programmed to sort books out. It would seem bad – a mistake in the program – if it said that the one book was to go into Philosophy and, inconsistently, into Civil Engineering. But it wouldn't be bad if the book had been entered differently on separate occasions – say, once as a book by the philosopher John Mackie (whose name the machine recognizes), and then separately as *The Cement of the Universe*.

Does the climber then believe *that* Snowdon is duller than Snowdon? He believes as much *of* Snowdon. If we dislike putting the contradiction inside the 'that'-clause we will need to modify the semantics in this way. We would say that although having any of a variety of universal thoughts, and being RR to Snowdon, is enough to count as thinking of Snowdon, only the right kinds of universal thought – ones involving some favoured Snowdony mode of presentation (MP_s) – permit you to be reported as thinking *that* Snowdon . . . Reports putting singular terms into the content of what is thought, doubted, etc. will have two responsibilities. The thinker will have to be thinking of the right object. And he will have to think of it in some favoured way.

My own view is that singular terms do not normally bear this dual responsibility (some do – see 9.7). Normally, we truly report someone as thinking that a was φ, provided his thinking bears RR to a. There is no further requirement that he think of it as a, or in a way especially tied to our own use of the name. So, for example, I can report someone as thinking that John was a spy, even if he would not recognize *our* John. Probably John was dressed queerly, behaving queerly, seeming quite unlike himself, when he was encountered. The subject need not have come across him in any favoured way, or under any particular mode of presentation. However, when different modes of presentation are in question we take more care. When it matters, for instance to the rationality of the subject, that the same object was encountered in two different ways, so that he did not realize that it was the same, we are likely to want to signal this. And choosing separate terms to relate the situation is a good way of doing it: it alerts the audience to the possibility that the subject failed to realize that it was the same thing twice over. On this account someone may truly be said to think that Snowdon is duller than Snowdon. But the true report is not the most helpful: reporting him as believing that Snowdon is duller than Yr Wyddfa enables the audience, especially when it knows that these are just two different names for the same mountain, to understand what happened.

This account will be highly congenial to the universalist. Underneath the reports made by relating people to objects (putting singular terms into reports of thought) there is another description of their thoughts, made via modes of presentation or universal features which do not tie them to particular objects. This description may not in practice be easily expressed, for we have already noticed that we often cannot put words to the features of things which impress us. But it is this theoretical description which matters when we are considering how logical people are.

Clearly any approach along these lines requires an account of the right relation, RR. But before sketching that, we should notice some other semantic problems to which it is relevant.

6. *The Contingent* A Priori *and Negative Existentials*

Suppose I know that someone has made the first ascent of the climb in Wales called Tensor. I know that $(\exists x)x$ climbed Tensor first. But I don't know who did it. Sitting in my armchair I can make identity-independent judgements, like the existentially quantified one just given. Suppose, however, that I attempt a different style of expression. I might say: 'Take whoever climbed Tensor first. Call him Cedric. Then Cedric climbed Tensor.' (Evans calls names introduced like this 'descriptive names.') Does my utterance 'Cedric climbed Tensor' express knowledge? Do I know Cedric climbed Tensor? If so, I seem to have a peculiar, armchair way of obtaining mountaineering history. For according to my usage, 'Cedric' is going to refer to some definite person: Joe Brown, say. Joe Brown actually climbed Tensor first. I know that Cedric climbed Tensor first; that is, I know of Cedric that he did this. Cedric is Joe Brown, so I know of Joe Brown that he did this.

Compare this case. The sentence 'I am here' has the peculiar property that whenever and wherever I utter it, it is bound to be true. Even if I am lost and do not know where I am, I can bravely say 'I am here', and know that I am expressing a truth. But how can this be so, if, as seems evident, the proposition or information making the content of this sentence is only true *contingently* – true, although it might have been false? To know where I am demands some kind of knowledge, in fact, precisely that which I don't have when I am lost. So we have the queer combination that I can say the sentence in perfect confidence, knowing that I have expressed a truth, although I am totally ignorant of which truth it expresses. But the puzzle is only superficial. By coming out with the utterance 'I am here' when I am lost I do not express knowledge of where I am, precisely because I do not *know* the reference of 'here', on the occasion. In the terminology of 9.1, I know the character of the sentence, since I am a perfectly competent English speaker and can use the word 'here' properly, but on this occasion do not know to which place it refers. Now it would be quite wrong of someone to say at some later time, indicating where I in fact was: 'Blackburn knew that he was here.' That is what I didn't know, being lost. When I came up with my sentence, I knew that it expressed a truth, but, being ignorant of where I was, I did not know which truth it expressed. This removes the appearance of a kind of sneaky way of having knowledge, without going through the normal empirical requirements of locating myself.

The same analysis suggests itself when we introduce 'Cedric'. Let us allow that the introduction of a name in this way is legitimate, so that the right thing to say is that 'Cedric' does indeed become a name of Joe Brown. And when I said 'Cedric climbed Tensor first' I knew I had expressed a truth. But I didn't know of Joe Brown (i.e. of Cedric) that he did this. I didn't know that of anybody at all: there was nobody whom I knew to have climbed Tensor first. Hence, I didn't know that Cedric climbed Tensor first. Again we can best see this by thinking of other people's report of me. Suppose I go through my little christening and subsequent utterance when Joe Brown is keeping quiet about having climbed Tensor, to tease the climbing fraternity. But it is known that Tensor has been climbed. People are wondering who did it. It later emerges that

Joe Brown did it, and my name 'Cedric' sticks to him. Even so, nobody can properly say 'Blackburn knew, that first evening, that Cedric climbed Tensor first'. Of course I didn't: for all the story shows, I was as ignorant of that as anybody else.

The alternative view would introduce a category of contingent, yet *a priori* truth: truths which could have been otherwise, yet which can be known "from the armchair". The idea that there should be such a category was first broached by Saul Kripke, in his famous lecture 'Naming and Necessity'. His examples were substantially similar: cases where a singular term is quite properly introduced on the basis of a description, and where it is then announced, of its reference (by using the term), that it satisfies the description. The trick is that we can do this from the armchair, yet it may be contingent that the particular thing we refer to has the properties used in the description. However, the above analysis suggests that the trick fails. For although the subject can utter a truth, and can know that his sentence is true, and can know what it means (the subject knows what 'here' means, and has himself defined the word 'Cedric'), yet it does not follow that he can be presented as knowing that a is φ, where a is the object referred to. The knowledge the subject does have, at the end of his christening ceremony, is just that which he had before, and it remains entirely identity-independent.

A closely related family of puzzles concern negative existentials. Consider the difference between:

Take whichever man climbed Tensor first: he exists, *and*
There is a man who climbed Tensor first.

The second is the kind of sentence to which a quantifier analysis is appropriate. It tells us that $(\exists x)(x$ climbed Tensor & not $(\exists y)(y$ climbed Tensor before $x)$). This would be true regardless of who got to the top first. The condition it puts upon a world is that something beat all other things up the climb. It could have been true even had Joe Brown never existed, provided someone else got up instead. But the same is not true of the first sentence. It is only going to be true provided the very man who did the climb – Joe Brown – exists. It is not true of possible worlds in which Joe Brown does not exist. (In case that terminology is unfamiliar, think of it like this. You can tell a story representing the world as though Joe Brown didn't exist, but someone else got up Tensor first. The first sentence I have put down is false of the world, as it is represented in your story, but the second is true.) The first sentence is an example of an identity-independent existence statement. In other words, part of the sentence functions as a singular term picking out an object, and the rest tells us that the object exists. We can do the same with names and demonstratives: Margaret Thatcher exists; this typewriter exists. Some such things we believe, and some we don't. For example, there are people who believe that I exist, but for all I know there are people who believe that I do not. They may be convinced that I am a fiction or unreal, and that my writings and other symptoms of my existence are unreliable. If there is a God, one day he may point out to me that I thought that *He* didn't exist, and I will have to admit it. But now what is it that I am supposed to believe of a thing, when I believe of that thing that it doesn't exist?

It would be easy if we could treat my belief as identity-independent: the belief that some combination of characteristics has no instance, expressed as its not being the case that $(\exists x) \ldots x$. But the argument of the last paragraph shows that this is too simple. It misrepresents the proposition, in the same way that 'D(MP$_s$) is φ' misrepresents the proposition that Snowdon is φ (p. 330). However we can profit from the universalist theory of that. On that view a person counts as thinking, of some particular, that it is φ if some of his thinking has the right relation, RR, to that thing. So a person can count as believing of a particular thing that it does not exist, just in virtue of believing some identity-independent, universal proposition, provided that this proposition has the right relation to the particular object. Thus in virtue of my belief that the universe has no particularly good creator with human welfare at heart I will count, if I meet anything much like the Christian God, as having believed that he does not exist. In virtue of believing that the name 'Simon Blackburn' is the alias for a committee of old bores, that my wife has no husband, and other such things, you would count as believing that I do not exist. Notice that only things that do exist can stand in the right relation to your thinking; one can only judge of things that do exist that they do not.

There used to be considerable controversy over whether 'existence is a predicate'. Russell in particular responded to the insights of quantification theory by denying that existence could be claimed or denied of an individual.[8] The only meaningful judgement, he thought, must be that a certain condition was met or was not met; existence became a second-level property – a property of properties. In this respect it is like number. When we say that there are seven oranges on the table, we are not describing the individual oranges (as if we said that there are mouldy oranges on the table); we are saying that the set of oranges on the table, or the property of being an orange on the table, has seven members or instances. And, in Frege's memorable phrase, 'affirmation of existence is in fact nothing but denial of the number nought'.[9] What then of existential statements and their denials which involve singular terms? We can appreciate a sense in which Russell was wrong, and a sense in which he was right. He was wrong in that, as we have seen, there are sentences saying of particular things that they exist or that they do not. But Russell may, again, have been right in his instinct: the fundamental kind of judgement can be seen as quantificational, and not dependent upon the existence of any actual thing for its identity. Such judgements count as affirming or denying existence of a thing if there is an object related to them in an appropriate way.

The light it casts upon these phenomena gives considerable credit to the universalist position. It is, in effect, by playing the universal judgement against the singular form of expression that we go some way to solving problems of substitutivity, negative existentials, and the contingent *a priori*. But these areas are highly controversial, and in the notes I give references to other points of view.

7. *The Right Relation*

What is the right relation, RR? We know of things in a multitude of ways: by perception, by memory, by inference, by testimony of others. Is there likely to be a clear-cut decision procedure, telling us that if someone's thought bears just such-

[8] Russell, 'The Philosophy of Logical Atomism', pp. 233 ff.
[9] Frege, *The Foundations of Arithmetic*, p. 65.

and-such relations to a thing, then he counts as thinking of it, whereas if they do not, then he doesn't? Here is Tyler Burge:

The paradigm of this relation is perception. But projections from the paradigm include memory, many introspective beliefs, certain historical beliefs, beliefs about the future, perhaps beliefs in pure mathematics, and so on. There is no adequate general explication of the appropriate non-conceptual relations which covers even the most widely accepted projections from the perceptual paradigm.[10]

In other words, we would have no clear rationale for drawing the dividing line in just one place.

For the universalist, a first thought might be that if a thing a actually bears the properties involved in X's thinking, then X is thinking of a. The right relation would simply be fitting the descriptions involved in the universal thought. But this seems wrong. Suppose I believe a piece of gossip to the effect that Princess Y is consorting with the world spaghetti-eating champion (perhaps my informant believes that Luigi Pastrami, who is consorting with Princess Y, is the world spaghetti-eating champion). Suppose that in fact Sister Maria Mozarella of the Blessed Convent is world spaghetti-eating champion. Then she would fit the description, but I do not on that account believe that Princess Y is consorting with her. That a thing fits my description is not enough to make it true that I am thinking of it, or referring to it. Nor is fit necessary – a thing may be quite unlike the way I am thinking of it, yet it might still be it which I am thinking of.

Certainly there are distinctive and important failures in our thinking. Notably, I might conceive of something as the wrong sort of thing in some fundamental way. Someone, for example, who fails to realize that I am a person, who believes something which he expresses by saying 'Simon Blackburn is a committee', may only doubtfully be said to believe that I am a committee; he is doubtfully thinking of me. Someone whose relation to any original informational episode involving a proposed object of thought is thin and garbled eventually loses any right to be counted as thinking of that thing. What about cases where the object played no role in the genesis of the thinking: where it didn't cause or explain why the subject is thinking as he is?

---

[10] 'Belief *De Re*', *Journal of Philosophy* (1977).

Surely then we are too far away from any informational episode to allow that thinking of an object is taking place. But if untutored reports are allowed, even these can be doubtful. If a prophet predicts in sufficiently detailed terms we may say that he predicted the coming of *this* person and not just predicted that there would be someone who . . . (in identity-independent terms). Or suppose the wife learns that the husband often takes out and adores a handkerchief with traces of the mistress upon it. So she buys a new one, identical except for the marks and substitutes it. She says, as she gloatingly learns of his strangled gasp of surprise when he took it out: 'He expected *it* to have lipstick marks on it!' She attributes an expectation to the husband relating him *de re* to the substitute handkerchief. But this had no causal influence on the husband's expectation at all.

Another idea is that you may count as thinking of some particular only if you would recognize it as the object of your thought under some favourable conditions or other. In some sense, you should be able to know what it is that you are thinking about. I believe that this flatters our relations with the past. For there is no practical sense in which I would recognize, say, the rabbit I had as a pet when I was a child. If it were resurrected I couldn't tell it from a million other rabbits. The fact that I am thinking of it is not manifested as a skill in identifying it. All that is true is that I do some thinking which is explained by my acquaintance with that rabbit. The thinking may need to satisfy some conditions in itself. For instance, I may need to have mastered various concepts – that of a rabbit, or of a scheme of temporally enduring objects amongst which we move (and which we frequently lose track of, distort in our memories, and so on). I can talk intelligently of rabbits and of the general nature of the world I inhabit. After that, my multifarious relations with particular items in that world can act and blend in any variety of ways to create my thoughts: why expect a principled cut-off point, before which I am thinking of some of them in particular, and after which I am not?

To think of things as they are – persons, ordinary physical objects, places, times – demands abilities. It demands what is commonly gestured at with the phrase 'mastery of a conceptual scheme'. At the very least this means being able to locate oneself, as an enduring object with one perspective on the world of similarly enduring and spatially arrayed objects. These are general abilities. But it does not follow at all that thinking of some particular thing or place or time demands any special abilities with respect to *it*, such as the ability to locate it or to keep track of it. On the face of it we can think of many things we have lost track of; that is what makes a great deal of our thinking so poignant.

8. *Perspectival Thinking*

In 9.5 I expressed the view that there is no convention or component of meaning to most singular terms which puts restrictions on the way a subject can think of their reference, when we report the subject by putting the term into a 'that'-clause. '*X* thinks that *a* is *φ*' allows for *X* to think of *a* under an indefinite variety of modes of presentation. Apparent failures of substitutivity – 'he thinks that Snowdon is dull, but he doesn't think that Yr Wyddfa is dull' – are handled pragmatically. That is, it is part of being helpful and avoiding misunderstandings that when a subject has failed to realize the identity of things he is dealing with, we take care, in reporting him, to give the audience clues that this is so. And changing the singular term is one way of doing this.

Putting things this way means identifying the content of these 'that'-clauses by reference. It is the reference of the singular terms in them which determines the particular truth or falsity to which the reported subject is related. The truth expressed by 'Snowdon is dull' is a truth about Snowdon and this is the truth to which *X* is related when we report that *X* thinks that Snowdon is dull. But just as the same mountain may present very different appearances, and as different mountains might present the same appearance, so these singular truths may be capable of different presentations. This leads to twin-earth cases and to cases of people maintaining conflicting attitudes to the very same singular thought. To unravel the puzzles we have been led to distinguish the universal element in thinking: the identity-independent or notional element, which depends upon the way in which the object of thought is known by the thinker.

Singular thoughts, identified through reference, do not obey a principle due to Frege. This is that if someone understands a sentence S, and understands a sentence S', then if S expresses the same thought as S' the subject cannot fail to realize that it does. According to this principle, thoughts should be, as it were, transparent to the thinker. There should be no possibility of his thinking that S, but not thinking that S', as there would be if thoughts, like mountains, could present different facets. But the singular thought can present as many different facets as the object to which reference is made. What we are really up against is the need to pull thoughts, identified as the truths and falsehoods about the world, away from thoughts identified as the objects of propositional attitudes. In the former capacity thoughts are well individuated by reference. Notice in this connection that X, thinking that water is φ on earth, may be thinking truly, whilst his *doppelganger*, thinking that XYZ is φ, may be thinking falsely, in spite of the identity of everything as it appears to them. Perhaps φ = 'is made of H_2O'. When thoughts are tied to truth and falsity, they must be individuated by reference. But when we turn to thoughts as things which characterize thinkers, it is not the singular thought we need, but the idea of a mode of presentation which it, like its object, can bear, and which is not tied to reference at all. If we avoid the category of singular thought, things are slightly easier. We can accept the same semantics for 'that'-clauses with singular terms. But we will not puzzle over the phenomenon of the one subject's different attitude to 'the same singular thought'. For that will be a bad way of putting the simple truth that someone can be said to believe that a is φ and that a is not φ when two consistent universal thoughts which he has are both RR to the thing a.

But is this adequate to all cases? Consider the example of the person who believes that *that* man's trousers are on fire (he points to the image in the mirror) whilst not believing that his own trousers are on fire. If singular terms substitute without fail, then he really believes that his trousers are on fire. This seems wrong; he doesn't behave like someone who believes that his trousers are on fire. He makes no attempt to put them out, for instance. He would be surprised on being told that his trousers are on fire. (Or at least he would if he were told this in a way which made him realize that it was himself. He wouldn't be surprised if he told it in a way which left him thinking of the victim as the man in the mirror.) Isn't it right here to admit a category of thought identified by something further than reference, so that the person already knowing of himself that his trousers are on fire, nevertheless learns something further when he learns that his trousers are on fire? The connection of thought and behaviour matters here. Consider:

X thinks that that person has his trousers on fire.
X thinks that he has his trousers on fire.

X thinks that a bomb will soon go off in Pembroke College.
X thinks that a bomb will soon go off here.

X thinks that the world ends at midnight, 1 January 1983.
X thinks that the world ends now.

It seems plausible to say that the second member of each pair tells us something different about X, even if X is so situated that the terms in the first report refer to him, to the place that he is, and to the time of his thinking (they are his trousers, he is in Pembroke College, and it is midnight, 1 January 1983). They tell us something different because they do introduce the way X thinks of the person, place or time. He thinks of it *as* himself, or as here or now. In other words, with these particular indexicals we have an exception to the general point I suggested, that ways of thinking of things are not conventionally or as a matter of meaning tied to particular singular terms. The point is vivid if we think of communication. If I try to tell X that his trousers are on fire, that that bomb will go off here, or that the world ends now, I just fail to communicate unless he realizes that this means him, here and now. It is not enough if he realizes that I am talking of that person, Pembroke College, and midnight, 1 January 1983. It is as though I am trying to communicate an essentially perspectival truth; one which needs appreciating in the light of its relation to him, there and then. And this essentially perspectival nature is not revealed if we locate the truth simply through the reference of singular terms used in reporting it. For substituting co-referential terms loses the essential relation to the here and now. These are the important cases for pressing the distinction between modes of presentation and reference. For they are precisely cases where the aspect under which things present themselves (as *me*, as *here*, as *now*) dominates the thinking that the subject does.

The reader may readily appreciate the difficulty that this category of truths is likely to cause. For what gives us the identity of these perspectival thoughts? If it is a different truth which I come to appreciate when I learn that my trousers are on fire, although I already knew of myself (but not *as* myself) that my trousers were on fire, then is this different truth the one which you also appreciate when you learn that my trousers are on fire? Is the thought that today is fine, entertained now, the same as the thought that yesterday was fine, entertained tomorrow, or has the perspective changed by then in such a way that the thought is different? Are perspectival thoughts strictly tied to one perspective on things, so that one which is apprehended *as* about me, here, now is then lost for ever, and only approximated to (referentially) by anyone who later thinks about him, there, then? Notice that there is a strong intuitive sense in which there is just one fact – today's fineness – which indifferently makes any of these apparently different thoughts true. There is no theory yet, in the philosophy of these things, which gives us a satisfactory picture of the "cognitive dynamics" of these cases: in other words, which tells us how to classify sameness and difference of thought across times, or across the utterly different mode of presentations under which I can think of myself, and under which you can think of me. It is this problem of individuating such thoughts which makes it so tempting to retreat into a purely referential classification, in which we think the same provided we attribute the same property to the same object, or time or place, no matter how we think of that object or time or place.

Adjusting the relations between these essentially perspectival thoughts, and thoughts conceived of in an objective, context-independent way (*timeless* truths and falsities), is one of the hardest problems in metaphysics. It is all very well to say that a particular angle on things is required when the subject thinks that he . . ., or that now it is . . ., or that here it is . . .; but what is it to apprehend a person as oneself, or a time as the present, or a place as the one which one occupies? It is even controversial whether one of these egocentric categories of thought is fundamental and can be used to explain the others, or whether there is no ranking. For example, one might suppose that if we understood self-awareness and self-reference then we could define *now* as the time of my utterance or experiences; *here* is of course the place where I am. But *now* is only the time of my *current* experiences or utterances; *here* is where I am *now*. And then reference to myself is plausibly argued to be possible only because I can conceive of myself as a being with a spatial position and a history in time.[11]

Further exploration of this takes us further into metaphysics, and into our general understanding of the way in which we know about the world we inhabit. It is one more of the great problems into which the philosophy of language blends. It would be the next step in a journey of which I have tried to provide the first step, which was to understand why the journey is worth taking, and to appreciate some of the directions it ought to take. In this part of philosophy there is no distinction between general problems of metaphysics and specific problems in the philosophy of language. The language we want to understand is that of people who have the puzzling perspective. This should not leave anyone pessimistic about the importance of the philosophy of language. The linguistic mode in which the problems are now couched is no disadvantage, for the lights provided by such thinkers as Frege and Russell are better lights in which to improve our understandings than any that existed before them. To remember the morals derived from the exploration of truth, there is no limit to the improvements we can struggle towards, even if we do not know whether the struggle is towards a final theory, fated to be agreed on by all enquiry. So we should not find it too pessimistic to conclude about reference and thought what Conrad concludes about the description of human beings in general:

And besides, the last word is not said – probably shall never be said. Are not our lives too short for that full utterance which through all our stammerings is our only and abiding intention? I have given up expecting those last words, whose ring, if they could only be pro-

---

[11] Evans, op. cit., ch. 7 is good on this. The relevant literature includes David Kaplan's work on demonstratives (unfortunately still only available in manuscript) and the seminal papers by John Perry, 'Frege on Demonstratives', *Philosophical Review* (1977), and 'The Problem of the Essential Indexical', *Noûs* (1979).

nounced, would shake both heaven and earth. There is never time to say our last word – the last word of our love, of our desire, faith, remorse, submission, revolt. The heaven and earth must not be shaken I suppose – at least not by us who know so many truths about either. (*Lord Jim.*)

Notes to Chapter 9

9.1 'Russell discovered the crucial . . .'
The best sources of Russell's views are the papers:

'Knowledge by Acquaintance and Knowledge by Description', in
   Mysticism and Logic.
'The Philosophy of Logical Atomism', in *Logic and Knowledge.*
Chs. XV and XVI of *Introduction to Mathematical Philosophy.*
'On Denoting', also in *Logic and Knowledge*, is relatively hard.

'. . . Tarski's achievement . . .' Can be appreciated informally like this:

Suppose we are given a metalanguage which enables us to name things, including the terms of an object language which we are to describe; which includes a stock of predicates, negation and conjunction operators, and constructions enabling us to say 'there are . . .' and 'everything is . . .';

Suppose we are to describe the ways in which the meanings of sentences in the object language, L, are built up;

Suppose we can say what the names of L are, and what it is that they refer to. What the primitive predicates of L are, and what they mean. Which expressions of L correspond to negation, conjunction, and the existential and universal quantifier;

Then the problem is to show what any arbitrary sentence of L means, by first giving a structural description of it – i.e. describing how it is made up from the stock of names, predicates, operators, and quantifiers – and having a set of rules determining what those things in those places do by way of contributing to meaning, or truth-conditions.

We can proceed by listing the translations we can. I shall use the convention that we underline object language expressions, and suppose that their translation is a non-underlined term of the same form.

> $\underline{a}$ *In L refers to a*
> $\underline{P}$ applies to things just in case they are *P*
> $\underline{Pa}$ is true iff *Pa*.

But in fact we don't go for truth directly. We go for the notion of an *assignment* satisfying a predicate (the implications of this I mention in a moment, after seeing how it works). This is to exploit the idea of treating a variable as an 'instantaneous name' of an object, as we range over a domain in order to evaluate general truths, as explained in the text. We shall call the assignment of a thing a to a variable $\underline{x}$, $(\underline{x} \rightarrow a)$ The denotation or reference of a variable, under an assignment s, we can call $s[x]$. So for instance, $(x \rightarrow a)[\underline{x}]$ is just the thing a. An assignment $(\underline{x} \rightarrow a)$ satisfies an open sentence or predicate $\underline{Fx}$ iff $F(\underline{x} \rightarrow a)[x]$: i.e. iff Fa.

A sentence with no variables in it can be evaluated or interpreted directly without making any assignment. We can say that the null assignment, Λ, satisfies $\underline{Pa}$, iff Pa. But for $(\underline{\exists x})Fx$ to be true, there must be an extension of the null assignment $(\Lambda + (x \rightarrow a))$ which satisfies Fx. In plain terms, there must be an object a, such that when 'F this?' lights on it, the answer is yes. The trick now is to show how the structure of a sentence is mimicked by assignments which progressively extend Λ.

Under any assignment, including Λ, the reference of a name stays the same. $s[a]$ is always a. Now we can treat both names and variables as terms, and collect together the informal explanations like this:

(1) s satisfies $\underline{P(t_1 \dots t_n)}$ iff $P(s[t_1] \dots s[t_n])$
(2) s satisfies $\underline{\neg \varphi}$ iff not s satisfies $\underline{\varphi}$
(3) s satisfies $\underline{\varphi \ \& \ \psi}$ iff s satisfies φ and s satisfies ψ
(4) s satisfies $\underline{(\exists x)\varphi}$ iff $(\exists \alpha)s + (\underline{x} \rightarrow \alpha)$ satisfies $\underline{\varphi}$
(5) s satisfies $\underline{(\forall x)\varphi}$ iff $(\forall \alpha)s + (\underline{x} \rightarrow \alpha)$ satisfies $\underline{\varphi}$.

A sentence $\underline{\varphi}$ is true iff Λ satisfies it.

$\underline{\varphi}$ here represents any open or closed sentence, i.e. any predicate or full sentence of the object language. $(\exists \alpha) \dots$ just says that there is a thing which . . .

These explanations give us a sequence of moves with which to construct the meaning of an object language sentence. For example:

Fa is true iff Λ satisfies it, i.e. iff Fa. (By (1).)
$(\underline{\exists x})Fx$ is true iff Λ satisfies it, i.e. iff $(\exists \alpha)\Lambda + (x \rightarrow \alpha)$
    satisfies $\underline{Fx}$. This will be so iff $(\exists \alpha)F(\Lambda + (\underline{x} \rightarrow \alpha)[\underline{x}])$, i.e. iff $(\exists \alpha)F\alpha$. (By (4) and (1).)

Notice that as with the description of the recursive structure of the numeral notation ANN (1.3) it is not the final result that is news. It is that going through the process of finding the translation into the metalanguage reveals the role of *that* quantifier or operator or name in *that* place, and in that sense reveals the structure of the language.

(Readers who are familiar with other expositions of this will notice that this way of putting it does not use the full panoply of satisfaction by sequences. This is because the notion of progressively extending the null assignment gets the same effect more naturally. It mimics the natural understanding of the quantifiers.)

What is the philosophical impact of *defining* truth in terms of satisfaction by an assignment – indeed satisfaction by the null assignment? Not much. It would be quite wrong to conclude that because we here treat both sentences and predicates as similar (both represented by φ) somehow the notion of the satisfaction of a predicate has a conceptual priority. On the contrary, everything hinges on an antecedent understanding of what it is for the atomic sentence, with just a predicate from the basic vocabulary and a name or set of names, $Pa_1 \ldots a_n$ to be true. Λ satisfies such a sentence iff $\underline{P(a_1 \ldots a_n)}$, which means that to determine whether Λ satisfies such a sentence you have to make a judgement; judgements are the bearers of truth and falsity. There is no way of squeezing past the priority of truth, unless, indeed, the other arguments for the redundancy theory are felt compelling (7.3).

The basic notation in this exposition is that of Neil Tennant, *Natural Logic*. There are reflections on the rivalry between truth and satisfaction in G. Evans, 'Pronouns, Quantifiers and Relative Clauses', *Canadian Journal of Philosophy* (1977). I agree with Dummett (*Frege*, pp. 519 ff.) against Evans, that the priority of truth imposes no need to avoid this kind of truth theory.

9.1 The issues arising out of Donnellan's case were discussed in a number of papers:

  A. F. MacKay, 'Donnellan and Humpty Dumpty on Referring', *Philosophical Review* (1968).
  S. Kripke, 'Speaker's Reference and Semantic Reference', in French *et al.* (1977).
  G. Evans, ch. 9.2 of his (1982).

Part of the debate concerns the same matters as 4.5: the potential conflict between what the speaker intends to convey, and the strict and literal meanings of the words he uses to convey it.

9.2 'The tension which dominates . . .'
A good collection for studying different views on this is A. Woodfield (ed.), *Thought and Object*. Other seminal papers include:

  J. Fodor, 'Methodological Solipsism Considered as a Research Strategy in Cognitive Psychology', *The Behavioural and Brain Sciences* (1980).

S. Schiffer, 'The Basis of Reference', *Erkenntnis* (1978).

T. Burge, 'Belief De Re', *Journal of Philosophy* (1977).

— 'Individualism and the Mental', in French *et al.* (1979).

9.4   This section is highly programmatic. One position which I find attractive, but which is not developed in the literature, would find a compromise between singular thought and universalists. The basis for a compromise is this. It is noteworthy that the best cases for the universalist concern items about which we know relatively little – historical personages, possible figures of myth, and the like. It is plausible to say that this is because we can keep so much of our thinking (fixed *de re*) constant, whilst as it were 'picking off' any single such individual. It may even be true that when we come nearer home we can imagine any single focus of thought to be absent or substituted, whilst the thinker is the same. But the essentially public and behavioural aspect of thinking could be protected not by denying sameness of thought in these single cases, but by claiming that they are necessarily exceptional (a similar move to that in the philosophy of perception which allows that any one experience could be illusory, but not that they could all be so). Such a compromise will not do justice to all the intuitions behind the universalist position, but it may be nearer the truth than either extreme.

9.5   I believe that it is plausible to see Russell as trying to express this argument, in a famous passage in 'On Denoting'. See:

S. Blackburn and A. Code, 'The Power of Russell's Criticism of Frege', *Analysis* (1978).

In effect, the point is that you cannot at all switch the semantic role – the reference or semantic value – of names between ordinary contexts and places when they occur inside reports of thought. A writer who emphasizes this requirement is D. Davidson ('On Saying That').

There are quite alarming consequences of the fact that every kind of term raises substitutivity problems. For at least in the cases of ordinary reference we can see what is going on. We know how it is that a speaker can come across an object under two different aspects. But predicates are supposed to express properties or features of things. If they fail to substitute, then how do we conceive of a subject "coming across" a feature under two different aspects? And they appear to fail in just the same way:

John realized that the figure was a circle.   *True*

John realized that the figure was the shape defined by the
    locus of a point equidistant from another point.   *False*

A circle just *is* that shape: so how can John realize the one truth and not realize the other: how is there room for two separate cognitive contents? The problem of the failure of even bona fide synonyms to substitute for one another in propositional attitude contexts is the 'paradox of analysis', discovered and explored by G. E. Moore. Myself I believe that some at least of the mystery is taken out of it if we realize that a person may exhibit understanding of a concept (and hence of a predicate expressing it) in his *actions*; hence he may act in ways sufficient to certify that he realizes that X is φ, although he is not aware of a true equivalence between being φ and being $\theta_1 \ldots \theta_n$. This can happen not because the person is ignorant of the meanings of the constituent terms, nor because his understanding of any of the concepts individually is deficient, but because he doesn't put together what he already knows. The importance of mentioning actions here is to remove a misleading model, according to which understanding a concept is having it as a literal, diaphanous presence in the mind (like an image – see 2.2). If it were like this, it would be hard to see how one could understand two synonymous terms without immediately seeing that they were synonymous. (Dummett endorses this principle in *Frege* , p. 95, and I express reservations about it in 'The Identity of Propositions'.) But as with ordinary referring expressions, there is still the semantic problem of saying how predicates contribute to the sense of utterances so that substitutivity fails, even if we feel we understand what is going on. The tradition Dummett is expressing thinks of 'what John realized' as an object – a Thought or proposition – with its own identity. The report of John relates him to just this thought, and if there is only one thought to be had, how is it that substitutivity fails? Again, I favour a pragmatically inclined answer: John's actions may show that he grasps the concept of a circle (he can recognize them, draw consequences from the fact that a circle is present, and so on), but also indicate that he does not connect this concept with that of the locus of a point. When this is so, it would be misleading to represent him as though he had made the connection, which is what the second report does.

'. . . singular terms do not normally bear this dual responsibility . . .'
The essential argument here is this: if ordinary names and demonstratives did bear such a responsibility, we might talk of the same thing by using one, and know ourselves to be doing so, but not communicate successfully (your term might bear a different sense and hence express a different thought from the one I take it to bear). But this seems not to happen. All that happens is that when someone does come across an object in a different way, it can sometimes be

important to realize that this is so. It does not follow from this that we do not understand what he says until we realize it.

9.6   For singular terms and existential statements, see:

B. Russell, 'The Philosophy of Logical Atomism'.

G. E. Moore, 'Is Existence a Predicate?', *Proceedings of the Aristotelian Society* (1936).

J. Mackie, 'The Riddle of Existence', *Aristotelian Society Supplementary Volume* (1976).

G. Evans, *The Varieties of Reference*, ch. 10.

For the contingent *a priori* and surrounding matters, see:

S. Kripke, *Naming and Necessity*.

K. Donnellan, 'The Contingent A Priori and Rigid Designation', in French *et al.* (1977).

S. Schiffer, 'Naming and Knowing', in the same volume.

G. Evans, 'Reference and Contingency', *The Monist* (1979).

9.8   The literature on perspectival thoughts includes, as well as the papers by Perry footnoted in the text, the following (difficult) contributions:

H. Castañeda, ' "He": a Study in the Logic of Self-Consciousness', *Ratio* (1966).

D. Lewis, 'Attitudes *De Dicto* and *De Se*', *Philosophical Review* (1979).

E. Sosa, 'Propositions and Indexical Attitudes', in Parret and Bouveresse (1982).

M. Dummett, 'A Defence of McTaggart's Proof of the Unreality of Time', in *Truth and Other Enigmas*.

Glossary

Analytic. The original definition (Kant) was that a proposition is analytic if the predicate is contained in the subject. The more general modern notion is that a proposition is analytic if it is 'true in virtue of the meanings of its terms'. The purpose of defining such a category is to find a harmless category of necessary truths; ones which are trivial enough not to raise worries of epistemology.

Atomic. An atomic sentence is one which contains no logical operators.

A posteriori. Not *a priori.*

A priori. A proposition can be known *a priori* if it can be known by merely thinking, by conceptual means alone.

Bivalence. The principle of bivalence states that every sentence is either true or false.

Cartesian. Doctrine associated with Descartes. A Cartesian view in the philosophy of mind sharply separates the mental from the physical. It may include the view that we have immediate private access to the contents of our own minds.

Conditional. A sentence of the form 'if . . . then . . .' expresses a conditional. The first gap is filled by the sentence expressing the antecedent, the second by that expressing the consequent.

Consistent. A set of propositions is consistent if no contradiction can be derived from it.

Content. See proposition.

Contingent. A proposition which is neither necessarily true, nor necessarily false.

Conventionalism. The attempt to explain some feature of our intellectual practices as the outcome of convention.

Convention. see 4.3.

Counterfactual. A conditional couched in the subjunctive: 'If . . . had been/were to be the case, then . . . would have been/would be the case.' The supposition made in the antecedent is (usually) taken to be contrary-to-fact.

Defeasible. A claim whose truth is open to defeat by any of an indefinite range of countervailing circumstances.

De dicto and *de re.* A belief or other propositional attitude is construed *de dicto* when the content is supposed to be a general one, specified by a sentence using quantifiers and general terms. It is construed *de re* when the subject is related to some specific thing. Thus 'John wants a sloop' may mean that John wants, in Quine's phrase, relief from slooplessness (*de dicto*) or it may mean that there is some particular sloop which John wants (*de re*).

Domain. The set of things in question in a given discourse; the universe of discourse or more formally the range of variables of a theory.

Empirical. An empirical truth is one which can be certified true by experience (see 5.4 and 7.4). An empiricist believes that all truths which we can know have this property.

Epistemology. The theory of knowledge.

Extension and intension. See 8.5.

Force. The force of an utterance is the speech act, in the sense of asserting, commanding, questioning, etc. which it is used to perform. The theory of force needs to find a way of classifying such acts, and saying what it is, in the way of speaker's intentions, etc., which determines the particular force of an utterance on an occasion.

Functor. A term expressing a function. '( )^2' is a functor expressing the mathematical function of the square of a number; if a term referring to a number is introduced as an argument, the overall expression denotes the square of the argument: this is the value of the function for that argument.

Holism. In the theory of meaning, the view that the meaning of an individual sentence is a function of its place in a larger whole, such as a theory or a language.

Idealism. The doctrine that reality is in some way dependent upon the mind.

Implicatures. Conclusions which may be drawn from the fact that an utterance was made (perhaps in a certain way). These are distinguished from strict logical consequences following from what was said. Implicatures may arise from conversational factors, or from conventional factors. See 4.5. and 9.2.

Indexical. A term used to refer, but whose reference is determined by some feature or features of the context of utterance. See 9.8.

Language. In the abstract, a language is characterized by a syntax, stating which sequences of signs make up well-formed sentences, and a semantics stating what meaning the sentences have, in virtue of the signs they contain and the order they are in.

Metaphysics. The theory of the kind of things and facts that there are.

Modal. The mode in which an assertion is made; as necessarily true or as possibly true. The extent of the analogy between these modalities and others (probably true? true now? true in the past?) is controversial.

Name. A term whose semantic function is to introduce an object, about which something is said.

Necessary. A proposition is necessary, or necessarily true, if it could not have been false; if it is true in all possible worlds.

Positivism. The view that scientific or empirical (q.v.) truth is all that can be understood. The logical positivists believed that by a process of logical analysis, any meaningful proposition could be reduced to an empirical one, and any others discarded. This thesis is the verification principle.

Pragmatics. The pragmatics of an utterance are those features which concern its effects, the likely consequences of its being made. Pragmatics is the study of force and of the conversational and conventional implicatures.

Predicate. Intuitively, the part of a sentence which can be used to say of a thing, or set of things, that something is true of them. In this work a predicate is a linguistic category.

Propositional attitude. A subject's propositional attitudes are described when he is said to believe, doubt, desire, expect, hope, regret, etc. that . . .; the gap is filled by a sentence identifying the content of his beliefs, etc.

Proposition. The content, or piece of information, or individual truth or falsehood expressed by a sentence.

Quantifier. An expression which can turn a predicate either into another predicate or into a whole sentence, whose satisfaction condition or truth-condition is then a matter of the presence or absence or quantity of things in the domain satisfying the original predicate. See notes to 9.1.

Realism. See 5.1.

Recursive account/definition. One which derives some value for a complex expression from repeated applications of function on the values of some set of base expressions.

Semantics. See language (see also 1.3, and 8).

Sentence. A unit of languge capable of expressing a single truth or falsehood.

Speech act. See force.

Syntax. See language (see also 1.3).

Synthetic. Not analytic.

Tautology. A tautology is strictly a truth-function (q.v.) which reduces to the value T or true whatever the values of its input arguments. The term is sometimes used loosely for any analytic statement.

Truth-function. A truth-function is one which, given a sentence or sentences with a definite truth-value as argument, yields another sentence, whose truth-value is a determinate function of the truth-values of the arguments.

Truth-value. The truth or falsity of a proposition.

Universal. The universal element in thinking is our ability to take different things to instance the same property or feature. See chapter 3.

Verification Principle. See Positivism.

Word. The presence of a word is a feature of a sentence which plays a role in determining its meaning.

Bibliography

Adams, E. *The Logic of Conditionals*, Reidel (1975).

Aristotle, *De Interpretatione*, ed. J. Ackrill, Oxford University Press (1963).

— *Metaphysics*, transl. W. D. Ross, Oxford University Press (1908).

Ayer, A. J. *Language Truth and Logic*, Gollancz (1936).

— *The Foundations of Empirical Knowledge*, Macmillan (1940).

Baldwin, T. 'Prior and Davidson on Indirect Speech', *Philosophical Studies*, xxv (1982).

Barker, S. and Achinstein, P. 'On the New Riddle of Induction', *Philosophical Review*, lxix (1960).

Bennett, J. F. *Rationality*, Routledge & Kegan Paul (1964).

— *Locke, Berkeley, Hume: Central Themes*, Oxford University Press (1971).

— 'The Meaning Nominalist Strategy', *Foundations of Language*, x (1973).

— *Linguistic Behaviour*, Cambridge University Press (1976).

Berkeley, Bishop. *The Principles of Human Knowledge*, Dublin 1710.

Blackburn, S. *Reason and Prediction*, Cambridge University Press (1973).

— (ed.) *Meaning, Reference and Necessity*, Cambridge University Press (1975).

— 'The Identity of Propositions', in (1975).

— 'Thought and Things', *Aristotelian Society, Supplementary Volume*, liii (1979).

— 'Truth, Realism and the Regulation of Theory', in French *et al.* (1980).

— 'Opinions and Chances', in Mellor (1980).

— 'Rule-Following and Moral Realism', in Holtzman and Leich (1981).

— 'The Individual Strikes Back', *Synthese* (1984).

Blackburn, S. and Code, A. 'The Power of Russell's Criticism of Frege: "On Denoting", pp. 48–50', *Analysis* (1978).

Block, I. (ed.) *Perspectives on the Philosophy of Wittgenstein*, Blackwell (1981).

Boorse, C. 'The Origins of the Indeterminacy Thesis', *Journal of Philosophy*, lxxii (1975).

Bosanquet, B. *Logic*, Oxford University Press (1911).

Bradley, F. H. *Essays on Truth and Reality*, Oxford University Press (1914).

Burge, T. 'Truth and Singular Terms', *Noûs*, viii (1974).

— 'On Knowledge and Convention', *Philosophical Review*, lxxxiv (1975).

— 'Belief *De Re*', *Journal of Philosophy*, lxxiv (1977).

— 'Individualism and the Mental', in French *et al.* (1979).

Butler, R. (ed.) *Analytical Philosophy, 1st Series*, Blackwell (1962).

Carnap, R. *Introduction to Semantics*, Harvard (1948).

— 'The Methodological Status of Theoretical Concepts', *Minnesota Studies in the Philosophy of Science*, vol. i, University of Minnesota Press (1956).

Castañeda, H. ' "He": A study in the Logic of Self-Consciousness', *Ratio*, vii (1966).

— 'Indicators and Quasi Indicators', *American Philosophical Quarterly*, iv (1967).

Carruthers, P. 'Frege's Regress', *Proceedings of the Aristotelian Society*, lxxxii (1981).

Chappell, V. C. (ed.) *The Philosophy of Mind*, Prentice Hall (1962).

Chisholm, R. 'Knowledge and Belief: 'De Dicto' and 'De Re' ', *Philosophical Studies*, xxix (1976).

Chomsky, N. 'Quine's Empirical Assumptions' in Davidson and Hintikka (1969).

— 'Knowledge and Language', in Gunderson (1975).

— *Rules and Representations*, Blackwell (1980).

— 'Principles and Parameters in Syntactic Theory', in Hornstein and Lightfoot (1981).

Coffa, A. 'Carnap's Sprachanschauung Circa 1932', *Philosophy of Science Association*, ii (1976).

Craig, E. J. 'The Problem of Necessary Truth' in Blackburn (1975).

— 'Meaning, Use and Privacy', *Mind* xci (1982).

Dancy, J. 'On Moral Properties', *Mind* xc (1981).

Davidson, D. 'Truth and Meaning', *Synthese*, vii (1967).

— 'True to the Facts', Journal of Philosophy, lxvi (1969).

— 'On Saying That', in Davidson and Hintikka (1969).

— 'On The Very Idea of a Conceptual Scheme', *Proceedings of the American Philosophical Association*, xi (1973).

— 'Radical Interpretation', *Dialectica*, xxvii (1974).

— 'Belief and the Basis of Meaning', *Synthese*, xxvii (1974).

— 'Mental Events', in (1980).

— 'Reality without Reference', in Platts (1980).

— 'What Metaphors Mean', in Platts (1980).

— *Essays on Actions and Events*, Oxford University Press (1980).

— *Inquiries into Truth and Interpretation*, Oxford University Press (1983).

Davidson, D. and Harman, G. (eds.) *Semantics of Natural Languages*, Reidel (1972).

Davidson, D. and Hintikka, J. (eds.) *Words and Objections: Essays on the Work of W. V. Quine*, Reidel (1969).

Davies, M. *Meaning, Quantification and Modality*, Routledge & Kegan Paul (1980).

Dennett, D. *Brainstorms*, Harvester (1978).

— 'A Cure for the Common Code', in his (1978).

Dennett, D. and Hofstadter, D. *The Mind's 'I'*, Penguin (1982).

Derrida, J. 'Signature, Event, Context', *Glyph*, i (1977).

Donnellan, K. 'Reference and Definite Descriptions', *Philosophical Review*, lxxv (1966).

Dummett, M. *Frege: Philosophy of Language*, Duckworth (1973).

— *Truth and Other Enigmas*, Duckworth (1978).

— 'Truth', *Proceedings of the Aristotelian Society*, lix (1958).

— 'What is a Theory of Meaning?', in Guttenplan (1975).

— 'A Defence of McTaggart's Proof of the Unreality of Time', in (1978).

— 'The Philosophical Basis of Intuitionistic Logic', in (1978).

Dworkin, R. 'No Right Answer', in Hacker and Raz (1977).

Edgington, D. 'Meaning, Bivalence and Realism', *Proceedings of the Aristotelian Society*, lxxxi (1980).

Evans, G. 'Identity and Predication', *Journal of Philosophy*, lxxii (1975).

— 'Pronouns, Quantifiers and Relative Clauses', *Canadian Journal of Philosophy*, vii (1977). Also in Platts (1980).

— 'Reference and Contingency', *Monist*, lxii (1979).

— 'Semantic Theory and Tacit Knowledge', in Holtzman and Leich (1981).

— *The Varieties of Reference*, Oxford University Press (1982).

Evans, G. and McDowell, J. *Truth and Meaning*, Oxford University Press (1976).

Feigl, H. and Sellars, W. (eds.) *Readings in Philosophical Analysis*, Appleton Century Crofts (1949).

Field, H. 'Tarski's Theory of Truth', *Journal of Philosophy*, lix (1972).

— 'Mental Representations', *Erkenntnis*, xiii (1978).

— 'Realism and Relativism', *Journal of Philosophy*, lxxxiv (1982).

Fodor, J. *The Language of Thought*, Harvester (1976).

— 'Methodological Solipsism Considered as a Research Strategy in Cognitive Psychology', *The Behavioural and Brain Sciences*, iii (1980).

Fraassen, B. van. *The Scientific Image*, Oxford University Press (1980).

Frege, G. *The Foundations of Arithmetic*, transl. J. L. Austin, Blackwell (1959).
— *Philosophical Writings: Translations*, P. Geach and M. Black, Blackwell (1960).
— *Posthumous Writings*, transl. P. Long and R. White, Blackwell (1979).
— 'On Sense and Reference', in (1960).
— 'The Thought: A Logical Inquiry', transl. A. M. and M. Quinton, in P. F. Strawson, ed. *Philosophical Logic*, Oxford University Press (1967).

French, P., Uehling, T. and Wettstein, H. (eds.)
Midwest Studies in Philosophy, vol. 2, *Studies in Semantics* (1977).
Midwest Studies in Philosophy, vol. 4, *Studies in Metaphysics* (1979).
Midwest Studies in Philosophy, vol. 5, *Studies in Epistemology* (1980).
University of Minnesota Press.

Fricker, E. 'Semantic Structure and Speaker's Understanding', *Proceedings of the Aristotelian Society*, vol. lxxxii (1982).

Friedman, M. 'Physicalism and the Indeterminacy of Translation', *Noûs*, ix (1975).

Geach, P. *Reference and Generality*, Cornell University Press (1962).
— 'Assertion', *Philosophical Review*, lxxiv (1965).

Goodman, N. *Fact, Fiction and Forecast*, University of London Press (1955).
— 'Symposium on Innate Ideas' in Searle (1971).

Graves, C. *et al.* 'Tacit Knowledge', *Journal of Philosophy*, lxx (1973).

Grice, H. P. 'Meaning', *Philosophical Review*, lxvi (1957).
— 'Utterer's Meaning and Intentions', *Philosophical Review*, lxxviii (1969).

Grover, D. *et al.* 'A Prosentential Theory of Truth', *Philosophical Studies*, xxvii (1974).

Guenthner, F. and Guenthner-Reutter, M. (eds.) *Meaning and Translation*, Duckworth (1978).

Gunderson, K. (ed.) *Language, Mind and Knowledge*, Minnesota Studies in the Philosophy of Science, vol. vii (1975).

Gustafson, D. *Essays in Philosophical Psychology*, Macmillan (1967).

Guttenplan, S. (ed.) *Mind and Language*, Oxford University Press (1975).

Haack, S. *Philosophy of Logics*, Cambridge University Press (1978).

Hacker, P. and Raz, J. (eds.) *Law Morality and Society*, Oxford University Press (1977).

Hanfling, O. (ed.) *Essential Readings in Logical Positivism*, Blackwell (1981).

Hare, R. *Moral Thinking*, Oxford University Press (1981).

Harman, G. *Thought*, Princeton University Press (1973).

Harrison, B. *An Introduction to the Philosophy of Language*, Macmillan (1979).

Heil, J. 'Does Cognitive Psychology Rest on a Mistake?', *Mind*, xc (1980).

Hempel, C. 'On The Logical Positivists' Theory of Truth', *Analysis*, ii (1935).

Hobbes, *Leviathan*, ed. M. Oakeshott, Blackwell (n.d.).

Hodges, W. *Logic*, Penguin (1977).

Holtzman, S. and Leich, C. *Wittgenstein: To Follow a Rule*, Routledge & Kegan Paul (1981).

Hornstein, N. and Lightfoot, D. *Explanation in Linguistics*, Longman (1981).

Hume, D. *A Treatise of Human Nature*, ed. Selby-Bigge, Oxford University Press (1888).

— *Enquiry Concerning Human Understanding*, ed. Selby-Bigge, Oxford University Press (1893).

Ishiguro, H. 'Imagination', in Williams and Montefiore (1966).

Joachim, H. H. *The Nature of Truth*, Oxford University Press (1906).

Jones, O. R. (ed.) *The Private Language Argument*, Macmillan (1971).

Jones, R. F. *The Seventeenth Century*, Stanford University Press (1951).

Kant, I. *Critique of Pure Reason*, transl. N. Kemp Smith, Macmillan (1929).

Kenny, A. 'The Verification Principle and the Private Language Argument', in O. R. Jones (1971).

Kim, J. 'Supervenience and Nomological Incommensurables', *American Philosophical Quarterly* xv (1978).

Kirk, R. 'Underdetermination of Theory and Indeterminacy of Translation' *Analysis*, xxxiii (1973).

Kneale, W. C. 'Are Necessary Truths True by Convention?', *Proceedings of the Aristotelian Society, Supplementary Volume*, xxi (1947).

Kripke, S. 'Is There a Problem about Substitutional Quantification?', in Evans and McDowell (1976).

— 'Speaker's Reference and Semantic Reference', in French *et al.* (1977).

— *Naming and Necessity*, Blackwell (1980).

— *Wittgenstein on Rules and Private Language*, Blackwell (1982).

Lakatos, I. 'Falsification and the Methodology of Scientific Research Programmes', *Philosophical Papers*, vol. i, ed. J. Worrall and G. Currie, Cambridge University Press (1978).

Lewis, D. *Convention*, Harvard (1969).

— *Counterfactuals*, Blackwell (1973).

— 'Radical Interpretations', *Synthese*, xxvii (1974).

— 'Attitudes *De Dicto* and *De Se*', *Philosophical Review*, lxxxviii (1979).

Lewy, C. *Meaning and Modality*, Cambridge University Press (1976).

Locke, J. *An Essay Concerning Human Understanding*, ed. P. H. Nidditch, Oxford University Press (1975).

MacIntyre, A. *After Virtue*, Duckworth (1981).

Mackay, A. F. 'Donnellan and Humpty Dumpty on Reference', *Philosophical Review*, lxxvii (1968).

Mackie, J. 'Simple Truth', *Philosophical Quarterly*, xx (1970).

— 'The Riddle of Existence', *Proceedings of the Aristotelian Society, Supplementary Volume*, i (1976).

— *Ethics: Inventing Right and Wrong*, Penguin (1977).

— *The Miracle of Theism*, Oxford University Press (1982).

Margalit, A. *Meaning and Use*, Reidel (1978).

Maxwell, G. 'The Ontological Status of Theoretical Entities', *Minnesota Studies in the Philosophy of Science*, vol. iii, University of Minnesota Press (1962)

McDowell, J. 'On The Sense and Reference of a Proper Name', *Mind*, lxxxvi (1977).

— 'Meaning, Communication and Knowledge', in van Straaten (1980).

McGinn, C. 'Charity, Interpretation and Belief', *Journal of Philosophy*, lxxiv (1977).

— 'Truth and Use', in Platts (1980).

— 'The Structure of Content', in Woodfield (1982).

Mellor, H. *Prospects for Pragmatism*, Cambridge University Press (1980).

Moore, G. E. 'Is Existence a Predicate?', *Philosophical Papers*, Allen & Unwin (1956).

— ' "Real" and 'Imaginary" ', *Lectures in Philosophy*, ed. Casimir Lewy, Allen & Unwin (1966).

Nagel, T. *The Possibility of Altruism*, Princeton (1970).

— *Mortal Questions*, Cambridge University Press (1979).

Neurath, O. 'Protocol Sentences', in Hanfling (1981).

Ortony, A. (ed.) *Metaphor and Thought*, Cambridge University Press (1979).

Parret, H. and Bouveresse, J. (eds.) *Meaning and Understanding*, de Gruyter (1981).

Peacocke, C. *Holistic Explanation*, Oxford University Press (1979).

— 'Causal Modalities and Realism', in Platts (1980).

— 'Rule Following: The Nature of Wittgenstein's Arguments', in Holtzman and Leich (1981).

Perry, J. 'Frege on Demonstratives', *Philosophical Review*, lxxxvi (1977).

— 'The Problem of the Essential Indexical', *Noûs*, xii (1979).
Pitcher, G. *Truth*, Prentice Hall (1964).
Plantinga, A. *The Nature of Necessity*, Oxford University Press (1974).
Plato. *Protagoras and Meno*, transl. W. K. C. Guthrie, Penguin Classics (1956).
Platts, M. *The Ways of Meaning*, Routledge & Kegan Paul (1979).
— (ed.) *Reference, Truth and Reality*, Routledge & Kegan Paul (1980).
Prawitz, D. 'Meaning and Proofs', *Theoria*, xxiii (1977).
Putnam, H. 'Symposium on Innate Ideas', in Searle (1971).
— 'The Meaning of Meaning', *Mind, Language and Reality*, Cambridge University Press (1975).
— 'Meaning and Reference', in Schwartz (1977).
— *Reason, Truth and History*, Cambridge University Press (1982).
Quine, W. V. O. *From a Logical Point of View*, Harper (1953).
— *Word and Object*, M.I.T. Press (1960).
— *Ontological Relativity and Other Essays*, Columbia (1969).
— *Philosophy of Logic*, Prentice Hall (1970).
— *The Roots of Reference*, Open Court (1974).
— 'Two Dogmas of Empiricism', in (1953).
— 'Notes on the Theory of Reference', in (1953).
— 'Epistemology Naturalized', in (1969).
— 'Reply to Chomsky', in Davidson and Hintikka (1969).
— 'On the Reasons for the Indeterminacy of Translation', *Journal of Philosophy*, lxvii (1970).
— 'Methodological Reflections on Current Linguistic Theory', in Davidson and Harman (1972).
Ramsey, F. *The Foundations of Mathematics*, Routledge & Kegan Paul (1931).
— 'General Propositions and Causality', in *Foundations: Essays in Philosophy, Logic, Mathematics and Economics*, ed. D. H. Mellor, Routledge & Kegan Paul (1978).
Rorty, R. *Philosophy and the Mirror of Nature*, Blackwell (1979).
— *The Consequences of Pragmatism*, Harvester (1982).
Russell, B. *Introduction to Mathematical Philosophy*, Allen & Unwin (1919).
— *An Inquiry into Meaning and Truth*, Allen & Unwin (1940).
— *Logic and Knowledge*, ed. R. Marsh, Allen & Unwin (1956).
— *Mysticism and Logic*, Allen & Unwin (1963).
— 'On Denoting' in (1956).
— 'The Philosophy of Logical Atomism', in (1956).
— 'Knowledge by Acquaintance and Knowledge by Description' in (1963).
Ryle, G. 'Mowgli in Babel', *On Thinking*, Blackwell (1979).

— 'Imagination', in Gustafson (1964).

Scheffler, I. *Science and Subjectivity*, Bobbs-Merrill (1967).

— *The Anatomy of Inquiry*, Harvard (1963).

Schiffer, S. *Meaning*, Oxford University Press (1972).

— 'The Basis of Reference', *Erkenntnis*, xiii (1978).

Schwartz, S. (ed.) *Naming, Necessity, and Natural Kinds*, Cornell University Press (1977).

Scruton, R. *Art and Imagination*, Methuen (1974).

Searle, J. *Speech Acts*, Cambridge University Press (1969).

— (ed.) *Philosophy of Language*, Oxford University Press (1971).

— 'Meaning and Speech Acts', *Philosophical Review*, lxxi (1962).

— 'Reiterating the Difference', *Glyph*, i (1977).

— 'Minds, Brains, and Programs', in Dennett and Hofstadter (1981).

— 'The Myths of the Computer', *New York Review of Books*, xxix, no. 7 (1982).

Shoemaker, S. 'On Projecting the Unprojectible', *Philosophical Review*, lxxiv (1975).

Sluga, H. *Frege* (Arguments of the Philosophers), Routledge & Kegan Paul (1980).

Sosa, E. 'Propositions and Indexical Attitudes', in Parret and Bouveresse (1981).

Sprat, T. *History of the Royal Society*, London (1667).

Stitch, S. P. 'What Every Speaker Knows', *Philosophical Review*, lxxx (1971).

— 'Grammar, Psychology and Indeterminacy', *Journal of Philosophy*, lxxix (1972).

Straaten, Z. van. (ed.) *Philosophical Subjects*, Oxford University Press (1980).

Strawson, P. F. 'On Referring', *Mind* (1950), and in (1971).

— *Individuals*. Methuen (1959).

— *Logico-Linguistic Papers*, Methuen (1971).

— 'Intention and Convention in Speech Acts', in (1971).

— 'Meaning and Truth', in (1971).

— 'Scruton and Wright on Anti-Realism', *Proceedings of the Aristotelian Society*, lxxvii (1976).

Stroud, B. 'Wittgenstein and Logical Necessity', *Philosophical Review*, lxxiv (1965).

Swift, J. *Gulliver's Travels*, ed. L. Landa, Oxford University Press (1976).

Tarski, A. *Logic, Semantics, Metamathematics*, Oxford University Press (1956).

— 'The Concept of Truth in a Formalized Language', in (1956).

— 'The Establishment of Scientific Semantics', in (1956).

— 'The Semantic Conception of Truth', in Feigl and Sellars (1949).

Taylor, B. 'On the Need for a Meaning Theory in a Theory of Meaning', *Mind*, xci (1982).

Teller, P. 'Goodman's Theory of Projection', *British Journal for the Philosophy of Science*, xx (1969).

Tennant, N. *Natural Logic*, Edinburgh University Press (1978).

Thomson, J. J. 'Grue' *Journal of Philosophy*, lxiii (1966).

— 'The Verification Principle and the Private Language Argument', in O. R. Jones (1971).

Williams, B. and Montefiore, A. (eds.) *British Analytical Philosophy*, Routledge & Kegan Paul (1966).

Williams, B. *Moral Luck*, Cambridge University Press (1981).

— 'Wittgenstein and Idealism' in (1981).

Williams, C. J. F. *What is Truth?* Cambridge University Press (1976).

Wittgenstein, L. *Philosophical Investigations*, Blackwell (1953).

— *Remarks on the Foundations of Mathematics*, Blackwell (1956).

— *The Blue and Brown Books*, Blackwell (1964).

— *On Certainty*, Blackwell (1969).

— *Remarks on Philosophical Psychology*, Blackwell (1980).

Woodfield, A. (ed.) *Thought and Object*, Oxford University Press (1982).

Wright, C. *Wittgenstein on the Foundations of Mathematics*, Duckworth (1980).

Ziff, P. 'On H. P. Grice's Account of Meaning', *Analysis*, xxviii (1967).

Index